# CANADA

## A PEOPLE'S HISTORY

# DON GILLMOR

## ACHILLE MICHAUD & PIERRE TURGEON

# CANADA
## A PEOPLE'S HISTORY
### VOLUME TWO

WITH AN AFTERWORD BY MARK STAROWICZ AND GENE ALLEN

M&S

**National Library of Canada Cataloguing in Publication**

Gillmor, Don
    Canada : a people's history. – Trade pbk. ed.

Published in conjuction with series, Canada, a people's history on CBC Television.

V.1 by Don Gillmor & Pierre Turgeon; with a foreword by Mark Starowicz and Gene Allen – V.2 by Don Gillmor, Achille Michaud & Pierre Turgeon; with and afterword by Mark Starowicz and Gene Allen.

Includes bibliographical references and index.
ISBN 0-7710-3324-9 (v.1). – ISBN 0-7710-3336-2 (v.2)

1. Canada – History.   I. Michaud, Achille   II. Turgeon, Pierre, 1947-
III. Canadian Broadcasting Corporation   IV. Title.

FC164.G54 2002        971        C2002-903221-0
F1026.G46 2002

We acknowledge the financial support of the Government of Canada through the Book Publishing Industry Development Program for our publishing activities.We further acknowledge the support of the Canada Council for the Arts and the Ontario Arts Council for our publishing program.

Typeset in Janson by M&S, Toronto
Book design by Kong Njo

Printed and bound in Canada

McClelland & Stewart Ltd.
*The Canadian Publishers*
481 University Avenue
Toronto, Ontario
M5G 2E9
www.mcclelland.com

1 2 3 4 5                06 05 04 03 02

CBC/Société Radio-Canada

Executive Producer              Mark Starowicz
Senior Producer and Editor      Gene Allen
Senior Editor                   Mario Cardinal
Visual Research                 Ron Krant and Mia Webster

McClelland & Stewart Ltd.

Chairman                        Avie Bennett
President and Publisher         Douglas Gibson
Senior Editor                   Dinah Forbes
Managing Editor                 Jonathan Webb
Copy Editor                     Catherine Marjoribanks
Art Director                    Kong Njo

Historical advisers

Ramsay Cook, General Editor, *Dictionary of Canadian Biography*
Jean-Claude Robert, Chair of the History Department,
    Université du Québec à Montréal

CONTENTS

# CANADA

## A PEOPLE'S HISTORY

# the TAKING OF THE WEST

CHAPTER 1

Confederation had been celebrated with fireworks and parades, and dominated by the outsized image of John A. Macdonald presiding over a delicately united country. British Columbia was wooed with the promise of a railway, the Maritime provinces appeased with money, and Ontario and Quebec had settled on a workable balance of power. Manitoba became a province in 1870, and four years later, Louis Riel, who had fought for French rights there, was living in exile in the United States.

Macdonald was by then something of a political exile himself, having resigned in November 1873, after the railway scandal brought down his Conservative government. A Liberal, Alexander Mackenzie, a former stone-mason from Sarnia, Ontario, succeeded him as prime minister. A stubborn man who had quit school at the age of fourteen, Mackenzie had a vision for the new country that was the opposite of Macdonald's. He advocated fiscal prudence and a measured approach to railway expansion. His success was hampered, however, by an economic depression that enveloped Europe and North America and would become the worst of the nineteenth century.

In central Canada, the small factories of the nascent industrial age were closing, and those that remained in operation took advantage of the large, desperate labour pool and lowered wages. Adults were laid off and children hired in their place. "There are examples of children under ten years of age

The North West Mounted Police at the Regina training camp, 1885. (*Canadian Pacific Archives* NS-5649)

working a ten hour day for $1.25 or $1.50 a week," reported Montreal's *La Presse*, "who, when Saturday arrives, after having given sixty hours of work to their master, owe a 75 cent balance because of the fines imposed on them." Montreal had the highest child mortality rate in North America, with one out of four children dying before the age of one. There were food riots in Montreal, Kingston, and Ottawa, and during the winter, thousands faced starvation. The cost of wood and coal to heat homes was out of reach, and some of the factories that were run by water power closed when the rivers froze, putting more out of work.

The most accessible recreation was found at the tavern, which provided a haven from cramped, miserable quarters, mind- and limb-numbing work, and scolding families. Montreal had a tavern for every one hundred and fifty citizens; Toronto, one for every seventy. They were located close to the factories and offered cheap rum from the Caribbean and local whisky, distilled for pennies and sold for dramatic profits. Whisky was prescribed as medicine, and children were given watered rum on cold mornings. Alcohol consumption reached epidemic proportions, and social ills inevitably followed. In Toronto, the jails were filled with people charged with "intemperance." "Mostly all offences are due either directly or indirectly to intemperance," said Montreal's police chief. "What is the cause of all larcenies? Drink. Of assaults? Drink. Disorderly conduct? Drink. Fights, furious driving, interference with the police, foul language, blasphemies? Drink! Of cowardly wife-beating? Drink!"

Women organized to fight the scourge of alcohol, and their campaign became an evangelical form of feminism, a liberating force. In Ontario, the Women's Christian Temperance Union (WCTU) spread its message through speeches and song:

> We're soldiers of the Water King
> His laws we will obey.
> Virtue and health are his rewards,
> We want no better pay.
> Then let us sing the Water King
> Good soldiers one and all.
> Our banners to the breeze we'll fling
> And down with alcohol!

In Picton, Ontario, Letitia Youmans and a group of churchwomen nervously addressed the city council, asking them to stop selling tavern licences. But the city's revenues from licences and the sale of liquor were too significant to give up. Inspired by the founding of the Dominion of Canada chapter of the WCTU in Owen Sound, Ontario, in 1874, Youmans formed a second chapter in Picton in December that year and lobbied citizens to sign pledges of abstinence. Alcohol, she argued, was causing both emotional and economic damage. "You men look at the temperance

**LETITIA YOUMANS** ◆ Youmans was present at the founding of the Women's Christian Temperance Union (WCTU) in 1874 at an international Sunday school conference in Chatauqua, New York. She later established a Canadian chapter in Picton, Ontario, and lobbied for temperance courses in public schools (causing the government to refer to the WCTU as "Women Constantly Troubling Us"). Youmans approached temperance as a moral and religious issue as well as a social concern, and her evangelical organization provided a vehicle to effect change at a time when women did not have the right to vote. By 1890, almost fifteen thousand children were enrolled in Ontario Bands of Hope, a WCTU-sponsored education program in which students listened to lectures, read the Bible, and sang temperance songs.

Touch not the foaming, tempting glass,
Nor look upon the wine!
A serpent vile is hid within
The liquid of the vine.

Its ruddy gleam invites you all
To taste the sparkling bowl,
And hides beneath the poison fangs
Which smite into your soul.
Touch not nor taste the seething ill
Flee from the tempting foe;
Let not its hue profane your lips.
Twill bring you bitter woe.

(*National Woman's Christian Temperance Union, Frances Willard Memorial Library*)

question in its financial aspect," she argued. "We women look at it as a bartering in souls and the temporal and eternal welfare of our husbands, brothers and sons. We look at it as an evil spirit devastating our homes and dragging our loved ones to perdition."

John A. Macdonald was a devout drinker, but Alexander Mackenzie was a teetotalling Presbyterian who supported the WCTU's demand that local authorities be allowed to impose prohibition in their districts. Because women could not vote, however, there was little political benefit to his position.

Macdonald attacked Mackenzie's faltering government in the House of Commons at every opportunity, blaming it for failing to bring the country out of the depression. "You have ruined our trade," he told the prime minister. "You have destroyed manufacturers, you have shaken our credit, you have deprived our workmen of work . . ." Workers had begun to leave the cities, which harboured the disadvantages of the industrial age (pollution, crime, overcrowding) without offering the advantages (employment). Some went south, seeking work in American factories. Others went west to the

Alexander Mackenzie (*National Archives of Canada*, PAC C-20052)

prairies, which offered space, fresh air, and free land, and seemed, from a distance at least, to be a paradise.

In 1869, the Hudson's Bay Company had sold Rupert's Land – almost 8 million square kilometres of territory that included parts of northern Quebec and northern Ontario, most of the prairies, and a portion of what is now Nunavut – to Canada, opening the west to settlement. Over the next twenty years, the west would go through a dramatic cultural and political transformation, a process hastened by the long-promised construction of a transcontinental railway. This sparked frantic land speculation, turning the raw prairie into real estate, and lured settlers from England, Europe, and Ontario.

The native peoples of the prairies would become the first casualties of the new settlement and the railway. "The iron road has frightened the game away and the talking wire stretches from sunrise to sunset," a Cree chief would later complain. The Cree, Blackfoot, Blood, Peigan, and other nations were being devastated by whisky, disease, and the starvation that came with the loss of the buffalo herds. They were courted with treaties and asked to trust in the beneficence of the Great Mother, Queen Victoria. The return of Louis Riel to the west provided a voice for the discontent of both Métis and natives, and, briefly, for the white settlers too.

**NORTH WEST MOUNTED POLICE** ◆ After the Hudson's Bay Company sold Rupert's Land (the North-West) to the government of Canada in 1869, the territory fell prey to whisky traders and violence. In May 1873, 20 Assiniboine natives were massacred by American hunters in the Cypress Hills. A year later, the first 318 members of the North West Mounted Police began a march westward to keep the peace. Recruited from Ontario, Quebec, and the Maritimes, they were farm boys and clerks who had been offered a good horse, a scarlet uniform, and seventy-five cents a day. Thirty-one deserted before the trek had even begun, and after one day of riding, five more disappeared. After almost three months of low rations, scant water, dying horses, and mosquito plagues, 251 men and 24 officers arrived at Fort Macleod, near the present-day city of Calgary. They quickly brought order to the territory with very little violence, thus making a very favourable impression on many of the Plains chiefs.

"The Great Queen Mother, hearing of the sorrows of her children, sent out the Red Coats," said Mistawasis, a Cree chief. "Though these were only of a number you could count on your fingers and toes, yet the cutthroats and criminals who recognized no authority but their guns, who killed each other on the slightest pretence and murdered Indians without fear of reprisal, immediately abandoned their forts, strong as they were, and fled back to their own side of the line. I ask you why those few men could put to flight those bad men who for years have defied the whole of the southern Indian nations? . . .

"Let me tell you why these things were so. It was the power that stands behind those few Red Coats that those men feared and wasted no time in getting out when they could . . ."

In the 1880s that relationship changed when the North West Mounted Police were called upon to enforce treaty agreements, so that they were viewed by some chiefs as agents of suppression rather than salvation. (Top: Colonel James Farquharson Macleod and Captain Edmund Dalrymple Clark, NWMP, *Glenbow Archives, NA-2206-1*. Below: NWMP circa 1890, *Provincial Archives of Manitoba, N-9304*)

Across the Red River from Winnipeg was the small, French-speaking Métis settlement of St. Boniface. As prime minister, John A. Macdonald had clashed with the Métis, led by Louis Riel, during the 1869 uprising known as the Red River resistance. "These impulsive half breeds have got spoilt by their *émeute* [insurrection]," Macdonald said then, "and must be kept down by a strong hand until they are swamped by the influx of settlers." And now the settlers were arriving. Hundreds of English Protestants came to Winnipeg or settled in homesteads on the Manitoba prairie, many of them hostile to the Métis, who had been farming the land with success for some time. "Instead of treating the Métis fairly," wrote Bishop Alexandre-Antonin Taché, who presided over the largest Catholic church in the area that was now known as the North-West, "the most fundamental manners have been forgotten. Instead of being treated in a gentlemanly way, the Métis have suffered vulgarities and insults."

The issue of schooling – Catholic versus Protestant – had been a contentious fixture of Canadian political life since the 1840s, and it proved to be even more divisive in the new province of Manitoba. The only protection for the French culture lay in the fragile balance of power between English- and French-speaking settlers that had been engineered by Louis Riel. The Red River resistance had preceded Manitoba's entry into Confederation, and protection for the French language and Catholic schools had been enshrined in the Manitoba Act. But it was being threatened by the waves of English settlers. "The old-timers seemed to feel a strange mood in the air," wrote Louis Goulet, a Métis who had been raised in the Red River area. "Newcomers, especially the ones from Ontario, were eagerly sowing racial and religious conflict, banding together to fan the flames of discord between different groups in the Red River Settlement. These émigrés from Ontario, all of them Orangemen, looked as if their one dream in life was to make war on the Hudson's Bay Company, the Catholic Church and anyone who spoke French."

Father Albert Lacombe, a missionary who had been living in the west since 1852, longer than any other member of the Oblate order, was the parish priest at St. Mary's in Winnipeg. Lacombe felt that the best way to preserve the French language was to encourage Quebecers to settle in Manitoba. A man who had survived prairie blizzards, grass fires, and attacks by Cree warriors, Lacombe saw the influx of Ontario Orangemen as a greater threat.

Father Lacombe met with Premier Charles Boucher de Boucherville of Quebec, asking for help in bringing Quebecers out to Manitoba, but de Boucherville had his own population problems. Quebecers were fleeing the depression and settling in New England factory towns – Lowell, Manchester, Suncook, and Keesville – which collectively had a larger French-speaking population than Manitoba, and so were known as the "Little Canadas." Priests had followed their parishioners and built new churches in the United States. Ten per cent of Quebec's people had emigrated, and de Boucherville was worried about the province's waning influence in Ottawa as its numbers

**ALBERT LACOMBE IN 1886 WITH BLACKFOOT MEN, CROWFOOT (LEFT) AND THREE BULLS (RIGHT)** ◆ After being ordained in 1849, Father Lacombe went to Red River for two years, then returned to Montreal for six months. "I did not relish the life of a parish priest and I would rather return to the world if I could not be a missionary. I wanted to make all the sacrifices – or none at all." He supervised the building of the first bridge in Alberta and established the territory's first school, at Fort Edmonton. He worked among the Cree and Blackfoot, advocating tribal peace, and spoke both their languages. The Blackfoot called Lacombe Ars-Okitsiparpi, "the Man of Good Heart." The CPR credited Lacombe with keeping Crowfoot from joining the North West Rebellion, and he was given a lifetime pass in recognition.

Lacombe died in 1916 at the age of eighty-nine, and both the Cree and Blackfoot claimed his body. A compromise was reached: his body was buried at St. Albert, in Cree country, while his heart went to Midnapore (south of Calgary), home to the Blackfoot. (*Glenbow Archives, NA-1654-1*)

dwindled. "Far from encouraging me in our business of colonization," Lacombe wrote of their encounter, "he assured me that he would do everything in his power to prevent Canadians from the province of Quebec from emigrating to Manitoba. He told me to go after the ones in the United States."

Lacombe did, seeking to lure them away from the factories and out to the bright spaces of Manitoba. "I want to speak to you about emigration to Manitoba," he told a group of transplanted Québécois. "We need French emigration if we are to preserve our position. Please be aware that an average of forty families arrive from Ontario each month. Manitoba is beautiful country, its wealth attracts our neighbours. Would you let them take lone possession of a land that belongs as much to us as to them? Come to Manitoba, you Canadians from the United States who want to see your homeland again, come there and you will find yourselves at home. . . . The prairies are there, waiting for you."

Lacombe was not the only French Canadian touring New England, looking for souls. The exiled Louis Riel was also there, seeking support for the Métis cause. "Everyone is for us, wherever I go," he said. "There was a meeting of French Canadians here yesterday. They passed the most sympathetic resolutions for the Métis, especially those who were being persecuted. They applauded. They demonstrated a generous affection for all of us." But

**LOUIS RIEL** ◆ "On the eighteenth of December 1874, while [I was] standing alone on a mountaintop near Washington, D.C., the same spirit that appeared to Moses in the midst of clouds of flame appeared to me in the same manner. I was astonished. I was dumbfounded. It was said to me: 'Rise, Louis David Riel, you have a mission to accomplish for the benefit of humanity.' The words, spoken in Latin, were addressed to me: I received my divine notification with uplifted arms and bowed head."

This is how Louis Riel, on August 2, 1885, described to a reporter from the *Montreal Star* the occasion on which he received the gift of prophecy. His journal entries at the time show an almost romantic attachment to death: "Death lies beside me in my bed. When sleep begins to close my eyes, she whispers. Her voice touches the bottom of my heart; it says that sleep is a rehearsal for death. 'Notice,' she says, 'how sleep comes to you. That is almost how I will greet you on the day you will have to meet me.'" (*St Boniface Historical Society*)

affection did not translate into emigration. They were not prepared to leave their factory jobs for an uncertain future in Manitoba.

The Quebec workers were held in contempt by the American factory owners, who paid them little and called them "the Chinese of the East." Riel ridiculed the workers' meekness in a satirical poem.

> I'll never work the soil
> like a bloody farmer
> Buried by sweaty toil
> A brutish commoner.
> I'd rather clean the works
> of a clanking machine
> or pose like dainty clerks
> a docile Canadian.

Riel's political lobbying developed religious overtones as he came to believe that God was speaking directly to him, commanding a divine mission. "When I speak to you," he told the New England Québécois, "it is the voice of God that sounds and everything I say is essential to you. I am the happy telephone who transmits the songs and messages of heaven. I help in a special way." He asked Father Primeau, the parish priest in Worcester, Massachusetts, to recognize him as a prophet of God. Primeau thought that Riel was delusional and sought help. In early January 1876, Riel was

**JOHN A. MACDONALD** ◆ "At the time we took the vote last year I went at considerable length into the subject of destitute Indians, the utter disappearance of the buffalo and the action of the American government which formed a perfected cordon to prevent buffalo from crossing the lines. Formerly the Indians in the North-west, except those tribes which had some little fish, subsisted on buffalo. Buffalo was their bread, wine and meat, and that supply utterly and totally failed. I am not at all sorry, as I have said before, that this has happened. So long as there was a hope that buffalo would come into the country, there was no means of inducing the Indians to settle down on their reserves. The total failure of the buffalo the year before last and last year, caused the Indians to be thrown on the mercy of the government of the North-west. We could not, as Christians and men, allow them to starve, and we were obliged, no matter what the cost might be, to furnish them with food. It was better to feed them than to fight them." John A. Macdonald, speaking in the House of Commons, May 9, 1883. (*National Archives of Canada, c-21596*)

diagnosed with megalomania and quietly taken to Longue Pointe, a Montreal insane asylum. He was soon after moved to the provincial asylum at Beauport, where he spent almost two years. His identity was kept secret to protect him from Canadian bounty hunters seeking the $5,000 reward offered by the Ontario government for his capture. Riel was still wanted in Ontario for the murder, during the Red River resistance, of Orangeman Thomas Scott.

When Riel was finally released, he found his old nemesis, John A. Macdonald, poised to return to power. Tired of Alexander Mackenzie's dour management, and weary of the depression, voters returned the Old Chieftain to office in 1878.

To deal with the depression, Macdonald instituted protective tariffs, which preserved the domestic market for Canadian manufacturers. His National Policy, as the plan was called, revived the construction of the Canadian Pacific Railway (CPR), which had languished under the cost-conscious Mackenzie. "Until that road is built," Macdonald said, "this dominion is a mere geographical expression and not one great dominion. Until bound by that iron link, we are not a dominion in fact." His proposed railway would stretch eight thousand kilometres through some of the most varied and difficult terrain in the world, through rock, along the vast prairies, and into the vertical maze of the Rocky Mountains. It would be one of the most impressive engineering feats in history, as well as one of the most expensive, and it would open the west for settlement. Farmers would have

**IMMIGRATION PAMPHLETS**

◆ Many of these pamphlets promoted the idea that, by settling in the clean, fresh prairies, the immigrant could not only improve his circumstances but improve himself: "All the charms that belong to youth, hope, energy, are found in the North West, and the bracing influence of the new free land on mind and character is remarkable. The Ontario farmer is a fine specimen of the yeoman, but three years in the North West raises him higher on the scale of manhood – while a commensurate improvement is noted in all classes and races from Europe who have come amongst us, having the essential qualities of capacity for work, perseverance, sobriety and intelligence." Nicholas Flood Davin, *Homes for Millions*, 1891. (*Canadian Pacific Archives*, BR-226)

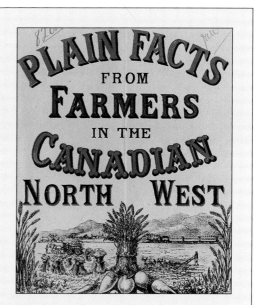

a means to get their crops to market and eastern manufacturers would have a commercial artery to consumers.

The land the railway was to pass through was advertised in central Canada, England, Scotland, and Europe. Lively pamphlets were published, extolling the virtues of the prairies in the hearty, unreliable prose of salesmen. One of the most inventive pamphleteers was Thomas Spence, who had served in Riel's short-lived provisional Manitoba government in 1870. Spence was known as the father of Western Immigration pamphlets. "Situated where the great stream of human life will pour its mightiest flood," he wrote, "beneficently endowed with nature's riches, and illumed by such a light, there will be no portion of all earth's domain surpassing in glory and grandeur the future of Canada's North-West. . . . Feeling himself every inch a man, as he gazes upon the unclaimed acres which shall reward his toil, the settler breathes a freer air, his bosom swells with a prouder purpose, and his strong arms achieve unwonted results."

There was competition for settlers from the United States, where wages were higher and the weather less severe. The Americans had their own lushly descriptive pamphlets: "the hope of the despairing poor of the world, boundless ocean of land; diversified by rolling hills and lakes and woods or swelling into the immense plains, waiting for the flocks and the fields." Canadian immigration literature dealt with the competition by warning of the warm, disease-carrying breezes and the wasting torpor of more southerly latitudes.

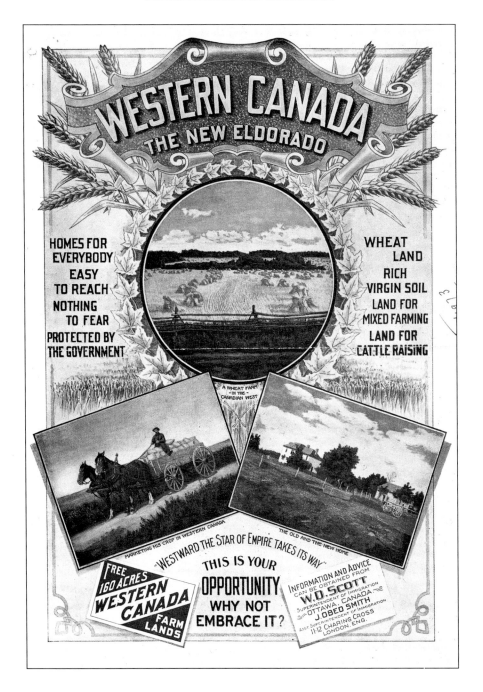

(*National Archives of Canada, C-85854*)

Pamphlets were tailored for specific markets. For English workers languishing in ill-paid servitude, trapped by class, they offered not just land but a new, egalitarian society. For those living in cities, the authors talked about the clean air and the pristine moral climate, free from the sin that crowded cities attracted. The west was a Utopian notion, a place where people could reinvent themselves. "The future citizen of the North-West of Canada will have Norse, Celtic and Saxon blood in his veins," Thomas Spence wrote. "His countenance, in the pure, dry electric air, will be fresh as the morning. His muscles will be iron, his nerves steel."

Macdonald's government was offering 160 acres (roughly 65 hectares) for a ten-dollar deposit, and people came trickling into the territory, hoping for a new life, one resembling the happy promise of the pamphlets. Once there, they were often overwhelmed by the realities of prairie existence. Jennie Plaxton and her husband left London, Ontario, in May 1879 and journeyed to Prince Albert, Saskatchewan, along crude cart trails out of Winnipeg. It was a wet summer, and they laboured through mud and were tortured by mosquitoes. "We travelled quite a distance when we met another couple – also a bride and a bridegroom," Jennie wrote in her memoir. "The bride was in torment with mosquitoes, just nearly crazed with them. . . . She asked her husband to shoot her and then kill himself. He merely laughed at her, but one morning while he was hunting his horses, the young wife found his revolver and shot herself. The poor woman was buried on the top of a hill where a wooden cross marks her grave."

The Plaxtons built a cabin that was finished on the day before Christmas, in temperatures of nearly minus-fifty degrees Celsius: "Even the police could not go out: their horses' noses would bleed from the cold. For the next few years we struggled on. We found it very lonesome. Every time a riverboat whistled on the river I hitched up my old black pony and drove it into town. I stood on the bank and watched the passengers disembark."

Mary Louisa Cummins came from London, England, with her husband, Colin, and settled at Grenfell, Saskatchewan. "At the time, the CPR was plastering the country with fascinating pictures of glorious wheat fields on the great western prairies," she wrote. "There was a fortune for everyone in three years not to mention glittering promises of practically free land. Hopes were high. So we, poor fools, fell into the trap."

Her husband went out first and built a house for them. "Am I to live in that?" she cried, when she saw the wooden box that was their home. It measured five metres (sixteen feet) square, with a partition down the middle to separate the kitchen from the bedroom. Mary Louisa had five children in quick succession, and she and her husband planted crops that barely sustained the family.

Harriet Neville and her family came to Cottonwood, Saskatchewan, from Hamilton, Ontario, beaten down by the depression and lured by the advertisements. "There was rather an excitement in the papers and otherwise about the opening of the North West Territories and the building of the CPR," she wrote. "My husband went to Winnipeg and from there . . . far west of the Saskatchewan River. I got a letter saying my husband had come to a station called Regina which might be the capital of Assiniboia and was going to stay there that winter building houses and he said he would make a homestead ready for me to come out in the spring." Harriet went expecting the clean, Anglo-Saxon gloss of the posters. "We got to Winnipeg and a mighty muddy city it was. If you stepped off the wooden sidewalks you sank deep into the prairie mire which stuck to you like glue. It was a rough looking place and not at all my idea of a city."

Nevertheless, Winnipeg was poised to boom, and the trickle of immigrants continued. But there was one aspect of the prairies that went unmentioned in every immigration pamphlet: their original inhabitants, the native peoples.

Crowfoot was a Blood native who was born around 1830 in the Belly River country, near present-day Lethbridge. He had a calm, patrician face with a long, fine nose. His father, Packs a Knife, was killed when Crowfoot was two, and his mother married a Blackfoot warrior. Crowfoot fought his first battle at fourteen and by the time he was twenty, he had survived eighteen more battles, mostly with the Plains Cree, and had been wounded six times, once by a bullet that was never removed. At twenty he was given the name Isapo-muxika (Crow Indians' Big Foot) after a daring raid on a Crow camp. He eventually became the Blackfoot leader, the most powerful chief on the prairies. Crowfoot was thoughtful, short-tempered, courageous. An agnostic, he did not embrace native spiritual beliefs, which set him apart. Strikingly, he wore an owl's skull tied into his hair his entire adult life.

Crowfoot's tenure as chief spanned a time of sudden and disastrous change: the destruction of the buffalo, the arrival of whisky, ongoing outbreaks of smallpox, and the dismal concept of the reserve. On the prairies, this profound change took no more than a decade.

The early missionaries had come to a political world defined by recent hostilities between the Blackfoot and the Cree. "The Blackfoot nation formed a people of whom it may be truly said that they were against every man and that every man was against them," said Father Albert Lacombe. "They possessed at the same time great eloquence, a savage pride and a wild love of freedom of their own."

Lacombe met Crowfoot when the Blackfoot were wintering along the Battle River and the priest was trying to gather his first souls out on the plains. Lacombe, raised on a farm near St. Sulpice, Quebec, and ordained in 1849, had been given "the mission of roaming the prairies in an attempt to evangelize the ever wandering Cree and Blackfeet." Lacombe had a Métis grandmother, and he had the advantage of speaking the languages of both tribes. Catholic missionaries had had success with the Woods Cree (though some became Methodists, to the fathers' dismay), but the Plains Cree remained unconverted and militant.

Lacombe's first attempt at evangelizing almost killed him. He was trying, unsuccessfully, to convert Crowfoot to Catholicism when the Plains Cree attacked the Blackfoot camp. "In an instant," Lacombe wrote, "some score of bullets came crashing through the leather lodge, and the wild war whoop of the Cree broke forth through the short and rapid detonation of many muskets . . . the groans of the dying, the yelling of the warriors, the harangues of the chiefs, and the noise of dogs and horses all mingled, forming a kind of hell."

Eight hundred Cree were attacking eighty Blackfoot. Lacombe tried to intervene. Silhouetted in his black cassock against the snow, he stood between the two armies with his arms raised, preaching harmony, until a

**CROWFOOT** ◆ "We all see the day is coming when the buffalo will all be killed, and we shall have nothing more to live on . . . then you will come into our camp and see the poor Blackfoot starving. I know that the heart of the white soldier will be sorry for us and they will tell the Great Mother who will not let her children starve. We are getting shut in. The Crees are coming in to our country from the north, and the white men from the south and east, and they are all destroying our means of living . . . we plainly see these days coming . . ." Crowfoot, speaking in 1877. (*Provincial Archives of Alberta, P-129*)

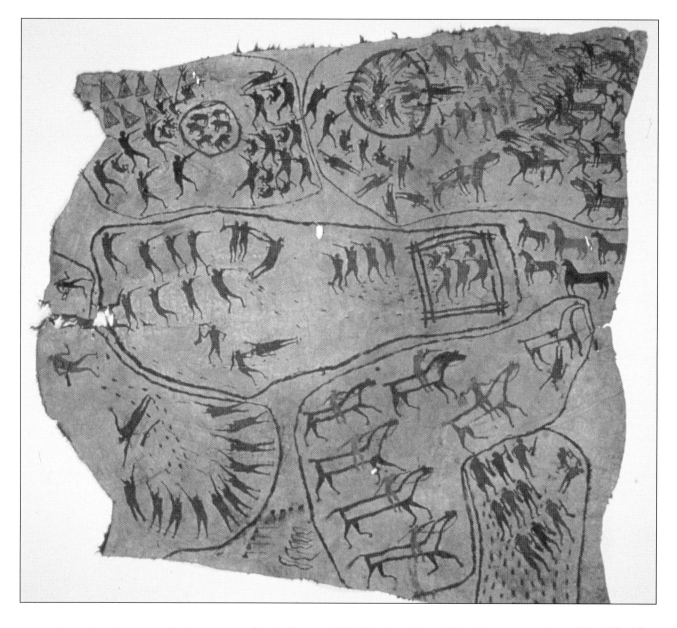

A battle on the plains recorded by the Sarcee, of the Blackfoot Confederacy. (*Royal Ontario Museum, HK-459*)

musket ball grazed his forehead, knocking him unconscious. Two Blackfoot warriors dragged him back to safety. It was one of the last bloody battles between the Blackfoot and Cree, a military struggle that ended finally in 1869, replaced by a quiet, wasting war with the federal government and alcohol.

The whisky traders first came up the Whoop-Up Trail, which extended from Fort Benton, Montana, to trading posts in southern Alberta and on into Blackfoot territory, near the confluence of the Bow and Elbow rivers. They came to trade rifles, blankets, pots, and, most profitably, whisky. Cheaply made from distilled alcohol mixed with chewing tobacco, red pepper, soap, molasses, and red ink, it was labelled Whoop-Up Bug Juice. The effects were immediate and devastating, causing more damage to the Cree and Blackfoot in three years than a century of tribal wars.

"The whiskey brought among us by the traders is fast killing us off and we are powerless before this evil," said Crowfoot. "We are unable to resist the temptation to drink when brought in contact with the white man's water. Our horses, buffalo robes and other articles of trade go for whiskey; a large number of our people have killed one another and perished under this influence."

In 1874, the North West Mounted Police (NWMP) arrived at the Oldman River, 165 kilometres south of the present site of Calgary, where they built a fort and set out to curb the whisky trade. Crowfoot was assured that his people would be protected. "My brother, your words make me glad," he said. "You say this will be stopped. We are glad to have it stopped."

The whisky trade was stopped, but there was a new worry: the disappearance of the buffalo, which provided food, shelter, and clothing to the Plains natives. In the 1870s, two technological advances spurred the slaughter of the buffalo: the means to tan buffalo hides for use as belt leather (previous methods had left it too soft, useful only as chamois), and the widespread use of the repeating rifle. There had once been as many as fifty million buffalo on the North American Great Plains, but their numbers were winnowed daily. A third factor was the U.S. government's policy of encouraging the slaughter as a military tactic, in order to destroy the "Indians' commissary," as General Philip Sheridan phrased it. "Let them kill, skin and sell until the buffalo are exterminated," he said. "Then your prairies can be covered with speckled cattle and the festive cowboy."

Crowfoot addressing the Marquess of Lorne at Blackfoot Crossing, Alberta, September 10, 1881. (*National Archives of Canada, C-121918*)

The slaughter of the buffalo took place in both Canada and the United States. Here, passengers and crew on the line of the Kansas–Pacific Railroad shoot buffalo for sport. (*Granger, 4E26.13*)

The "festive cowboy" was joined by the equally festive British sportsman, who came west and shot hundreds of the animals. In the early 1870s, there were still herds of buffalo so vast that it took several days to pass by them on horseback. But within five years, tens of millions had been slaughtered for sport, profit, or military gain. The buffalo were pursued almost to extinction in the United States, and buffalo hunters burned the grasslands at the Canadian border to keep the few remaining animals from heading north. When Canadian settlers started farming, the first cash crop for some was buffalo bones, sold by the ton for fertilizer.

As the railway moved west, it became necessary to establish treaties with the natives, whose land it would cross. In the United States, native land was being occupied by force, resulting in bloody wars. In Canada, the hope was to achieve peaceful transfer of land in exchange for compensation.

On August 15, 1876, two thousand natives camped on the plains outside Fort Carlton on the North Saskatchewan River, waiting to meet with treaty commissioner Alexander Morris and sign the largest land treaty in the history of the continent. The transfer of more than 325,000 square kilometres was being negotiated. Morris opened the ceremony with his vision of the natives' future: "I see the Queen's Councillors taking the Indian by the hand saying we are brothers, we will lift you up, we will teach you, if you will learn, the cunning of the white man. All along that road I see Indians gathering, I see gardens growing and houses building; I see them receiving money from the Queen's Commissioners to purchase

Buffalo bones.
(*Canadian Pacific Archives*, NS-6679)

clothing for their children; at the same time I see them enjoying their hunting and fishing as before, I see them retaining their old mode of living with the Queen's gift in addition." Each family would receive one square mile of land to farm, about 2.5 square kilometres.

Morris's offer was not well received by everyone. Poundmaker, a Plains Cree chief, responded, "This is our land! It isn't a piece of pemmican to be cut off and given back to us. It is our land and we will take what we want." Some Cree were wary of the treaty, which had been accompanied by ill omens, they felt. Two men, the Reverend George McDougall, and Superintendent Leif Crozier of the North West Mounted Police, had been sent by the government to sell the idea of the treaty to the Plains natives. McDougall was found frozen to death, and Crozier went mad, wandering the landscape aimlessly until the Cree found him. The natives associated these events with the treaty, and a further curse was attached when a Cree chief, Sweet Grass, was given a shotgun as a gift for signing the treaty and it went off accidentally, killing him.

Big Bear was another Cree chief who was not seduced by the treaty. "He was to be seen every day riding around the camp on an Indian pony, haughty and defiant," an observer noted, "his face and body adorned with war paint, and his long black hair decorated with eagle feathers while he carried a gaudy parasol over his head." Big Bear was a small, tough leader who had once had a vision that foretold the coming of the white man and the "bounteous presents from the Great Mother," which he saw simply as a bribe. "We want none of the Queen's presents!" he declared. "When we set a fox trap, we scatter

**POUNDMAKER AND HIS WIFE** ◆ "Next summer, or at the latest next fall, the railway will be close to us, the whites will fill the country and they will dictate to us as they please. It is useless to dream that we can frighten them; that time has passed; our only resource is our work, our industry, our farms. The necessity of earning our bread by the sweat of our brows does not discourage me; there is only one thing that can discourage me – what is it? – if we do not agree amongst ourselves; let us be like one man, and work will show quick, and there will be nothing too hard. Oh! Allow me to ask you all to love each other; that is not difficult. We have faced the bullets of our enemies more than once, and now we cannot bear a word from each other." Poundmaker, January 1, 1882, addressing his people at a feast. (*Canadian Pacific Archives, NS-8411*)

**CANADIAN PACIFIC RAILWAY CONSTRUCTION WORKERS** ◆ The building of the CPR was an audacious and troubled enterprise that threatened personal fortunes, imperilled governments, and took the lives of hundreds of construction workers. Through the Rocky Mountains, avalanches were a constant threat, one that continued even after the line was built. The first CPR transcontinental train left Montreal on the evening of June 28, 1886, and arrived in Port Moody, British Columbia, at noon on July 4. At CPR president William Van Horne's insistence, the trains were luxuriously appointed. First-class fare from Montreal to Vancouver was twenty dollars. (*National Archives of Canada*)

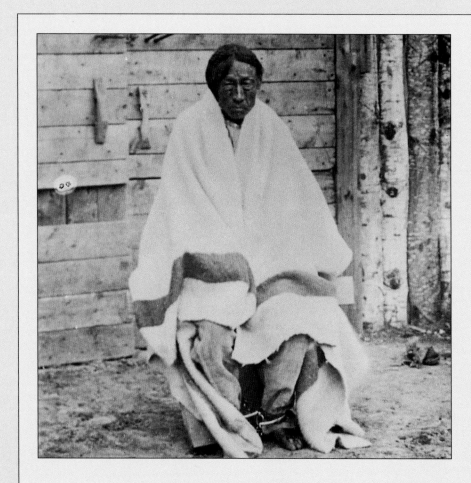

**BIG BEAR IN 1886** ◆ "It has come to me as through the bushes that you are not all united. Take time and become united, and I will speak. The government sent to us those who think themselves men. They bring everything crooked. They take our lands, they sell them and they buy themselves fine clothes. Then they clap their hands on their hips and call themselves men. They are not men. They have no honesty. They are an unsightly beast. Their faces are twisted from the appearance of honest men." Big Bear, speaking at the Duck Lake Council, 1884. (*National Archives of Canada*, PA-25514)

**THE SIGNING OF THE 1876 LAND TREATY WITH THE SASKATCHEWAN CREE** ◆ "I do not differ from my people, but I want more explanation. I heard what you said yesterday, and I thought that when the law was established in this country it would be for our good. From what I can hear and see now, I cannot understand that I shall be able to clothe my children and feed them as long as the sun shines and water runs." Poundmaker, speaking to Alexander Morris, lieutenant governor of the North-West Territories, 1876. (*National Library of Canada*, 64741)

pieces of meat all around, but when the fox gets into the trap, we knock him on the head. We want no baits! Let your chiefs come like men and talk to us." Big Bear – who was young, and not swayed by the influence of the missionaries – was one of the few chiefs willing to confront the government.

The prevailing mood was one of weary resignation. The buffalo were almost gone, and the tribes had been devastated by whisky and smallpox. Most of the Plains chiefs signed the treaty, at least symbolically. None actually signed his name, or even marked an X. They simply touched the pen that someone else had used on their behalf (though Crowfoot later claimed that he had not done even that). In return they were promised land, a plough, a harrow, and seed; they would become farmers. There was a tentative peace.

Big Bear went south to Montana, contemptuous of the process. While searching for the last of the buffalo, he kept in touch with events through a subscription to the *Saskatchewan Herald*. Big Bear used the press to state his case and sent a letter to the editor declaring that he was neither a monster nor a fugitive; he was simply waiting to see if the government would keep its promises.

Father Lacombe worried about the growing white settlement and the progress of the railroad. "I would look long in silence at the road coming on like a band of wild geese in the sky, cutting its way through the prairies opening up the great country we thought would be ours for years. I could see it driving my poor Indians before it and spreading out behind it the farms and towns . . ."

The transcontinental railway was necessary to consolidate the nation that Macdonald had envisioned, but it already had a tawdry, troubled history. The original contract to build it had gone to Montreal shipping magnate Hugh Allan in 1872, a gift in recognition of Allan's generous contributions to Macdonald's election campaign that year (roughly $350,000). The railway scheme collapsed in the well-publicized "Pacific Scandal" when leaked documents showed requests from Conservative Party members that read like children's letters to Santa ("Dear Sir Hugh, The friends of the government will expect to be assisted with funds in the pending elections . . . Sir John A. Macdonald $25,000; Hon. Mr. Langevin $15,000 . . .").

Part of the line had been constructed under Allan, and there were a few isolated sections that had been completed by other contractors, but the bulk of the line, across the prairies and through the Rocky Mountains, remained unbuilt. Its completion had been promised as a condition of British Columbia's entry into Confederation, and in 1878 the deadline agreed on was only three years away.

A new railway syndicate was formed, led by George Stephen, president of the Bank of Montreal. It included James Jerome Hill, John S. Kennedy, Richard Bathgate Angus, and a silent but powerful partner, Donald Smith. Smith's name had been omitted from the government contract because

**DONALD A. SMITH** ◆ Donald Smith came from the Scottish Highlands to work for the Hudson's Bay Company and spent thirty years in the wilderness. When he came to Montreal at the age of forty-nine, he was a rustic, untutored man whose tastes had been formed in log cabins and tents. He quickly adjusted, however, and made a fortune by investing in furs, American railroads, and banks. With his newfound wealth he bought a Franco-Victorian mansion on Dorchester Street. His extensive renovations included a $50,000 mahogany staircase that was built without nails – all the pieces were carefully dovetailed by cabinetmakers – and a space to house his collection of paintings by Raphael, Gainsborough, and Titian. He had an English butler (a delicious irony for a Highlander) and twelve servants, and he entertained more lavishly than anyone in the city. This photograph was taken moments before he drove in the last spike of the Canadian Pacific Railway. (*National Archives of Canada, c-3693*)

Macdonald detested him, and Stephen thought it might jeopardize their chances. During the Pacific Scandal, Smith, as the member of Parliament for Selkirk, Manitoba, had loudly denounced the corruption in the Conservative Party, a fact that Macdonald, with his long political memory, had not forgotten. The government guaranteed the syndicate a $25-million loan and granted it title to 25 million acres (10 million hectares) of prairie land – an enormous real estate deal. It was also effectively given monopoly status. Stephen thought it would cost $45 million to construct the line. Sandford Fleming, the CPR's chief engineer, who had laid out much of the route already, estimated the cost at $100 million. Both estimates turned out to be low.

Stephen went to England to raise money but was met with a barrage of negative press, retailing the horrors of prairie life as seen from central London. "Men and cattle are frozen to death in numbers that would rather startle the intending settler if he knew, and those who are not killed outright are often maimed for life by frostbites," read an article in the optimistically named *Truth* magazine. Mosquitoes bore a malarial plague, the article cautioned, and chances of survival on the plains were slim. Stephen tried to engineer favourable coverage in the London papers, but his efforts were hijacked by the animal-loving English population's interest in Jumbo the elephant, then touring England with the Barnum circus. It was rumoured that the elephant was dying, and his imminent demise dominated the front pages. As it turned out, Jumbo survived and lived another four years (until hit by a train at, ironically, St. Thomas, Ontario).

The government loan was quickly depleted, and little new money had come in to allow work to continue. Contractors were going unpaid, and a sense of desperation plagued the project. The route that Sandford Fleming had mapped out (which went northwest from Red River through Saskatoon, Edmonton, and on through the Yellowhead Pass in the Rockies) was rejected by the syndicate. They felt it would be cheaper to take a southern route, which would also allow them to capitalize on land speculation at new and unclaimed sites.

The syndicate received a blast of energy when William Cornelius Van Horne took over the construction of the line in 1882, promising to build 500 miles (800 kilometres) in a single year. Van Horne had started his railway career at the age of fourteen as an apprentice telegrapher and worked his way up to general manager of the Chicago and Milwaukee Railroad. He looked a bit like Edward VII, and his personal philosophy was the opposite of that adhered to by the sober Scots with whom he came to fraternize in Montreal: "I eat all I can, drink all I can, I smoke all I can, and I don't care a damn for anything." He had heroic work habits, at times performing hard physical work on the railway himself, eating five meals a day, drinking till dawn, and returning to the job the next day. Under his management, the railway roared ahead, sometimes by as much as ten kilometres of track a day.

Against his will, Father Albert Lacombe was called away from his mission among the Blackfoot and Cree to act as chaplain for the CPR crews. He accompanied the line's progress, counselling the often blasphemous workers after their killing workdays and before their nights filled with drink. His efforts to bring the word of the Lord to these men were wasted, he felt, and he returned happily to Fort Macleod, where he set up a mission for the natives.

When it was confirmed in 1881 that the railway would run through Winnipeg, the city experienced a giddy expansion. Fleming had proposed taking the railway through Selkirk. Winnipeg, he pointed out, was on a flood plain. "It is futile to assume that the Red River shall never again overflow its banks," he said. "Man is utterly powerless to prevent its occurring periodically." And the larger the population, he argued, the larger the disaster. But the city of Winnipeg lobbied the government, offering tax-free

**WILLIAM CORNELIUS VAN HORNE** ◆ Van Horne was an oversized man with an almost barbaric energy who made a habit of eating, drinking, and working all to excess. He would eat a pound of caviar accompanied by whisky and followed by Havana cigars. He occasionally worked on the railway he was supervising, putting in long hours as foreman or labourer and eating dinner with champagne at midnight.

Van Horne lacked a formal education and declined all the honorary degrees that were offered him. But he was refined in surprising ways. After moving from his house on Dorchester Street in Montreal, he commissioned CPR architect Bruce Price to design an addition to an existing home on Sherbrooke Street and had its fifty-two rooms decorated by Edward Colonna, who provided some of the first art nouveau design in Canada. Van Horne needed the space to house what was then one of the largest private art collections in North America. He had impressive examples of Japanese pottery and oriental wall hangings, and more than two hundred paintings by Rembrandt, Cézanne, Courbet, and Toulouse-Lautrec, among others. In one room were his own paintings; he was a passionate, if limited, landscape painter. He once said that he had been tired only twice in his life. (*Canadian Pacific Archives*, NS-8889)

land in perpetuity, free land for a train station, $200,000 in cash, and the construction of a $300,000 bridge over the Red River.

In return, the city reaped the benefits of the ensuing boom. Within months, there were three hundred real estate offices in Winnipeg. Speculators divided the surrounding prairie into grids and flipped land like pancakes, sometimes selling property in nearby towns that did not yet, and in some cases never would, exist. Land was sold in bars and offices, on wagons and sleighs. The city grew in an awkward burst, its population quickly doubling. Carpenters worked around the clock to keep up with demand. There were 180 telephones in operation, a novelty for the newly rich commercial class. "Diamond pins and diamond brooches and diamond rings were greatly in evidence," wrote George Ham in the *Toronto Mail*. "The city was all-ablaze with the excitement of prospective riches. Champagne replaced Scotch and soda, and game dinners were very common. Auction sales were held daily and nightly, and in the auction rooms of Jim Coolican, Walter Dufour and Joe Wolf people bought recklessly. Property changed hands. If ever there was a fool's paradise, it sure was located in Winnipeg. Men made fortunes – mostly on paper – and life was one continuous joy ride."

It was not a joy ride for everyone. "The Canadian people and those who governed them, thought only about the expanse and wealth of the vast domains of which they were taking possession," said Alexandre-Antonin Taché, the archbishop at St. Boniface. "The unfortunate Manitoba boom has gripped the North West and many a greedy man sees it as the promised land for wealth he has not had to work for. The region is not ready for such

**WINNIPEG, 1882** ◆ The land boom in Winnipeg lasted little more than a year, but in those months, the price of land on Main Street went as high as $2,000 per foot of frontage. By 1882, it was worth a fraction of that, and it would be ninety years before prices reached that level again. Ontarians came to Winnipeg to make their fortunes and lived in tents until houses (some built in as little as twenty-four hours) could be constructed. Jim Coolican was the largest of the land speculators, and he was known as the "Marquis de Mud." In one two-week period, Coolican sold a million dollars' worth of real estate. (*Provincial Archives of Manitoba, N-3077*)

large numbers of these men." The Métis, many of whom did not have title to the land they farmed, were excluded from the profit-taking, and the boom played itself out after a year and a half. A few months later, Sandford Fleming's prediction came true when the 1883 flood washed out the bridges. By that time, however, the opportunists had moved west along the route they expected the railway to follow.

Edmonton was supposed to get the CPR line, and there was a brief, abortive land boom there until it was announced that the track would instead go through Calgary. Along the proposed route, all kinds of towns sprang up. One, called Cannington Manor, was founded by a failed London banker named Captain Edward Mitchell Pierce and populated by British remittance men who wanted to recreate England on the prairie. Located south of the present site of Moosomin, Saskatchewan, it was described by Alice Hewlett, one of the early arrivals: "Once upon a time there was magic in the name of Cannington Manor. . . . In those days it was a gallant adventure upon which the early settlers set out. The railway had come no nearer than Brandon; reports were what they had to go upon, reports of a fair land where milk and honey could be made to flow. So they set out from England and Scotland

and from Ontario, and by devious paths found their way to the virgin prairie east of the Moose Mountains."

The town replicated English life, with cricket, tennis, fox-hunting, poetry reading, and scientific discussions. "Tea was served on Tennis Courts by the Ladies, and indeed it was a bright and happy scene," Hewlett wrote. "Intermingling with the pretty summer frocks of the ladies could be seen young men in flannels wearing the blazers and colours of all the best known English and Scottish public schools and even varsity blues. . . . Then back, usually in a buckboard, home to dress for dinner, to dine with friends or attend some public or private dance, card party, midnight frolic, drive or ride to the lake."

When the railroad bypassed Cannington Manor by sixteen kilometres, the town withered, then disappeared. But the British traditions would be upheld farther west, in the ranching country of the foothills.

In 1879, Crowfoot and his Blackfoot band went south to search for buffalo, which had largely vanished from the Canadian plains. The chief was encouraged by Indian commissioner Edgar Dewdney, who saw this as an opportunity to save money: "I advised them to go and gave them provisions. . . . They continued to follow the Buffalo further and further south until they reached the main herd. . . . I considered their remaining away saved the government $100,000 at least." By the spring of 1880, the buffalo were scarce everywhere, and the U.S. army was threatening. Crowfoot wrote to Dewdney, asking if the Great Mother would feed them. Dewdney responded that they should continue to pursue the buffalo. The last remaining herds took refuge in the Judith Basin in central Montana, attracting a crowd of Blackfoot, Cree, and Sioux, who joined in the hunt, the last one of any consequence.

By the fall, Crowfoot and his traditional enemy, Big Bear, were camped near Fort Carrol, Montana. Not far from these unlikely neighbours was Louis Riel. Since his release from the Beauport insane asylum in 1878, Riel had been teaching school in Montana, living quietly with his wife and two children. He had hopes of returning to Canada to claim a parcel of land he believed was rightfully his. He met with Big Bear, warning that the government would not honour the treaties it had signed with the natives. "Riel wanted me to raise all the men I could but I wouldn't," Big Bear said of the meeting. "Many wanted to fight in 1879 but I stopped them." A second meeting was cancelled after U.S. troops moved into the area, but the spectre of a rebellion had been raised.

The whisky traders found Crowfoot's band in Montana, with disastrous results. The Blackfoot traded away their horses for whisky, and some sold their women into prostitution. They died of measles, starvation, and exposure through the cold winter. On August 4, 1881, they prepared to walk more than six hundred kilometres home. It took six weeks to reach Fort Walsh, in the Cypress Hills.

Driving buffalo into a pound
(*Metro Toronto Reference Library*)

Augustus Jukes, a North West Mounted Police doctor, toured their encampments. "They are literally in a starving condition," he wrote, "and destitute of the commonest necessities of life. The disappearance of the buffalo has left them not only without food, but also without robes, moccasins and adequate tents or 'tepees' to shield them from the inclemency of the impending winter. Few of their lodges are of buffalo hide, the majority being of cotton only, and many of these in the most rotten and dilapidated condition. . . . Their clothing for the most part was miserable and scanty in the extreme. . . . It would indeed be difficult to exaggerate their extreme wretchedness and need, or the urgent necessity which exists for some prompt and sufficient provision being made for them by the government."

Treaty 6 was one of a series of treaties that were signed throughout the west and the north in the 1870s. It contained a clause that required the government to support the natives in the event of pestilence or famine. But in the early 1880s the economy was faltering, and the prime minister was looking for ways to cut back government spending. The deputy-superintendent of Indian affairs was Lawrence Vankoughnet, and he toured the western reserves and wrote to Macdonald: "Careful consideration after personally visiting localities convinced me that there has been much needless expenditure." He proposed cutting rations. The local Indian agents and NWMP argued against such a disastrous policy, but Vankoughnet insisted that the discretionary power of field agents be reduced, and that the decision-making power be concentrated in Ottawa. The natives received

This page, top left: Cree Women at Fort Walsh (*Provincial Archives of Alberta, AA-18806*). Top right: A Blood warrior (*Provincial Archives of Alberta, P85*). Bottom: Crowfoot and his family (*Glenbow Archives, NA 1104-1*). Opposite page, top left: Unknown warrior (*Saskatchewan Archives Board R-B2839*). Top right: Yellow Dog, a Blackfoot man (*Minnesota Historical Society*). Bottom left: Siupakio and Sikunnacio, Sarcee girls (*Provincial Archives of Alberta, B-10595*). Bottom right: Horse Child, son of Big Bear (*Glenbow Archives, NA 635-3*)

rations every other day, in a policy that became known in bureaucratic circles as "feed one day, starve the next."

The beef doled out as rations came from newly created ranch operations in the foothills. With the buffalo gone, the grazing lands of southern Alberta were perfect for raising cattle.

In 1881, the first large-scale operation, the Cochrane Ranch Company, was inaugurated by Matthew Cochrane, a Tory senator from Quebec. In response to Cochrane's request, Macdonald's government drafted regulations that allowed land to be leased for one cent an acre. Cochrane eventually leased 360,000 acres (145,700 hectares), mostly west and south of Calgary, and in 1881, the first cattle were introduced to Alberta: 9,400 head of polled black Angus and Shorthorns that were driven up through Montana to the border by American cowboys. A Canadian outfit then moved them north at a rate of twenty-five kilometres a day and forded the Bow River near Calgary in the autumn. The cattle drive was going on at the same time, and roughly the same rate, as Crowfoot's tragic northern march, the demoralized remnants of Plains culture moving beside the commercial future of the foothills. A few hundred cattle died or strayed en route, while Crowfoot's band buried its dead on the trail.

The ranch was administered from the east, through Cochrane and a group of Montreal merchants who were his partners. The first winter was mild and the cattle could graze. Hoping for another mild winter, the eastern partners did not put up any feed, and when more than a metre of snow fell and temperatures dropped to nearly minus-thirty degrees Celsius most of the herd starved. When the snows finally cleared, thousands of dead cattle filled the ravines, bloating in the spring sun. The Blackfoot found temporary employment skinning them where they lay, for twenty-five cents a hide.

Most of the ranches were owned by absentee landlords, British parliamentarians and eastern merchants who saw cattle as a good investment. They sent their sons to run the ranching operations, and a society grew up that was largely conservative, anglophile, and Anglican. There were formal balls, polo matches, cricket games, and "fox" hunts, where coyotes were substituted. These ranches supplied beef to the North West Mounted Police and to the natives on their reserves.

But little of the beef arrived; there was not enough to sustain the natives. During the winter of 1883–84, an estimated one in ten of the Plains natives died of starvation. "The bodies of the dead were strung up in trees as is the Indian custom," wrote a reporter from the *Manitoba Free Press*. "Spring found some fifty or more ghastly corpses dangling from limbs of trees surrounding the teepees of the remaining members of the band."

For five years, the government pursued a policy of coercion, trying to force natives onto reserves, using food as a weapon. Big Bear finally went to a reserve but refused to stay there, seeing it as a slow death for his people. Poundmaker agreed to try, but he lamented the shortage of resources and supplies that had been promised in the treaty. "We want teachers to instruct and educate our children. We try to do what the farm instructor has told us and we are doing the best we can but we need farm implements. I speak for my children and grandchildren who will starve if they do not receive the help that they so much need."

The white settlers were not having an easy time either. In order to borrow money needed to buy supplies and machinery, they had to have legal title to the land they were farming. But their pleas were met with indifference in Ottawa. Macdonald's protective tariffs, which had been greeted with enthusiasm by eastern manufacturers, were punishing the settlers, who now had to pay more for farm implements. The high price of shipping grain east added to their resentment.

William Jackson, a University of Toronto philosophy student who settled in Prince Albert in 1879, helped organize the Settlers' Union. "Gentlemen," he told the farmers, "we are starting a movement in this settlement with the view of attaining provincial legislatures for the North West Territories." Jackson blamed federal legislators for the recession and advocated a populist revolt. "The best day that ever dawned for my native Province of Ontario was that cold December morning of 1837," he said, "when William Lyon Mackenzie rebelled. When he took up arms in defence of our civil and religious liberties."

Jackson approached Métis farmers, asking them to join in an alliance against Ottawa. Dominion surveyors were staking out the land that the Métis had claimed, and they were ready to listen. Even the *Prince Albert Times*, a Tory paper, took up the cry and chastised the federal government: "The Dominion Government . . . occupies the contemptible position of a greedy grasping overbearing bully who has however totally misjudged the fighting powers of the subject it has chosen to oppress. . . . They need not look for their friends among the Canadians, half-breeds or Indians as they are likely soon to be made aware of in a manner at once startling and unpleasant."

This brief solidarity among westerners against the federal government quickly fractured along various lines, separating the Métis from the white settlers, the militant from the conciliatory, and the natives from everyone else. Within months, the *Prince Albert Times* had abandoned its rebellious tone and reverted to its Tory voice.

Big Bear tried to ally the Plains nations to present a united political voice. In June 1884, he organized a gathering of more than two thousand natives on Poundmaker's reserve, under the guise of a traditional Thirst Dance. It was probably the largest gathering of Cree chiefs in history. His goals were political rather than military, as he believed an actual war would be disastrous.

A troop under the command of Superintendent Leif Crozier, who had recovered from his bout of bush fever, arrived and tried to arrest a man who had assaulted a farm instructor when he was refused flour. The Mounties

**HOMESTEADERS** ◆ "[The wheat] looked so grand and golden on August 24 and the next day the binders were to come but that night a heavy frost fell and our grain was all black and withered in the morning. It was not worth the twine to bind it. . . .

"The weather we endured all those 14 years ranged from aching frost to unendurable heat. I have seen 60 degrees below zero registered on our Negretti & Zambra thermometer outside our door. It cuts one's breath to take in air at that temperature but the air is generally still when it is as cold as that. Then the summers when the hot winds were terrible and hail storms with stones bigger than your fist would level the crops. I remember seeing the box off our wagon being blown clear over our house at Rillington and that was no small undertaking for it was quite a wide house." Mary Louisa Cummins (1869–1939), who came from London, England, to homestead at Grenfell, Saskatchewan (*Glenbow Archives*, NA-424-30)

were quickly surrounded by Cree warriors. "The chiefs, including Big Bear, were doing all they could to have the man give up quietly," Crozier reported. "They said however if an attempt were made to arrest him forcibly they felt sure bloodshed would follow. . . . What made me most anxious to avoid a collision was the fear that the first shot fired would be the signal for an Indian outbreak with all its attendant horrors." The day ended without violence, but it was clear that the department of Indian affairs had badly mismanaged the situation, and that the government would either have to feed the natives or fight them. However, Big Bear's attempt to ally the bands was a failure – there was simply too much infighting – and their political voice remained splintered.

Crowfoot was viewed by the government as the most powerful Plains chief, and to discourage militancy, Edgar Dewdney, now governor of the North-West Territories, organized a trip to Winnipeg for Crowfoot and Red Crow, a Blood chief, in 1884. He wanted the chiefs to witness the military strength of the white man and the power of his civilization. Their visit was covered by George Ham, from the *Toronto Mail*: "In taking them to the theatre that night, the electric lights were turned on; gazing up at them he put his hands over his mouth and exclaimed oh my oh my the white man is wonderful. He has plucked a lot of little stars from the skies and put them on the poles to light the village with." Officials showed Crowfoot the Stony Mountain Penitentiary and the armoury, with its impressive cache of weapons. He asked how many ration days a week the people of Winnipeg had.

It was into this climate of hostility, resentment, poverty, and disillusionment with the federal government that Louis Riel returned, like Moses coming down from the mountain. He crossed the border on July 1, 1884, after a group of Métis farmers came to Montana and asked him to counsel them. But his name and actions had long been invoked among frustrated settlers. "If history is to be taken as a guide," wrote Frank Oliver in the *Edmonton Bulletin*, "what could be plainer than that without a rebellion the people of the North-West need expect nothing, while with rebellion, successful or otherwise, they may reasonably expect to get their rights. . . . Was it not by armed rebellion coupled with murder that Manitoba attained the rights she enjoys today from the very men who hold the reins of power in Ottawa?"

Macdonald was acutely aware of Riel's charisma and leadership qualities, and was kept abreast of his movements. "At this moment, Riel has gone into the North West on the invitation of the half-breeds, and requires to be watched," he warned. "One cannot foresee what he may do, or what they, under his advice may do."

His fears were quickly borne out. Riel and Will Jackson, head of the Settlers' Union, formed an immediate bond, and in August, Riel again solicited the support of the Blackfoot and Cree. Though he was wary of making a military commitment, Big Bear met with Riel, and the fact that the two had met was enough to spread alarm. Both men were considered by the government to be dangerous; an alliance between the two could be disastrous. "Big Bear is an agitator and always has been," Hayter Reed, the assistant to the minister of Indian affairs immediately wired to Macdonald, "and having received the moral support of the half-breed community, he is only too glad to have an opportunity of inciting the Indians to make fresh and exorbitant demands." This was not true, but Big Bear's authority was eroding, and his warriors were restless. Macdonald asked Bishop Vital-Justin Grandin to go to the Métis settlement of Batoche and find out what Riel was planning.

Church authorities worried that Riel, with his combination of personal charisma and religious mysticism, was usurping their control. "The Métis spoke to me of Riel with an extraordinary enthusiasm," Grandin reported. "For them he was a saint; I would say rather a kind of God." Riel began to see himself in those terms too, showing flashes of the religious mania he had displayed in New England before being taken to the Beauport asylum. He announced that his presence in the North-West was a divine mission sanctioned by God. The Métis were the chosen people, he said, their blood a unique mixture of European Catholic and the uncorrupted innocence of the native, and God would protect them. "Riel is a dangerous man who could cause real trouble," Grandin wrote to Archbishop Taché. It was Taché who had first spotted Riel's potential and sent him to Montreal to study for the priesthood twenty-five years earlier.

In December, Saskatchewan settlers and Métis signed a petition written by Will Jackson that demanded the early issuance of land deeds, tariff reductions, control of natural resources, and the right to vote for elected representatives. Riel sent it to Ottawa and waited through a desolate Christmas for the response. Crops had been poor for three years, and most settlers were facing famine. Riel himself was penniless, forced to accept charity.

By the middle of February, the only response from Ottawa was the wan suggestion of a commission to look into Métis land claims. Riel's religious delusions sharpened through the long, barren winter, and his visions became more apocalyptic. He advocated a battle to the death. "The petitions sent to the Government are not listened to," he said. "The Original half-breeds are determined to save their rights or to perish at once." Riel reverted to the tactics that had been successful for him in 1869, setting up a "provisional government of the Saskatchewan" at Batoche and defying local authority.

Despite this alarming news, Macdonald did not take action. He had other troubles: the CPR was facing bankruptcy. On March 26, 1885, Macdonald received a letter from George Stephen saying that, without immediate government money, the railway would have to be abandoned. "I need not repeat how sorry I am that this should be the result of all our efforts to give Canada a railway to the Pacific Ocean," he wrote. "But I am supported by the conviction that I have done all that could be done to support it." Macdonald was growing weary of the ongoing travails of his railway. "Stephen asks for a loan for a year of 5 millions," he lamented. "Everyone is reaching the limits of endurance. How it will end God knows, but I wish I were well out of it."

Faced with two concurrent crises, Macdonald decided to use one to solve the other. The threat of Riel's rebellion could justify the expense of the railway, which would provide transportation for federal troops. It had taken ninety-six days to get Lieutenant Colonel Wolseley's men to Red River sixteen years earlier to quell Riel's rebellion. While the railway was behind schedule and effectively broke, it was complete as far as the Rocky Mountains and could quickly move eastern troops out to the plains. It was a necessary and practical instrument of government.

On the day that Stephen's cable arrived, Superintendent Crozier advanced toward Batoche with fifty-six Mounties, forty-one Prince Albert volunteers, and a seven-pound artillery piece. Riel had earlier demanded that Crozier surrender Fort Carlton to him, which Crozier had refused. The superintendent felt that Riel's drive had to be stopped before it reached

Fight at Duck Lake.
(*National Archives of Canada,*
*958-140-4* )

the natives. There were perhaps one thousand Métis under Riel's control, and a few hundred settlers who were allied with his cause, and they did not represent a significant military threat. But if the thousands of Plains natives joined Riel, the Mounties might be facing the kind of war that was playing out in the American west. Crozier felt that a show of strength was necessary to keep the natives neutral.

Riel's military commander was Gabriel Dumont, a buffalo hunter who was legendary as both a horseman and marksman. He was fiercely loyal to Riel and believed that God did indeed speak through him. Dumont's brother Isidore and a Cree native approached Crozier's men at Duck Lake, Dumont waving a white blanket. A Mountie interpreter rode out to meet with them, but the Cree pushed the Mountie's rifle away. Crozier interpreted the gesture as an attempt to grab the gun. He could see Métis moving in the nearby bush. Suspecting an ambush, he ordered his men to fire, and both the Cree and Isidore Dumont were killed. But Crozier's men were in the open, and were quickly cut down by Métis shooting from behind cover. Crozier was forced to retreat, with twelve dead, eleven wounded, and five horses killed. Only four Métis and one native were killed

**GABRIEL DUMONT**

◆ Before he became a rebel, Dumont was a peacemaker who drafted a treaty between the Métis and Blackfoot, negotiated with natives, and settled local disputes. In 1886, he was paraded in Quebec at election time as a living reminder of the injustice that had struck down Riel. But Dumont was inarticulate and uninterested in politics, and he quickly left the campaign trail. He was granted amnesty in 1890 and returned to Gabriel's Crossing near Batoche, where he lived until his death of natural causes in 1906, at the age of sixty-eight. (*Montana Historical Society, 942-022*)

at Duck Lake. "God has been pleased to grant us the victory," Riel announced, "and as our movement is to protect our rights, our victory is just and we offer it to the Almighty."

But the clash with the NWMP caused panic elsewhere. Some of the white settlers were with Riel, but their endorsement stopped short of armed insurrection. After Duck Lake, he lost the support of most of them, although Will Jackson remained loyal. The skirmish also raised the threat of a native uprising, provoking two responses among white settlers: fear and indifference.

Jennie Plaxton wrote about the situation at Prince Albert: "We employed a family of Indians to work for us, a father, mother, daughter and son-in-law. We built a little log shack for them, and my husband broke an acre of land for them. We paid these Indians in goods from the Hudson's Bay store. . . . When the rebellion broke out in 1885, there was great excitement. We noticed there was something wrong from the behaviour of our Indians. They dressed themselves up in their war paint and left for Duck Lake, where they took part in the fight there, although they were Sioux. All the people on the outskirts of Prince Albert were advised to go in to town. . . ."

For some settlers, the rebellion was simply another troublesome detail in their already difficult lives. Mary Louisa Cummins wrote about Riel with a dry understatement: "There was a lot of fighting to the west of us. . . . The

North West Mounted Police were after [Riel] and arrived at our place when they heard he was sneaking up the valley. If he was, they certainly made enough clatter to show where they were. They came full tilt along our trail with their wagons clattering and rattling, men and horses looking very warlike and imposing. The children were wildly delighted to see them while the men got a big kick out of it all.

"Colin put in another crop in 1885 but it was frozen before it was up a foot and all that labour was lost. The 1886 crop was also frozen and so our Golden Wheat Fortune faded away."

At Fort Edmonton, settlers left their farms and sought refuge inside the fort. Frank Oliver, the editor of the *Edmonton Bulletin*, thought that the settlers would be safe as long as the natives continued to camp nearby. "I returned home passing the Indian tents again on the way," he wrote. "I slept without thought of danger, for the drum was the last sound I heard before going to sleep. In the morning there was not a tent in sight. The removal of the tents was accepted by all parties as notice that a state of war existed." The settlers prepared themselves for battle, breaking out unused weapons; the women sewed powder sacks.

"This insurrection is a bad business, but we must face it as best we may," Macdonald wrote. "I telegraphed Father Lacombe stating that I was sure that his people would be all right, but he had better see them." Macdonald hoped that Lacombe could influence Crowfoot, but Lacombe's report was not encouraging. "The Blackfeet were well armed with rifles and they had plenty of cartridges," he later wrote. "Among the Indians of the North-West there was a kind of general feeling with the old and the young that the time was at hand to finish with the white policy. Many influential Indians were at the time fomenting the fire of rebellion."

Militias were marshalled in Halifax, Toronto, and Winnipeg. In Quebec, the 9th Voltigeurs were mustered to mixed response. "People whom we met by the hundreds on the street would tell us that we were going to wage war on our brothers; on Frenchmen like us," said George Beauregard, a militia-man. "That we would be piteously massacred and we were being sacrificed as cannon fodder." The various militias were under the command of General Frederick Middleton, a British officer who had a walrus moustache and a healthy contempt for the abilities of his colonial troops. Eight days after Duck Lake, the first troops arrived in Winnipeg, and within a week, Middleton set out for Batoche.

Riel's position was tenuous; he had only about half of the Saskatchewan Métis behind him, and he had lost the support of the Settlers' Union. He needed the natives.

Crowfoot believed that war with the whites would lead to slaughter, but he used his position to political advantage and lobbied for more food for his people. Macdonald ordered that rations to Crowfoot's band be increased and supplies be sent to where "the tomahawks are sharpest." Crowfoot dictated a telegram to the prime minister pledging support: "Continued reports and many lies are brought to us and we don't know what to believe, but now that we have seen the Governor and heard him speak, we will shut our ears and only listen to and believe what is told to us through the Governor. Should any Indians come to our reserve and ask us to join them in war, we will send them away."

Riel's best hope was with the Cree. Big Bear's band was camped near Frog Lake, in the district of Saskatchewan, hungry after their rations had been cut and emboldened by the Métis victory at Duck Lake. A group of warriors under Wandering Spirit painted their faces red, preparing for war. They attacked the settlement, taking prisoners and looting the store, then killed nine white men, two of them priests. "I could hear gun shots and whoops coming from everywhere," said Louis Goulet, who had been taken prisoner. "The Indians were drunk with ferocity. I saw Father Marchand, one of the two priests, fall on his knees arms crossed, yes, raised to heaven. He was gunned down on the spot. I never saw him move again. . . . I had this feeling I was all along in a horrible nightmare."

Big Bear had not endorsed Riel's actions at Duck Lake, but his warriors were in no mood for negotiation. "I felt sorry when they killed those men at Frog Lake," Big Bear said. "But the truth is, when the news of the fight at Duck Lake reached us, my band ignored my authority and despised me because I did not side with the half-breeds." Big Bear and his band went north to escape the army, rather than join Riel at Batoche.

There were other skirmishes, with natives mostly raiding food stores. Starvation haunted the Plains nations; every band was acquainted with hunger. On March 29, 1885, some Stoney natives demanded flour from James Payne, a government farm instructor, and when he refused, they shot him. The next day they killed a rancher. In the course of these skirmishes, it was not clear what shape the rebel forces would take, whether these isolated parties would form a cohesive army behind Riel. The chiefs had either lost power or ceded it to their war chiefs. The natives were an unknown quantity.

The militiamen from eastern Canada, untested in battle, were themselves an unknown quantity. At Fort Qu'Appelle, the staging ground for the advance on Batoche, General Middleton reviewed his men with a growing sense of discouragement: "I went down the ranks of the 90th and questioned each man and found that many of them had never fired a rifle, some had never fired any weapon at all. This was not a cheerful outlook after receiving a telegram dwelling on the excellence of the shooting of the half-breeds."

Riel was becoming more erratic and mystical, convinced that God was directing his military efforts. His general, Gabriel Dumont, advocated guerrilla warfare tactics, engaging the enemy en route, demoralizing them with quick strikes. Dumont suggested they blow up the railway, an effective military tactic and a shrewd symbolic strike. But Riel wanted an epic, biblical battle.

The Surrender of Poundmaker to Major General Middleton at Fort Battleford, Saskatchewan, May 26, 1885. (*National Archives of Canada*, C-2769)

Dumont was sent out to delay Middleton, in the hope that some natives could be recruited to the rebel cause. With 135 fighters he waited for Middleton's 800 troops at Fish Creek ravine, about twenty-seven kilometres south of Batoche, taking defensive positions in the dense cover. Dumont's men were better marksmen, and he held the favourable ground. Middleton lost six men, with forty-nine wounded, to Dumont's four casualties.

Riel sent agents to the Cree, led by Poundmaker, near Fort Battleford, and had them read an edict: "To the Indians of Battleford, Rise up and face the police. If it has not been done take Battleford. Destroy it. Keep all the merchandise and food and come to join us. You can easily send us 40 or 50 men."

Poundmaker, like Big Bear and Crowfoot, felt it unwise to engage in war with the white troops, but his young warriors were already raiding food stores. Middleton sent Colonel W. D. Otter to confront Poundmaker's band, in retaliation. With 325 men, artillery, and a Gatling gun, Otter attacked Poundmaker's camp on May 2, 1885. But his troops found themselves exposed to sniper fire from the woods, and they retreated after a day of fighting left them with eight casualties.

"A number of Indians had mounted and were about to start after the retreating soldiers," said Robert Jefferson, a government farm instructor

The dead, North West Rebellion. (*National Archives of Canada, C-3451*)

who had been taken prisoner, "but Poundmaker would not permit it. He said that to defend themselves and their children was good, but he did not approve of taking the offensive. They had beaten their enemy off; let that content them. So there was no pursuit."

Riel now realized that the natives would never join his rebellion. His religious visions became more frequent. While Dumont was holding off the Canadian militia at Fish Creek, Riel was planning to move the seat of the Holy Roman Empire to Montreal and appoint a new pope. He changed the holy day from Sunday to Saturday. He had a vision of the final battle at Batoche: "I have seen the giant, he is coming. He is goliath. I pray to intercept the communications of the enemies. . . . Oh my God, grant us the favour of meeting for that we beat them one after another."

Dumont pulled back. Middleton approached the settlement of Batoche with eight hundred men and spent three frustrating days firing uselessly at the concealed Métis and suffering casualties. Riel walked among his troops with a crucifix, commanding them to "Fire, in the name of the Father! Fire, in the name of the Son! Fire, in the name of the Holy Ghost!"

On the fourth day, Middleton planned a pincer attack from two sides, but only one of the untrained groups attacked on cue, and the day ended in another disappointment.

Middleton was disgusted with his soldiers, and they were equally fed up with his imperial pretensions. Ignoring his orders, the troops mounted a frontal assault on Batoche that overwhelmed the Métis, killing twelve of them. The rest fled into the woods, followed by Canadian scouts. They found Gabriel Dumont, who said he had ninety cartridges left for anyone who wanted to capture him. They left him alone and he fled.

On May 15, Riel was found by two scouts and surrendered, wild-looking and cold. "He is dressed in a poorer fashion than most of the half-breeds captured," a North West Mounted Police scout reported. "While talking to General Middleton as could be seen from the outside of his tent, his eyes rolled from side to side with the look of a hunted man."

Middleton telegraphed Macdonald: "Riel is my prisoner. What is to be done with him? I await instructions here." The rebellion was over. Riel was taken to a temporary jail in Regina.

The Dominion troops returned east, welcomed as heroes, waving from parades, sitting through speeches in their honour. Every militiaman was given a silver medal sponsored by Queen Victoria for his part in the country's first successful miliary campaign. "Canada is delirious with enthusiasm upon the return of our volunteers," Macdonald announced. "This has done more to weld the provinces into one nation than anything else could have done."

On the plains, the Dominion forces rounded up anyone who had taken part in the rebellion, or any related native battles and skirmishes. Dumont was by then in Montana, where he briefly joined Buffalo Bill's Wild West Show as a marksman, billed as "The Hero of the Half-breed Rebellion." Louis Goulet had escaped from Big Bear but was arrested by the NWMP, mistakenly assumed to be a Métis supporter of Riel. "We found ourselves with everybody who'd taken part in the rebellion one way or another," he wrote. "There was Riel and his council, the people who were at Duck Lake, Fish Creek, Batoche, as well as Indians who'd taken part in the uprising and others who'd been attacked: Poundmaker and his band. The prison was full to overflowing. We lived under canvas in that pen for a whole week until they put us in a large building which they soon divided into cells."

Riel pondered his defence in the confusion of the jail. He wanted a trial before the Supreme Court of Canada, where he would convince the world of the purity and religious necessity of his cause.

There was significant political pressure from Ontario's Orangemen to hang Riel for treason, though it was not an offence that carried the death penalty. Bitterness still lingered over the murder in 1870, on Riel's orders, of Thomas Scott, an Irish Protestant from Ontario. Scott had been an unsympathetic figure in life, but had grown more appealing with time, evolving into a martyr, the subject of a romantic novel and a lengthy, heroic poem.

In Quebec, Riel was considered a champion of the rights of Catholics and French-speakers in the west, and sympathy for him was building. But Macdonald had always seen the province as an unmovable stronghold of Tory support, and he felt he could risk angering the voters over Riel. Ontario was politically more uncertain, and Macdonald wanted to solidify support there. With the concurrence of justice minister Alexander Campbell, Macdonald invoked a British law from 1342 and levelled the charge of high treason, which did carry the death penalty.

Winnipeg was briefly considered as a site for the trial, since a superior court convened there, but Chief Justice Lewis Wallbridge wrote to Alexander Campbell, warning him that in Manitoba Riel could insist that half the jury be Métis. "In Regina," the judge suggested, "the prisoner would not be entitled to a mixed jury." In Regina, the judge was a federally appointed local magistrate, Hugh Richardson, who chose the jury by putting

Overleaf: The Capture of Batoche (*National Archives of Canada*, C-2424)

the names of thirty-six people he knew into a jar and picking six. None was French-speaking or Catholic.

The trial began in the prairie heat of July 20, 1885. Asked how he pleaded, Riel responded, "I have the honour to answer that I am not guilty." To prove high treason, the Crown had to show that Riel had waged war against the government. Their most compelling evidence was a letter that Riel had sent the North West Mounted Police, demanding the surrender of Fort Carlton and threatening a "war of extermination." The strategy of the defence team (a quartet of competent eastern lawyers – François Lemieux, Charles Fitzpatrick, T. C. Johnstone, and J. N. Greenshields) was to prove that Riel was insane and that the letter was the product of a delusional mind rather than a legitimate military threat.

Will Jackson, who had stayed by Riel's side, was also on trial. He was not planning an insanity defence, but the two doctors who examined him declared that he was, in fact, insane. "I have always declared myself perfectly responsible," he announced, "that is to say as Riel's secretary and I wish to share his fate whatever it may be." The Protestant jury felt that any Methodist who had followed this unstable Catholic must be mad, and he was declared so after a trial that lasted thirty minutes. He was committed to the Selkirk Lunatic Asylum in Manitoba, though he escaped a few months later and fled to the United States.

After Jackson's insanity verdict, Riel's lawyers were confident they could get their man acquitted in the same way. Dr. François Roy, who had treated Riel for megalomania at the Beauport asylum, was testifying on his behalf, as was Dr. Daniel Clark of the Toronto Asylum for the Insane. The legal definition of sanity hinged on whether a person could appreciate the difference between right and wrong at the time the crime was committed. Dr. Clark argued that the law was arbitrary and unscientific. "It is all nonsense to talk about a man not knowing what he is doing simply because he is insane," he argued. "I could convince any lawyer if they will come to Toronto Asylum, in half an hour that dozens in that institution know right and wrong in the abstract and in the concrete and yet they are undoubtedly insane."

General Middleton and others testified that Riel did know right from wrong. And Riel himself rejected the defence. To give his cause legitimacy, he had to be seen as sane: "I suppose that after having been condemned, I will cease to be called a fool, and for me, it is a great advantage. I have a mission, I cannot fulfill my mission as long as I am looked upon as an insane being. . . . If I am guilty of high treason I say I am a prophet of the new world."

His trial lasted four days. Riel addressed the court, listing the undemocratic treatment of Métis on the prairies and outlining his vision for a diverse society. "Through the grace of God I am the founder of Manitoba," he told the assembly.

It took the jury less than an hour to return a guilty verdict, though they asked the judge for mercy, to forgo the death penalty. Judge Richardson

**RIEL'S TRIAL** ◆ "The North West is my mother. She is the mother country of my nation. . . . God cannot create a tribe without locating it. We are not birds. We have to walk on the ground. . . . The North West Council is a sham legislature and not representative government at all. . . . British civilization has defined such government as irresponsible, and by all the science which has been shown here yesterday, you are compelled to admit if there is no responsibility, it is insane. The federal government . . . besides doing nothing to satisfy the people of this great land, it has even hardly been able to answer once or give a single response. That fact indicates an absolute lack of responsibility, and therefore insanity complicated by paralysis." Louis Riel, speaking at his trial, August 1, 1885. (*Top: Riel addressing the jury. National Archives of Canada, C-1879. Inset: Principal witnesses at the trial. National Archives of Canada, PA-118747*)

ignored their request. "You are to be taken now from here to the police guard room at Regina . . . and that you be kept there until the 18th of September next then the 18th of September you will be taken to the place appointed for your execution and there be hanged by the neck till you are dead and may God have mercy on your soul."

The verdict was applauded in Ontario. A letter to the *Toronto Mail* read, "Right thinking men of all parties felt that Riel has had a fair trial. The sentence of death pronounced upon him was fully warranted by his crimes. The blood of Thomas Scott cries for vengeance." In Quebec, his conviction was seen as vengeful and motivated by crass political calculation. That a sane, English-speaking Protestant was acquitted due to insanity and Riel condemned to die was insupportable. "Riel is condemned to be hanged," read an editorial in *La Presse*. "We can't be surprised, the whole thing was arranged from the beginning. Upper Canada needed a victim. It was decided Riel would be offered up. . . ."

If Riel thought he was speaking for God, Macdonald was acting like an Old Testament Jehovah consumed with retribution. He was initially unconcerned with the protest from Quebec. "The conviction of Riel is satisfactory," he said. "There is an attempt in Quebec to pump up a patriotic feeling about him, but I don't think it will amount to much." Macdonald had taken a huge political gamble, and it appeared to be paying off. "He shall hang though every dog in Quebec bark in his favour," Macdonald said.

Riel's pending execution polarized the country, to a far greater degree than Macdonald had imagined. His Quebec ministers warned him of deep and lasting alienation in Quebec should Riel hang. "Riel must not be hung," cautioned secretary of state Joseph Chapleau. "Bad blood exists today and must not be increased. Consider matters carefully. Riel's execution means our downfall." The entire Quebec bloc threatened to desert Macdonald. They proposed an inquiry into Riel's mental state, to demonstrate that he was in fact insane. To pre-empt this, the prime minister secretly ordered that Riel be examined by three hand-picked doctors: two anglophones – a police surgeon and a Conservative supporter who had been appointed warden of the Kingston Penitentiary – and a francophone, Dr. François Valade.

Macdonald's secret commission reflected the country's linguistic and political schism. The two English doctors pronounced him "foolish and peculiar" but sane. Valade disagreed: "After having examined carefully Riel in private conversation with him and by testimony of persons who take care of him, I have come to the conclusion that he is not an accountable being, that he is unable to distinguish between wrong and right on political and religious subjects." Macdonald reported to his cabinet that the three doctors were unanimous in their opinion that Riel was sane and accountable; Riel would hang on November 16. His Quebec ministers objected but did not desert their leader, believing that their open dissension would further inflame tensions between French and English.

In his Regina cell, Riel was unsurprised at the verdict and oddly relieved. "For fifteen years they have pursued me in their hate," he wrote, "and never yet have they made me waver; today still less, when they lead me to the scaffold, and I am infinitely grateful to them for releasing me from this dreadful captivity that weighs on me."

As Riel's cause was dividing the country along linguistic, religious, and political lines, that great unifying force, the railway, was reaching completion. The daunting task of building a line through the final section of the Rockies would be costly, both in money and lives.

The route was chosen by Albert Bowman Rogers, a Yale-trained engineer who chewed tobacco, wore his overalls backwards, eschewed baths, and had a gift for obscenities and getting results. The Selkirk and Monashee ranges posed particular engineering problems. Eagle Pass could be used to cross the Monashees, but for the Selkirks, Rogers would take the line through the pass later named for him, an intricate, daring route that wound six hundred metres above the Columbia River. Hundreds of men died during the laying of track in the mountains, and the project was delayed by avalanches, clay that was too soft to support the track, collapsed bridges, and record snowfalls.

While the line was nearing completion, it came close to bankruptcy yet again. There were strikes among the workers and threats from unpaid contractors. George Stephen once more approached the government for new loans, and Macdonald used the Riel rebellion as a lever to extract more money for the railway from Parliament. Had it not delivered troops to the west in mere days and saved the country? Had it not peopled the plains? (Though it had not really accomplished this, not yet, it had become a powerful symbol of settlement.)

After vigorous debate in the House of Commons, it was decided by the Conservative majority to lend more money to the CPR syndicate. The rebellion had been politically useful, and Macdonald had managed it carefully. "We have certainly made it assume large proportions in the public eye," he noted of Riel's brief uprising. "This has been done however for our own purposes, and I think wisely done."

On November 7, 1885, at Craigellachie in the Eagle Pass, Donald A. Smith drove in the last spike in the railroad, a personal vindication for being excluded from the contract documents. The most famous photograph in Canadian history shows the white-bearded Smith holding a sledgehammer, bent like Methuselah, surrounded by a sea of sombre men. It was galling for Macdonald to have the detested Smith as the lasting image of such an extraordinary accomplishment, but he was accustomed to taking his political victories as he found them.

On November 16, a cold, clear morning nine days after Donald Smith's historic hammer swing, Riel was woken in his cell to face the gallows. He told the sheriff, "I am glad that at last I am to be released from my sufferings." He recited a psalm and invoked a blessing for John A. Macdonald: "I pray that God will bless Sir John and give him grace and wisdom to manage the affairs of Canada well." Carrying a small ivory crucifix set in silver, Riel was led from his cell by a group of North West Mounted Police in their red tunics, and two priests, Father McWilliams and Father André. He recited the Lord's Prayer with Father André.

At 8:20 the trap door was released by Jack Henderson (who had been Riel's prisoner sixteen years earlier), and Riel swung before the four witnesses present. On December 9, his body was returned to his native Red River on board a CPR train and buried at the cathedral in St. Boniface. He was forty-one years old.

In Ontario, Riel was burned in effigy, but in Quebec flags flew at half-staff, while merchants draped their windows in black and displayed Riel's picture. Students wearing black armbands marched through the streets. The *Montreal Herald* condemned Macdonald's actions as a craven political gambit: "The government was only interested in the effect of their action on elections to come two years from now in the province of Ontario! Partisan demands were permitted to stifle the national conscience; merciful intentions were smothered under threats of partisan vengeance." A crowd of fifty thousand came to Montreal's Champs de Mars to listen to thirty-seven speakers condemn the decision to execute Riel. One of the speakers was a Liberal politician named Wilfrid Laurier. "If I had lived on the shores of the Saskatchewan," he told the grieving throng, "I would have taken up a rifle to defend my property." Laurier offered a prophetic warning. "Race and religion are about to dominate politics in Canada," he said. "Not justice, not mercy, not liberty – race and religion, and with that an abyss will separate our two people."

Out of the Montreal rally, a new party was born, the Parti National, formed by Liberals and enraged ultramontane Catholic Conservatives. Led by Honoré Mercier, the former leader of the opposition Liberals, it was decried in the *Toronto Mail* as "the party of race and revenge."

Joseph Chapleau had hoped to avoid this sectarian tension: "A violent wind is blowing over Quebec at this moment, threatening to overturn the Conservative party and the government. May it please God that be the limits of the disaster, and that the nation we belong to is not more seriously damaged by it." He tried to convince Macdonald to defer Parliament to let tensions ease. Macdonald responded by boarding a ship at Quebec City and sailing to London, away from the tempest of national argument.

Eleven days after Riel's hanging, at Battleford, the last, unheralded drama of the rebellion played itself out. On November 27, eight natives were hanged for murders committed during the rebellion. The eight included six Cree (Wandering Spirit, who was Big Bear's war chief, Miserable Man, Bad Arrow, Round the Sky, Iron Body, and Little Bear) and two Assiniboine (Ikteh and Man Without Blood). They sang their death songs as they waited for the trap door to be sprung. Few members of the press were there, but the hanging was witnessed by natives from surrounding reserves. Macdonald's pitiless coda echoed over the proceedings. "This will show the red man that the white man rules," he wrote in a letter to the Indian commissioner. In little more than a decade, the natives who had guided the whites into the territory had been marginalized, shunted aside to facilitate settlement.

Foremost Man, a Cree chief, offered a lament for what the prairies had been less than a generation earlier: "Where are the buffalo? Where are our horses? They are gone and we must follow them. You people have my lands. Let them send the buffalo back, and take their own people to the reserve where they come from. Give us the prairies again and we won't ask for food. But it is too late. It is too late; it is too late."

In Ottawa, on June 28, 1886, Macdonald boarded the first transcontinental train. It had started in Halifax and was bound for Vancouver. Macdonald saw the west for the first time from a special luxury car, observing the calm plains through his window.

Immigration to the west had stalled, due to the rebellion, harsh winters, and failed crops, and only the most determined stayed. Harriet

Neville was still farming near Cottonwood, in the Saskatchewan district: "In the spring of 1886, we bought seed and sowed all the wheat which we had and prepared and planted a large garden. Everything made a fair start in growth, then suddenly descended upon us so stifling a heat that we could scarcely breathe and in two days even the grass crackled under our feet. The wheat had headed but dried before ripening. Potatoes wilted and ripened before half grown. All over the country it was the same. . . . Some people went back to Ontario and England. Others would have gone if they had money."

Macdonald stopped along the route to campaign – an election was only months away. In the foothills he met with Crowfoot. "My chiefs fear for their children, that food would not be given them," the chief told Macdonald. "I ask you Sir John to help banish these fears." Macdonald gave him a new suit and William Van Horne sent him a permanent pass for the CPR.

The Plains chiefs who had witnessed the destruction of their traditional culture and livelihoods did not survive long into the new era. Big Bear was convicted of treason in Regina and sentenced by Judge Richardson to three years in Stony Mountain Penitentiary, the prison that Crowfoot had toured months earlier. Big Bear argued that he had not been in control of his warriors, to no avail. He languished in prison, as many natives did, and spent as much time as possible in the warden's private zoo, which contained several tame buffalo and two bears. He was released after fourteen months, shrunken and sick, and put on a train to Regina. From there a freight wagon took him north to Little Pine reserve, and he died in his cramped cabin a few weeks later, shunned by his people.

Poundmaker, like Big Bear, had been a conciliatory force in the rebellion. "I gave myself up," he said at his trial. "You have me because I wanted peace. I cannot help myself, but I am still a man. You may do as you like with me." He was sentenced to three years in prison. Crowfoot, who was Poundmaker's adoptive father, worried that his son would die in prison. Of Crowfoot's twelve children, only four had made it to adulthood, and by 1886 they too were dead of starvation or tuberculosis. "I have a feeling of lonesomeness of seeing my children dying every year," he wrote to Poundmaker. "And if I hear that you are dead, I will have no more use for life." Crowfoot lobbied Macdonald for Poundmaker's release and the prime minister obliged. Four months after Poundmaker left the penitentiary, he visited Crowfoot at the Sun Dance of July 4, 1886, and died of a lung hemorrhage.

On the afternoon of April 17, 1890, Crowfoot himself lay dying in his tent near the present site of Gleichen, Alberta, surrounded by friends. His mother, who was well into her nineties, was among his last living relatives, a small, mute witness to a century of change. "A little while and I will be gone from among you," Crowfoot told them. "From nowhere we came; into nowhere we go. What is life? It is the flash of a firefly in the night. It is the breath of a buffalo in winter time. It is the little shadow that moves across the grass and loses itself in the sunset." At the end of a long obituary

John A. Macdonald's funeral procession. (*National Archives of Canada*, C-7125)

in the *Macleod Gazette*, Father Lacombe wrote, "He is no more. No one like him will fill his place."

Macdonald won a comfortable majority in the 1887 election, his political gamble paying off, though Riel's death would linger in the national consciousness for decades. In 1891, Macdonald suffered a stroke that left him without speech, and he died a week later, on June 6. His colleague Hector Langevin delivered the eulogy in the House. "Mr. Speaker," he said, "I would have wished to continue to speak of our dear departed friend, and spoken to you about the goodness of his heart, the witness of which I have seen so often, but I feel that I must stop; my heart is full of tears. I cannot proceed further."

Noble, intemperate, heroically energetic, articulate, and entertaining, Macdonald personified the country in all of its graces and most of its sins. "We are all miserable sinners," he once remarked. His legacy was Confederation, which had been driven by his stubborn spirit and moulded in his image. His funeral procession moved slowly through the crowds along Ottawa's Rideau Street on June 10 and was assaulted by an abrupt thunderstorm. His body was carried to Kingston on a CPR train draped in black, and he was buried in the cemetery that held his parents, his first wife, and his long-deceased child.

Macdonald was followed as prime minister by John Abbott, who served from 1891 to 1892. Abbott in turn was succeeded by Sir John Thompson, who died in office in 1894 an hour after meeting with Queen Victoria at Windsor Castle. Their terms were dwarfed by Macdonald's achievements: a nation – born of historical tensions, serial hostilities, and two religions and languages – that had improbably managed to build the longest railway in the world.

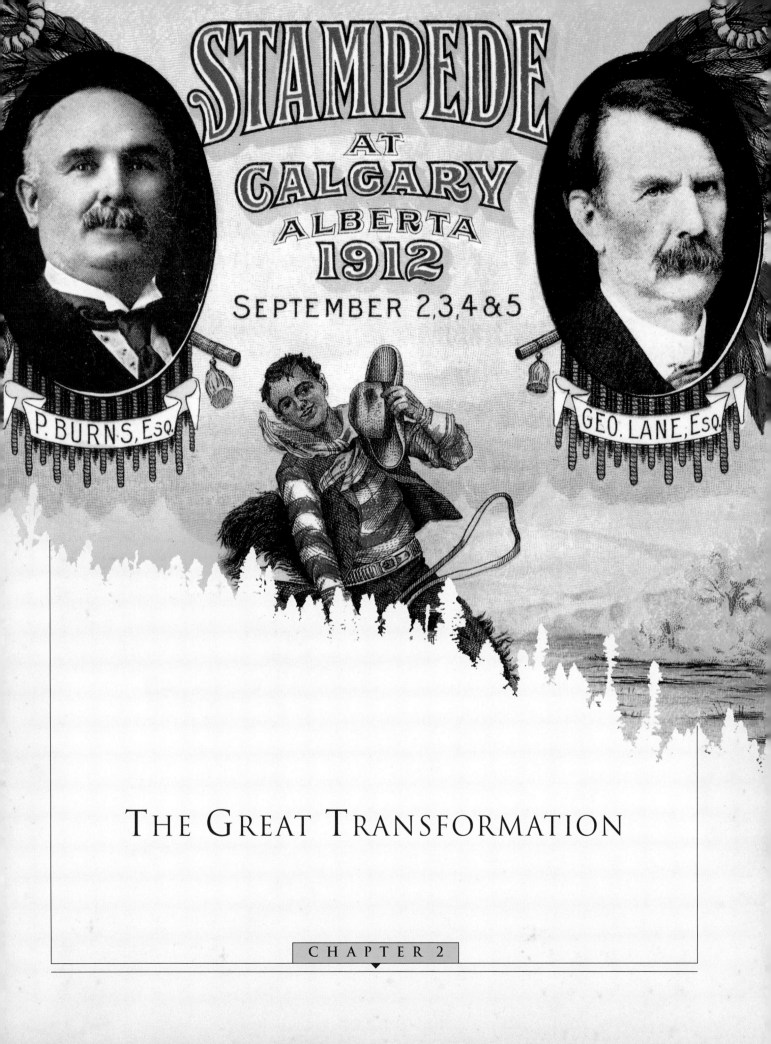

STAMPEDE
AT
CALGARY
ALBERTA
1912
SEPTEMBER 2, 3, 4 & 5

P. BURNS, Esq.

GEO. LANE, Esq.

# The Great Transformation

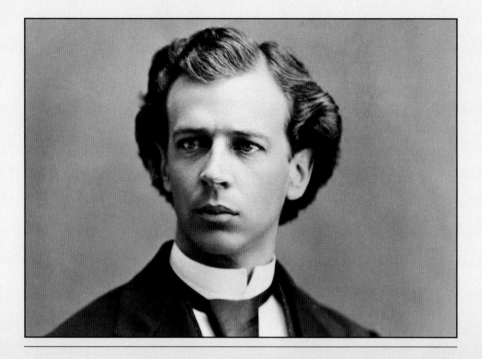

In 1904, Prime Minister Wilfrid Laurier famously announced: "the twentieth century shall be the century of Canada. . . . For the next . . . hundred years, Canada shall be the star towards which all men who love progress and freedom shall come."

A harbinger of the country's explosive growth was the discovery of gold in the distant Klondike region of the Yukon in 1896, the year Laurier was elected prime minister. After twenty years of slow economic growth or outright depression, the news was welcome. It would take a year for word to leak out to the world, and so the handful of Klondike miners who made the discovery had one brief, isolated season to make their fortunes.

At 6:00 a.m. on July 17, 1897, the steamboat *Portland* came into the Seattle harbour, carrying sixty-eight new millionaires. That morning's edition of the *Seattle Post Intelligencer* offered the headline, "GOLD, GOLD, GOLD – A TON OF GOLD." The secret was out. Five thousand people waited to greet the *Portland*, infected with that most American of notions: the possibility of quick, immense wealth. The idea of finding a fortune in the wilderness spread like a plague, and tens of thousands of Americans went north.

Among them was Martha Purdy, a thirty-one-year-old Chicago socialite who left her two small children to join what would become known as the Klondike Gold Rush. "To me it was a quest that had all the allure of a 'Treasure Island' or 'Aladdin's Lamp,'" she wrote in her memoir. "I had only to go to the world-famed goldfields . . . and collect the gold. I pictured myself and my children living in luxury the rest of my days."

The least expensive route to the goldfields was up the coast by boat, then through the mountain passes at the northern end of the Alaska Panhandle. Purdy's husband decided to stop in San Francisco, so she continued on with her brother. Shortly after she reached Chilkoot Pass, she discovered that she was two months pregnant. "As I looked directly before me at the fearful mountain pass that was to go down in history as 'the worst trail this side of hell,'" she wrote, "I thought of my New England forbears, women who had bravely faced the hardships of pioneering."

Tappan Adney, a journalist for the American magazine *Harper's Weekly*, described the parade through the mountains. "There is nothing but the grey wall of rock and earth. But stop! Look more closely. The eye catches a movement. The mountain is alive. There is a continual moving train; they are perceptible only by their movement, just as ants are. . . . They are human beings, but never did men look so small."

This huge foreign influx presented problems for the North West Mounted Police, who had the task of keeping order. In the 1898 NWMP annual report, Inspector Robert Belcher wrote, "This pass being the gateway into British territory, many of these people had to alter their customs and ideas to such an extent that it appeared to me to be the first lesson in a long course of education they would undergo before reaching Dawson." He had a tiny customs house at the summit of the Chilkoot, and he was given a machine gun to keep the peace. The gun froze in its packing crate and was never taken out.

Before the men could fight each other for gold, they first had to fight the elements. On April 4, 1898, a heavy snowfall resulted in an avalanche on the approach to Chilkoot Pass that buried sixty people in seconds. One of the prospectors, Duncan Clark, an Iowa farm boy, described the aftermath: "Not less than 1,000 men with shovels on backs went to look for the dead. It was a horrible sight to see big, robust men, the very picture of health dug from the snow, put on a sled and hauled to the morgue. Forty of the dead were found the first day. They were placed in a row for identification – my brother John among that number. . . . I got a box made out of two inch lumber and took my brother down to Dyea [Alaska] and buried him in the government yard. There is not a preacher in town to my uttermost surprise. When the corpse was lowered down into the grave, an old resident stepped up to the head of the grave and offered up the Lord's prayer." Duncan Clark continued into the goldfields alone. Several years later, he was found dead, his body only a few metres from his tent, and it was assumed that he had been murdered.

In the spring of 1898, there were twenty thousand men camped on the shores of Lake Bennett, at the head of the Yukon River, waiting for the ice to

Opposite: Wilfrid Laurier. "We are French-Canadians, but our country is not confined to the territory overshadowed by the citadel of Quebec; our country is Canada, it is all that is covered by the British flag on the American continent. Our fellow countrymen are not only those in whose veins run the blood of France. They are all those, whatever their race or whatever their language, whom the fortune of war, the chances of fate, or their own choice have brought among us, and who acknowledge the sovereignty of the British Crown. . . . What I claim for us is an equal share of the sun, of justice, of liberty. . . . I do not want French Canadians to domineer over anyone, nor anyone to domineer over them." From a speech given at the St. Jean Baptiste celebration in Quebec City, June 24, 1889. (*National Archives of Canada*, PA-25390)

**KLONDIKE** ♦ "You could buy anything in Dawson City in its heyday. . . . Anything from oysters to opera glasses. You could buy a dance-hall queen for her weight in gold, and one man did. His name was Chris Johanson, and he lived on Whisky Hill. . . . Of the tens of thousands who came here, only a handful found the gold they were seeking, and yet very few I think regretted the journey to Dawson City. The great stampede was the high point of their life. The winter of 1897. The gold rush was something like a war, it caused many casualties, but those who survived it and learned from it were strangely ennobled. These men found their Eldorado." An anonymous Dawson resident. (*Top: National Archives of Canada, c-6648, Bottom: National Archives of Canada c-28652*)

**MARTHA BLACK** ◆ "It was a wild winter in Dawson that winter of '98. As I look back to it I have an infinite pity for the men of those days, many of superior breeding and education. They were lonely, disillusioned, and discouraged. There were so few places to go where it was bright and cheerful. They gathered with the others in the saloons and dance halls. They joined the party with the first round, and then they drank to drown their woes. The continued arctic darkness contributed to their debauchery. Revellers lost all sense of time as to day and night periods, and attuned themselves to the ever-present night until they passed out from sheer exhaustion." (*Munger Archives, Kansas*)

melt so they could continue toward Dawson, still eight hundred kilometres farther north. In June, seven thousand homemade rafts and boats moved slowly downstream, a homely armada of hopeful miners seeking their millions. Dawson was a small outpost sitting on a wedge of frozen swampland. "On landing," Martha Purdy wrote, "even in our most enthusiastic moments, we could not have said the place was beautiful. It was like every other new town in the making; disordered and untidy."

Within a month, its population had swelled. "It is a motley throng," wrote Tappan Adney. "Every degree of person gathered from every corner of the earth. . . . Australians with upturned sleeves and a swagger; young Englishmen in gold stockings and tweeds . . . Japanese, Negroes – and women, too, everywhere. It is a vast herd; they crowd the boats and fill the streets, looking at Dawson." It was an American town on Canadian soil, infected with a single idea.

Martha Purdy found a cabin on a hill overlooking the town. "While I did not enter into the gaiety, I did have what sporting editors would call a ringside seat. We did not know when we squatted . . . that we had established ourselves above the red light district." Men outnumbered women twenty-five to one. "Lousetown" and "Paradise Alley" ran behind the main street, and each residence had a name on the door: Montreal Marie, Spanish Janette, Golden-Gut Flossy. The gold was elusive, but entertainment was available everywhere. In dance halls and theatres and saloons, Gussy Lamore and Snake-Hips Lily sang and danced. Feda Maloof's hootchie-kootchie dance was banned, but not Klondike Kate's Flame Dance, in which she slowly unravelled two hundred metres of tightly wrapped red chiffon from her body in front of mesmerized, unwashed prospectors. "An angel couldn't keep good in Dawson City," one miner warned. For all that, it was a surprisingly law-abiding place.

By the summer of 1899, after a chaotic run of only a few years, the territory was nearly panned out. There were rumours that gold was washing up on the beaches of Nome, Alaska, and within a week, half of Dawson had emptied, following the circus to a new location. "Hundreds of people are leaving the country daily," Martha Purdy noted. "But this creates a greater opportunity for those who remain. . . . Health, determination and self-denial are necessary for success here." In January 1899 she gave birth to her third son, Lyman. She went into the gold mining business and eventually established a successful sawmill in Dawson City. In 1904 she married a lawyer named George Black. Black became commissioner of the Yukon Territory and a member of Parliament for the Yukon. In 1935, seventy-year-old Martha Black became the second woman elected to Parliament, replacing her ill husband. She died in the Yukon at the age of ninety-one.

Though Wilfrid Laurier was a tremendous proponent of Canada's predominance in the twentieth century, he himself was a product of the nineteenth century. He deplored innovations like the telephone and the automobile, and disdained even photography. He was a man of great contradictions; it was one of the qualities that made him a skilful diplomat. Though he had originally been opposed to Confederation, by the turn of the century he was its staunchest champion. "My object is to consolidate Confederation," he said, "and to bring our people, long estranged from each other, gradually to become a nation. This is the supreme issue. Everything else is subordinate to that idea."

Laurier faced every divisive issue with a spirit of diplomacy and earned the nickname "the Great Conciliator." "Is it the British lion that is to swallow the French lamb," he asked rhetorically, speaking to the issue of the nation's linguistic and cultural divide, "or the French lamb that is to swallow the British lion? There can be more than one race, but there shall be but one nation. I do not intend to forget my origin, but I am a Canadian before anything." He would repeat a version of this speech hundreds of times over the course of his lengthy political career.

Laurier helped to define Canada in the early years of the century, as he shepherded the country through the greatest transformation in its early history. Between 1896 and 1911, Canada was a riot of boastful statistics: the prairies had produced 8 million bushels of wheat in 1896, but by 1911 the total was 75 million. Cities sprang up and flourished: the population of Saskatoon rose from 113 people in 1901 to 12,000 in 1911; Regina grew from 2,000 to 30,000; Winnipeg from 42,000 to 136,000; Vancouver from 27,000 to 100,000. Under Laurier, the country became more industrialized and ethnically varied, and John A. Macdonald's vision of filling the empty west was finally realized.

Laurier was tall and charming with a soulful face that conferred a sense of nobility, a poet's face. His chronic bronchitis contributed to his frail, romantic look. A French anglophile, he was eloquent in both languages. When defending Louis Riel, he had been accused of being too French, but by the turn of the century, Charles Tupper, who served briefly as prime minister, complained, "He's too English for me."

"Laurier was nearly all things to all men . . . a human solar system," the *Toronto Star* noted. "He was sometimes many things to himself. One moment he could be as debonair as Beau Brummell, the next as forbidding and repellent as a modern Caesar."

Laurier began life as the son of a poor Quebec surveyor. In 1868, he married a shy piano teacher named Zoé Lafontaine. Soon after, however, he became entranced by his neighbour, Emilie Lavergne, who had just returned from an extended stay in London. Lavergne, who was married to Laurier's law partner, Joseph Lavergne, recognized Laurier's potential. "I saw very quickly that this young politician was still, in certain ways, only the little greenhorn," she later wrote in her unpublished memoir. "His wife was not the person who could teach him even those elements of etiquette that a man of the world should know. . . . I made him understand that this lack of etiquette would hamper him among the English elite, with whom he would

**HENRI BOURASSA** ◆ "I regret every time I go back to my province . . . to find developing that feeling that Canada is not Canada for all Canadians. We are bound to come to the conclusion that Quebec is our only country because we have no liberty elsewhere." (*National Archives of Canada. C-4956*)

be called upon to mingle in Ottawa. I taught him then to eat, to dress with taste, in a word, all that a gentleman should know." Lavergne helped construct the perfect political candidate: a man comfortable with both the rural poor and the urban sophisticate, a bilingual charmer.

Emilie's marriage to Joseph Lavergne seemed to be rooted more in convenience than in passion, and she and Laurier struck up a friendship that lasted for twenty-five years. Though the relationship was, to all appearances, simply platonic, it was rumoured that Emilie's children, Gabrielle and Armand, were fathered by Laurier. Armand bore a strong resemblance to Laurier, and it was Laurier, not Lavergne, who paid for Gabrielle's schooling. Almost a third of Laurier's letters to Emilie dealt with the welfare of the children. In Ottawa there was a persistent whisper about their relationship.

"I would like to see you, my friend . . ." he wrote to Emilie in one of his many, careful letters, "simply to see you, to hear you, to look in your eyes, to listen to your voice, to feel that it is you, to be sure of it, to enjoy the consciousness of it. . . . I crave all the more to see you."

Laurier was elected a member of Parliament in 1874, and for seventeen years he sat opposite John A. Macdonald, observing his rhetorical flourishes, political gifts, and talent for excess. Laurier ascended to the leadership of the Liberal Party in 1887 and waited patiently for the country to tire of the Conservatives.

In the spring of 1896, he recruited Henri Bourassa as a political candidate in the upcoming election. Bourassa boasted an enviable political lineage: he was the grandson of Louis-Joseph Papineau, the leader of the failed 1837 rebellion in Lower Canada. Bourassa vividly recalled his grandfather's death. "I was only three when he died," he wrote. "I remember it as if it happened yesterday . . . the room where my grandfather died and where we were led to receive his last blessing." He would be guided always by Papineau's legacy.

Bourassa was Laurier's opposite in almost every way. He was solitary, mystic, and pious where Laurier was pragmatic and always surrounded by friends. Bourassa's close-cropped hair and robust appearance looked almost Prussian next to Laurier's tall, ethereal presence.

"I am ready to accept it," Bourassa said when asked if he would be a Liberal candidate, "but for two conditions. I retain the right to vote for or against my party according to my convictions. And to be free to act accordingly, I don't want a single penny of the election fund to enter my riding."

Laurier's campaign slogan was the cheerfully optimistic "Sunny Ways," but it was enough to get him elected in what was seen as a Conservative loss rather than a Liberal victory. In 1896, at the age of fifty-four, Laurier became Canada's first French-Canadian prime minister.

His first challenge came with the Manitoba school crisis. In 1890, the provincial government, in a violation of the Manitoba Act, had abolished the guarantee of separate schools for Catholics in Manitoba, schools in which French was the language of instruction. The federal Tory government had recognized this as a political quagmire and had been unable to pass remedial legislation to resolve the issue with Laurier in opposition, leading the charge against the government's bill. Now Laurier approached the issue with the spirit of compromise that would be his governing trademark. He reached an agreement with Manitoba premier Thomas Greenway that did not restore the separate schools but granted minor concessions to the Roman Catholics, such as allowing public schools to teach religion between 3:30 and 4:00 p.m. "The settlement which we have obtained from the government of Manitoba satisfies every sensible man in Canada," Laurier wrote to a M. Drolet on December 15, 1896, "but the clergy of the province of Quebec will not pardon us." His imperfect solution also left the door open for minority school questions in other provinces, which would nag him throughout his tenure.

The following year, 1897, marked Queen Victoria's sixtieth year on the throne. Laurier was given a prominent place in the Diamond Jubilee celebrations. He received a knighthood, and he was given the honour of riding in the carriage that followed the queen's in the procession through the streets of London. At a reception later, Laurier gallantly offered a pledge to his British hosts. "If a day were ever to come when England was in danger," he said, "let the bugle sound, let the fires be lit on the hills . . . whatever we can do shall be done by the colonies to help her."

He was taken up on his offer two years later, in October 1899, when the Dutch settlers who had colonized the Transvaal and Orange Free State at the southern tip of Africa invaded the British South African colonies, declaring war. In the beginning, the Boer War appeared to be just another in a series of nineteenth-century imperial skirmishes for Britain, all of which had been dispatched with relative ease. But the Boers were expert horsemen and marksmen, and they employed guerrilla tactics that surprised the British army. What had begun as a skirmish grew into a difficult and costly war.

Canada was quickly divided along linguistic lines: the majority of English Canadians wanted to assist Britain, while most French Canadians viewed this as a war of imperial expansion, a foreign battle being waged on a distant continent. Laurier initially said that the country would not be involved, then changed his mind under pressure from English Canada. His compromise solution was to send volunteers but to have Britain pay them. "If there is anything to which I have given my political life," he said in the House of Commons, "it is to try to promote unity, harmony, and amity between the diverse elements of this country. I shall not deviate a line from the policy that I have traced out for myself."

His decision was not popular among his Quebec MPs. "I will oppose imperialism as long as I am in Parliament," Henri Bourassa said. "I will vote against each and every imperialist project, whether red [Liberal], blue [Tory], or quail-coloured." For him, the Boer War was an issue of British imperialism, and on October 12, 1899, he and other Quebec MPs met at Laurier's residence to challenge him on the issue of Canada's involvement.

"Do you take account of opinion in the province of Quebec?" Bourassa asked him.

"My dear Henri," Laurier responded, "the province of Quebec does not have opinions, it has only sentiments. The circumstances are extremely difficult."

"It is because they are difficult that I ask you to remain faithful. To govern is to have the courage, at a given moment, to risk defeat in order to maintain a principle."

Laurier's word had been given variously to Britain, to English Canada, and to Quebec. "Ah, my dear friend," he responded, "you have not a practical mind."

A few days later, Bourassa announced that he would resign his seat, listing his reasons in a letter to Laurier. "The question is whether Canada is ready to . . . return to the primitive state of a crown colony," he wrote.

Laurier took the resignation in stride. "My honourable friend is young and enthusiastic," he said, addressing the House of Commons. "He is at that age when brilliant and chivalrous theories matter more than practical qualities." Bourassa later won a seat in a by-election, by acclamation, and returned to Parliament as an independent.

Laurier's pragmatic qualities had already been glimpsed in 1897, when he broke off his relationship with Emilie Lavergne, concerned, perhaps, that, as prime minister, he could not afford the whispered scandal that followed them. He appointed her husband a judge in 1896 and eventually transferred him to Montreal, and he had a messenger return to Emilie all the letters she had written him. Emilie never forgave him. "He was a man," John Dafoe, editor of the *Manitoba Free Press*, wrote of Laurier, "who had affinities with Machiavelli as well as with Sir Galahad."

For Henri Bourassa, the Boer War was Britain's problem, a war of imperialism. But many English Canadians saw the conflict as an opportunity for the young nation to take its place on the world stage, as an ally rather than a colony. For some, it was the embodiment of British adventure, evoking the heroic battles celebrated in *Boy's Own Magazine*.

Growing up in Guelph, Ontario, John McCrae had been weaned on these stories of military valour, and he had come to resemble their heroes: a tall, handsome, award-winning cadet. He studied medicine at the University of Toronto, graduating at the top of his class and serving as an officer in the military reserves. The Boer War began the year he graduated, and he carefully followed its progress. Rudyard Kipling, author of *The Jungle Book* and the most prominent champion of British imperialism, had written a poem, "The White Man's Burden," that McCrae pasted into his scrapbook.

Take up the White Man's burden –
Send forth the best ye breed –
Go, bind your sons to exile
To serve your captives' need;
To wait, in heavy harness,
On fluttered folk and wild –
Your new-caught sullen peoples,
Half devil and half child.

McCrae had been heading for Montreal's McGill University to take up a teaching position, but he was determined now to join the fight in South Africa. "Ever since this business began," he wrote to his mother, "I am certain there has been not 15 minutes of my waking hours that it has not been in my mind. . . . I shall not pray for peace in our time. One campaign might cure me – but nothing else ever will, unless it be old age."

McCrae joined the Canadian volunteers as a lieutenant, assigned to lead the right section of D Battery, which included fifty-four men from his home town. There was a parade on the day of their departure, January 4, 1900, and the mayor of Guelph declared a holiday. Each soldier was given a Bible, and, as an officer, McCrae received a set of binoculars.

In his first week in Cape Town, McCrae met Kipling. "Met the high priest of it all," he wrote to his mother. "I had a 5-minute chat with him – Kipling I mean. . . . He is little, fat like his pictures, & very affable. He says 'Up country it is just *Hell*.' He told me I spoke like a Winnipegger."

The next two and half months were spent waiting restlessly in Cape Town. Then, in mid July, the battery finally encountered the enemy. "21 July 1900, Our baptism of fire," McCrae wrote in his diary. "They opened on us from the left flank. . . . One shrapnel burst over us & scattered on all sides of us. I felt as if a hail storm were coming down & wanted to turn my back, but it was over in an instant." The only casualty in that first battle was a horse.

More men died of disease than in combat during the Boer War, and the glories of battle were eclipsed by the ignoble deaths in poorly run field hospitals. "For absolute neglect and rotten administration, it is a model," McCrae wrote of the British hospital. "I am ashamed of some members of my profession. . . . Every day there are from 15 to 30 Tommies dying from fever and dysentery. Every one that dies is sewn up in a blanket, and four shillings are taken out of the pay for the blanket. The soldier's game is not what it's cracked up to be."

A year later, the Boers were still stubbornly resisting the onslaught of British troops, which now numbered in the hundreds of thousands, and Britain was being criticized for what had become an unpopular war. Even Kipling was unnerved by the lack of progress. "We have 40 million reasons for our failure," he wrote in the London *Times*, "but not one excuse. Consequently, the more we work and the less we talk, the better it will be. If we learn this lesson of imperialism, we will keep our empire."

**RUDYARD KIPLING** ◆
Novelist and poet Rudyard Kipling held the imperialist view that Britain was inherently superior and had a moral responsibility to the world. He had a mythic sense of the British empire as something that would maintain order and relieve suffering among the less enchanted nations of Africa and the Indian subcontinent. (*Library of Congress*)

**BOER WAR** ◆ In 1897, Queen Victoria's Diamond Jubilee celebrated the inevitability and grandeur of the empire. Two years later, that confidence was dealt a blow in South Africa when what had started as a small war against an inferior opponent turned into a series of military disasters. In October 1899, the Boers attacked the towns of Ladysmith, Mafeking, and Kimberly, and what the British had predicted would be a short conflict (over "by Christmas") turned into a protracted and bloody guerrilla war that claimed the lives of 22,000 British soldiers, 25,000 Boer civilians, and 14,000 Africans.

The Boer War brought together an interesting group: Mohandas (later Mahatma) Gandhi was a stretcher-bearer in the British medical corps; Sir Arthur Conan Doyle, doctor and creator of Sherlock Holmes, ran a field hospital; Winston Churchill was involved in several major battles, wrote two books about his experience, and parlayed his military exploits into a political career; Sir Robert Baden-Powell helped defend Mafeking and later established the Boy Scouts; Rudyard Kipling, who went on to win the Nobel Prize for literature in 1907, worked as a journalist for an army newspaper. (*Top: The Manitoba Transvaal Contingent. National Archives of Canada,* PAC *C-12272. Right: Fusiliers at Honey Nest Kloof, South Africa, National Archives of Canada* C-24604)

Despite its military superiority, Britain was making little progress, frustrated by Boer ambushes and the dynamiting of trains. Most of the Canadian troops, including McCrae, had returned home by the time British troops finally resorted to burning Boer farms and putting civilians, including women and children, into badly run concentration camps. The last Boer guerrillas surrendered in May 1902; by that time, 25,000 Boer civilians and 14,000 natives had died in the British camps, of famine or disease. The British kept South Africa.

McCrae came back to Guelph, to cheering crowds and a proud speech from the mayor, his boyish enthusiasm for war having withered. The war was an inglorious debacle, but it provided Canada with an opportunity to define itself within the empire, and the imperialist issues it raised became a touchstone for English-Canadian nationalism.

Across the country, Canada was undergoing an economic boom, and its cities were being defined by waves of immigrants. Among them was Israel Medres, who came to Montreal to escape the oppressive living conditions in the Russian empire. He found work on the docks and in the Canadian Pacific Railway (CPR) yards, where he joined an army of immigrants doing hard manual labour for very little gain. "A lot of people talked about their problems," he wrote. "They cursed Christopher Columbus . . . the first words of English these immigrants learned were 'hurry-up,' 'come-on,' 'time is money,' 'help yourself,' and 'never mind.'" On Boulevard St-Laurent, Yiddish was the dominant language in the fetid tailor shops where immigrants stitched clothing. Medres observed the wretched conditions and began writing columns in the Yiddish newspaper the *Jewish Daily Eagle*, a voice for the workers. "Many of them hoped that the sooner they could learn English, the faster they could leave behind the workshops with their foremen and their 'hurry-ups,' and manage to establish a small shop of their own," he reported. Many did, but not Medres, who remained a journalist and editorial writer at the *Daily Eagle*.

Montreal was a city of oversized accomplishments, boasting the Victoria Bridge, an engineering marvel that spanned one of the largest rivers in the world. The city was headquarters to the Canadian Pacific Railway, the world's longest railway, and Montreal was the largest city in the country, with a population that had grown from 216,000 in 1891 to 528,000 in 1911, the result of a huge rural influx, international immigration, and the amalgamation of outlying suburbs.

Not far from the sweat shops on St-Laurent was the excess of the Square Mile, home to most of the country's largest industrialists and financiers. Two-thirds of Canada's wealth was controlled within its borders, on the southern slope of Mount Royal, and its occupants lived in an opulence not seen anywhere else in the country. It was an architectural mélange of grand Second Empire, Italian Renaissance, and Neo-Gothic homes (sometimes with several styles incorporated in a single house), as the new

**EMILE NELLIGAN** ◆ Emile Nelligan was one of the country's first modern poets, and his work was greatly celebrated in Quebec. All of his poems were written by the time he was twenty, the age at which he was admitted to a mental hospital near Montreal. He spent the next forty-two years there. His sonnet "The Golden Ship" describes his fate. (*National Archives of Canada*, C-88566)

commercial aristocracy tried to recreate a European notion of wealth. Before 1917 there was no federal income tax, and capital gains tax was an idea of the distant future, so money could be accumulated without hindrance. Many of Montreal's fortunes, however, were the product of a dour, Presbyterian work ethic that self-made Scots industrialists had brought from their homeland. Sir William Macdonald, the founder of the tobacco company that carries his name, lived in a modest house, never married, and felt a gramophone was too great an expense. His bedroom contained an old iron bed and the walls were bare. He did not smoke and threatened to fire a nephew unless he quit the "filthy habit." Macdonald gave $15 million to charity, however, an extraordinary sum at the time.

Sir Herbert Holt was an austere multi-millionaire who did not drink, smoke, or belong to a club, and who took up his first leisure activity – bridge – at the age of seventy-five. At the end of a lost game, Holt accused his partner of ineptitude and punched him in the face. When Holt's death was announced during a baseball game at Delorimier Stadium, the crowd cheered.

There were also elaborate costume balls, however, with champagne fountains and visiting royalty. Bored society women speculated in the stock market. John McCrae went to Montreal to resume his medical fellowship and mixed with the city's elite. "Last night I went to the annual dinner at the Shakespeare Club," he wrote to his mother in April 1902. Later in the year, he wrote, "Tonight I have to go to the Neurological Class and improve my mind. Later, the Dean of the Arts Faculty is giving an At Home to W. B. Yeats, whoever he is: he is a writer 'of sorts' as the Englishmen say." Yeats had already made a reputation as a poet, though his genius would not be celebrated for several years. McCrae was writing poetry himself that was being published in the *McGill University Magazine* and *Saturday Night*.

"The rich in Montreal enjoyed a prestige in that era that not even the rich deserve," wrote Stephen Leacock. McCrae met Leacock as a member of the city's Pen and Pencil Club. "I have been asked to join the 'Pen and Pencil Club,'" McCrae wrote to his mother, "a small club of about 14 or 15 which has existed about 30 years; they elect about one man a year, and are supposed to be 'the very elect' – at least by themselves."

Leacock had yet to gain fame as a humorist; he was at McGill in the political science and economics department, working on a textbook, *Elements of Political Science*. He and McCrae shared a love of literature and had similar ideas about Canada's role in the Empire. They were strongly attached to Britain but felt Canada was ready to be treated more as an equal and less as a junior partner. In some circles, the notion of imperialism "is too much associated with a truckling subservience to English people and English ideas and the silly swagger of the hop-o'-my-thumb junior officer," Leacock wrote. "I am an Imperialist," he declared, "because I will not be colonial." He advocated an imperialism that was distinctly Canadian, "the imperialism of the plain man at the plough and the clerk in the counting house, the imperialism of any decent citizen that demands for his country a proper place in the councils of the Empire and in the destiny of the world. In this sense, imperialism means but the realization of a Greater Canada."

The governor general, Albert Grey, the fourth Earl, heard Leacock speak in Ottawa and was impressed enough to arrange for the author to tour the world, speaking about the imperial cause. In London, at the fourth colonial conference, Leacock boldly stated, "We will be your colony no longer. Make us one with you in an Empire, Permanent and Indivisible." His blunt remarks offended his hosts, and a newspaper article written by Leacock was dismissed by Winston Churchill as "offensive twaddle."

In Montreal, McCrae had a punishing work schedule that included a private practice, academic responsibilities at McGill, and the writing of medical papers. But in the evenings he made time for a glittering social crawl, fraternizing with the governor general, Earl Grey, and the city's wealthiest families, the Allans and the Molsons among them. "I am having an awful time dodging invitations: I don't like to seem to pick my friends," he wrote to his mother, "but the pace is too great. I don't like to seem a society man at all, – but it fairly pours on me." He lamented that he had no time for poetry and that, approaching the age of forty, he was still single. "What a – stale thing is life!" he wrote to a friend. "I have so damned many things on my soul at present that I can't sit down." One of his many research papers was titled "An analysis of two hundred autopsies upon infants," a grim reminder of the vast gap between the Square Mile and the city's poor. Montreal (along with New Orleans) had the highest infant mortality rate in North America, a rate that was on a par with Calcutta's.

In his novel *Arcadian Adventures with the Idle Rich*, Stephen Leacock wrote about the stark contrast: "Just below Plutoria Avenue [Sherbrooke Street], the very pleasantest place imaginable, and parallel with it, the trees die out and the brick and stone of the city begins in earnest. Even from the avenue you see the tops of the sky-scraping buildings in the big commercial streets, and can hear or almost hear the roar of the elevated railway, earning dividends. And beyond that again the city sinks lower, and is choked and crowded with the tangled streets and little houses of the slums. In fact, if you were to mount to the roof of the Mausoleum Club on Plutoria Avenue you could almost see the slums from there. But why should you? And on the other hand, if you never went up on the roof, but only dined inside among the palm-trees, you would never know that the slums existed – which is much better."

The slums were south of the Square Mile, in Griffintown, a tangle of shanties and crowded apartments inhabited largely by Irish and French Canadians. And yet, in 1904 André Siegfried, a political scientist from France, observed: "An attitude adopted in Anglo-Canadian circles is that of ignoring deliberately the very presence of the French. From their whole bearing and conversation, you might spend many weeks among the English of Montreal without anyone letting you realize that the city is two-thirds French. Many travellers never suspect this."

**STEPHEN LEACOCK** ◆ "We have tolerated with a smile the bribery of voters, the corrupting of constituencies, the swollen profits of favoured contractors, the fortunes made in and from political life, the honours heaped upon men with no other consideration than their bank accounts." Stephen Leacock, from *Democracy and Social Progress*. (*Corbis-Bettman*)

Like John McCrae, Toussaint Stephen Langevin was a Montreal doctor, an obstetrician who had trained in the city. Born in 1885 in Scottsville, a small village south of Quebec City, he had set up his practice in Montreal's Plateau Mont-Royal, a working-class district of three-storey apartment buildings, and he was chief doctor at the Hôpital de la Miséricorde, where he took care of unmarried pregnant women. "The typhoid epidemics in the Mile End district contributed to the rapid rise of my practice," he wrote in his memoirs, "since the existing doctors were overwhelmed by the number of sick people."

His patients were the working poor: "I visited some truly needy families. It was a tearful sight to see those six, seven or eight children, almost naked in a frigid home, heated by a stove filled with old papers, those beds without mattresses, a single flannel blanket on the springs. It is easy to understand why all of these children, born during this nefarious period, were influenced physically and morally by mothers who were exhausted, hungry and too often, demoralized."

Langevin's patients were often unable to pay. "My beginnings in practice were modest, since my women patients were nicknamed the 'yellow-stomachs,' 'the black feet,' living as they did in a district called 'Pipes and Chimneys.' That district was located between Mont-Royal Street and the Canadian Pacific train tracks. The scarcity of potable water in this sector explained why they never or seldom washed. . . . These mothers, surrounded by numerous infants born in sequence, lived in hard conditions. How many times did I hear, at the step of these slums, the same tune, 'Thank-you, dear doctor, I will come to pay you on Saturday.' Alas, how many of these Saturdays were forgotten, how many invoices lost. . . . After having helped with the delivery for a great part of the night, people still dared to borrow three or four dollars to pay for baptism the day after." The hospital refused the unmarried women painkillers or chloroform during childbirth. "It was a pity to hear three or four patients in the waiting room crying in pain. 'You sinned, my child, you have to expiate,' that's what was given to them under the guise of consolation! It was the motto of the Department. These tears and these cries were, in my mind, a useless and dangerous torture." Langevin felt there was enough misery in their lives. "I dared to lessen these painful contractions by bringing my chloroform."

Alfred Charpentier lived on the Plateau, in the neighbourhood where Langevin worked. The eldest of thirteen children, Charpentier started working at thirteen, then apprenticed as a bricklayer with his father at the age of sixteen. The end of his apprenticeship in 1907 coincided with a recession that left little work for bricklayers, and lower wages for those who were employed. Charpentier and his father went into business for themselves, building houses, then selling them. "But we went bankrupt after one year," Charpentier wrote in his memoir, "as a consequence of errors made by me in the calculation of estimates for the few contracts that we did. As a result, we lost our properties."

**MONTREAL** ◆ Below Montreal's Square Mile, where two-thirds of the country's wealth was concentrated, lay Griffintown and Point St. Charles, where working-class Irish and French Canadians lived.

"While you walk in the streets of the upper city, you see tall and handsome houses, stately churches and well-built schools, but descend the hill, by Cathedral, Mountain and Guy, and their characteristics change, the tenement house replaces the single residence, the factory with its smoking chimney is in evidence on every side . . . the sanitary accommodation of 'The City Below the Hill' is a disgrace to any 19th century city on this or any other continent." Sir Herbert Ames, businessman, social reformer, and resident of Montreal's Square Mile. *(Notman Photographic Collection, Musée McCord Museum)*

The family moved into an apartment on St-Denis Street. "We were fifteen at the family table, and I was still the only one, along with my father, to provide for the family's needs. Twenty-three years separated me from the youngest child. . . . During the following four years, disease was continually present in our home, hitting my mother and many of the children. Then the depression frequently forced my father and I out of work."

As the cities became more industrialized, the working class grew and became more organized. A member of the fledgling bricklayers' union, Charpentier suffered through two bitter strikes. "The first one lasted for a week, in 1908, the second lasted for six weeks in 1910. The family was in financial straits for many years to come." Charpentier became more involved in the union; first elected secretary of the Montreal bricklayers' union in 1908, he was made president in 1911.

Charpentier was joined by rural French Canadians who were arriving in droves, seeking factory work, and changing the urban landscape. "The fact is that in Canada, industrialism has been suddenly thrust into what was essentially an agricultural society," wrote James Shaver Woodsworth, a Methodist minister from Winnipeg who would later be elected to Parliament. "Many of our laws are not modern. Improvement comes slowly and is resisted, because the Canadians who largely dominate the situation do not understand the new social order."

The new social order retained many of the inequities of the old social order, and survival was a difficult task. In 1912, a Montreal social welfare committee reported that a worker earning $1.75 for a twelve-hour day and working six days a week could make $550 annually: "To get this much, a man must have continuous work with no sickness, no changes in jobs, and he must not waste his money on drink or dissipation. Granted all this he can give a family of five a mere existence. No allowance is here made for sickness, recreation, church, house furnishings, lectures and savings." The family would also have to live, the report stated, "in insanitary quarters, sometimes below street level."

While Montreal was drawing labour from both the hinterland and abroad, the west was filling with immigrants, and Henri Bourassa argued that the prairies needed a greater French-Canadian presence. "If we want the west to become homogeneous and to stay Canadian, to take part in our national life," he said in a speech at the Monument National in Montreal, in April 1905, "it is not sufficient to build cities there, to grow crops, and to create a flow of commerce by building railways. The most efficient means of producing this national unification, perhaps the only one, is to transplant in the west a segment of the old French-Canadian trunk and surround it with an atmosphere that will preserve its native sap and original qualities. . . . Then let come the American, the Doukhobor, the Galician. The old trunk resisted every assault along the banks of the St. Lawrence, so the new tree will endure prairie storms; and the future of a united Canada will be preserved."

The minister of the interior, Clifford Sifton, was looking for Americans and British immigrants first, but when they did not arrive in sufficient numbers, he extended his search to Doukhobors, Poles, Finns, Icelanders, and Galicians (Ukrainians). A "stalwart peasant in a sheep-skin coat, born on the soil whose forefathers have been farmers for ten generations, with a stout wife and a half dozen children is good quality . . ." Sifton said. "I am indifferent as to whether or not he is British born." For the first time, Canada was attracting large numbers of people who were neither French nor British in origin. During Sifton's terms in office, the population of the west increased from 300,000 to 1.5 million.

**IMMIGRANTS ARRIVING ON THE ATLANTIC LINE** ◆ "Workingmen from the cities and towns are the most helpless people in the world when they are placed upon the prairies and left to shift for themselves. It takes two generations to convert a town-based population into an agricultural one. Canada has no time for that operation." Clifford Sifton, minister of the interior. (*Glenbow Archives*, NA-1687-37)

To attract settlers, Sifton hired agents who went abroad to deliver glowing lectures on the country's advantages. He brought American reporters up on junkets, hoping for favourable press, and set up a clandestine company that paid steamship agents to bring immigrants from western Europe. But his most effective tool was the immigration pamphlet, expanding on previous efforts by Thomas Spence and others under the Macdonald administration. In 1900, Sifton sent out one million pamphlets. They contained practical information on transportation, soil, and climate (omitting the winter temperatures), and offered helpful, untruthful parallels ("The frontier of Manitoba is about the same latitude as Paris"). Testimonials of those who had flourished on the plains were included: "I was thin and pale, had a cough," wrote a former Chicagoan who had moved to Lacombe, Alberta. "When winter came, I found it to be the most pleasant part of the year, as the dry, cold air was bracing and entirely different from the damp, chilly wind I was used to." The pamphlets had an editorial exuberance that offered land, freedom, and spiritual sustenance – a chance to live like Adam on the empty plains. They spoke of "the building of Jerusalem in this pleasant land." Sifton worked to get landless eastern Europeans to come, translating the advertisements into more than a dozen languages and distributing them across the continent. "All the fabled mutations of wand and enchantment sink into insignificance before the change which this free world works in the serf of Europe," read one pamphlet, ". . . something better anyway than the tear-drenched, blood-stained tapestry of the old world's past."

Among those who came west to escape the blood-stained past was Petro Svarich. He was twenty-two, living in Tulova, a small village in Galicia (a part of the Austro-Hungarian Empire that later became Ukraine), when he sent away for information on what was rumoured to be free land in Canada. His family was wealthy by the standards of his village, but they were only a generation removed from serfdom. The pamphlet offered them 160 acres of land (65 hectares) and complete freedom. "My father, after long deliberation, decided to sell his entire estate, and emigrate to Canada," Svarich wrote in his memoir. "He said, 'In Canada there are no taxes, no compulsory military service, no gendarmes. Paradise! Complete paradise!'" The Svarich family left Galicia and, on March 3, 1900, joined with a small group who left Hamburg on the *Arcadia*, bound for Halifax.

Svarich arrived in Winnipeg in April and reassessed paradise: "My experience in this first Canadian hostel I shall not forget for the rest of my life. In one night I was bitten so bad by fleas and bedbugs that the next day I could hardly clean myself of them. My mother wept when she saw me – all miserable, wretched and discouraged." The family travelled across the prairies, intimidated rather than buoyed by its emptiness. Months earlier, a group of fifty-nine Galician immigrants had taken the same route, and there were fifty-five graves marking the trail; all but four children had died of scarlet fever.

Svarich and his parents continued to the Edna-Star district, a handful of farms spread over the parkland east of Edmonton. Other Galician immigrants farming there had sent letters postmarked from Edna, a place that Svarich had built up in his mind to be a thriving town. "Thus I find my Edna," Svarich wrote, "in the bush, lost on the bank of a creek. The Edna I had realized in my dreams! I had fantasized that it was some sort of El Dorado, drawing me nigh." It consisted of a few farms, a postal station, a store, and the house of the man who had suggested they come west. "I could not believe my eyes: the house was like a pigsty, the stable but a crude shelter, both covered with sod; a second well was being dug and there was no water. . . . Our hearts sank with what we saw and what obviously awaited us too. We turned to our hosts and began to scold them. They had deceived us with their letters."

The Svariches continued their search over old buffalo trails, through forests. Svarich's father finally declared, "This forest must be mine," and they settled there, calling the district Kolomea, after a Galician town. They brought in their first harvest six months after arriving. "My parents were very satisfied with the harvest, for the total yield was three times as much as

Top: A Galician
immigrant family
(*National Archives of
Canada*, C-4745)
Left: Mrs. Herman
and her children,
settlers in Alberta
(*Glenbow Archives*,
PA-2685-49).

**WINNIPEG, 1905** ◆ By 1902, Winnipeg was the largest grain-handler in North America, dealing with 57.8 million bushels annually, compared to Chicago's 37.9 million. An immigration pamphlet boasted that "Winnipeg is founded on the prairie, and the vitality, the immense potentiality and ever advancing prosperity, of which the prairie soil of Western Canada is the greatest reservoir in the world, is in Winnipeg's blood. The city is only on the threshold of its greatness. The transformation that is being wrought now is for all time, and is only beginning." (*Provincial Archives of Manitoba, N-10338*)

they would have in the old country. . . . My father now felt like a wealthy man and would not return to his old farm in the Old Country for anything, for if he accomplished this much in one year, imagine how much he would have in five or even ten years."

Not everyone was as enthusiastic. Petro Kotyk, who had been working in the mines at Frank, Alberta, wrote, "As a reminder to those who want to go to Canada . . . he'll suffer as much on that large farm as the man in the old country who has no house, nor field, and works on the landlord's estate. And he'll have to suffer that way for not only a year or two, but for the rest of his life. No one really writes the truth."

After less than a year on the farm, Petro Svarich did what young rural men were doing in the east, what they have always done: he left the farm for the city. "I felt it was a waste of my youth and talent to remain on the farm in the bush," he wrote. "I hoped to improve my English, find some work in a store, earn some money and, some day, open my own store . . . and set up a post office and get some farm machinery agency in my district as well." He moved to Edmonton and worked as a type cleaner at Frank Oliver's *Edmonton Bulletin* for a dollar a day.

In the early years of the new century, Edmonton would enjoy an economic boom based in part on land speculation; the city's population increased from 4,000 in 1901 to 57,045 in 1911. But the boom had yet to make an impression when Svarich moved there in 1901, and he found too many men looking for too few jobs. He left Edmonton to work on the CPR, but he was quickly discouraged by the monotony and hardship of tamping wooden railway ties into gravel beds ten hours a day. "My whole body seemed broken and twisted and hurt at every movement," he complained. "I could not even sleep because my body hurt so much." He was able to get work at the CPR roundhouse at Lake Louise, where he filled the coal chutes that were dumped into the locomotives that stopped to refuel. In 1901, the Prince of Wales (soon to be King Edward VII) was visiting Canada and expressed an interest in touring Lake Louise on horseback. "An order was wired from Calgary that a road needed to be cut through the trees to the lake," Svarich wrote. "I was the first to volunteer for the work, together with six Italians. It took us two days to clear a suitable trail to the lake, on the shore of which we raised a large Union Jack on a tall flagpole." The prince arrived, cantered to the lake with his entourage, had lunch, and left on the train.

Svarich injured his hand working for the CPR and moved to Rossland, British Columbia, to try mining, which paid $3.00 per day, twice what the railway did and ten times what he would have made on the farm. After five months, Svarich had saved $400. He sent half back to his parents and used the other half to book passage to the Klondike. He was late for the gold rush, but he decided to take his chances anyway. By the time he got to Dawson in 1902, most of the adventurers had either left for Alaska or been deported by the Canadian authorities, but larger gold mining operations still worked the area. Svarich got a job in one and stayed for two years, until he became homesick and left for Vancouver.

He was paid in gold, which was assessed at $2,150 at a government office in Vancouver, and he thought about staying on the coast and maybe working in a sawmill. "I became convinced that it would not be so easy to find a job," he wrote, "due to the large number of Chinese and Japanese who worked everywhere for very low wages." Instead he returned to Alberta, to start a store in Vegreville, where a Ukrainian community had grown up. He sought comfort in religion and joined the Presbyterian church, but he left after a year. "I became convinced that the Ukrainian soul will never be satisfied nor nourished by the charity which the Protestant religion offers to its faithful. Our disposition is more natural, poetic, rich in meaning; it loves ritual, singing, ceremony, the grandeur of church decorations and religious mysticism, which the Protestants lack. Everything is dry, abstract and empty with them."

**PABLO PICASSO** ◆ In 1907, Pablo Picasso, along with Georges Braque, pioneered the Cubist style. Picasso's first work in this mode, *Les Demoiselles d'Avignon*, borrowed from African sculpture and showed a fractured, modern image that broke with the more linear representations of the previous century. (*The Museum of Modern Art, New York*)

To the south of Vegreville, Calgary was also growing at a tremendous rate: from 5,000 people in 1900 to 75,000 in 1912. Downtown property that was bought for $2,000 in 1904 was sold for $300,000 six years later.

In 1912, an American trick roper named Guy Weadick inaugurated the first Calgary Stampede with the backing of four local businessmen. It would include "Indians," rodeo events, and his wife, trick rider Flores LaDue, and he boasted that it would be the greatest show on earth, "devoid of circus tinsel and far-fetched fiction." Weadick did rely on one romantic fiction, though: an American interpretation of the west that mythologized the cowboy, appealing to the eighty thousand Americans who had come north to settle in Alberta. Weadick used Methodist missionaries to convince local native people to participate in the Stampede's parade, to lend it authenticity. Eighty thousand people watched the event, more than the population of the city itself.

At the same time that Weadick was presenting his version of the west, a British planner and architect named Thomas Mawson offered Calgary an urban plan that was intended to transform it into the Paris of the prairie. He gave a speech to the Canadian Club titled "The City on the Plain and How to Make it Beautiful." Impressed, the city council commissioned him to produce a model, and after several months, he delivered one that incorporated spacious plazas and three-storey Beaux-Arts buildings set on wide streets. There were monuments and grand bridges and a boating reach on the Bow River, a relentlessly European urban plan that had the scale the city felt fitted its ambition.

While the cost of implementing this plan was being debated, the Dingman Discovery Well #1 in Turner Valley blew in. On May 14, 1914, Archibald Wayne Dingman announced that "oil of a very specific gravity has been struck in the company's No. 1 well, and the quality is equal, if it does not excel, the finest grades found in any oil territory." Within weeks, more than five hundred new oil companies had incorporated. Lacking experience, employees, equipment, and leases, they attracted investors nonetheless, and the city was consumed by the possibilities that came with a major oil strike. But only six of the oil companies drilled wells to completion, and none found oil. It was later revealed that the Dingman well had not struck oil, after all, but naphtha. The local excitement turned to anger, then depression, and the hustlers and entrepreneurs moved on to the next opportunity. City council not only lacked the money to implement Mawson's grand plan, it could barely pay him his fee.

While the men in the sheepskin coats were populating the prairies, another group of immigrants was arriving that was far less welcome. Between 1880 and 1885, fifteen thousand Chinese men were brought to British Columbia and paid a dollar per day to do the most dangerous and difficult work in building the railway through the mountains. They came to British Columbia to escape poverty and war at home but found little solace. Hundreds of Chinese workers died building the line between Vancouver and Calgary, from exposure, crushed by falling rock, blown to pieces by dynamite, or suffocated in avalanches. Aside from the killing work on the railway, there was the loneliness and despair of living without women. With the railway complete, some wanted to return to China and take their chances there, but few could afford the return fare.

**SIGMUND FREUD** ◆ In 1900, Austrian psychiatrist Sigmund Freud published *The Interpretation of Dreams*, launching the concept of psychoanalysis. He was the first to treat mental illness as something caused by psychological factors, believing that neurotic symptoms were the result of a struggle between subconscious sexual urges and defences built up against them. His 1905 book *Three Contributions to the Sexual Theory* introduced the concepts of the Oedipus complex and penis envy. "They regard me rather as a monomaniac," Freud said of response to his psychoanalytic theory, "while I have the distinct feeling that I touched on one of the great secrets of nature." (*Corbis Bettman*)

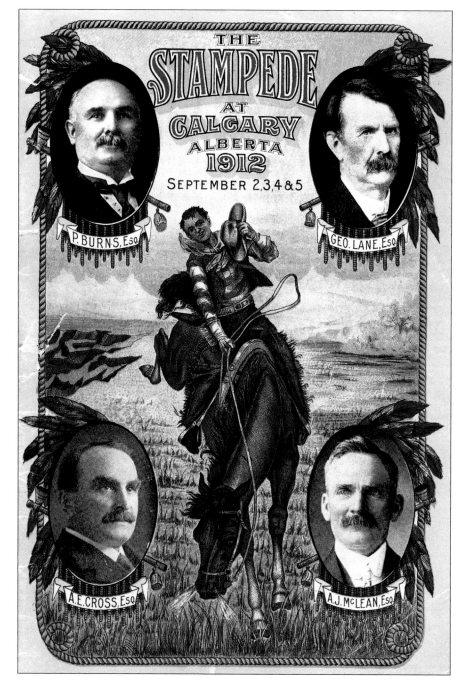

The first Calgary Stampede. Ranching was in a state of crisis in 1912, with ranchers facing financial ruin and the dominance of American meat-packing plants. In an effort to boost the flagging livestock industry, Calgary's "Big Four" cattlemen – Pat Burns, A. E. Cross, George Lane, and Archie McLean – put up the $100,000 needed to finance the first Stampede. (*Glenbow Archives*, NA-604-1a)

"Some of these men went back," said Won Alexander Cumyow in testimony to a 1902 royal commission on Chinese and Japanese immigration. "But others had no means to pay their way back, and many who remained were in great straits for a long time. The Chinese . . . usually congregate in one part of the city. The chief reason for this is companionship. Besides the Chinese know that the white people have had no friendly feeling towards them."

Won was among the first of the Chinese born in Canada, and he spoke English as well as several native languages. He ran a drugstore owned by his father, and he was well aware of the prejudice that existed. "Canada would be strengthened by exclusion of the Chinese race," the Reverend Leslie Clay

**CHINESE RAILWAY LABOURERS** ◆ Chinese immigrants first gained a reputation as cheap, reliable labour in the building of the Central Pacific Railroad in the United States. The six thousand Chinese who worked on that railway in 1866 were celebrated for their "industry, economy, sobriety, and law-abidingness." By the time the Canadian Pacific Railway (CPR) began to build the line through the Rocky Mountains, cheap Chinese labour (they were paid $1.00 per day, as opposed to between $1.50 and $2.50 for white workers) was a virtual necessity, since the railway flirted regularly with bankruptcy. John A. Macdonald thought that the Chinese would never assimilate into Canadian society, but he realized that they were fundamental to the railway's construction. "It is simply a matter of alternatives," he said. "Either you must have this labour or you can't have the railway." The other advantage that CPR contractors quickly noticed was the mobility of the Chinese workers. Two thousand workers could break camp, move forty kilometres, and set up within twenty-four hours. By contrast, it took a week to move that many white workers.

The Knights of Labour and the Anti-Chinese Society were among the groups that thought the Chinese dragged down the wages of white labourers and sought to keep them out. Ultimately, the groups had little impact: fifteen thousand Chinese worked for the CPR between 1880 and 1885. They suffered from scurvy (due to a diet restricted to rice and ground salmon) and were relegated to the tasks that were the most difficult (grading the hills) and dangerous (blasting tunnels with dynamite). Hundreds died during the construction of the railway. (*Western Canada Pictorial Index*)

reported to the commission. "It has a tendency to deter white immigration. They depress wages . . . lower the standard of living. They ignore our religious services. They create a laxity of sentiment and feeling and the social evil [prostitution] is likely to increase. I think they are injurious in present numbers."

The Chinese presented a conundrum. They had been brought in to perform cheap, dangerous labour, and continued to do so in the sawmills and fish canneries. Employers found them industrious, sober, and cheap – but the general population resented their presence for roughly the same reasons. "It is a mystery to me as it must be to other observers that so many people in all ranks of life are so ready to employ Chinamen to do their work," Won Alexander Cumyow told the commission. "This seems to nullify the allegations that they are either offensive or detrimental to the development of the country."

A fifty-dollar head tax was levied on Chinese immigrants, but this did little to slow the rate of their arrival. By 1900, the Chinese population of British Columbia was growing by four thousand annually. That year the head tax was increased to one hundred dollars. The royal commission reported in 1902 that the Chinese are "unfit for full citizenship. . . . They are so nearly allied to a servile class that they are obnoxious to a free community and dangerous to the state." In 1903 the head tax was raised to five hundred dollars, which had the desired effect; the number of Chinese immigrants dropped from five thousand in 1904 to eight in 1905. But in May 1907, there was an unexpected Asian influx with the arrival of the *Kumeric*. "Eleven hundred and seventy-seven of the little brown men are on the steamer," reported the *Vancouver Province*. "The decks were crowded with swarming Japanese, who cover her from stem to stern like a swarm of ants."

On September 7, a newly formed group called the Asiatic Exclusion League of Vancouver organized a rally at city hall, which was a block from Chinatown and the adjacent Japantown. Almost half of the city – thirty thousand people – turned out for the rally, wearing white ribbons that said "For a White Canada." After rousing speeches that advocated an exclusively white, Christian society, seven thousand men headed for Chinatown. "The mob soon left the Chinese quarter and headed in the direction of Japtown," reported the *Vancouver Province*. "The crash of glass was continual. Window after window was shattered in other stores and boarding houses as the riotous gang pushed farther into the thoroughfare lined with nests of Japanese." The rioting continued, unimpeded by police, for three days. "On Saturday night we have all the windows smashed," recalled Shum Moon, president of the Chinese Board of Trade. "And Sunday, we have a few windows broken again. On Monday night we were informed by one gentleman at City Hall, there was a party going to set fire to Chinatown, so that is the worst night we ever had."

The rioting waned, but the sentiment remained. Won Alexander Cumyow was working as an official court reporter in Vancouver, dealing with not just Chinese but natives, providing translation. He became politically active and lobbied for voting rights. "Unless we have a vote and exercise other privileges where we reside we will always be looked upon as nobody, but once we have a vote we have the power. . . . I do think that if the Chinese pay admission to this country, and if they have the education qualifications they should not only be allowed the privileges of the franchise, but be treated otherwise as men and as British citizens."

Won became one of the first Chinese Canadians to enter the middle class, but his own children still faced barriers: his eldest son was not accepted into the Law Society, and his daughter was barred from nursing school. In 1923, on July 1, Dominion Day, all Chinese immigration was halted, and this became known among Chinese Canadians as "Humiliation Day." The Exclusion Act was not repealed until 1947. Two years later, Won, then eighty-eight, became the first Chinese Canadian to cast a ballot in a federal election.

Chinese Canadians were not the only disenfranchised group seeking the vote. Women were organizing and demonstrating for the right to cast their ballots as well. In Washington, three hundred American suffragists presented their demands in February 1906. In England, a group of suffragettes stormed Parliament, resulting in sixty arrests and dozens of injuries. Canadian women, emboldened by their example, leaped into the fray.

One of the leaders of the Canadian movement was Nellie McClung, a Manitoba woman whose earliest teenage ambitions were chiefly literary: "I wanted to write; to do for the people around me what Dickens had done for his people. I wanted to be the voice for the voiceless. . . . I wanted to reveal humanity; to make people understand each other; to make the commonplace thing divine."

After getting married and moving to Manitou, Manitoba, McClung joined the local Women's Christian Temperance Union, which, in addition to its campaign for the legal prohibition of alcohol, supported such early feminist causes as women's right to vote and mothers' allowances. "No one could deny that women and children were the sufferers from the liquor traffic. Any fun that came from drinking came to men exclusively, and the men themselves would be the first to admit that," McClung said. She felt that the only way to implement temperance legislation was to gain political influence. "Has nature excluded woman from the ballot?" she asked rhetorically. "I think not. Any man who can make his cross, drunk or sober is counted intelligent enough. . . . Our worthy opponents will emphasize the fact that women are the weaker vessel – well I should think that a woman who cooks for the hired men, washes and bakes and scrubs and sews for her family could stand the extra strain of marking a ballot every four years."

McClung was also interested in improving the dismal conditions of working women, and to that end she convinced Manitoba's Conservative premier Rodmond Roblin to tour a factory with her. "On his way to the factory, the premier, who sat between us with his plump hands resting on a gold-headed cane, gave us his views on women working in factories," McClung later recounted. "He advised us not to allow our kind hearts to run away with us. Most of the women in the factories, he understands, were from foreign countries, where life was strenuous. . . .

"We conducted the Premier down dark slippery stairs to an airless basement where light in mid-day came from gaunt light bulbs, hanging from smoky ceilings. The floor was littered with refuse of apple peelings and discarded clothing. There was no ventilation and no heat.

"He was shocked at the filth of the place. . . . 'For God's sake, let me out of here,' he cried at last. 'I'm choking! I never knew such hell holes existed!'"

Despite the tour, Roblin could not endorse McClung's feminist position. "Placing women on . . . political equality with men would cause domestic strife," he argued. "The majority of women are emotional, and if given the franchise would be a menace rather than an aid." McClung's response was a play titled *A Women's Parliament*, which was staged at Winnipeg's Walker Theatre with McClung playing the role of a female premier in a country where men wanted the vote. "If men were to get the vote who knows what would happen," McClung's character argued. "It's hard enough to keep them at home now. . . . Politics unsettle men and unsettled men means unsettled bills, broken furniture, broken vows, and divorce. . . . There is no use giving men the vote. . . . Man has a higher destiny than politics."

**NELLIE McCLUNG** ◆ In 1913, Nellie McClung approached Manitoba premier Rodmond Roblin on the subject of voting rights for women. Roblin said that nice women did not want the vote.

*McClung*: By nice women, you probably mean selfish women who have no more thought for the underpaid, overworked woman than a pussycat in a sunny window for the starving kitten on the street. Now in that sense I am not a nice woman. . . . I care about those factory women, working in ill-smelling holes, and we intend to do something about it, and when I say 'we' I'm talking for a great many women, of whom you will see more as the days go on. I'll not be back, Sir Rodmond; not in your time . . . but it's just possible that you will hear from me, not directly, but still you'll hear; and you may not like what you hear, either.
*Roblin*: Is that a threat?
*McClung*: No, it's a prophecy.

(*Glenbow Archives*, NA-1641-1)

Finding no sympathy from Roblin, McClung turned to the Liberal leader, T. C. Norris, who said he would endorse female suffrage. In 1915, Norris's Liberals won the provincial election, and on January 28, 1916, women in Manitoba became the first in the country to gain the right to vote.

While the west moved slowly, inevitably forward, the Maritime provinces looked to the technological innovations of the new century while continuing to suffer the industrial grittiness of the previous one. On December 19, 1900, the blast furnace of the Dominion Iron and Steel Company was fired up, and in the "Age of Steel" it was anticipated that Nova Scotia would take a prominent place. Dominion characterized the new industrial spirit of the twentieth century with its scale and organization. "Coal is king," said Mayor D. M. Burchell, "and we have every reason to feel that at no distant date, Glace Bay will take its place among the leading cities of Canada."

Matthius "Tius" Tutty, whose father had died at sea, looked at the two stark options that faced local men and chose mining over fishing. "When I was fourteen I went into the mines," he would later recall, "at Bridgeport . . . between Glace Bay and Dominion." Coal had been taken from the area for two hundred years (initially used to fuel the French fortress at Louisbourg), and thousands of children had preceded Tutty underground. "We had a little lamp, something like a teapot hooked in your cap. A little spout on it. And a wick in it, seal oil. Yes, I had my light go out in the mine. Different times. Dark? Well, you couldn't be any darker . . ." Tutty drove the horses that

Cape Breton coke oven workers in 1910. (*Beaton Institute, Eachdraich Archives, University College of Cape Breton*)

hauled boxes of coal along the tracks, a kilometre underground, six days a week, twelve or thirteen hours a day. The children ran the horses until they were old enough to swing a pickaxe and handle blasting powder. "There were horses killed," Tutty remembered. "Runaway boxes. Now there was a driver he wasn't killed but he got hurt pretty bad – he never got over it. . . . The driver was going up this headway and the box came down and hit the horse. Killed the horse and broke the driver, pretty bad. . . . There was an explosion about four years before I started. It was eight men killed. The manager – his name was Johnson. All they found was his lamp, his finger still in the hook."

After a few years Tutty got a pickaxe to swing against the dark face of the seam, and he loaded the coal with a pan shovel. He was paid for each box of coal he delivered to the surface, but he had to pay for his own equipment, explosives, and clothes. Glace Bay was a company town, where Dominion owned the stores and housing and determined the wages and the working conditions. Thousands lived in Dickensian gloom.

Ironically, directly above the primitive operations of one of the largest coal mines in the world, the technological promise of the twentieth century was being realized. The Italian physicist Guglielmo Marconi had come to Cape Breton to experiment with wireless communication, attempting to connect Europe and North America. The previous year, he had successfully transmitted the Morse code signal for "S" from Cornwall, England, to St. John's, Newfoundland, but his results had been publicly doubted. Prime Minister Laurier saw Marconi as an investment in the future and granted the inventor concessions to build transmission towers, as well as the exclusive right to send telegraph messages should his idea work. "Excitement around town is intense," the *Sydney Record* reported, "and all kinds of news is going the rounds concerning events the future will unfold." In December 1902,

The *Silver Dart* on Baddeck Bay. (*A. G. Bell National Historic Site*)

Marconi sent a wireless message across the Atlantic to international attention, revolutionizing communications.

Also in Cape Breton, Alexander Graham Bell worked at his magnificent summer estate on the Bras D'Or Lake, sketching kites and helicopters and experimenting with flight. The Wright Brothers' 1903 manned flight at Kitty Hawk, North Carolina, had been the first, but Bell's *Silver Dart* airplane, which was much more sophisticated and manoeuvrable, was ready for testing on February 23, 1909, on the frozen Baddeck Bay in Bras D'Or Lake. "Before some people realized what was taking place, the buzz of the engine could be heard and the machine was seen advancing rapidly," wrote Charles Fox, a reporter who witnessed the attempt. "She had done about 90 feet along the ice when she rose gracefully into the air to an elevation of about 20 to 30 feet at about 40 miles an hour before she glided down. . . . Everyone seemed dumbfounded." The *Silver Dart* flew just less than a kilometre, higher and longer than the Wright Brothers' plane, making it the first manned flight in the British empire.

Tius Tutty was still working up to seventy hours a week in the coal mines, earning little and risking his life. "I had a lot of accidents," he remembered. "There's no question about it. If there's something to get I got it. I remember I wasn't feeling too good, my eyes bothered me – lost the sight in my eye ever since. . . . I had that skull fracture . . . a big piece of the roof came down, that's all I remember." But he stayed there, mostly because, with little education, he had no other option. "I got to make a living and there's no other place to go. I said, I'm not a coward. If I die down there well I'll die down there."

The year that Bell was testing the *Silver Dart* and ushering in Canadian aviation, the Cape Breton miners embarked on a violent, protracted strike. The newly organized United Mine Workers of America had

**ALEXANDER GRAHAM BELL** ◆ Alexander Graham Bell invented the telephone in 1876 and later turned his energies to flight. In 1905, he constructed a tetrahedral kite which he towed behind a steamboat, lifting a man fifty-one metres into the air. His experiments culminated in the *Silver Dart*, an airplane that used the ice of Baddeck Bay in Cape Breton as a runway to take off and fly eight hundred metres in 1909. It later flew thirty-two kilometres. Bell died in 1922 at the age of seventy-five and was buried in Cape Breton, at the top of Beautiful Mountain. (*A. G. Bell National Historic Site*)

challenged the dominance of the large companies in the United States, and now the Canadian miners joined the fight. Five hundred Royal Artillery troops stationed in Halifax were shipped across the Strait of Canso to deal with the potential unrest. Tius Tutty joined the union, and for ten months he lived nervously under the sights of machine guns, without pay or relief. Children died of cholera and starvation. The men finally went back to work.

"Maybe I should have kept fishing," Tius Tutty said. "I don't know how I'm living. I really don't." Tutty lived his entire life in Glace Bay and died there at the age of ninety-five.

Through the first decade of the century, the careers of Wilfrid Laurier and Henri Bourassa were intertwined, though the two were not friends. Bourassa blamed Laurier for the erosion of the French language through unrestricted immigration, and he was worried that the west was ceasing to be a bicultural society – French and English – and was instead becoming multiethnic, with francophones a small minority. While he personally liked the prime minister, he felt that his compromises too often arose from weakness rather than a grand, unifying vision. "Upon his arrival at the gates of Paradise," he wrote, "Mr. Laurier's first action will be to propose an 'honourable compromise' between God and Satan."

Laurier complained that Bourassa "fights his friends with the same violence as his enemies; he becomes intoxicated with his own words. . . . Bourassa is a man of great ability, but his ability is negative and destructive. . . . He was at one time a close friend of mine, but we separated. His aim was to isolate the French population from the rest of the community and make them a separate body."

By 1910, Laurier was in his fourth term, sixty-nine years old, and still elegant and dapper. But he was losing his taste for political battle. "As I advance in years," he wrote to the rector of Laval University, Olivier-Elzéar Mathieu, "difficulties appear to resurface constantly under my feet. Until now I have been fortunate enough to overcome them all. . . . It is quite likely that one day or another, a failure could happen to me."

The most pressing possibility of failure lay in the thorny issue of imperial relations. Germany had been building a massive navy; Britain was alarmed and asked for help from her colonies. The *Toronto Globe* and many English Canadians urged Laurier to aid Britain with money and ships. But Henri Bourassa attacked Laurier in the inaugural edition of the Montreal newspaper *Le Devoir*, on January 10, 1910, stating his position that Canada should not commit any ships to Britain. Laurier, as always, sought a middle way, and on January 12 he introduced the Naval Services Bill in Parliament. "I do not pretend to be an imperialist," he stated. "Neither do I pretend to be an anti-imperialist. I am Canadian first, last, and all the time." Ships would be built, he said, but for a Canadian navy that could serve at Britain's side if needed.

Laurier's compromise found little support. The proposed navy amounted to a few cruisers and destroyers, already outdated at a time when the Germans were creating massive armoured vessels. Rodmond Roblin accused Laurier of commissioning a "tin pot navy" of little use to anyone, while Bourassa worried that the Naval Services Bill would lead to Canada's entanglement in imperial wars. In *Le Devoir* he wrote, "It is the gravest blow our autonomy has suffered since the origin of responsible government."

In the spring, Laurier left the political bickering of Ottawa for a two-month tour of the west, a public relations exercise that buoyed both him and his western constituents. "The immensity of this country is the subject of perpetual amazement, however one is prepared for it," he wrote to a friend,

Rodolphe Lemieux. In Winnipeg, ten thousand greeted him at the railway station. In Prince Albert, Laurier stopped to chat with a fifteen-year-old newspaper boy named John Diefenbaker, who concluded the conversation by saying, according to legend, "Well, Mr. Prime Minister, I can't waste any more time. I have to deliver my papers." Farmers everywhere engaged Laurier on the issue of reciprocity, lobbying for free trade with the United States, which would mean lower costs for farm machinery manufactured in eastern Canada and protected by a tariff barrier.

In Medicine Hat (a town Rudyard Kipling had predicted great things for, calling it the "New Ninevah"), Laurier gave a version of his standard speech. "I have imbibed the air, spirit and enthusiasm of the west," he said. "I am a true western citizen; no, I should say a true Canadian." After Medicine Hat, the train took him to Montreal for the twenty-first Eucharistic Congress of the Roman Catholic Church, held at Nôtre Dame church. Laurier had lost his religious faith in his twenties, and he had written to Emilie Lavergne, "You have the faith; you can pray. I do wish that I also,I could believe & pray." But he had remained, nominally and politically, Catholic.

As a lapsed Roman Catholic living in Quebec and operating in a political arena dominated by English-speaking Protestants, even his religious position afforded Laurier a balance. "Whenever it shall become my duty to take a stand upon a question whatever," he had said in a speech in the House of Commons, "that stand I will take not upon grounds of Roman Catholicism, not upon grounds of Protestantism, but upon grounds which can appeal to the conscience of all men."

Henri Bourassa was also attending the congress, an inflexible, pious man who did not separate his faith from his politics. He was surprised, then, to find language the main issue on this occasion when Archbishop Francis Bourne of Westminster stood up at the Congress and delivered an unanticipated speech advocating English as the primary language of the Catholic Church in North America. "God has allowed the English tongue to be spread over the civilized world," Bourne told the largely French-speaking audience. "Until the English language, English habits of thought, English literature, in a word, the entire English mentality, is brought into the service of the Catholic Church, the saving work of the Church is impeded and hampered."

Some anglophones in the church applauded, but most of congregation greeted this view with a stunned silence. Bourassa was scheduled to speak, but he abandoned his prepared text to deliver what became a historic speech challenging Bourne's views. "Among three million Catholics," Bourassa said, "descendants of the first apostles of Christianity in America, the best safeguard of the Faith is the conservation of the language in which, during three hundred years, they have adored Christ." He pointed out that 75 per cent of the continent's clergy had come out of Quebec. "Let one beware," he warned, "let one be carefully aware, of extinguishing this fire,

**THE GROUP OF SEVEN** ◆ In 1910, Frederick Varley, Tom Thompson, and Arthur Lismer were among the Canadian painters who were giving Canadian landscapes a new life. Their work was a vibrant, almost violent response to the previous century's pastoralism: "There is a small party of us here, the young school, just 5 or 6 of us and we are all working to one big end. We are endeavouring to knock out of us all the pre-conceived ideas, emptying ourselves of everything except that nature is here in all its greatness." Frederick Varley, writing to his sister Ethel, in 1914. Left to right: Frederick Varley, A. Y. Jackson, Lawren Harris, Barker Fairley, Franz Johnston, Arthur Lismer, and J. E. H. MacDonald (*Art Gallery of Ontario*, N-10594). Top: *Forest* by Tom Thompson (*Art Gallery of Ontario*)

with its intense light which has illuminated a whole continent for three centuries." Two bishops left the stage as he spoke, uncomfortable with the political freight in his speech. "We are only a handful," Bourassa continued, "it is true, but in the school of Christ I did not learn to estimate right and moral choices by number and wealth." The congress erupted in applause, and Bourassa received a standing ovation. Concern that he had offended Rome with his political response was dispelled when the cardinal legate, Vincenze Vanutelli, the pope's emissary, rose to embrace Bourassa, leaving Archbishop Bourne mute and isolated.

Back in Ottawa, the debate over the naval issue had not gone away. Laurier's bill was defeated on November 3, which left him depressed. "Governments can't last forever because they are made to grow old and then to die," he wrote to a friend. He tried to revive his political fortunes with the issue of trade reciprocity, but it ran into opposition. Western farmers and consumers wanted it, but eastern manufacturers were opposed. Reciprocity, argued Conservative leader Robert Borden, would turn Canada into a commercial annex of the United States. "Should we, at the time of our greatest successes and realizations," he asked, "lose hope and abandon the battle for our national existence?" Unsurprisingly, the Americans who favoured free trade were not attuned to the political and national nuances of their neighbour. "I hope to see the day when the American flag will float over every square foot of the British North American possessions clear to the North Pole," said Champ Clark, speaker of the U.S. House of Representatives and an advocate of free trade.

Among the opponents of reciprocity were Rudyard Kipling and Stephen Leacock. Kipling, who disliked Laurier for little reason other than his natural elegance (a friend of Kipling's had called him "that damned dancing-master"), was quoted in the *Montreal Star* saying that to embrace the United States was to dance with the devil. "It is her own soul that Canada risks today," he said. Leacock wrote dozens of articles criticizing what he felt was Laurier's reckless policy. "The ravenous maw of American industry opens wide, the restless eye of the trust looks abroad for new fields. . . . And meantime smile, if you can, with the simper of the fool's content at the sale of your little peck of potatoes in the Boston market. Clutch tight the Yankee nickel of your profit. You may well treasure it. You have sold it for your birthright and your future."

It was Clifford Sifton, once Laurier's closest ally, who did the most damage to his cause, tying reciprocity into the issue of imperial relations. "Now we come to a point where we may be of use to the Empire, when we can send men and ships if necessary," he said, "when we can be of some use to the Empire that gave us our liberty and our tradition of citizenship – at the first beckoning hand from Washington we turn to listen."

Laurier could not count on support in Quebec to offset English Canada's concerns about reciprocity. "Formerly I also cried hurrah for Laurier," Henri Bourassa said. "But Laurier has sacrificed his own in the West. . . .

**EMILY CARR** ◆ After studying in England and France, Emily Carr returned to Victoria, British Columbia, in 1913 to build a house and settle there: "The world is moving swiftly and the tempo of life has changed. What was new a few years back is now old. There have been terrific expansions in the direction of light and movement; within the last few years these have altered everything. Painting has felt the influence. Isn't it reasonable to expect that art would have to keep pace with the rest? The romantic little stories and the mawkish little songs don't satisfy us any longer. Why should the empty little pictures? The academic painting of the mid-nineteenth century in England had entirely lost touch with art in running after sentiment." From a speech to the Victoria Women's Canadian Club. (*BC Archives*, F-01220. *Top: Skidegate, Graham Island, The Bridgeman Art Library/ Art Gallery of Ontario*)

**CARD PARTY AT RAVENSCRAG** ◆ Ravenscrag, the Montreal home of shipping magnate and railway pirate Hugh Allan, was the largest in the Square Mile, situated high enough on Mount Royal to allow Allan to see his ships in the harbour. He commissioned architect John Hopkins to design an Italian Renaissance structure that originally had thirty-four rooms (more were added). Allan's son Montagu donated the home to the Royal Victoria Hospital in 1942 and it became the Allan Memorial Institute, a psychiatric facility. (*Notman Photographic Archives, Musée McCord Museum, MMM VIEW-14013*)

Laurier imposes on us a costly navy, which will serve no purpose except to kill our own sons in the wars of England. Laurier forces me today to choose between him and the country. I choose the country."

Laurier's policy of compromise had left him with little defensible ground. "I am accused in Quebec of having betrayed the French, and in Ontario of having betrayed the English. . . . In Quebec I am attacked as an Imperialist, and in Ontario as an anti-Imperialist. I am neither . . . I am a Canadian. Canada has been the inspiration of my life." In the fall of 1911, his Liberals were voted out, and Robert Borden, a Halifax lawyer, became the country's eighth prime minister. Laurier conceded defeat at St. Peter's Market in Quebec City and the next day returned to his Ottawa home, less than a kilometre away from the majestic, unfinished hotel that would be named for him, the Château Laurier.

**ROBERT BORDEN AND WINSTON CHURCHILL, 1913** ◆ Robert Laird
Borden suffered three defeats as leader of the Conservative Party before
becoming prime minister in 1911. He was the opposite of Laurier: plodding,
patient, ineloquent. "Our recognition of this war as ours," he said in 1914,
"determines absolutely once and for all that we have passed from the status
of the protected colony to that of the participating nation." (*National
Archives of Canada, C-2082*)

The country's fortunes mirrored Laurier's. After eighteen years of extraordinary growth, the boom that had populated the west and transformed the
cities came to a dramatic end. By 1914, Canada was mired in the depression
that had enveloped much of the world. A familiar cycle began, with factories
closing, fewer consumers, and depressed markets. The prairies were hit by a
severe drought that exacerbated the problem. Laurier's open-door immigration policy ended. After record numbers had been allowed into the country,

**THE KISS** ◆ In 1891, Thomas Alva Edison introduced the Kinetoscope, a film projector that had a coin slot attached to it. Patrons could look through the lens and watch short, jerky versions of vaudeville acts. Edison had based his invention on the "*chronophotographe*" of Frenchman Etienne-Jules Marey. The French, in fact, largely pioneered the film era; it was Louis Lumière who invented the film process and Charles Pathé who industrialized it. Lumière made the public projection of films possible so that it became a collective experience, rather than the individual viewing afforded by the Kinetoscope. The French also elevated the form past a carnival gimmick, filming plays and historical dramas. In 1908, foreign films accounted for 70 per cent of the American market. Thomas Edison tried both thugs and lawsuits to gain control of the market but settled finally on a cartel that worked to keep foreign films out.

The first public film screening in Canada was on July 21, 1896, at Ottawa's West End Park, where hundreds of people paid ten cents to see a series of short (less than a minute) films, including *The Kiss*. The first Canadian films were made by James Freer, a Manitoba farmer who filmed life on the prairies in 1897. The following year his work was screened in England as immigration propaganda, in an attempt to lure settlers to the prairies.

Louis Lumière lived to see film become entrenched as a commercial medium. "Had I been able to foresee what the cinema would become," he lamented, "I never would have invented it." (*Hulton Getty/Archive Photo, JH9579*)

376 Sikhs aboard the *Komagata Maru* were turned away from Vancouver Harbour. The Canadian navy escorted the ship back out to sea, shutting the door on the Laurier era.

In Europe, a dark mood prevailed as the dominant powers faced off against one another. On one side was the Triple Alliance (Germany, Austria-Hungary, and Italy), and on the other was the Triple Entente (France, Russia, and Great Britain). The two sides were separated by accelerating nationalism, rival imperialistic visions, and an aggressive military buildup on both sides that was reaching a critical point. This uneasy staring contest needed only a spark to ignite it.

On June 28, 1914, the spark was provided when Archduke Franz Ferdinand, heir to the Austrian throne, was assassinated by a Serbian nationalist during a trip to Sarajevo. The result was war, falling into place with a domino effect: Austria declared war on Serbia; Russia, as self-declared protector of the Slav nations, mobilized; Germany demanded a promise of non-intervention from Russia and France, which was not forthcoming. Germany then declared war on Russia on August 1, and on France two days later. On its way to France, the German army invaded neutral Belgium, which drew Britain into the fray. The British demanded that the Germans withdraw, a demand they ignored, and on August 4, Great Britain was at war.

As a colony, Canada was automatically at war when Britain was. And initially, the country was politically united concerning the war effort, supportive of sending troops to aid Britain. Laurier, as the Liberal leader sitting in opposition, applauded Robert Borden's actions in the House. "It is our duty," Laurier said, "to let Great Britain know and to let the friends and foes of Great Britain know that there is in Canada but one mind and one heart and that all Canadians are behind the mother country, conscious and proud that she has engaged in this war, to save civilization from the unbridled lust of conquest and power." Henri Bourassa agreed, in a rare moment of accord. He was in France when war was declared and he wrote in *Le Devoir*, "[It is] Canada's national duty to contribute according to her resources. . . . I have not written and will not write one line, one word, to condemn the sending of Canadian troops to Europe."

Nellie McClung was at her cottage north of Winnipeg when she heard the news that the country would go to war. Her eldest son, Jack, was one year shy of the minimum age to join up and anxious, like many, to get into the war before it was over. "Instinctively we felt that we had come to the end of a very pleasant chapter in our life as a family; something had disturbed the peaceful quiet of our lives; somewhere a drum was beating and a fife was calling," she wrote.

John McCrae was forty-one, but he joined up and went to Valcartier, Quebec, where an army camp had been carved out of the bush to house 33,000 recruits. After the Boer War, he had few illusions about the upcoming battle. "It will be a terrible war," he wrote to a friend, "and somebody's finish when all is said and done." Because of his age and training, McCrae could have volunteered in the medical corps, but he chose to be a gunner in the artillery and to serve as the unit's medical officer.

On October 3, 1914, the first troops of Canada's Expeditionary Force boarded thirty ships and sailed for England. Optimistic, poorly equipped, and hastily trained, they were joined by the *Florizel*, with its five hundred members of the Newfoundland Regiment. The convoy stretched thirty-four kilometres over the Atlantic. Three more months of training in England awaited them, practising manoeuvres in the rain, sliding in the mud of Salisbury Plain, impatient to get to the front. John McCrae then joined the eighteen thousand soldiers of the First Canadian Division who took up positions near Ypres, the last Belgian city not occupied by the German army. To their left were Algerians and Moroccans of the French army. To the right were British troops.

The war had started nine months earlier and was being conducted along the broad guidelines of condoned violence that had defined European warfare for more than a century. But modern warfare and its attendant horrors arrived on Thursday, April 22, 1915, and the Canadians were its first witnesses. In the late afternoon, a heavy, green-yellow cloud moved over the French lines, hugging the ground and falling into the trenches, the first wave of chlorine gas settling on the Algerian soldiers.

Chemical warfare changed the nature of war; what had been combat was now extermination. Now that this new brutality had been introduced, both sides would use it, and the industrial sector would quickly gear up to produce the gas and ship cylinders filled with it to the front lines. Men would sit in the trenches, praying for favourable winds. But on April 22, it was still a gruesome novelty, unexpected and impossible to defend against.

The French troops who were not immediately overcome fled to the Canadian trenches. Lieutenant Colonel Ian Sinclair described the scene: "Our trenches were shortly filled with them crowding in from our left. They were mostly blind and choking to death, and as fast as they died were just heaved behind the trench."

The Germans waited for the gas to dissipate, then moved into the abandoned French trenches, and the Canadians were given the order to stop their advance at any cost. Facing superior numbers and firepower, the Canadian soldiers fixed bayonets and charged into the German machine-gun fire. "Oh mother!" wrote John Carroll, a gunner from Paris, Ontario. "It seemed like a miracle to me our little company was not swept out of existence amidst that hail of shrapnel, shells and bullets pouring at us like rain. We drove the Germans back, a few hundreds of us Canadians against thousands of Germans. But I don't think they knew there was such a small number of us. It was getting dark and probably they did not like the look of our flashing bayonets."

At 3:30 a.m. on Saturday, April 24, a six-metre wall of green gas moved toward the Canadian trenches. The men were ordered to soak their handkerchiefs with urine and tie them around their mouths and noses as a crude

## JOHN McCRAE

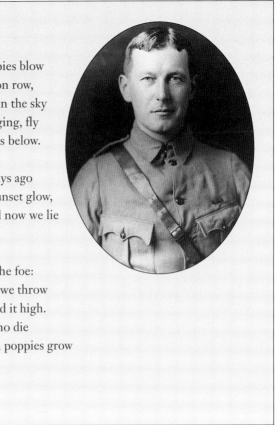

In Flanders fields the poppies blow
Between the crosses, row on row,
That mark our place; and in the sky
The larks, still bravely singing, fly
Scarce heard amid the guns below.

We are the Dead. Short days ago
We lived, felt dawn, saw sunset glow,
Loved and were loved, and now we lie
In Flanders fields.

Take up our quarrel with the foe:
To you from failing hands we throw
The torch; be yours to hold it high.
If ye break faith with us who die
We shall not sleep, though poppies grow
In Flanders fields.

*(Guelph Museum)*

defence. But the gas moved through their ranks, filling their lungs, clouding their eyes, and leaving dreadful sacs of blood hanging on their skin.

"On the front field one can see the dead lying here and there," observed McCrae, "and in places where an assault has been they lie very thick on the front slopes of the German trenches."

Chemical warfare did not discriminate between soldiers and civilians. "On the road we began to see the French stragglers: men without arms, wounded men, teams, wagons, civilians, refugees," McCrae wrote, "all talking, shouting – the very picture of debacle. . . . Of one's feelings all this night – of the asphyxiated French soldiers – of the women and children . . . I could write, but you can imagine."

On Sunday, May 2, the artillery fire resumed, and McCrae's close friend Alexis Helmer was killed. "Heavy fire again this morning," McCrae wrote. "Lieut. H[elmer] was killed at the guns. His diary's last words were, 'It has quieted a little and I shall try to get a good sleep.' His girl's picture had a hole right through it and we buried it with him. I said the Committal Service over him, as well as I could from memory."

The next day, while sitting on the back of an ambulance, McCrae composed a poem, "In Flanders Fields," describing the scene.

The two-week battle at Ypres resulted in six thousand Canadian casualties, amounting to a third of the division. A thousand men lay dead on the battlefield. "The general impression in my mind is of a nightmare," McCrae wrote to his mother. "We have been in the most bitter of fights. For seventeen days and seventeen nights none of us have had our clothes off, nor our boots even. . . . In all that time while I was awake, gunfire and rifle fire never ceased for sixty seconds. . . . And behind it all was the constant background of the sights of the dead, the wounded, the maimed, and a terrible anxiety lest the line should give way."

McCrae received orders to report to a new hospital unit, No. 3 Canadian General Hospital, raised by McGill University. In June, the hospital was set up on the northern coast of France, it was later moved to a Jesuit college in the town of Boulogne. McCrae worked on his poem "In Flanders Fields" during these months and finally sent a finished copy to *The Spectator* in London, where it was rejected. But a journalist who visited the hospital in Boulogne took a copy back to *Punch* magazine, which printed it. Within months it became the most popular poem of the war.

By 1917, McCrae was suffering from severe asthma attacks and bronchitis. In January 1918 his condition was diagnosed as pneumonia. He was appointed consulting physician to the First British Army, the first Canadian named to the post. He died five days later, on January 28, of pneumonia and meningitis.

# ORDEAL BY FIRE

With the Battle of Ypres, the Canadian public had its first glimpse of the horrors being unleashed on European battlefields. But a different war was being waged at home. Several hundred thousand Canadians, recent immigrants from Germany and the Austro-Hungarian empire, were suspected of disloyalty. These people, most of them farmers or workers enticed to come to Canada by federal government incentives, were now feared and mistrusted, suspected of harbouring an allegiance to their homelands. Once welcomed with open arms, they were now forced to register, to carry around special identity papers, and to report regularly to the authorities. Some were sent to internment camps.

The hostility increased after German U-boats, on May 7, 1915, torpedoed the *Lusitania*, a large passenger liner en route from New York to England. The ship sank off the coast of Ireland and 1,200 people were lost, including 100 Canadians, most of whom were women and children on their way to meet husbands or fathers serving overseas. Among the dead were two young daughters of Sir Montagu Allan, a banker and shipowner and one of the richest businessmen in Montreal. In response, Canadians angrily attacked German shops in Victoria, Montreal, and Vancouver.

In 1916, the Anti-German League was created in Toronto. Foreign newspapers were censored, and in 1918 it was forbidden to publish newspapers in

The internment of enemy aliens was a potent symbol of the domestic tensions that war created. Internment camps could be turbulent places: Philip Yasnowskyj, originally from Galicia (Ukraine), was interned near Kapuskasing, Ontario, when a riot broke out in 1916 over the inmates' refusal to work. Yasnowskyj saw the incident as a turning point. "We all resolved to ignore every order to go to work. Needless to say, I never again showed up for my job of gathering litter. . . . Our food rations were reduced by half, but we did not worry about that. Persuasion did not move us, and threats did not scare us." (*Glenbow Archives, NA-1870-6*)

the language of the enemy. In 1916, the city of Berlin, Ontario, whose population was largely of German origin, decided to rename itself Kitchener (after the British war secretary Lord Kitchener). The king of England abandoned the Germanic name of Hanover and announced that the family would henceforth adopt the surname Windsor. In the midst of the anti-German hysteria, Beethoven's music was even briefly outlawed.

"Enemy aliens" who failed to report once a month, or to register, or was suspected of collusion with the enemy were interned. Between 1914 and 1920, 80,000 "enemy aliens," the majority of them Ukrainians, but also Germans, Bulgarians, Turks, Croats, and Serbs, had to register. A further 8,579 were also interned in twenty-four work camps scattered across Canada. The Canadian government confiscated the internees' money, their farms, and their houses.

"When Ottawa imprisoned my family, I was six years old," remembered a former detainee, Mary Manko, who had been born in Canada to Ukrainian parents. "I did not do anything wrong. My parents came to Canada in search of liberty. They were invited here. They worked hard, helped build the country with their blood, toil and tears. A lot of tears. At the age of two and a half, my sister Nellie caught pneumonia and we had to bury her there, at Spirit Lake." Mary Manko was interned in Quebec, in the Spirit Lake camp near Amos, in the Abitibi region, surrounded by four hundred kilometres of forest. For two years, 1,200 prisoners, including 60 women and children, were held there at gunpoint.

The Hague Convention prohibited treating the internees as criminals or convicts. "At first," said Nicola Sakaliuk, another Ukrainian interned at Spirit Lake, "they told us that we could work or not work, as we saw fit. But these conditions only lasted one month or two. Then, if you refused to work, they put you on dry bread and water. And if that didn't work, they stopped feeding you. I was convinced that they didn't have the right to act like that."

Some chores were compulsory: making meals, doing housework, chopping and carrying firewood. Prisoners who did additional work – cutting wood, clearing land, building houses and roads, and doing maintenance work on railway lines – received 25 cents per day. Municipalities were happy to send the unemployed aliens they were responsible for feeding and housing to federal internment camps. In 1914 and 1915, some cities took advantage of the widespread fear to imprison men who had been laid off owing to railway bankruptcies. In 1916, though, nearly all those interned were released to relieve the labour shortage caused by the presence of so many men at the front.

After heavy losses at Verdun, the French implored their allies to launch an offensive against the Germans. In January 1916, Joseph Joffre, commander-in-chief of the French forces, and Sir Douglas Haig, commander of British troops in France, decided to launch the first large, combined Franco-British offensive. Although it held no strategic importance, they chose the

**FRANK MAHEUX AND HIS FAMILY** ◆ When Frank Maheux enlisted, he was married, a father, and at thirty-four much older than the average recruit. He left his wife, Angéline, to raise their children alone in the remote logging community of Baskatong Bridge, Quebec. Like other soldiers, Maheux was plagued by homesickness, and his thoughts were often with his family. To his wife, he wistfully confided: "I'll say to myself Angéline is sleeping now. I don't know what I'll give to be beside you, instead I'll have my rifle beside me." (*Courtesy of Mary Ethel Ladas*)

Somme valley as their target, as it was close to the meeting ground of the French and English sectors on the western front.

On the morning of July 1, 1916, 100,000 British troops advanced in broad daylight into No Man's Land as if they were marching on an exercise. Staggering under the weight of thirty kilograms of gear, they walked across a crater-filled field in long orderly lines that were easy targets for German machine-gunners. More than 20,000 British soldiers lost their lives that day, the worst loss in British military history. The 1st Newfoundland Regiment was nearly annihilated at Beaumont Hamel during the first half hour of the attack: of 800 soldiers who joined in the attack, 310 were killed and only 68 emerged unscathed. It took days for the survivors to recover the dead and bury them.

Two months later, on August 30, the Canadian Expeditionary Force joined the Battle of the Somme, supporting the first tank attack on the western front. The lumbering tanks were almost useless in the muddy landscape. Sergeant Frank Maheux, a Quebec logger who had enlisted in the 21st Ontario Battalion, wrote to his wife, Angéline, that the tanks were like unwieldy elephants pulled to pieces by artillery and bogged down in shell holes.

On September 15, 1916, the Quebecers of the 22nd Regiment received orders to capture Courcelette, a village in the Somme valley that was occupied by the Germans. It was the regiment's first major operation, an improvised and nearly suicidal attack, as Lieutenant-Colonel Louis-Thomas Tremblay well understood. "We know very well," he wrote in his diary, "that we are heading to the slaughterhouse. The task seems nearly impossible, considering how ill-prepared we are, and how little we know the layout of the front. Even so, morale is wonderfully high and we are determined to show that we Canadians are not quitters. . . . It is our first big attack. It will have to be a success for the sake of the honour of all the French Canadians that we represent in France." At the cost of many human lives, Courcelette made famous the name of the 22nd Regiment – widely known in English Canada as the "Van Doos" – and several officers and soldiers were decorated for their courage.

Sergeant Frank Maheux took part in the assault with the 21st Ontario Battalion and described the outcome to his wife, Angéline: "All my friends have been either killed or wounded. There are only a few of us left, but we have succeeded in reaching our objective. My dear wife, it is worse than hell here. For miles around, corpses completely cover up the ground. But your Frank didn't get so much as a scratch. I went to battle as if I had to cut wood with my bayonet. When one of my friends was killed at my side, I saw red: some Germans raised their arms in surrender, but it was too late for them. I will remember that all my life."

Canon Frederick Scott, an Anglican priest from Quebec City, was the head chaplain of the 1st Canadian Division. Three of his sons signed up along with him: William, Harry, and Elton. On October 13, 1916, Canon Scott wrote to his wife: "Darling Harry is up in the front trenches. . . . I can see his tent on the hillside as I write. May God save him. He is a splendid fellow and the idol of his battalion." A week later Harry was killed. He was twenty-six years old and had married just four months before leaving for Europe. "He died with nobility," Canon Scott wrote to the family, "just as he led his company into battle. He didn't suffer. I hope to recover his body later. May God give you strength and courage." The chaplain wandered into No Man's Land in the hopes of finding his son's grave: "There on a sort of ridge stood a lonely white cross. . . . So I got my man to dig. . . . After he had taken off a few shovelfuls of earth something white was laid bare, and there

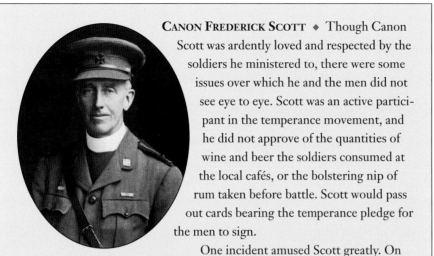

**CANON FREDERICK SCOTT** ♦ Though Canon Scott was ardently loved and respected by the soldiers he ministered to, there were some issues over which he and the men did not see eye to eye. Scott was an active participant in the temperance movement, and he did not approve of the quantities of wine and beer the soldiers consumed at the local cafés, or the bolstering nip of rum taken before battle. Scott would pass out cards bearing the temperance pledge for the men to sign.

One incident amused Scott greatly. On his way to his quarters one night he tripped over a guy rope, and a soldier looked out of his own tent, in concern. As Scott made his way off in the darkness, he heard the young man say to his tent mates, "It's only old Scott drunk as usual." (*Courtesy of Helen Morrison*)

was darling Harry's left hand with the signet ring on his little finger. It was like a miracle – to think that I had found him on that waste on which I could see many bodies still unburied – to think that I was able to touch his dear old hand once more and to know that he was there."

As the Battle of the Somme dragged on, the ground became a grim hell. "We were walking on dead soldiers," Frank Maheux wrote to his wife. "I saw poor fellows trying to bandage their wounds [while] bombs heavy shells were falling all over them. Poor Angéline, it is the worse sight that a man ever wants to see."

Some of the recruits could not deal with the slaughter. Sergeant William Alexander of the 10th (Alberta) Battalion deserted and was found two days later in a nearby village. He was court-martialled and sentenced to death. Canon Scott tried to have the sentence commuted, without success. "He turned to me and said: 'Sir, is there any hope?'" Canon Scott wrote. "I said: 'No, I am afraid there is not.' . . . He took the matter very quietly. . . . I urged him to go out and meet death bravely."

Alexander was shot by his fellow soldiers at 6:10 a.m. the next day, and Canon Scott presided at the funeral: "I have seen many ghastly sights in the war, and hideous forms of death, I have heard heart-rending tales of what men have suffered, but nothing ever brought home to me so deeply, and with such cutting force, the hideous nature of war and the iron hand of discipline, as did that lonely death on the misty hillside in the early morning."

After five months, the Battle of the Somme finally ended, when rain, snow, and sleet made further fighting impossible. It was difficult to tell victor from vanquished. The Allies had pushed 13 kilometres forward along a 35-kilometre front, and lost 623,907 men, while the Germans, who would call this battle "*das Blutbad*" (the Bloodbath), lost 660,000 infantrymen. The Canadian divisions, which numbered 100,000 men, counted 24,000 dead and wounded. "If hell was as atrocious as what I saw at Courcelette," wrote Lieutenant-Colonel Tremblay, "then I could not wish it on my worst enemy to go there." General Ferdinand Foch had undertaken the offensive and Joffre had ordered it: both lost their commands, only to have them returned after the personal intervention of Georges Clémenceau, president of the French Commission on Defence and External Affairs.

At the beginning of 1917, Canadian electoral law still stipulated that idiots, madmen, criminals, and judges were not allowed to vote. It did not specifically exclude women, but as only male property owners were enfranchised, they were *de facto* excluded. But tens of thousands of women had taken the places of men in factories, banks, and offices. How, they asked, could they be denied the vote when they were the ones making the economy work and manufacturing the weapons and munitions? Women were determined to use their increased political clout to bring ten years of struggle for the vote to fruition.

Nellie McClung and others had unsuccessfully lobbied Manitoba premier Rodmond Roblin to grant women the right to vote. Roblin resigned in 1915 after a bribery scandal, and during the election campaign that followed, the Liberal candidate, T. C. Norris, promised that he would extend the franchise to women. But once elected, he stalled for time. On December 23, 1915, a delegation handed him a stack of petitions, one of which was presented by a ninety-four-year-old suffragist, Mrs. Amelia Burritt, of Sturgeon Creek, who had gathered 4,250 signatures. On January 27, 1916, the Manitoba provincial legislature finally put the issue to a vote. The gallery was packed, and when the bill passed unanimously, making Manitoba's women the first with the right to vote and hold public office, there was thunderous applause and riotous celebration.

Prime Minister Robert Borden was not keen on the idea of women voting, but on May 16, 1917, he declared in the House of Commons that women deserved the vote and should participate in the government of the country. This change of heart was not a shift in personal beliefs: Borden wanted to use women voters to support his conscription bill. Borden's proposed Wartime Elections Act would remove the right to vote from conscientious objectors, certain religious groups, and Canadians born in enemy countries and naturalized within the previous fifteen years, unless a close male relative was already on active duty. Women could vote, but only if they were related to soldiers.

The bill was met with indignation. Many saw its discriminatory half-measures as an overt attempt to serve the imperial cause rather than the cause of women. But in spite of a general outcry, the measure became law in September 1917, and in December of that same year some 500,000 Canadian women voted in a federal election for the first time.

**MILITARY NURSES AT THE POLLS, 1917** ◆ When Canadian nurses cast their ballots at the front, they became the first women to vote in a federal election. Military nurses, "sisters" as they were called, were officers, and as such they were given the right to vote by the Military Voters Act of August 1917. Overseas postings were eagerly sought – many more nurses applied than could be accommodated – and the requirements were strict: nurses had to be unmarried, healthy, between the ages of twenty-one and thirty-eight, and graduates of a recognized nursing college. In return, they earned a good wage of two dollars a day and found adventure, camaraderie, and a chance to apply their skills where they were most needed. They also worked long hours and cared for the injured and dying in conditions unlike anything they had ever seen in Canada. Red Cross nurse Ella Bongard, from Picton, Ontario, expressed the pressures in verse:

Sister has gone for a rest in bed,
Fainted on duty – so they said,
After a long day of stress and strife,
Came news of a Red Cross train in sight,
Bringing the wounded from Cambrai,
Two or three hundred on the way.

(*National Archives of Canada*, PA-2279)

On May 24, 1918, Parliament extended the right to vote to Canadian women twenty-one years old and over, not including native, Japanese, and Chinese women. Borden declared that the women would exert a good influence on public life, to which the humorist Stephen Leacock responded sarcastically: "Now that women have the right to vote, what are they going to do? Nothing at all, unless it is to elect men to the government."

By 1922, women had the right to vote in all provinces except Quebec. Many people there remained opposed to the women's vote, notable among them the Catholic clergy. "The entrance of women into politics, even by suffrage alone, would be unfortunate for our province," wrote Cardinal Pierre Bégin, archbishop of Quebec, on March 22, 1922. "Nothing justifies it, neither natural law, nor the interest of society." One of Quebec's best-known journalists, Olivar Asselin, once in favour of the women's vote, now claimed that the right to vote had been given to "thousands of bird brains." Henri Bourassa, publisher of *Le Devoir*, wrote that female suffrage was "the introduction of feminism in its most harmful form, the woman-voter who would soon generate . . . the woman-man, a hybrid and dreadful monster that would kill the woman-mother and the woman-wife." The women's vote would bring about a drop in the birth rate, he predicted; it would undermine the authority of fathers and destroy families. Nevertheless, on February 9, 1922, four hundred women marched on the Quebec legislature to claim this right. Among the demonstrators was Thérèse Casgrain, a tireless campaigner for women's suffrage. "After having listened to us politely," wrote Casgrain, "Premier Louis-Alexandre Taschereau told us in private: 'If the women of Quebec ever get the right to vote,

**HENRI BOURASSA AND HIS FAMILY, 1915** ◆ In the spring of 1915, conscription was not yet the dominant issue on the political agenda. However, the sting of Ontario's law banning French language instruction in its schools was still strongly felt in Quebec, and there was continued resistance to the efforts of recruiters. Henri Bourassa wrote to an acquaintance in London about the growing tension: "The relations between French and English are also getting more distant and bitter. In the largest English Province, Ontario, the government is pursuing an anti-French policy in matters of education, worse than the Prussian régime in Alsace-Lorraine. As you may well imagine this is not tending to convince the French-Canadian that the blessings of British rule are such that he ought to rush to the defence of Great Britain on the battlefields of Europe. It is in vain that we endeavour to make a distinction between British rule as it is practised in Great Britain and the narrow and intolerant spirit prevailing in English Canada. To him, British rule is what he tastes of it here at the hands of the English-speaking majority." (*Archives nationale du Québec à Montréal*, P97.D9024-22)

then I won't be the one to give it to them.'" Year after year, Quebec women would make this pilgrimage to Quebec City to claim the right to vote. They would not get it until 1940, nearly twenty-five years after women in western Canada.

Prohibition had always been closely tied to the issue of women's suffrage, and during the war that link was intensified. "There are a certain number of deeply religious, patriotic and estimable people," observed Stephen Leacock, "who actually believe that in passing a law to make it a crime to sell a glass of beer they are doing the work of Christ on earth." Nellie McClung equated alcohol with the German brand of warfare. "We despise the army of the Kaiser for dropping bombs on defenceless people, and shooting down women and children," she wrote. "We say it violates all laws of civilized warfare. The liquor traffic has waged war on women and children all down the centuries. Three thousand women were killed in the United States in one year by their own husbands who were under the influence of liquor. Noncombatants!"

Beer became a symbol of German infamy. In 1915, King George V went on the wagon for the duration of the war. That same year, Saskatchewan adopted Prohibition. In 1916, all other provinces outlawed alcohol, except for Quebec, which in 1918 adopted a weak prohibitionist law that was abolished as soon as the war ended. In 1917, the federal government forbade the manufacture, interprovincial transport, and import of beverages with more than 2.5 percent alcohol content, with the exception of beverages for medicinal use. After decades of struggle, the Prohibition movement had finally succeeded.

**PROHIBITION** ◆ In 1916, police enforcing the Canada Temperance Act emptied barrels of beer into the gutters of Moncton, New Brunswick. Such scenes were the cause of consternation for some and celebration for others. It was a glowing victory for the Women's Christian Temperance Union, which had been lobbying for prohibition for a generation, and whose popular slogans denounced alcohol in all its forms. "Liquor enslaves, prohibition sets free!" "The last to be hired, the first to be fired, is the man who drinks!" "The liquor traffic, not prohibition, destroys human liberty!" (*Enforcing the CTA, Moncton, N.B., circa 1916. United Church of Canada Archives, 93.004P/TN*)

It was a short-lived triumph, though. Federal laws banning alcohol were not enforced after the end of the war. The provincial governments – with Quebec taking the lead – opted for a more profitable solution: to sell alcohol themselves in government stores. By the end of the 1920s, only Prince Edward Island still had Prohibition.

Early in 1917, the Allied Command proposed that the Canadians take Vimy Ridge, an objective that had already cost the lives of thousands of French and British soldiers. The task fell to British Lieutenant-General Julian Byng, who was the commander of the Canadian Corps. The icy, snow-covered ridge seemed impregnable. From the top of this plateau surrounded by fields, 150 kilometres from Paris, the Germans commanded a perfect view of the region; it was impossible to take them by surprise. The slopes of the ridge were filled with trenches, shelters, and tunnels protected by barbed wire and machine guns. The enemy had electric lighting, telephones, and munitions wagons.

The Canadians made elaborate preparations for the assault throughout the winter of 1916–17, the coldest Europe had seen in forty years. "Towards the end of winter," wrote Lieutenant Claude Williams, the twenty-one-year-old son of a Methodist minister in Hamilton, "the infantrymen and

SIR ARTHUR CURRIE ◆ Nicknamed "Guts and Gaiters" because of his aloof nature, Arthur Currie was nonetheless respected by his troops. He visited them often in the trenches and took the time to speak to his soldiers individually. Following the losses that led up to the capture of Cambrai in October 1918, Currie asked the officers of the 42nd Battalion for advice: "I want to know exactly what you are thinking, whether you believe mistakes have been made by higher commanders or not. I want you to feel quite free to speak to me man to man and nothing you say will be held against you." This former school-teacher and real estate salesman stood in stark contrast to some of the less popular English generals, career officers who barked orders at their men with little thought to their well-being.

Currie was promoted to brigadier general in 1915, and in 1917 he was given command of the entire Canadian Corps, the first Canadian to be awarded that honour. Through his use of innovative tactics and battle-readiness in the ranks, Currie inspired an *esprit de corps* that many believe led to the Canadians' success at Vimy. Currie said simply, "I am a good enough Canadian to believe, if my experience justifies me in believing, that Canadians are best served by Canadians." (*National Archives of Canada*, PA-1370)

machine gunners began to train for the spring offensive on Vimy. Through the fields, long ribbons had been unwound that represented trenches, roads, villages and barbed wire located behind the German lines." Kilometres of telephone and electric cables were installed. The Allies even built a fake ridge, an exact copy of the one at Vimy, including an identical maze of caves and tunnels. Soldiers trained there until they knew the terrain as well as the Germans. "If old Kaiser Bill only saw the preparations that have been made," wrote Claude Williams, "he would throw up the sponge, I am sure."

On the morning of Easter Monday, April 9, 1917, the Canadian divisions prepared to attack. Canon Scott rose at 4:00 a.m. Of his two surviving sons in the military, one was on leave and the other had been wounded. He ate the breakfast he had prepared the night before, then took his position in order to be able to witness the coming artillery barrage: "It was a thrilling moment. Human lives were at stake. The honour of our country was at stake. The fate of civilization was at stake."

For the first time, the four Canadian divisions were all on the same battlefield: fishermen from British Columbia, prairie farmers, workers from Ontario and Quebec, and miners from Nova Scotia prepared to climb the snow-covered ridge. The attack began at 5:30 a.m. with the roar of more than three thousand pieces of artillery. "I knelt on the ground and prayed to

**CLAUDE WILLIAMS** ◆ Williams, a young lieutenant from Hamilton, Ontario, wrote to his family about life in the trenches in 1916:

Dear Mother and All,

Talk about mud here though, there is nothing but mud, mud, and more mud and nothing but mud to look forward to until next spring. You should see us coming out of the trenches, plastered from helmet to heel with it, inches thick, even our hands and face. The only way you could believe what it is like would be to take in Canada a person who has been in a snow storm for hours, you know how he would be covered with snow, well substitute the snow with mud and there you have a Tommy coming out of the trenches. One of Jim's runners the other day got stuck in it for half an hour up to his waist and couldn't get out, afterwards he was pulled out but had to leave his waders behind in the glue and was in his stocking feet. But after all mud is a small thing, we have plenty to eat and a pretty decent place to sleep, so what more does a soldier want.

Lovingly,
Claude

(*Courtesy of Helen Boody*)

the God of Battles to guard our noble men in that awful line of death and destruction," Canon Scott wrote, "and to give them victory."

The men were ordered to move in small groups and take out the heavy machine guns, instead of advancing in closed ranks. They moved along increasingly dangerous terrain. "At one place, we heard a Canadian who was lying deep in a shell hole calling out, 'Water, water!'" Lieutenant Williams wrote. "The top of his head had been blown off, exposing his brain. We could do nothing. Orders were that we were not to stop to attend the wounded. They must wait for the stretcher bearer." Faced with the relentless advance, the Germans abandoned their trenches, some fleeing and others surrendering.

Among the Canadian soldiers was Mike Mountain Horse, a Blood native from Alberta. His brother Albert had been gassed at Ypres and died at the age of twenty-two, and Mike and his brother Joe had enlisted to avenge his death. "The spirit of revenge for my brother's death manifested itself strongly in me as I gazed down on Albert lying in his coffin that cold winter day in November 1915," Mike wrote. He joined the 91st Battalion and was part of the assault on Vimy. "As I listened one night to an enemy bomber droning like a huge bumble bee over the allied lines," he wrote, "the thought came to my mind, where is the God that the white man has taught the Indian to believe in? Why does he allow this terrible destruction? And I prayed that He might yet bring the nations to their senses."

**THE 29TH (VANCOUVER) BATTALION ADVANCES ACROSS NO MAN'S LAND AT VIMY RIDGE** ◆ On April 10, the day after the Canadians launched their attack on Vimy, newspapers at home screamed of their grand success. "On Monday, we attacked," read *Le Devoir*. "Canadian troops, under heavy enemy fire, went over the top with great élan, and took the enemy trenches – the result of months of deadly planning. In successive waves, the brave Canadians circled the slopes of the hill, and locked the defenders of Vimy Ridge in an iron gauntlet. They pushed far beyond the first line of trenches, all the way to the little forest that runs north of the ridge. There, they regrouped to launch the final assault that would bring total victory." (*National Archives of Canada*, PA-1020)

Mountain Horse – an acting sergeant who was wounded twice in action and buried for four days in a German trench – was one of the few survivors of his regiment. He marked captured German artillery with designs of the Blackfoot Confederacy. When he was discharged in 1918, he painted his war experience onto a cowhide robe, depicting twelve separate incidents. "The attitude of my people during World War One," he wrote, "is sufficient proof of their right to be called British subjects. . . . When duty called, we were there. . . . Our people showed all the bravery of our warriors of old."

The Battle of Vimy Ridge lasted four days, leaving 3,598 Canadians dead and 7,004 wounded. Despite this painful toll, the victory – the first major one for the Canadian Expeditionary Force – gave rise to immense pride back home. Canadians had begun the war as colonials, as subordinates, but were now allies; they had succeeded where others had failed. General Currie noted in his journal, "A wonderful success. Every line was captured on time, every battalion doing equally well. The grandest day the Corps has ever had. . . . The attack was carried out exactly as planned. The sight was awful and wonderful." The *New York Tribune* wrote that Canada had fielded a better army than Napoleon's, and a French newspaper spoke of Canada's Easter gift to France. After Vimy, Arthur Currie was knighted on the battlefield by King George V and named commander-in-chief of the Canadian Expeditionary Force, succeeding Sir Julian Byng. For the first time, Canadian soldiers would be led by one of their own. At Vimy, they had

**THE TAKING OF VIMY RIDGE** ◆ Lieutenant Claude Williams was among the Canadians who attacked Vimy Ridge in April 1917. After the battle, he wrote to his mother: "Just came in from sending a cable to you reporting 'All Well.' They say you will receive it tonight. I thought you might be a little anxious after seeing the account of the battle in the paper. The papers here are full of it: The French especially wish to congratulate the 'gallant canadians' for capturing 'Vimy Ridge'…. It was absolutely the finest experience of my life – wouldn't have missed it for anything – there are of course lots of sights we are trying to forget as well as we can. A battle is a grand thing when you see pictures of it and descriptions, but they only show up the bright side of the affair but we see the shady side – the horribly mangled dead, and mutilated wounded, at first one feels an absolute nausea at these sights, but in the excitement soon reaches a surprising callousness and never thinks twice of them." Elated by the Canadians' success, Claude Williams believed this victory might well signal the end of the war – a hope that proved to be sadly mistaken. (*Richard Jack*, The Taking of Vimy Ridge, Easter Monday, 1917, *Canadian War Museum, 8178*)

captured more land, cannons, and weapons, and taken more prisoners (4,000), than all previous British offensives in two and a half years of war. Four Canadians were awarded the Victoria Cross, the Commonwealth's highest military decoration for bravery.

While Vimy had united the country, another issue was tearing it apart: conscription. Canada had lost ten thousand men at Ypres and Vimy, and the casualties outnumbered new recruits. The war had created employment, and young men preferred working at home to fighting at the front. Recruitment rallies were organized throughout the country, at which returning veterans appealed to fellow citizens to join up. They met with less success in the country than in the city, and with the least success in Quebec: only a modest percentage of volunteers were French Canadians.

On July 22, 1915, in Sohmer Park in Montreal, a crowd turned out to protest the efforts at recruitment. The following day, in Lafontaine Park, recruiters were bombarded with stones by students and workmen. At a patriotic evening in the Champs de Mars, the army had to intervene to prevent violence. Quebecers did not see why they should die for France, a country they had had little contact with for a century and a half. Nor did they feel any attachment to the army, a predominantly English-Canadian institution. Officers in the Canadian army were mainly of British origin. Between 1867 and 1914, the Royal Military College in Kingston had trained only 11 French-speaking officers out of 255 graduates. Orders were given in English, a language the vast majority of French-Canadian soldiers did not understand.

And there were other grievances, including Ontario's decision to make English the only language of instruction in its schools. Four thousand schoolchildren had been sent home because they wanted to be taught in French. "If they ask us to fight for England, we will answer: give us back our schools!" said Armand Lavergne, Quebec nationalist and provincial MLA (rumoured to be the illegitimate son of Wilfrid Laurier). "It is not in the trenches of Flanders that we are going to get the right to speak French in Ontario. . . . Every French Canadian who signs up is shirking his duty. I know that what I say is high treason. I can be thrown in jail tomorrow, but I am not worried about that. We are being told that it is a question of defending liberty and humanity but that is a monumental farce. If the Germans are our persecutors, then there are worse persecutors at the very doors of our society. . . . I am not afraid of becoming a German subject. I wonder whether the German regime could not be favourably compared to the regime of the Krauts in Ontario."

One-third of the eleven thousand native people old enough to fight signed up, a proportion twice the national average. The native population had already suffered terrible losses on their own soil in previous centuries, and now they would risk death on foreign soil. One who had earlier enlisted was Lieutenant Cameron Brant, a descendant of Mohawk chief Joseph Brant; he was gassed at Ypres. Iroquois chiefs tried, without success, to prevent recruitment on their reserves, but in January 1918 they managed to exempt their people from conscription.

In Ontario, recruitment propaganda urged women to refuse the romantic advances of their lovers and husbands if the men did not turn up in uniform. If there was a sexual blockade, however, it did not have much effect. Recruits were rare, and officers were now occasionally willing to accept even vagrants and the feeble-minded. In October 1916, a survey of recruitment concluded that only one recruit in five was in shape for military service. A patriot from Guelph, Ontario, aged seventy-nine years, showed signs of senility. Another soldier had signed up five times in Montreal and made the

**RECRUITMENT RALLY, MONTREAL, 1916** ◆ Beneath the colours of the empire, Sir Wilfrid Laurier addressed a Montreal crowd on the need for more men to do their duty and sign up for military service. Across the country, the social pressure to enlist was enormous, and the politicians' rhetoric was the least of it. Billboards with enlistment slogans dominated the city streets and newspapers printed lists of who was signing up. Recruiting officers continued to prowl small towns and even visited young men at work in the fields.

Robert Swan, a bank employee from Yarmouth, Nova Scotia, felt the pressure wherever he looked: "The poster was Lord Kitchener pointing at you, 'We need you,' 'Why are you not in the army?' Young girls were going along and they would meet what looked like a pretty good able-bodied man and they'd pin something white on them – called them a coward in other words, because they weren't in the army. 'What are you doing in civilian clothes when all my brothers are in the army?' That sort of thing. That's the kind of pressure. There was pressure through the press and through the communities to persuade the men to enlist." Eventually Swan signed up. (*National Archives of Canada, C-14952*)

transatlantic crossing twice, despite a record of alcoholism, fits of violence, and obvious reduced mental capacity.

In 1916, Robert Borden's Conservative government announced its intention to double the ranks of the Canadian contingent in Europe from 250,000 to 500,000 men. It was clear that it would take more than recruiting propaganda to meet this target, and on May 18, 1917, Borden announced the introduction of a bill that would make military service compulsory, retreating from his promise that there would be no conscription. He hoped that the bill would provide an additional 100,000 soldiers. His opponents retorted that conscription was feared by Quebec and rural English Canada alike. And with the United States having joined the war a month earlier, was such a drastic step necessary to ensure victory for the Allies?

With the fate of the conscription bill undecided, Borden proposed to Wilfrid Laurier, leader of the Opposition, that the Liberals and Conservatives join forces in a coalition government, ensuring support for the bill in the House. But Laurier was opposed to conscription, and he refused the offer. This decision drove a wedge between English-speaking and French-speaking Liberals, and Laurier's chief lieutenants abandoned him in favour of Borden. "At the present time, I find myself separated from colleagues who are as dear to me as brothers," wrote Laurier. ". . . I obey my conscience, and they obey theirs, but this situation indicates that we are in the presence of a separation that, if it is not checked, could send shock waves across the country as a whole."

English Canada rejected Laurier, but he was supported in Quebec. In an effort to keep the debate from boiling over, he proposed a referendum on the issue of conscription. "All my life, Mr. Speaker," he declared in the Commons, "I have fought coercion, all my life I have encouraged mutual understanding, and the motive that inspired me to take this position shall forever be my guide, to my dying breath." But Borden rejected the idea of a referendum.

On May 22, 1917, the archbishop of Montreal, Paul Bruchési, wrote to the prime minister: "Men have signed up. . . . As a result, more than 400,000 men have freely answered the call to arms. You would like to sign up 50,000 or 100,000 more. . . . Don't you believe, given the size of our population, that we have done more than our fair share? . . . But now, Prime Minister, the measure of conscription has been announced. . . . There is much disquiet among the people. . . . In particular, in the province of Quebec, regrettable uprisings are to be expected. Protest gatherings are being announced. Riots are not improbable."

Borden responded by citing German atrocities committed in France. If the enemy triumphed in Europe, he claimed, they would then invade Canada. The archbishop was unimpressed with Borden's apocalyptic warning and wrote back, on June 2, 1917: "This law will shock the entire country. Do you realize that? You want to make it as palatable as possible. It won't make any difference, because people will not support it. By what means will you force the citizens to accept the law and to obey it?" The prime minister replied that during the four days of recent debate on soldiers' voting rights, 5,500 Canadians in France had fallen, close to Lens. "I would feel," he concluded, "that their blood and the blood of all the other victims of the war would be on my hands if this bill did not pass, and I was unable to send reinforcements to replace our soldiers." Frank Maheux, on the front in Flanders, agreed with this argument and wrote to his wife that he was going to vote for Borden in the upcoming election. "I vote to the last minute for Borden.

**VOLUNTEERS** ◆ Many Canadians answered the call to arms in 1914, believing the war would last a few weeks and would be over by Christmas. Young recruits piled onto trains headed to Valcartier, in Quebec, for training before being shipped overseas. Cheering crowds filled the streets to see the men off and lined the tracks as the trains passed through their communities. The fanfare left Ontario volunteer Roy Macfie in good spirits: "It was a great trip coming. I had my head out of the window all the time it was daylight. Every town we passed there were crowds at the station waving flags and yelling goodbye and at every farm house the women would be out waving their aprons, dish cloths and anything they could get hold of." (*City of Toronto Archives*, SC 244-824)

**SIR ROBERT BORDEN** ◆ After his visit to the front in 1917, Prime Minister Robert Borden was determined to proceed with conscription: "We have sent the Canadian Expeditionary Force to the battlefront in the name of Canada: it is idle and shameless hypocrisy to pretend, as the chief faction opposed to this law do, that because these men went voluntarily we at home have no obligation to support them. We encouraged them to go, we organized, trained and equipped them. They have offered themselves for the supreme sacrifice on our behalf. More than thirty thousand of them are under the sod, having died that we may live and that our inheritance may be preserved. To desert them now on the grounds of quibble that they were merely volunteers would be as ignoble an evasion of moral responsibility as any country in all history was guilty of." (*National Archives of Canada*, PA-2747)

**ANTI-CONSCRIPTION RALLY, MONTREAL, JULY 15, 1917** ◆ Despite demonstrations and rallies throughout the summer of 1917, conscription was imposed, and many young men found themselves ordered to report for duty. Alfred Tremblay, a farmer's son from Hébertville, in the Saguenay-Lac-St-Jean region of Quebec, was twenty-two when he was conscripted in 1918: "The government passed the conscription bill, and I was called to arms. I was to report to the military depot in Quebec City, and I didn't refuse to go. Others decided not to show up. It wasn't bravery on my part; I thought I'd be exempted because of health problems that I had as a kid. But the medical exam was a joke. They weighed me, they took my measurements, and told me to step into a uniform, and that was that. They didn't listen to my heart, nothing. There was nobody there to help me. . . . A friend of mine got a discharge, but I wasn't so lucky." Alfred Tremblay left for military training, but the war ended before he ever reached the front. (*La Presse*)

We want some body to take our place. If he don't keep his promise we will cut his xxx off."

During the summer of 1917, crowds of up to three thousand people took to the streets of Montreal chanting "Down with Borden." Meetings protesting conscription were held, to no avail. The Military Service Act was passed in the Commons on July 24, 1917, thanks to the support of nearly all English-speaking MPs, and in spite of the opposition of nearly all French-speaking MPs. English and French Canadians had not been so divided since the Riel affair.

On August 7, a Montreal electrician named Elie Lalumière founded the anti-conscription Constitutional League, which later dynamited the Outremont residence of Senator Beaubien and the Cartierville residence of Lord Atholstan, owner of the *Montreal Star*. On August 28, the conscription bill was given royal assent by the governor general, the Duke of Devonshire, and this was followed by two days of violence in Montreal. Store windows were smashed and tramway rails ripped up. One hundred and fifty policemen were called in to disperse the crowd, and four were wounded, along with two demonstrators. The following evening, a demonstrator was killed in Philips Square.

Opposition to conscription was not restricted to Quebec. In 1917, a trade union supporter, Fred Dixon, who had been elected as an independent to the Manitoba provincial legislature, encouraged a crowd in Winnipeg's Market Square to burn their recruitment orders and to resist conscription.

On August 2, 1918, there was a general strike in Vancouver protesting the death of Albert "Ginger" Goodwin. Goodwin had been declared unfit for the draft because of tuberculosis but was suddenly called up while organizing a strike in the city of Trail, British Columbia. He then fled to Vancouver Island, where he was taken in by a group of conscientious objectors. Goodwin was subsequently shot to death by a policeman, who claimed the shooting was in self-defence. Vancouver workers believed he had been murdered and walked off the job in protest.

A federal election was called for December 1917, and it would be fought on the single issue of conscription. On October 12, Borden announced that he had formed a Union government, in which the Conservatives' power was bolstered by the support of most English-Canadian Liberal MPs. Under wartime legislation, Borden was able to distribute the votes of soldiers as he saw fit, allocating them to ridings where he needed extra support. He had already deprived immigrants from enemy nations of the vote, a group that traditionally voted Liberal. Laurier objected to these tactics, and he wrote to a friend in Winnipeg: "What do you see in the infamous law that has just been adopted and that deprives so many of our fellow citizens of their rights: the sign that the government wants to win the war or that it wants to win the election?" In Ontario, the attacks on Laurier increased. He was accused of being a traitor, and the servant of Henri Bourassa; it was suggested that "a vote for Laurier is a vote for the Kaiser!"

In Quebec, the few people who favoured conscription did not dare speak out in public. Albert Sévigny, the only French-Canadian minister in Borden's government, tried to broach the issue with the citizens of his Dorchester riding. They jeered him and he had to seek refuge in a hotel; he was later escorted out by an armed detachment.

On December 17, 1917, the Borden government was re-elected, with 113 Conservatives and 39 Unionist Liberals. Laurier's Liberals had 82 members on the Opposition benches, 62 of them from Quebec. The Unionists were jubilant: Canada would fulfill its duty as part of the empire and would avoid national shame. But Quebec found itself even further isolated from the rest of Canada.

Shortly after the election, in January 1918, the Liberal member for Lotbinière, Joseph-Napoléon Francoeur, tabled the first separatist motion in the Quebec assembly, proposing that Quebec leave Confederation: "This House is of the opinion that the province of Quebec is inclined to accept the rupture of the Act of Confederation of 1867, if, in the other provinces, it be considered to be an obstacle to the union, to the progress and the development of Canada." The legislature discussed this ambiguous secessionist proposal in the days that followed, before it was finally withdrawn.

Conscription dictated that all able-bodied men between twenty and thirty-two years of age who were bachelors or widowers without children had to sign up. In Ontario 124,965 men registered, and 116,092 asked for exemptions – 3,000 more than in Quebec, where 115,602 were called up.

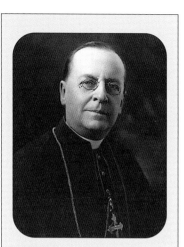

**MONSEIGNEUR PAUL BRUCHÉSI** ◆ Monseigneur Bruchési, the archbishop of Montreal, could not in good conscience allow the conscription legislation to pass without a final word of protest. On August 31, 1917, he wrote to Prime Minister Robert Borden: "Do not be offended by what I am about to say: I think this law is a calamity. My predictions will be borne out. This law will trigger a disastrous civil war in our country whose outcome is impossible to forecast. . . . Will you resort to prison, and armed repression, to stifle the protests? What do you stand to gain if blood is spilled in the streets? And you really think to serve the Allied cause this way? . . . Consider, I beg you, the responsibility that weighs on your shoulders, and, above all, think of the welfare of our dear Canada." (*National Archives of Canada*, PA-30244)

Roughly 93 per cent of all eligible men in Canada asked for exemptions. Both anglophones and francophones pleaded that they were the sole support of their families, or were disabled, or students, or members of a profession that was vital to the economy. Courts were set up to adjudicate the hundreds of thousands of requests. When the Borden government did not reach its recruitment objectives, it announced that it was cancelling all exemptions. Thousands of conscripts, particularly French-speaking ones, refused to be sent to the front and went into hiding.

Fearing that he would be enlisted, young Jules Lachapelle sought refuge in the countryside with his wife, Anna. When she learned that recruiters were searching the region, she asked her sister-in-law to lend them her eighteen-month-old girl and they would pass the baby off as their own. "After nineteen days, the detective came round," Anna Lachapelle wrote. "My baby was ready for bed. I had washed her and was rocking her. I told my husband: watch out, there is a man on his way here. My husband told me to stay calm, just rock the baby, don't let anything show. He came to the house. He knocked. My husband opened the door – 'Good evening, sir' – and offered him a chair. He came straight over to me, and said 'So, you have a lovely little baby. There's no denying it.' She had blond hair just like me. He spoke to us a little while. Then he said: 'I will be on my way.' Then he passed through the doorway and it was over. Sweat was flowing down my back. I couldn't take it any longer." Jules did not go to war, and later on, they would have five children of their own.

To many Canadians, the Lachapelles and others looked like cowards. Some people even proposed rounding them up. A man named Louis Friedenberg wrote to the military authorities in Montreal: "The majority of them are called the night birds. They are never seen in the daytime, but if you will take my advice and give me a special commission. I will do everything to bring these slackers to serve the country." Instead, Ottawa sent the North West Mounted Police after the deserters. In Quebec, twenty-three-year-old Joseph Mercier was arrested in a bowling alley because he did not have his exemption papers with him. He was let go only when his family turned up with the documents. But the incident sparked retaliation: a crowd looted the offices of the army registrar, pitched files out in the snow, and smashed the windows of English-owned shops. The police did not intervene, but the army did. Rumours swirled that the federal police were ripping up exemption papers in order to force young men awaiting the judgment of the courts to leave for the front. On Easter Monday, April 1, 1918, after five days of rioting, Ottawa sent soldiers into Quebec City. On rue Bagot, they tried to drive the demonstrators back but met with a hail of rocks. "We heard a regiment from Ontario . . . galloping around through the streets of Saint-Sauveur," wrote Canon Scott's son Frank, who was in Quebec City at the time. "The electric lights had been cut off by the rioters; the whole of lower town was in fog and in darkness that night, and we heard shouts. Then all of a sudden we heard machine-gun fire. It was deafening and it sounded as though there was a general massacre going on down there." Official casualties: four dead and more than seventy wounded.

One hundred thousand men were finally called up and put in uniform; half that number crossed the Atlantic and only 25,000 reached the front before the end of hostilities. They were often badly received by the volunteers, who made up 95 per cent of the Expeditionary Force. "Whatever warnings our officers have issued, there isn't going to be anything friendly about the welcome we are holding out for these conscripts," wrote Claude Williams. "Nearly everybody here is waiting for the chance to punish these reluctant soldiers and to take it out on them."

The war was the engine driving the Canadian economy. By 1917, the Imperial Munitions Board (IMB), a body set up to contract supplies from Canada for use by the Allied war effort, had coordinated a billion dollars' worth of contracts, making it Canada's biggest business. It oversaw more than 600 weapons factories, employed 150,000 workers (tens of thousands of them women), and did $2 million in business daily. While the IMB was providing for Allied needs, the Canadian government was spending just as much money on its own war effort, buying ammunition, aircraft, ships, vehicles, chemical products, gases, and explosives. Companies like Canadian Car and Foundry, Canada Steamship Lines, and the Angus factories in Montreal flourished, as did manufacturers of uniforms, boots, and other goods needed by the army. Prairie wheat was in great demand and prices were rising (they would drop again after the war, leaving many farmers heavily indebted). The factories of central Canada and the foundries and refineries of British Columbia were operating at full capacity.

It was Sam Hughes, the defence minister, who orchestrated the industrial war effort between 1914 and 1916. Newspapers often published stories about the sudden fortunes made by his close associates, who trafficked their influence. "We have turned out 250,000 soldiers," Hughes said in 1916. "Our manufacturers, at the present time are capable and ready for any undertaking. . . . There has been added to the wealth of Canada, through the action of the Shell Committee, $250,000,000; or $30 each for every man, woman and child in the country." But the shareholders of munitions factories seemed to profit more than anyone else.

Hughes insisted on equipping the army with the Ross rifle, and he granted a subsidy of $18 million to Charles Ross, its manufacturer. But the rifle, which was designed for great accuracy, tended to jam in the dust and mud of the battlefield, leaving soldiers weaponless. Ultimately, Hughes was forced to resign in November 1916, a year after Borden named Joseph Flavelle chief executive of the Imperial Munitions Board. This millionaire philanthropist, who had made his fortune in canned salt pork, decided that the quality of munitions was more important than profits, especially when the lives of soldiers were at stake. In 1917, under his leadership, the Board's five nationalized factories sent 23,786,206 shells to Europe, close to

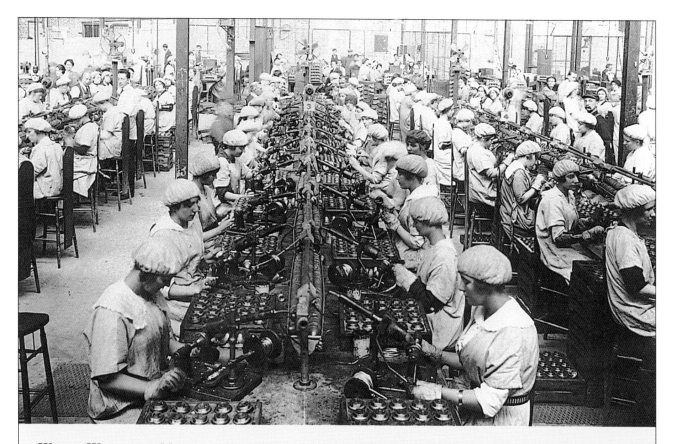

**WOMEN WORKING IN MUNITIONS FACTORY** ◆ "Twelve months ago, in Canada, no thought of woman labour was in the mind of any manufacturer. Experience has proved that there is no operation on shell work that a woman cannot do, and as a matter of fact, is not doing . . ." This was reported by the Imperial Munitions Board in 1916.

For some women, munitions work meant a much needed source of income; for others, it was an opportunity to support the war effort. Either way, a job at the factory involved long shifts, sometimes overnight, and difficult conditions. "I don't remember any great tragedy but there could have been, your clothes getting caught or something getting caught," said Elsa Neil, who worked at the Fairbanks-Morse munitions factory in Toronto. "Oh, and on the other side of the wall where my back was, there were great big blasting furnaces that these shells came out of, so if ever there'd been a fire, there was absolutely nothing would have saved us. Nothing could have saved us."

Not only did women prove that they were capable of this difficult work, they lobbied hard for safe working conditions and appropriate pay. In 1917, when munitions production was at its height, there were at least 35,000 women employed in munitions plants in Ontario and Montreal. (*National Archives of Canada, c-18734*)

one-third of all munitions used by the Allied artillery. When the labour unions asked for higher salaries for munitions factory workers, Flavelle retorted that there was no chance – although he did recommend to industrialists that women be paid equally with men. Not a single business leader complied with this mild recommendation.

In 1917, King George V made Flavelle a baronet. At nearly the same time, however, newspapers revealed that Flavelle had pocketed record profits by selling bacon to the English. *Saturday Night* magazine accused him of having starved soldiers while creating an artificial shortage to drive up the price of pork ("the most sordid and despicable trafficking, namely the

**SAM HUGHES** ◆ Colonel Sam Hughes, Canada's minister of militia for the first two years of the war, was forced from office by Prime Minister Borden in 1916. The scandal of the Ross rifle, championed by Hughes but hated by the Canadian soldiers who had to use it, will always be associated with his name. One soldier who vividly remembered the rifle's shortcomings was Bert Remington of Montreal: "All of our equipment was a leather bag and a water bottle and a haversack – and the Ross rifle! Don't ever forget the Ross rifle! What a bastard! It was a good weapon, but for service – uh,uh. It was a political gag with Sam Hughes and the Ross rifle. I'd like to cram it right . . .! Anyway, our watchmen would curse Sam Hughes and the Ross rifle and the Canadian government. Germans coming on in mass, and the rifle wouldn't fire, the bolt wouldn't close, the steel wasn't tempered. They'd try to drive it open and they'd blow their brains out." (*National Archives of Canada, C-2468*)

**SIR JOSEPH FLAVELLE** ◆ This sketch of Joseph Flavelle, head of the Imperial Munitions Board, is the work of Frederick Varley, who spent the last year of the war as an artist for the Canadian military. In the midst of an uproar about the quality of Canadian-manufactured munitions in 1916, Flavelle went to Europe, to see the battlefields of the Somme and witness the war directly. From an artillery observation post, Flavelle saw the Allies drop shells on German lines and watched German planes being kept at bay by anti-aircraft fire. The horror of trench warfare left a searing impression: "… as I looked at them, tens of thousands of them, guns booming on every side and shells whistling over my head as they went on their dread message to the other side, this one thing came back to me again and again: My God! What have these men done? What have these men done that they must be punished in this way?" (*Frederick Varley, courtesy of Michael Bliss*)

accumulation of great wealth out of the blood and agony of those who fight in the trenches"). He was asked to resign from the IMB immediately. A royal commission exonerated Flavelle, although it noted that his food enterprises showed profits of 80 per cent, enough to brand him a war profiteer in the public imagination. "This is a new experience," he wrote to his wife. "Why should I be exempt from what better men have suffered? . . . I am thankful, so thankful, to be without a shadow of reproach in myself. I am often wrong, but not in this." Flavelle refused to resign, but he lost all his political credibility.

On the morning of December 6, 1917, the weather in Halifax, Nova Scotia, was clear. There was no snow on the ground, and a light mist floated over the harbour, the key departure point for Canadian men, munitions, and supplies bound for Europe. The wounded brought back from the front were disembarked from hospital ships, and soldiers on leave celebrated among the waterfront bars.

That morning, the Norwegian ship *Imo* was getting ready to leave the harbour. The *Mont-Blanc*, a French vessel loaded with ammunition, was approaching from the opposite direction. It was about to join an Allied convoy to be escorted across the Atlantic. A small craft forced the *Imo* to change course, putting it in the path of the *Mont-Blanc*. Both ships blasted their horns in warning, then collided. The *Imo* tore a three-metre gash in the hull of the French vessel, which only the crew knew was carrying 2,766 tonnes of wet and dry picric acid, 200 tonnes of TNT, 10 tonnes of gun cotton, and 35 tonnes of benzol, a new type of solvent.

The crash initially caused just sparks, black smoke, and flames. Curious, excited children ran toward the harbour. In schools, factories, and homes, men, women, and children gathered at the windows to observe the extraordinary fire. The crew of the *Mont-Blanc* jumped into lifeboats and paddled madly for the shore, trying to warn onlookers to flee. Sparks set fire to the barrels of benzol lashed to the deck of the *Mont-Blanc*, and fire spread slowly inside the hold. It took twenty minutes to reach the explosives.

At 9:06, the *Mont-Blanc* was disintegrated by the largest man-made explosion the world had known (it would be twenty-eight years before a larger one, at Hiroshima). Windows were broken seventy-five kilometres away, and the shock waves were felt at a distance of more than three hundred kilometres. The shaft of the ship's anchor, weighing half a tonne, was recovered three kilometres away. Shards of iron, wood, and steel flew in all directions. People standing close to the shore were propelled through the air, sucked up by the firestorm and brought down ten metres away, slashed, bruised, their clothes torn to shreds, their laced boots missing, their bodies smeared with black soot. A few of them miraculously survived; others disappeared under the ruins. Some bodies, vaporized by the force of the explosion, were never recovered.

People who watched from their windows lost eyes, and their faces were ripped by the shattering glass. The shock wave of the explosion sent the sea into a boil, building up a monster wave that rolled disastrously to shore. Houses, factories, schools, and churches were knocked down. Millions of glass panes twirled in the air. Bricks and concrete disintegrated. Trees and poles snapped, and railway tracks were twisted and thrown up into the air. Houses with coal furnaces and cellars filled with coal burned like stacks of paper. The ruins smouldered for a week. Six square kilometres of Halifax were simply wiped out.

More than two thousand were killed and nine thousand wounded, which compared to the worst military losses of the Canadian troops. Among the survivors, almost a hundred were blinded. The explosion knocked out all telegraph and telephone wires, and for several hours Halifax was isolated from the rest of the world. The city was evacuated. Blood-soaked, silent, traumatized refugees, covered in soot, took to the streets clutching whatever they could take with them, some of them almost naked in the December cold. The explosion was quickly followed by a terrible snowstorm, and the charred blackness of the miserable city was soon covered with a pristine white.

**HALIFAX EXPLOSION** ◆
The explosion that devastated
Halifax harbour on December 6, 1917, was witnessed
by Lambert Griffith, a sailor
in the Royal Canadian Navy.
Griffith's ship, HMCS
*Niobe*, was anchored just 850
metres from the *Mont-Blanc*,
the French munitions ship
that exploded at 9:06 a.m.
"All at once there was a most
hideous noise & I saw the
whole boat vanish, a
moment after I saw something coming can't describe it. I was hurled on the deck & there was an awful noise going on. I got to my feet & ran with a whole lot of fellows. My one fixed idea was to get below. We all tried to get down the one ladder without any success. I had the presence of mind enough to dig my head in between all kinds of legs. . . . After that I ran along the deck & heard all kinds of things falling. It was shrapnel & bits of the side of the ship.... I managed to get to the gangway unhurt & found that the ship had broken her big cable & the gangway gone. As she crashed in to the jetty I jumped off & got ashore just before she shoved the jetty over." With little time to get his own bearings, Griffith set immediately to work clearing ammunition stored nearby. Twenty sailors of the Royal Canadian Navy lost their lives in the explosion. (*Nova Scotia Archives and Records Management, N-37*)

Some believed that the city had been attacked by Germans. The *Halifax Herald* held the Kaiser responsible for the explosion. Citizens of German origin were arrested, then let go. Rumours of sabotage spread like wildfire. The disaster area was surrounded by soldiers, and a special permit was required to enter.

Committees were formed to locate the missing, to identify unidentified victims, to interview parents looking for lost children, and to ensure that children were cared for and orphans found families willing to take them in. More than one thousand people throughout North America offered to adopt them. Children with blue eyes and blond hair were the most sought after.

The search for the missing continued for months; bodies were still being recovered the following spring. Charles Upham looked for the remains of his family. With his brother and his son, Archie, he searched through the debris of his home: "We collected all that was left of my mother, my two sisters and my brother – some bones – and we put them into a shoe box and brought it to the Fairview cemetery. By then, it was already summer time."

The Jacksons all lived close together next to the port, in the working-class district of Richmond. Most of the extended family died. Among the survivors was Mary Jean Jackson, a forty-year-old mother who lost her ten children, her husband, her mother, four brothers, two sisters, and many nephews and nieces. Another son, James, was born in 1918. "I never once heard her complain or grieve aloud over her losses," James wrote. "In fact, I was never aware of her tragedy until the age of twelve, when I heard parts of the story from other people. Occasionally, when I was that age I would come home from school and knew she had been crying."

Mary Jean mentioned the explosion only once a year, on the night before All Souls' Day. "From the time I was old enough to write and until the year she died," James said, "my mother named the names of the dead who were to be prayed for at that special mass. She named them softly, slowly and lovingly, without any emotion other than perhaps a slight tinge of sadness. As young as I was, I sensed these were very special people and this was a very solemn occasion. There were far too many names to fit the form supplied by the church. They were listed on two sheets of writing paper. In my best penmanship I carefully copied each name – the grandmother, uncles and aunts, half-brothers and sisters and all the cousins I never knew. They were always in the same order; she never forgot even one. There were fifty-four names."

In Europe, Henri Philippe Pétain, commander-in-chief of the French forces, decided that the French army, now much weakened, would play a defensive role while it waited for the Americans, who had declared war on Germany but had not arrived at the front. His British counterpart, General Douglas Haig, did not want to leave the British Expeditionary Force idle, and he judged that the momentary absence of two allies from the battlefield offered the prospect of a huge victory for which he could take credit. He launched another big offensive in Flanders, near Ypres, on July 31, 1917, ignoring the forecast of heavy rain.

The opening artillery barrage did not surprise the German forces, who had observed the preparations for the offensive from their hilltops and had sought refuge in their bunkers to escape the bombardment. Once the British infantrymen launched their attack, the forecasted rain started pouring down in sheets, transforming the land they had to cover into vast fields of mud, which swallowed up whole regiments, along with their equipment. Haig's offensive continued until the end of October. General Currie, commander of the Canadian Expeditionary Force, protested when his turn to enter the action came, arguing that this was not the moment for an attack. He predicted that the Canadians would lose sixteen thousand men, and it would be a meaningless sacrifice. Haig insisted, and the Canadians joined the Battle of Passchendaele, which began on October 30. The Allies were trying to expel the Germans from northern Belgium, from Ostend and Zeebrugge, which was used as a naval base for enemy submarines.

Arthur-Joseph Lapointe, who had left the Gaspé Peninsula to join the 22nd Regiment, described Passchendaele in his journal: "Before us, some two kilometres away, stretched the ridge of Passchendaele. At the foot of this ridge, lay a low plain, pockmarked with countless shell holes filled with stagnant water. Everywhere was an air of desolation. Not a house was to be seen, as far as the horizon. Only the bare, terribly scarred plain, over which a cataclysm seemed to have passed. It was as if life could never return to these killing fields. In a flooded trench, corpses of Germans, their stomachs grotesquely bloated, floated in slushy water. Here and there were bodies buried in the mud with only an arm or a leg showing above the surface. Macabre faces appeared, blackened by their long stay on the ground. Everywhere I looked, all I could see was corpses covered in a shroud of mud."

Haig had been predicting a decisive victory without significant losses. But on November 6, he ordered a stop to the offensive. The Canadian soldiers had reached the ruins of Passchendaele, just five kilometres away from their starting point. General Currie's frightening prediction of losses came true; there were 15,654 casualties. The air was putrid with decay. Haig lost 325,000 British infantrymen in an operation that had succeeded in taking only five kilometres of muck, which the British would abandon to the Germans six months later. As for the enemy's relatively minor losses, they did not offer the general the consolation of saying he had lived up to his motto: "Kill more Germans." British prime minister David Lloyd George wrote that Passchendaele "would count among the greatest, most difficult, most sinister, most futile and bloodiest battles ever fought in the entire history of warfare." Winston Churchill was blunter: "This adventure was a pathetic and unprecedented waste of bravery and human life," he said. But Douglas Haig was a protégé of King George V's, and so he kept his command, in spite of the angry outcry from the British press.

The morale of the troops was badly shaken by the losses at Passchendaele. Nearly forty thousand of France's two million soldiers deserted. In the fall of 1917, Pétain ordered forty-nine of them to be executed, to set an example. The Canadian Expeditionary Force decided to execute those soldiers accused of having fled. Lieutenant-Colonel Thomas Tremblay sent five of his men of the 22nd Regiment to the firing squad. Arthur-Joseph Lapointe described how a fellow soldier was punished: "We entered a huge courtyard surrounded by a stone wall. The condemned man appeared all of a sudden in between two policemen. As he walked past us, he threw us such a sad glance that I was moved to tears. He disappeared behind a large taut canvas which had been thrown up so we could not see him. Beyond this canvas was the firing squad. All of a sudden, we heard the shots of a fusillade ring out. A command was given and we stood at attention. It was a tragic moment, during which military justice had just been satisfied. . . . Now, we had to march past the victim. It was a cruel duty to impose on us. The entire rearguard marched past the body of the poor wretch bound to his seat. Blood was splashed on his tunic and his head had fallen on his chest. On his face there remained such an air of resignation that it was as if he were still smiling softly in death."

Once the Americans joined the fray in 1917, the Germans became more desperate. In early 1918, they risked everything in a series of offensives

**ARTHUR-JOSEPH LAPOINTE**
◆ Lapointe enlisted voluntarily, but, unlike many volunteers, he felt no ill will toward the conscripts: "I know some of the conscripts we met yesterday. I am sorry for them with all my heart. They were sent in here against their will, while the rest of us took on this heavy task voluntarily. A dozen of their companions, who got here yesterday, were killed overnight. Their bodies now lie in a corner of the trench, waiting to be taken to the rear and buried in a little cemetery."
(*Courtesy of Yvette Lapointe*)

*Canadian Gunners in the Mud,*
*Passchendaele, 1917,*
Alfred Bastien
(*Canadian War Museum, 8095*)

on the western front that almost handed them victory. But during the last months of the war, the "Hundred Days," Canadians broke through German lines near Amiens, which had remained thus far impregnable, and pushed all the way to Mons, in Belgium. For the Kaiser and his allies, this was the end.

The Armistice was signed at the eleventh hour of the eleventh day of the eleventh month. In London, recovering from a foot injury, Canon Scott observed the celebrations: "There was wild rejoicing in the city and the crowds went crazy with delight. But it seemed to me that behind the ringing of those peals of joy there was the tolling of spectral bells for those who would return no more. The monstrous futility of war as a test of national greatness, the wound in the world's heart, the empty homes, those were the thoughts which in me over mastered all the feelings of rejoicing."

Ottawa was the first city in Canada to announce that the war was over. Early in the morning, bells began ringing out, and factory and fire station sirens screamed. Several thousand people gathered on Parliament Hill to celebrate the peace. In every region of the country, people held spontaneous parades. Kaiser Wilhelm was burned in effigy. In Toronto, shops closed, and everybody – including brass bands – took to the streets. But the celebrations were short-lived; the country had lost sixty thousand men. It was exhausted. And a new crisis quickly descended.

**WAR IN THE AIR** ◆ Before the war, many Canadians had never seen an airplane. For the soldiers, that would change as soon as they made it overseas. Watching airplanes fight it out in the skies was a fascinating pastime. Despite the danger, serving in the elite Royal Flying Corps was an ambition for many young men. Basil Morris was convinced that battling in the skies had to be better than the muddy trenches, and he was thrilled to accept a transfer. He wrote with excitement to his sister: "We had a scrap with a couple of Hun machines and it surely was some scrap. It was great shooting at the blighters and their machine-gun bullets were cracking all around us. I don't think I hit either of them but hope so. It was my first try over the line and so was quite a good initiation. I didn't feel at all nervous up in the air during the scrap but was a bit shaky after we got back. The pilot certainly shot our machine around in all sorts of ways." On March 17, 1917, ten weeks after he took to the skies, Basil Morris died when his plane was shot down over Belgium. A third of the Royal Flying Corps's pilots, among them 1,600 Canadians, lost their lives. (*C. R. W. Nevison*, War in the Air, *1918. Canadian War Museum, 8651*)

In 1918, Spanish influenza raged across the face of the earth. It started in China, broke out in a U.S. army camp in Kansas, then took hold in Britain. In the interests of bolstering the war effort, the spread of the epidemic was not widely reported. Spain was a neutral country, and it was the first to announce the threat of the deadly virus, thus giving it its name. Influenza killed more than twenty million people around the world. More than fifty thousand Canadians died, almost as many as those who were killed in the war.

For Cecilia DeLory, on Prince Edward Island, Armistice Day would always be a day of mourning and desolation: "My mother, my oldest sister and my four brothers caught the flu," she wrote. "After eight days, Mother, who was only forty years old, contracted pneumonia and died. My father and I attended her funeral at four o'clock on November 11, 1918, just as the bells were ringing in honour of the Armistice."

Influenza struck soldiers stationed in Europe first. On returning home, they transmitted the virus to civilians. One Canadian in four got it, and it affected almost every home. Hearses filled the streets. Schools, shops, and factories closed their doors to avoid contagion, as did courthouses, restaurants, theatres, and dance halls. On October 25, 1918, the Alberta government ordered all citizens to wear a mask when they went outside their homes. In Regina, whoever sneezed, coughed, or spat in public was subject to a fine. Trams and churches were disinfected. In the north, whole Inuit villages were annihilated.

The day after the Armistice, in Red Deer, Alberta, Ella Persons became worried about her husband, who was a physician. "Dear mother," she wrote, "for the last two weeks, all people talk about here is the influenza. Dick calls on his patients from dawn till midnight. We are more or less all right, but a little downhearted. So many physicians died that I worry about Dick, but he is OK." Ironically, Ella was the one to die, a few days after mailing this letter, leaving behind her husband and healthy sons.

Hospitals were overflowing, and doctors were at a loss. Influenza victims were isolated, given syrup, and treated with cupping glasses. The public desperately tried anything: bags of camphor and smoked herring worn around the neck; swallowing alcohol, garlic, raw onions; concoctions of hot milk, ginger, and black pepper. People stopped shaking hands. They took to prayer. A healthy man could suddenly find himself unable to walk, beset by shivering, headaches, back pain, coughing, and fever. The disease could vanish, or it could degenerate into a deadly pneumonia.

In Montreal, Brother Alphonse Rodriguez of the Frères de l'instruction chrétienne risked death each day while taking care of forty patients from every different background and faith. "For the first time," he wrote, "I took a dead body down to the charnel house. What an impression – what a dreadful odour. For two days, corpses had been kept in the hallway, where coffins were lined up. . . . The remains were placed in a coffin already all spattered with blood. I could not stay long since the place . . . filled me with such horror."

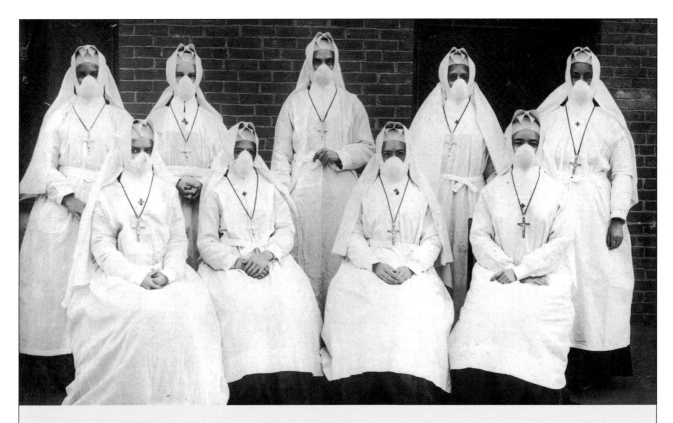

**INFLUENZA EPIDEMIC, 1918-19** ◆ Among the hardest hit by the "Spanish flu" were those who tended its victims, such as these Sisters of the Good Shepherd in Quebec City. As the disease spread, Canada faced an acute shortage of medical personnel; many doctors and nurses were still with the troops in Europe. The call went out for volunteers. St. John's Ambulance, the Red Cross, the YMCA, the Imperial Order of Daughters of the Empire, the Women's Canadian Club, and community groups across the country responded. Harold Fisher, the mayor of Ottawa, said, "I want to make it absolutely clear that people are dying in our midst because they are not provided with proper care. They are not dying because we do not know about them. We know where they are, but we have nobody to send. Knitting socks for soldiers is very useful work but we are now asking the women of Ottawa to get in the trenches themselves." Teachers, now with empty classrooms, also tended to the afflicted. Eleanor Beaubier, in Saskatchewan, went door to door caring for the sick until she, too, took ill and died, just twenty-four years old. Neighbours remembered the sacrifice of this young teacher and renamed their town Beaubier. (*Soeurs du Bon-Pasteur de Québec*)

A few months before the end of the war, Arthur-Joseph Lapointe had a nightmare in which his younger sister appeared to him, dressed in mourning. She guided him past a row of graves and with her finger indicated the names of his brothers and sisters. "I am dead myself," she said to him before disappearing. Lapointe woke up and noted in his diary what he had dreamed. When he returned to the Gaspé, the train dropped him near his home in Mont-Joli at 2:00 a.m. His brother Alphonse hurried toward him, followed by their father, who told him, "This dreadful influenza epidemic has brought the death of three of your brothers and your two sisters in the space of nine days." Arthur-Joseph was devastated by the news and looked to his brother. "He is the only one I have left," he noted in his diary.

The war separated English from French Canadians, the foreign-born from Canadians, patriots from deserters. But it also separated those who had taken part in the war from those who had remained in Canada. Returning soldiers were often changed: wounded, mentally fragile, devastated. Some had caught tuberculosis or venereal diseases. Marriages suffered and families were destroyed. Returning soldiers were not finding the better world they had been promised. War factories were shutting down, and there were bankruptcies and unemployment. Some men got their jobs back when the women who had replaced them were sent home again. Others were forced to look for work, and they often blamed the immigrants who had taken their places. Wages were low and the cost of living was continually rising, partly because of strong demand for products that had long been rationed. Housing for demobilized soldiers was in short supply, and rents were exorbitant. The government granted land and pensions to veterans, who were for the most part dissatisfied with these stopgap measures. They were out of work and unhappy, and many joined the throngs of dissatisfied labourers who could not keep up with inflation.

From Halifax to Vancouver, a storm was brewing, but it was in Winnipeg that it broke loose. On May 15, 1919, the Trades and Labor Council called for a general strike, and by 11:00 a.m. that day thirty thousand workers had walked off their jobs in support of metal workers who were seeking higher wages, an eight-hour day, and union recognition. "In Germany, I fed on grass and rats. I would prefer going back to eating grass than give up the freedom for which I fought so hard and suffered so much," Blackwood, a veteran, wrote in the striking workers' newspaper. Elevators shut down, trams stopped, postal and telephone communications came to a halt, and nothing moved without approval from the strike committee. The spectre of a Bolshevik revolution was raised. Arthur Meighen, the solicitor general, stated: "The leaders of the general strike are all revolutionists of varying degrees and types, from crazy idealists to ordinary thieves."

James Shaver Woodsworth, a Methodist minister in a working-class Winnipeg district, disagreed. "In fact it has nothing to do with revolution," he said. "It is an attempt to meet a very pressing and immediate need." He joined the strikers. "And now!" he wrote. "Now, we are being told to celebrate peace! Whereas the profiteers reign triumphant, and the cost of living keeps rising. These men did their fair share. Now the rich should pay theirs!"

Many of the strike leaders were British immigrants, and a federal law was passed allowing them to be deported without due process. Foreign-born strikers were also made targets. "They say one of our leaders was a German," said Helen Armstrong, the daughter of a socialist tailor from Toronto and the wife of George Armstrong, one of the strike leaders. "I don't care what a man is if he's whole under the skin and a worker. The only enemy alien we have in Canada is the capitalist and the strike breaker." Deporting immigrants was not enough to restore order. Policemen who refused to promise not to strike were fired and replaced by a special militia that was paid more than the police. Each of the "Specials" received a horse and a baseball bat to keep order.

Fred Dixon, who wrote for the *Western Labor News*, urged the strikers to avoid armed confrontation, knowing that violence would work to the advantage of their adversaries. "Strikers, hold your horses!" he said. "This is the hour when you can win. Steady, boys, steady. Keep quiet. Do nothing. Keep out of trouble. Don't carry weapons. Leave this to your enemies. Continue to prove that you are the friends of law and order."

On the night of June 17, after a demonstration that went badly, Prime Minister Borden sent twelve union and immigrant leaders to Stony Mountain penitentiary, forbade the publication of the *Western Labor News*, and ordered the NWMP to put down demonstrations with whatever force should prove necessary. On June 21, veterans organized a parade that directly challenged the restrictions on assembly imposed by Mayor Charles Gray. A crowd of six thousand people gathered in front of the city hall as Gray read the Riot Act, his voice not carrying through the crowd. Demonstrators tipped over a tram and set it on fire. Brandishing baseball bats, the "Specials" charged the crowd. "Then with revolvers drawn," Fred Dixon reported, "[the NWMP] galloped down Main Street, turned, and charged right into the crowd on William Avenue, firing as they charged. One man, standing on the sidewalk, thought the Mounties were firing blank cartridges until a spectator standing beside him dropped with a bullet through his breast. . . . Dismounted red coats lined up . . . declaring military control."

On "Bloody Saturday," two strikers were killed, dozens more were wounded, and the police made thirty-one arrests. The Winnipeg General Strike had been crushed. On June 25, the strikers returned to work under threat of losing their jobs.

The events shook Canon Scott, who was in Winnipeg at the time. "I am getting old," Scott said, "but I am going to dedicate the rest of my life to fighting labour's battles. . . . I shall go back to the east and tell to all. . . . My sympathies are with the strikers."

Fred Dixon was arrested and charged with sedition, and J. S. Woodsworth was charged with seditious conspiracy. At his trial, Fred Dixon told the jury: "Liberty of opinion . . . that is what is on trial. . . . I advised men to use their ballots and keep the peace. . . . In your hands is placed the question of liberty of speech. Whether a man has a right to criticize government officials or not." Dixon was acquitted, and the charges against Woodsworth were dropped. Public opinion remained divided over the strike, but Woodsworth was elected to Parliament two years later, a popular figure.

Prairie farmers were facing their own problems, including falling wheat prices and large debts. They also had to pay heavy taxes to finance the construction of roads and schools needed to accommodate the influx of immigrants. Farmers were abandoning the land to move to cities. And as a result of the difficult conditions, there was a resurgence of agrarian political

**WINNIPEG GENERAL STRIKE, JUNE 4, 1919** ◆ On this day Charles Gray, the mayor of Winnipeg, addressed members of the Loyalist Veterans' Association, a group opposed to the general strike. Tempers were running high. Thousands had joined a sympathy strike in Vancouver the previous day, and in Winnipeg strikers and their opponents had followed that up with new demonstrations, narrowly avoiding a confrontation outside the Manitoba legislature. While many returning soldiers supported the strikers, others, angry about their inability to find work, directed their frustration at the recent immigrants who played a prominent part in the strike and who, they felt, had taken jobs that rightly should have been theirs. With the Russian Revolution still on everyone's mind, there was also widespread fear that the strike would spread Bolshevism to Canada. (*Provincial Archives of Manitoba, 1691*)

**WINNIPEG GENERAL STRIKE, JUNE 21, 1919** ◆ Fred Dixon, a labour activist and reporter for the strike newspaper, the *Western Labor News*, witnessed the events of Bloody Saturday: "On Saturday about 2:30 p.m., just the time when the parade was scheduled to start, some fifty mounted men swinging baseball bats rode down Main Street. Half were red-coated Royal North-West Mounted Police, the others wore khaki. They quickened their pace as they passed the Union Bank. The crowd opened, let them through and closed in behind them. They turned and charged

through the crowd again greeted by hisses and boos, and some stones. There were two riderless horses with the squad when it emerged and galloped up Main Street. The men in khaki disappeared at this juncture but the red-coats reined their horses and reformed opposite the old post-office." (*Provincial Archives of Manitoba, N-12296*)

movements. "We as farmers are downtrodden by every other class," said Henry Wise Wood, a farmer who had immigrated to Alberta from Missouri in 1906. "We have grovelled and been ground into the dirt; we are determined that this shall not be. We will organize for our protection; we will nourish ourselves and gain strength, and then we shall strike out in our might and overthrow our enemies."

Wood found a natural ally in Irene Parlby, an Englishwoman who had fallen in love with the prairies: "Here was a land where the spirit of the wilderness still held sway; where so far as traditions were concerned, the page was clean, and where the only conventions were the roughly defined codes of chivalry towards women, and honour between man and man. I revelled in the sense of freedom, the quiet loveliness of the great empty spaces."

In 1921 and 1922, the farmers' parties won elections in Alberta and Manitoba, having already taken power in Ontario. Irene Parlby was elected to the Alberta legislature. "We must work for a higher standard of business and political morality," she wrote, "which last will never be achieved until we destroy, root and branch, the whole system of patronage which spreads its malignant tentacles through every fibre of our national life."

In 1921, the Conservatives called a federal election. The fact that Prime Minister Borden had resigned, replaced by his solicitor general, Arthur Meighen, was not enough to quell discontent. Agnes Macphail, an Ontario schoolteacher, declared her candidacy for a seat in the Commons under the banner of the Progressive Party. This new national party was sharply critical of the existing party system and proposed that MPs be allowed to vote on their own initiative, at the request of their electorate, even if it meant going against the political program of their party. "There is another battle to fight, a victory to claim," declared Macphail, "and then our country will be freed once and for all from the greedy hands of the profiteers." Farmers in Ontario and the west had not forgotten that the Conservatives had broken their promise not to send their sons to war. On September 6, Macphail became Canada's first female member of Parliament.

Quebecers had not forgotten the Conservatives' broken promises either; not a single Conservative was elected from Quebec. The Progressive Party, with the support of farmers in Ontario and the west, won sixty-five seats, enough to form the official Opposition. But their distrust of the Ottawa political game was such that they refused the role, and the privileges that came with it. The Liberals were in power once more under William Lyon Mackenzie King, but the Progressives had put an end to the dominance that the Liberals and Conservatives had enjoyed in Parliament for more than fifty years.

In the aftermath of the war and the conscription crisis, Quebec nationalism became more vigorous. Abbé Lionel Groulx, a priest born into a modest family, believed that French Canada's survival depended on faith, the family, and language. In the 1920s, he took part in many debates, published the

**IRENE PARLBY** ◆ Before Irene Parlby was elected to the Alberta legislature in 1921, she was president of the United Farm Women of Alberta. In her first report for the UFWA, Parlby demanded that the work of farm women be recognized: "The day has forever fled, when the woman can confine her interests within the four walls of her home. Our duties are ever pushing us out further into the great world. We cannot work there alone. We must have the whole hearted cooperation of the men, to bring about the sane and Christian civilization for which the world today is in travail." (*Glenbow Archives, NA-273-1*)

monthly *L'action française*, distanced himself from Henri Bourassa, flirted with separatism, and wrote: "We have to choose either to be masters of our own destiny or to resign ourselves forever to being a subjugated people."

Some consider Groulx to be the spiritual father of Quebec nationalism. But for others his nationalism is embarrassing, since it would have granted the Church a central political role and it seemed to extol a form of corporatism in which each social class would have its place in a society guided by the values of Catholicism. He left his mark on an entire generation of Quebec nationalists and changed the way French Canadians saw themselves, by giving them pride in their past. "A history three centuries long," he wrote in 1921, "the almost complete possession of the soil by a determined race, the deep imprint that this race left through its moral values and its original institutions, the special status which was acknowledged in each political constitution since 1774, made of Quebec a French State which must be recognized in theory and in fact."

Groulx was not alone in his views. Jean-Marie-Rodrigue Villeneuve, the future cardinal of Quebec, wrote in *L'action française* in July 1922, "It will be possible during this century for a Catholic and French State to take shape in the Saint Lawrence River valley: quite a few people feel that this is no longer a mere pipe dream but an ideal worthy of ambition, a hope firmly established." In 1921, Quebec premier Louis-Alexandre Taschereau declared that Quebec was at a crossroads: what awaited the province was either the status quo or the rupture of the federal state.

The United States loomed much larger in both the Canadian imagination and the national economy than it had before the war. Americans replaced the British as Canada's most important trading partners, and the country was drifting away from Britain politically. When Turkey threatened a British garrison in Chanak, a seaport on the Dardanelles, Britain asked for Canada's military help. Prime Minister Mackenzie King refused, arguing that Canadians did not want to take part in another war. Then, in 1926, Britain's Balfour Report officially described the dominions, including Canada, Australia, and the Irish Free State, as equal partners of Britain, henceforth to be known as "autonomous nations of an Imperial Commonwealth," rather than as subordinates. For the first time, Canadian ambassadors were named abroad: in Tokyo, Paris, and Washington. Vincent Massey became the first Canadian ambassador to the United States.

Along with a closer economic relationship, Canada was losing its citizens to the United States. The 1920s started with three difficult years of recession, caused by falling prices and demand following the galloping inflation of the war years. Even banks declared bankruptcy. In 1923, the Home Bank, with seventy-one branches (forty-seven of them in Ontario), closed its doors. Small depositors, especially farmers, would never recover their savings. War was no longer driving manufacturing, and factories closed. The Maritimes were especially hard hit. Unemployment reached record levels in Halifax and in the mines of Nova Scotia. In Glace Bay, Cape Breton, strikes and lockouts led to violent incidents like those in Winnipeg. Ottawa was forced to send half of all Canada's militiamen to the region.

Maritimers and Quebecers migrated to factories in New England. During the 1920s, nearly a million Canadians moved south. In 1925, the *Halifax Citizen* declared that there were more Nova Scotians in Massachusetts than in Nova Scotia. The population of both Nova Scotia and Prince Edward Island declined between 1921 and 1931. On the prairies, Winnipeg's outsized confidence had been shaken by the General Strike, and its geographic advantage had been compromised by the construction of the Panama Canal, which made it possible to ship goods cheaply to the west coast by sea; Vancouver was the new "Gateway to the West." Canadians from the prairies drifted to Chicago and Detroit.

Canada was becoming increasingly urbanized; for the first time, the majority of Canadians lived in cities. Thirty-two-year-old Florentine Maher left the small Quebec village of Warwick, following her husband, who had just been appointed a government dairy inspector in Montreal. "At last, my dreams of youth were being fulfilled," she wrote. "I was going to live in the city, where I could indulge my tastes: theatre, movies, reading, stores!"

People were lining up to see Charlie Chaplin in *The Gold Rush*, and to watch the frantic comedies of Harold Lloyd and Laurel and Hardy. Toronto-born Mary Pickford and her husband, Douglas Fairbanks, were Hollywood stars, and they tried to convince Stephen Leacock to write for the movies, but he was not tempted. "It is freely stated," he wrote, "that the moving pictures are four-fifths piffle and the other fifth poison; and that they are made up altogether of sex-stuff, sob-stuff, crime-stuff, and hysteria and vanity mixed up together."

But Florentine Maher did not care what Leacock thought. "I didn't miss an opportunity," she wrote. "I had been deprived for so long of these entertainments. . . . I often went to the Plaza Theatre, on Sunday afternoon. . . . I was young and I liked to laugh." It was the time of jazz, and smart girls who dared to smoke in public and wear pants. The divorce rate was six times what it had been before the war. Florentine had a newfound sense of freedom, and a new car. "Our second car was a McLaughlin-Buick," she wrote, and she and her husband drove to the country with friends on the weekends.

The automotive age had begun in earnest, changing the way Canadians lived, how and where they vacationed, and how Canada's cities developed. By the mid-1920s, the French planner and architect Le Corbusier was already sounding a warning: "No city of today has a *programme for dealing with traffic*." In Canada, the automobile's putative start had come with Confederation (a steam-driven car was built by a Quebec watchmaker in 1867) and there had been experiments with electric cars before the fledgling manufacturers turned to the unreliable salvation offered by the internal combustion engine. Forty-eight Canadian companies were manufacturing cars before the war, but by the 1920s, almost all had either gone bankrupt or been bought by larger concerns. The Russell Car Company, an offshoot of

**FLORENTINE MAHER**
◆ When Florentine Maher moved from a small town in rural Quebec to Montreal in 1922, she seized the new opportunities and diversions there were for women. She often went to the movies and the theatre, read the latest books, and was inspired by the fashion magazines she read: "So I learned how to sew, and I made my whole wardrobe. I also sewed wedding gowns, engagement dresses. I made outfits for my daughters out of my husband's clothes. I sewed like a real expert." *(Courtesy of Maher family)*

**SUNNYSIDE BOARDWALK, TORONTO, 1923** ◆ Canada's emergence from the post-war recession was accompanied by radically changing attitudes – and fashions. Women bobbed their hair, and the more daring cropped it short as a schoolboy's. Hemlines jumped to the knee, and arms were left uncovered. Garments were loose, without a waistline; many women stopped wearing tight underbodices and wore silky slips instead. The new styles took a bit of getting used to for Jane Walters of Welland, Ontario: "There was a time at that stage when they wore dresses absolutely straight and flat across here, and some of them used to bind their bosoms to get into these dresses! I had a singer's body and believe me, I had a big bosom, and I had the most awful time getting dresses, all the girls did. We just went through that stage of flat bosoms. It was a bad time. You can't buck nature and not get some bad results from it." (*City of Toronto Archives*)

Canada Cycle and Motor (CCM), had a promising start but was sold to Willys Overland in 1915. Sam McLaughlin, a carriage maker, had gone to Detroit in 1905, trying to get the licence to build Buicks in Canada. He eventually got the rights to the Buick engine and used it to power his own car, the McLaughlin, which was built in Oshawa. It was a twenty-two-horsepower, two-cylinder touring car that sold for $1,400. He later sold his company to Chevrolet, following a trend in the industry that would see a quick winnowing of companies. In 1923, there were 113 exhibitors at the automobile show in New York, including Saxon, King, Liberty, Lincoln, Columbia, Gray, Commerce, Dodge, and Ste. Claire. Within a decade, the field had been reduced to a few dominant giants, Ford and General Motors most prominent among them.

Detroit was the main conduit for bootlegged liquor coming from Canada. Michigan had gone dry in 1918, a year before the Volstead Act brought Prohibition to the United States, and the state had had a year to develop illegal networks. Because it had the auto industry, it also had a well-developed road system, providing effective transportation routes for enterprising criminals.

By 1920, Prohibition was already disappearing in Canada, which then became the main supplier to the United States. Most provinces allowed the manufacture of alcohol, provided it was for export. Between 22 and 45 million litres of alcohol entered the United States illegally each year. On the prairies, in the Maritimes, in Ontario, in Quebec, and on the west coast, smugglers made fortunes supplying alcohol to American gangs. A case of spirits that cost eighteen dollars in Ontario could be sold for nearly seven times that amount south of the border.

Bootleggers were endlessly inventive: bottles were stuffed into the carcasses of pigs; canned fruit tins were filled with gin; cars, trains, airplanes, and boats were converted so that they could be filled with cases of whisky. Corruption was rampant, and customs officers, Mounties, and government officials might turn a blind eye for a price. Bootleggers had little fear of the police, but they were on guard against competition. In the United States, Al Capone ruthlessly defended his empire, executing his enemies. Rocco Perri's gang in Toronto was responsible for an estimated seventeen murders. And it was not just criminals who joined the fray. A Methodist minister from Ontario, J. O. L. Spracklin, waged war against smugglers who fired shots at his presbytery. He organized raids on inns, picked fights with bootleggers, personally patrolled the Detroit River, and, in 1920, killed the owner of an inn (he was later acquitted).

Detroit needed workers for its assembly lines, to build factories and housing, and it drew its labour from the southern states, from the rural hinterland, from Europe, and from Canada. In 1921, 27,000 people were enrolled in "Americanization" classes, learning how to greet people with a firm handshake, to brush their teeth once a day, and to speak English. The U.S. government was concerned that the American way of life was being threatened by the foreign influx, and Congress appointed a nine-member commission to examine the effects of immigration. They produced a report which concluded that immigrants were "poisoning the pure air of our otherwise well-regulated cities; and if it were not for them there would be no congestion, no filth, and no poverty in the great industrial and commercial centers of America." Canadians, it noted, accounted for 6.9 per cent of the nation's juvenile delinquents (far behind the "insanity-prone" Irish, at 20.5 per cent). The Immigration Act was revised in 1924, and immigration quotas were greatly reduced.

While America was growing increasingly concerned about the effect of immigrants on its way of life, some Canadians were becoming nervous about American influence within their own borders. In 1923, the first American president to visit Canada, Warren G. Harding, declared in Vancouver's Stanley Park: "We think and live the same way, we cherish the same aspirations. Since the end of the war, Americans have invested $2.5-billion in Canada. It is a lot of money and I don't doubt it is being used wisely for us and in very useful ways for you."

Quebec's premier, Louis-Alexandre Taschereau, solicited American investment, hoping it would stem the tide of Quebecers moving south. "I am not afraid and I will never be afraid that our French Canadians will become Americanized because of an inflow of American capital," he said. "They have resisted other dangers and other trials, and as I have said many times, I prefer importing American dollars to exporting Canadian workmen." Taschereau offered land deals, and Quebec towns like Shawinigan and Arvida boomed as American capital flooded into the province.

Henri Bourassa was concerned about the corrupting influence of foreign money. "At this rate," he warned, "American capital will soon run Canada and Canadians. We could and should be alarmed. It's not surprising. It's the direct result of the folly of our wartime spending spree. We wanted to play the part of a grand nation: we've gone bankrupt to save 'civilization' and 'democracy.' We are now at the mercy of our neighbours. They've made money while we're facing financial ruin."

The relationship with the United States was not limited to investment and ownership. With the advent of new technologies, Canadians were also increasingly exposed to American culture. Movies and magazines brought American politics, music, and personalities into Canadian lives, and radio, which burgeoned in the 1920s, broadened that exposure. "The first time I heard a radio, I could have believed I was in a fairy tale," said Nathan Nathanson, who lived with his wife and children in Cape Breton. "The idea that something could move in the air without the help of any wire seemed incredible. I felt I was dreaming all that." Stephen Leacock offered another perspective: "I realized a new plague had spread across the world." But Nathanson understood what an extraordinary opportunity radio represented: "All the little radio sets had to be sold. And people had to be able to listen to something." He created his own radio station, CJCB; the J was for his wife, Jenny, and the CB for his native Cape Breton.

In 1923, Foster Hewitt described the first hockey game on radio, featuring teams from Toronto and Kitchener, and inaugurated his trademark catchphrase: "He shoots, he scores!" Canadians listened to American broadcasts but had mixed feelings about the influence of their neighbours. They admired their prosperity and popular culture, but they did not want to be Americans. They wanted a recognizable, distinct culture of their own, a national identity. Painter Arthur Lismer said, "Most creative people, whether in painting, writing or music, began to have a guilty feeling that Canada was yet unwritten, unpainted, unsung. . . . After the war was over, a lot of things began to happen to artists and people in Canada. Canada was growing up. The war, destructive of life, was yet the turning point in the development of Canada as an entity. Canadians began to realize that they knew little about themselves."

In 1920, Lismer had joined with fellow painters Frederick Varley, A. Y. Jackson, James Macdonald, Lawren Harris, Frank Carmichael, and Franz Johnston to form the Group of Seven. "We are no longer humble colonials," A. Y. Jackson said. "We've made armies, we can also make artists, historians and poets." The group had produced the most striking art of the First World War, and in the 1920s, they were intent on re-imagining the Canadian landscape.

Emily Murphy was the author of the popular "Janey Canuck" books, which celebrated the west ("It is a great place this Canadian West – the country of strong men, strong women, straight living and hard riding. . . . Who wants to go to heaven?"). "Canada is not statistics," she declared. "Canada is not a map, not a government. A great nation cannot be made, cannot be discovered and then coldly laid together like the pieces in a picture puzzle."

Emily Murphy was also the first woman in the British empire to be appointed a judge. On her first day in court, she was told by lawyer Eardly Jackson that the judgment she was about to pass would not count, since under the law she was not considered a person. The British North America Act of 1867 did not take a stand on the status of women as persons, and this, according to some, excluded them from this legal category. Murphy fought this interpretation and launched a struggle in which she was supported by four other women: Nellie McClung, Louise McKinney (one of the first women elected as a member of a provincial legislature), Irene Parlby, and Henrietta Edwards. In 1928, the Supreme Court of Canada ruled that women were indeed not persons. Murphy appealed the ruling all the way to Canada's ultimate legal authority: the British Privy Council in London. Nellie McClung noted that "On the morning of October 18th, 1929, newspapers all over the British Empire carried the black headlines: Privy Council Declares That Women Are Persons! It came as a surprise to many women in Canada at least who had not known that they were not persons until they heard it stated that they were."

Six days later, the stock market crashed in the United States, ending the brief euphoria of the 1920s and ushering in the Depression.

# HARD TIMES

"I landed in Canada, a refugee from unemployment and want in England with the youthful naive idea of finding work and prosperity in the new country," wrote Ronald Liversedge in his published memoir. "It soon became apparent that there were no jobs and for a couple of days I hung around the CPR depot, dozing on benches."

By the time he came to Canada at the age of twenty-nine, Liversedge had already seen more of the world than he would have liked. In 1916, he had enlisted in the British army and fought at the Somme. He survived that slaughter but was wounded in a later battle. After the war, Liversedge went to Australia for five years where he worked as an itinerant labourer, returning to London in time for the 1926 general strike, which saw four million men walk off the job, first halting coal mining, then transportation and newspapers as others joined the strike.

Liversedge left the bleak, lingering post-war malaise of Britain for the expansive promise of Canada, but instead he found the Great Depression beginning to take shape. From Halifax, he took a train to Winnipeg, but he could not find work there. In Saskatchewan, he found a farm job for the summer, and afterwards he rode the rails west to Calgary. "I learned of the life of the transient unemployed," he wrote. "I learned of freight riding, of

Riding the rails during the Great Depression. "Men have been swindled by other men on many occasions. The autumn of 1929 was, perhaps, the first occasion when men succeeded on a large scale in swindling themselves." – John Kenneth Galbraith, *The Great Crash*, 1929. (*National Archives of Canada*, RD-1001)

life in the jungles, cooking mulligan stew with a chunk of bummed meat, and stolen potatoes, of being hounded by police from town to town. The freight trains, the long, cold, hungry rides on box cars, oil tankers, lumber cars, any place that was available. We were not professional hoboes, but unemployed men, many recent immigrants, the beginning of a mighty army."

In 1930, it was still a modest army that moved across the country, looking for nonexistent work and increasingly scarce food and shelter. In Sudbury, Ontario, Liversedge and other recent arrivals were confronted by the harsh surprise of the Canadian winter, and by the crowded conditions in the local jail when they were picked up for vagrancy. After serving thirty days, they sought refuge in the city's only soup kitchen: "In this dimly lit small basement were tables around which the men stood to eat. Each man coming down from the kitchen had to wait on the stairs with his rapidly cooling plate of beans [to] stand at this veritable feast of the passover.

"The atmosphere was like that in a chilly mouldy crypt. The tables were covered with ice and beans and pieces of wet bread. The meals were always the same. The exception was the shooting of a bear by a Sudbury businessman who gave the bear to the city who then sent it to the soup kitchen with the result that a few hundred men suffered violent diarrhea."

Liversedge's bad luck would continue for the next decade; his only talent, apparently, was for finding himself at the centre of each new crisis that the 1930s offered.

The prime minister at this time was William Lyon Mackenzie King, a Liberal, grandson of William Lyon Mackenzie, the "firebrand" of the 1837 Upper Canada rebellion. For eight years King had overseen Canada's growing prosperity and increasing role in global trade. The country now supplied half the world's wheat and more than 60 per cent of its newsprint

A Montreal soup kitchen in 1931. (*National Archives of Canada*, PA-168131)

and benefited from healthy exports of minerals and manufactured goods. The federal government had only one economist, and he worked for the Department of Foreign Affairs; the economy was supposed to take care of itself. But there was no question that unemployment was on the rise, and the prime minister was clear on one point: Canada was in no need of jobless immigrants. King's government issued an order-in-council in 1930 that restricted newcomers to farmers, residents' wives, Americans, and Britons.

King was dull, reliable, and largely friendless. His most profound attachments were to his deceased mother and his dog Pat, an Irish terrier. He was a closet spiritualist who sometimes contacted his mother through a medium, and sought her advice.

It was a medium who told King that 1930 would be a good year to call an election. The American stock market had crashed the previous year, bringing Canadian stocks down with it, and European markets were failing. Global trade had collapsed, and there was less demand for Canada's resources. The result was a rash of bankruptcies and another wave of unemployment. In an effort to shore up local industry, many governments instituted protectionist policies, which only exacerbated the problem. A cycle of diminishing demand was being played out among western democracies. King, however, was unfazed by the global chaos.

The prime minister's political opponent was Conservative leader Richard Bedford Bennett, a former lawyer for the Canadian Pacific Railway and wealthy Calgary businessman who proposed to apply his hard-headed business skills to the task of dealing with the Depression. "The Conservative Party is going to find work for all who are willing to work, or perish in the attempt," he told an audience in Moncton, New Brunswick, while on the campaign trail. "Mr. King promises consideration of the problem of employment. I promise to end unemployment. Which plan do you like best?"

The voters preferred Bennett's forceful promise, and the Conservatives won a commanding majority. But King took the defeat in stride. He could see that hard times were coming, and he doubted there was much that any politician could do about it. "Bennett for a while," he wrote in his diary on July 29, 1930. "Then a Liberal party with a long lease of power later on." It was a prophecy that would prove accurate.

On the prairies, the five years leading up to 1930 had been a time of renewed immigration, expansion, and optimism. In that farm culture, wheat was nearly deified. "I first became aware of wheat when I was in elementary school," wrote Anne Bailey, a farmer's wife who kept a diary. "Our teacher, a farmer's daughter, drew a very large kernel of wheat on the blackboard and beside it another kernel showing the different parts of its make-up. We learned it from memory. . . . I loved every minute of harvest time, especially when I was allowed to haul the wheat to the elevator. It was worth working and waiting for all summer. And the order to Eaton's for winter clothes – the most exciting of all."

**WILLIAM LYON MACKENZIE KING** ◆ King initially failed to recognize the scale and consequences of the Depression, an attitude that was revealed in a House of Commons debate on April 3, 1930, when he gave what would be known as the "five-cent piece" speech.

"With respect to giving monies out of the federal treasury to any Tory government in this country for these alleged unemployment purposes, with these governments situated as they are today, with politics diametrically opposed to those of this government, I would not give them a five-cent piece." (*National Archives of Canada*, C-55540)

Top: Dust Storm, Fort Macleod, Alberta. (*Glenbow Archives*, NA-2928-26). Bottom left: The prairie becomes a desert in 1937, near Elva, Manitoba. (*Provincial Archives of Manitoba, N-18333*). Bottom right: Farm equipment abandoned in a drift of dust. (*Glenbow Archives, NA-2291-2*)

By the end of the 1920s, when Bailey was working her own farm, there was a glut on the world wheat markets that led to reduced demand. The price of wheat went from a dollar a bushel to thirty-four cents. In 1930, most of the crop was destroyed by drought, and the next year was no better.

"My son came running into the house greatly excited," Bailey wrote. "'Come quick, Mom,' he shouted, 'there's a big black cloud coming in the sky.' He ran out ahead of me and pointed to the western sky where sure enough there was the blackest most terrifying cloud I have ever seen on the horizon. It was moving very quickly and the edge of it was rolling along." Rain would have provided much needed relief for the parched fields. But it was not a rain cloud, it was the dried topsoil of a hundred farms lifted into the air. "Panic rose in me. What should I do? Where should we go? The house was sure to be blown away and our nearest neighbour was a mile away. At the rate the cloud was moving I could never make it as I would have to carry the baby. I shut the door tight, picked up the baby and yelling at the other two to follow, I ran for the dug out barn. Already the shadow of the cloud was upon us.

"When it was light enough for me to see the forms of my cattle I knew it was safe to open the door, so once again I looked outside. A cloaking silence enveloped the whole outdoors, yet dust hung in the air so thick it was clearly visible. Everything – land, air, sky – was a dull grey colour. With the baby in my arms and the boys close behind me I went to the house. Our feet sank in sand almost to our ankles and we breathed and tasted sand."

The cities of the prairies followed the fortunes of the farmers. Winnipeg had grown at a precipitous rate during the 1920s but it now went into a swift decline. In 1929, $11.1 million worth of building permits had been issued in Winnipeg. Five years later, that figure fell to $700,000. As the prairies dried up and emptied, farmers came to the cities to find work and were disappointed. Prime Minister Bennett introduced a federal relief program that offered $20 million for the unemployed and indigent, and the municipalities made their own policies to administer the funds. In 1928, 500 people registered for Winnipeg's emergency relief fund; six years later, 44,000 people were on relief.

Among them was James Gray. In 1926, after working as an accountant and saving his money, Gray had bought a mini-golf course, offering diversion to Winnipeg's new leisure class. But when the Depression hit, his new enterprise suffered. "I was not yet twenty-five," he wrote in a memoir, "but I could look back on ten years of psychopathic concentration on getting ahead in life. Then my number came up and I was confronted with the ego-shattering discovery that there wasn't a single employer in all Winnipeg who would give me a job. It was my own fault. I couldn't feed my family."

The relief vouchers he received provided just enough for himself, his wife, and their daughter. "We received no cash," he wrote. "Vouchers covered food, fuel and rent." But there was no money for anything other than bare subsistence, and the work he did in exchange for the vouchers was of little practical use. "The closest any of us on relief ever got to socially useful labour was sawing cordwood, but we were drafted periodically for all the makework projects, like raking leaves, picking rocks, digging dandelions, and tidying up back lanes. . . . It was all justified on the grounds that exercise would be good for us, that working would improve our morale, and that, by providing us with a token opportunity to work for our relief, we would be freed of the stigma of accepting charity. None of these propositions had much validity." Gray was 180 centimetres tall (five-foot-eleven) and his weight dwindled to fifty-four kilograms (118 pounds). The doctor assigned to treat relief recipients gave him the bad news: he had contracted tuberculosis. Gray went to a sanatorium to recover and spent his time reading and writing.

After he was cured, he found work as a reporter for the *Winnipeg Free Press* at twenty dollars a week. He drove across the prairies, reporting on conditions in what would be known as the Dust Bowl. "The cloud of dust that trailed after us began to seep into the car," he wrote. "Our clothes stuck to us, and the seat of the car was damp with sweat. I could feel blisters developing on my feet from the concentrated heat of the floorboards. From Lethbridge to Winnipeg, temperatures rose to the 100 degree mark [37 degrees Celsius] and stayed there for days on end. Each day seemed hotter than the day before. The hot winds grew stronger and the dust clouds that hung over the whole of the mid-continent grew thicker and thicker. By the second week in July the crop was gone."

Saskatchewan was hardest hit: the fields were dead, the crops burned. Hundreds of millions of tonnes of topsoil were blown away, black clouds that moved across the prairies and continued east, leaving a residue on the ledges of skyscrapers in New York City. In their wake, like a biblical plague, grasshoppers came in their millions, eating whatever was left: crops, gardens, even clothes left on the line to dry – an unexpected cloud that passed with a mechanical hum. "Anybody who lived in Regina that summer and could not get over being squeamish about walking on wall-to-wall grasshoppers stayed indoors," Gray wrote. "Clouds of the insects obscured the sun." In Weyburn, Saskatchewan, Gray stopped at a gas station. "We made a deal with the son of a garageman to clean the grasshoppers off our car for a dollar. It took him almost two hours and a gallon of coal-oil." There were small gestures of relief from other parts of the country: Maritimers sent salt cod, and Torontonians sent money.

To lead them out of the desert, some Saskatchewan farmers looked to the Co-operative Commonwealth Federation. The CCF was born in a Calgary legion hall on July 31, 1933, and later that year hundreds of farmers, labourers, preachers, trade unionists, socialists, and academics came to Regina to hammer out the goals and structure of a political movement that would incorporate socialism and a splash of Christian theology. A crusading Baptist minister named Tommy Douglas, history teacher Frank Underhill, J. S. Woodsworth, and Montreal lawyer and poet Frank Scott were all there. For the new party's platform the convention agreed on socialized banking, a form of national health care, a minimum wage, and farm security. It was a radical departure from free-market economics, and this policy became known as the "Regina Manifesto."

Some of the central ideas had been debated in Frank Scott's Montreal home. Scott was optimistic about the party's future, though nervous about some of the people it had attracted. "There are dangerous movements in the CCF," he wrote in a letter. "B.C. has some queer people. Then members of the Communist party are known to be in the CCF – two or three were delegates here – and are taking their orders from the party to which they really give their allegiance. The result is a good deal of suspicion all around. Just the same, the convention showed a general unity that was quite encouraging.

**THE CO-OPERATIVE COMMONWEALTH FEDERATION (CCF) CAUCUS IN 1935** ◆ In 1934, the CCF, which proposed a socialized economy, published four major planks in its political platform:

"1) *Finance*: – The CCF is against the private monopoly and control of financial institutions. A CCF government will release the community from this control by the socialization of all our banking and financial machinery including the Central Bank.

"2) *Agriculture*: – The CCF through co-operation with the provinces or by amendment to the B.N.A. Act if necessary will protect the farmer from foreclosure or eviction under pressure of mortgage companies and other creditors and from exploitation by packers, millers, dairy corporations and others ...

"3) *Labour and Social Services*: – The CCF will bring to an end the system which makes poverty and insecurity the prevailing condition of the workers in this land of plenty, and as a preliminary to this will initiate an immediate large scale program of socially useful public works.

"4) *Peace*: – We recognize that modern war arises primarily from the clash of interests in a world economy based on competition; therefore the establishment of permanent world peace depends on abolishing competition and on building the Co-operative Commonwealth."

*(Left to Right: Tommy Douglas, Angus MacInnes, A. A. Heaps, J. S. Woodsworth, M. J. Coldwell, Grace McInnis [caucus secretary], Grant MacNeil – the first CCF members elected to Parliament. Yousuf Karsh, National Archives of Canada, PA-181423)*

. . . I shall not forget the denunciations of capitalism hour after hour and the raging thunderous applause afterwards."

The leader of the new party was J. S. Woodsworth, member of Parliament for Winnipeg North Centre and a former Methodist minister. Woodsworth declared that unemployment was not the fault of the individual, it was a function of the system. He explained the Depression in a way that lifted the burden from the jobless and placed it on the government. Woodsworth held dear the notion of a prairie paradise, of the rural landscape as a place where people could live in harmony with nature and with God. Though this utopian idea had been largely defeated by the Dust Bowl, Woodsworth believed that the CCF would embody the biblical concept of the brotherhood of man; their shared vision would lead to a New Jerusalem.

In Ottawa, R. B. Bennett could not find a way out of the Depression, but he found a scapegoat in Communism, the spectre that had haunted democracies since the Russian Revolution in 1917. "We know that throughout Canada this propaganda is being put forward by organizations from foreign lands that seek to destroy our institutions," he said. "And we ask that every man and woman put the iron heel of ruthlessness against a thing of that kind."

While Bennett denounced Communism, he himself was cited as the chief cause of its rise in Canada. "Red is a state of mind," said Bill Knight, the mayor of Blairmore, Alberta. "Back in 1929 there were no Reds. Things were prosperous, everyone was well-fed. It is different today. You talk about Communists, the Communists in Canada were made by Bennett." In 1933 Blairmore's town council elected a slate composed entirely of members of the Workers Unity League – a group founded by the Communist Party of Canada – and it declared itself a Communist town.

The *Times* of London reported that Moscow had sent operatives to Canada to organize mine workers, and Communists were making themselves known at some demonstrations. Winnipeg had a Communist sitting as a municipal alderman. In Ottawa, there was genuine fear about the spread of Bolshevik ideas.

Bennett's military chief, General Andrew McNaughton, warned cabinet that the unemployed could launch a Communist revolt. "In their ragged platoons," he said, "here are the prospective members of what Marx called the 'industrial reserve army, the storm troopers of the revolution.'" McNaughton suggested that young, unemployed men be sent to nationwide rural labour camps, known as Unemployment Relief Camps, where they could neither vote nor organize. There they were given clothes, meals, and medical care and were paid twenty cents a day, one-tenth of what an employed labourer would make doing the same work. The camps were voluntary, but those who resisted going could be arrested for vagrancy. Ronald Liversedge ended up in a logging camp north of Nanaimo, British Columbia. "In those bunkhouses," he wrote, "there were more men reading Marx, Lenin and Stalin than there were reading girlie magazines." Bennett had unwittingly provided basic training camps for the army of unemployed, and within months, they would become militant.

Bennett also decided to enforce Section 98 of the Criminal Code, which outlawed Communist association and required the accused to prove his innocence. This law was used to arrest Tim Buck, leader of the Communist Party of Canada, and eight other Communists in 1931. One of the men was released for lack of evidence, but the other eight were convicted of "being members of an unlawful association" and "being party to a seditious

**RICHARD BEDFORD BENNETT** ◆ During Bennett's term as prime minister (1930–35), his policies failed to stem the nation's misery, but he tried to effect change on a more personal level. Most evenings he spent alone at the typewriter in his seventeen-room Château Laurier suite, answering the letters that came to him by the thousands. It was said, unkindly, that Bennett's most intimate friend was himself, and during his last years in office this became increasingly true. (*National Archives of Canada*, PA-148530)

Kingdom, Saskatchewan                 *Sept 28, 1933*

Dear Prime Minister RB Bennett
It is with a very humble heart that I take the opportunity of writing this letter to ask you if you will please send for the underwear in the Eaton catalogue. My husband will be 64 in December and he has nuritis very bad at times in his arms and shoulders. We have had very little crop for the last three years. Not enough at all to pay taxes and live and this year crops around here west of Saskatoon are a complete failure. My husband is drawing wood on the wagon for 34 miles and had to draw hay too, for feed for horses, this winter. He has to take two days for a trip and sleep under the wagon sometimes. I have patched and darned his old underwear for the last two years, but they are completely done now. If you can't do this I really don't know what I'll do.
                                    Mrs. Thomas Perkins


Kingdom                               *Nov 15, 1933*

Prime Minister RB Bennett
Dear Sir received your kind favour of underware for my husband. We wish to thank you very much for it. We sure are thankful for your kindness.
                                    Mr and Mrs. Thomas Perkins.


Passman, Saskatchewan                 *Oct. 16, 1933*

Dear Sir,
I am a girl thirteen years old and I have got to go to school everyday its very cold now already and I haven't got a coat.
                                    My name is Edwina Abbott.

Premier Bennett, Parliament Building
Ottawa, Ontario, Canada

We you know have nothing up here dryed out & eat out with grasshoppers nothing to eat outside or in horses no oats for years asking help my children has not enough to eat. Please try and do some thing. farmer suffering so much in every way come & see for yourself you can't believe till you see, try & come
                                    Mrs. G T McTavish


Murray Harbour, PEI

Dear Sir,
I am writing to see if their is any help I could get. As I have a baby thirteen days old that weighs one pound and I have to keep in cotton Wool & Olive Oil, and I haven't the money to buy it, the people bought it so far and fed me when I was in bed. if their is any help I could get I would like to get it as soon as possible their is five of a family, Counting the baby. their will be two votes for you next election Hoping to hear from you soon.
                                    Yours Truly,
                                    Mrs. Jack O'Hannen


Port Cobourg, Ontario,                *May 9, 1934*

Dear Mr Benet I can spel very good to right I think my women is coming to see me this summer from Detroit Mish. I didn't see her for 4 years and I have no close have you some old close you could sent me and I cout meat my wife and I will do a good tarn for you yours truly
                                    Mickey Ratelle
Write soon

Tim Buck, speaking to a crowd at Blairmore, Alberta, in 1932. (*Glenbow Archives*, NC-54-2042)

conspiracy." A play titled *Eight Men Out*, which unentertainingly catalogued the injustices to Buck and his colleagues, was performed nightly at a Toronto theatre until police interrupted a show and shut it down.

Buck was convicted and sent to Kingston penitentiary, where he claimed that he was shot at by prison officials while in his cell. He was subsequently released after serving half of his five-year sentence and welcomed at a rally in Toronto that drew seventeen thousand people. Bennett had helped fashion a martyr for the disenfranchised. J. S. Woodsworth introduced a bill into the House of Commons asking that Section 98 be repealed, in that it curtailed essential freedoms, but it was voted down. Nevertheless, Bennett could see that it was an unpopular piece of legislation, and he avoided using it again.

The prime minister tried other means to deal with the growing social unrest. Believing that immigrants, particularly those from eastern Europe, had brought alien and dangerous ideas with them, Bennett's government expelled ten thousand people from the country without a trial: "We will take action as will free this country from those who have proven themselves unworthy of Canadian citizenship."

While Bennett might have inadvertently strengthened the forces of Communism with his actions, he also roused an anti-Communist, anti-foreigner sentiment in other Canadians. This new xenophobia gave added support to those who were already moving toward the fascist, racist policies that were gaining ground in Japan, Italy, and Germany. "Jews are like cockroaches and bugs," wrote Adrien Arcand, leader of Canada's National Social Christian Party. "Don't be fooled. There are many around. It is too bad we cannot exterminate them with insecticides, but we can count on the good sense of our countrymen. The Jew is everywhere."

In 1933, this anti-Semitic prejudice erupted in violence at a baseball game between a Jewish team and a non-Jewish community team at a ballpark in Toronto's Christie Pits, a former sand quarry. Ten thousand people had come out to see the teams play, among them members of the Balmy Beach Swastika Club, an anti-Semitic group from across town. One of their members waved a swastika and repeatedly yelled "Heil Hitler!" A fight broke out, starting with fists and escalating to bats and truncheons. Police failed to arrive at the scene, though they had been warned of impending violence. Instead, they were busy monitoring a meeting of a dozen Communists. The fight at Christie Pits went on for six hours, ending finally at 2:00 a.m. In Winnipeg, six thousand people showed up at a Nazi picnic to eat sandwiches, play touch football, and praise Hitler. As the Depression persisted, the country's political mosaic became more complex and antagonistic.

After four years of economic crisis, Bennett decided to radically remodel both his policies and his image. With no money for fuel, it was common for people to take the engines out of their Chevrolets and Ford Phaetons and hitch the chassis to a team of horses; these hybrid vehicles were derisively called "Bennett Buggies." To revamp his policies, Bennett borrowed ideas from American president Franklin Roosevelt, who had introduced his New Deal to combat the Depression. Roosevelt spoke regularly on the radio, telling Americans in his "Fireside chats" that things were looking up, that God was on their side. Bennett had no gift for broadcasting – his delivery was rapid and unsure – but he went on the radio and outlined his own New Deal, a repudiation of the laissez-faire principles he had lived by. It would involve progressive taxation, unemployment insurance, health insurance, government regulation, and social reforms. "In the last five years great changes have taken place in the world," he told his listeners. "The old order is gone. We are living in conditions that are new and strange to us. Canada on the dole is like a young and vigorous man in the poorhouse. . . . If you believe that things should be left as they are, you and I hold contrary and irreconcilable views. I am for reform. And in my mind, reform means government intervention. It means government control and regulation. It means the end of laissez-faire."

In the United States, Roosevelt's innovations came under the scrutiny of the conservative Supreme Court, which ruled that some of the individual acts were unconstitutional. But the president was re-elected with an unprecedented majority, and the Supreme Court then allowed most of his new plans to be put into effect. Most of Bennett's proposals were also ruled *ultra vires* by Canadian courts, but he did not have Roosevelt's popularity to buoy him. His reforms were stillborn.

Mackenzie King had predicted that Bennett's new programs would be overturned by the courts. King was biding his time, waiting for an opportunity to return his Liberals to power. While out of office, he explored in depth the spiritualism he had flirted with during the 1920s. In 1932, he attended a seance conducted by Mrs. Etta Wriedt, a medium from Detroit: "There can be no doubt whatever that the persons I have been talking with were the loved ones & others I have known and who have passed away. It was the

**THE NEW DEAL** ◆ "I pledge you, I pledge myself, to a new deal for the American people," Franklin Delano Roosevelt said in accepting the Democratic nomination for the presidency in 1932. His New Deal involved the creation of dozens of agencies to help counter the effects of the Great Depression. The Civilian Conservation Corps provided work for three million men in reclamation projects in national parks and forests. The Public Works Administration employed men to clear slums and build highways, public buildings, and airports. Under the Agricultural Adjustment Administration, farmers were paid to curtail their yields. The Federal Theater Project supplied money for plays, and the Federal Writers' Project paid for books, among them James Agee's *Let Us Now Praise Famous Men*, in which he wrote about southern sharecroppers. Here, Roosevelt is cheered by workers at a PWA project in 1933. (*Library of Congress, US262.096633.205839*)

spirits of the departed . . . it is hard to believe. It is like those who had Christ with them in His Day." In 1933, he progressed to "table rapping," where he and others sat with their hands on a table and unseen spirits rapped out answers on it, spelling their replies, using one rap for A, two for B, and so on. He also experimented with numerology and reading tea leaves. King was an insecure man, and his beliefs in the spirit world comforted him. The messages he received bolstered his confidence ("You were predestined to be Prime Minister. . . . The fate of Canada is in your hands"). The spirits rarely instructed him; more often they simply confirmed his own views. But he spent a lot of time communicating with departed relatives and the famous dead. In 1934, he returned from Europe having made friends with Leonardo da Vinci, a member of the de Medici family, Louis Pasteur, and Philip the Apostle. He was ready to challenge Bennett for his old job.

**WILLIAM ABERHART** ◆ Aberhart's view of his differences with Mackenzie King was encapsulated in a 1937 letter to the prime minister:

"The fact is your advisors are chiefly bankers and lawyers who, unfortunately too often, think that THE PEOPLE are made for the systems and not the systems for THE PEOPLE."

Aberhart was premier of Alberta for seven years. He died in office in 1943 at the age of sixty-four. (*National Archives of Canada, C-9447*)

In Alberta, those looking to their politicians for salvation could turn to William "Bible Bill" Aberhart, an earnest-looking Baptist preacher and high school principal. He stepped in to fill the political void left when the ruling party, the United Farmers of Alberta, was brought down by a sex scandal. Vivian MacMillan, a twenty-two-year-old government stenographer and organist with the Baptist church, had brought a lawsuit against Premier John Brownlee alleging seduction. She claimed that the premier had first forced himself on her in October 1930, and they had been having unwelcome sex for three years. The trial, which involved political intrigue (the claim that the whole thing was a Liberal plot), romance (Vivian MacMillan was engaged to a handsome young medical student, John Caldwell), and the extremely rare opportunity to hear detailed descriptions of sex, kept the entire province rapt. The jury sided with MacMillan, but its verdict was overturned by Chief Justice William "Cowboy Billy" Ives, who perhaps subscribed to the Liberal conspiracy theory. Ives's decision was itself overturned on appeal, and Brownlee resigned in disgrace.

Aberhart, with his Old Testament rectitude, was the perfect candidate to replace him. He was one of the first preachers to use radio, and his

Sunday afternoon broadcasts were a beacon for Albertans in the first grim years of the Depression. In 1931, Edmonton had 14,573 people on relief, out of a population of 79,197. Aberhart preached to this flock, suffering in the wilderness. "He had a voice that made the pilot lights on your radio jump," one listener said. "You simply had to believe him. Sometimes when I heard him, I used to say to my wife: 'This man seems to be in direct contact with the Supreme Being.'"

In 1932, Aberhart read a book by a British engineer named Major C. H. Douglas, who introduced an obscure economic theory he called "social credit." It entailed the government distributing money to bolster purchasing power and drive production, stimulating the economy. Aberhart incorporated Douglas's fiscal ideas into his message of deliverance, and a political party was born. At a Social Credit picnic Aberhart spoke to the thousands who sat on the hills eating hot dogs. "Do not the common people need leaders and shepherds today the same as in the days when Christ had compassion on them and fed the five thousand with five loaves and two small fishes?" he asked rhetorically. "There is salvation. God will work a miracle to bring people into the place of joy and prosperity. Is that not a message for believers in Social Credit?"

Aberhart's Prophetic Bible Institute in Calgary became the headquarters for a new economic gospel that was illuminated by the light of faith and obscured by esoteric catchphrases ("monetization of natural resources," "fountain-pen money"). "You remain in the Depression because of a shortage of purchasing power imposed by the banking system," Aberhart told his followers. "Social Credit offers you the remedy. If you have not suffered enough, it is your God-given right to suffer more. But if you wish to elect your own representatives to implement the remedy, this is your only way out."

Aberhart promised twenty-five dollars a month to each family as a way to jump-start the economy. The United Farmers of Alberta had been crippled by the Brownlee scandal, and in the 1935 election Aberhart won a landslide victory: of the province's sixty-three members of the legislative assembly, fifty-six were Social Credit, none with any legislative experience. Within days, the army of jobless men that Ronald Liversedge had described began arriving from other provinces, pouring out of boxcars, looking for their twenty-five dollars. At the same time, Aberhart was confronted with his first bitter taste of political reality: there was not enough money in the treasury to meet that month's government payroll, let alone pay 400,000 people twenty-five dollars each.

His solution was to have Alberta print its own money, a move that was denounced in the press as dictatorial. "The spirit of Christ has gripped me," Aberhart responded. "I am only seeking to feed, clothe and shelter starving people. If that is what you call a dictator then I am one." His scheme did not work. Provincial employees were paid with "prosperity certificates," but even the beer stores, which were owned by the province, would not accept them. The Supreme Court declared that the certificates were not legal

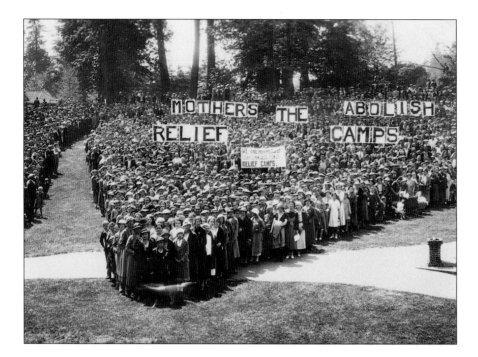

The Mothers' Picnic in Stanley
Park, Vancouver, 1935. (*Glenbow
Archives, NA-3634-10*)

tender, and most were redeemed for cash by the government; the rest were
kept as souvenirs.

Bennett's troubled tenure was facing another challenge as the relief camps he
had created started to mobilize. In the early spring of 1935, four thousand
men from B.C. camps went on strike and congregated in Vancouver, declaring that they would occupy the city until the government found work
for them. The strike organizers were looking for public sympathy and instructed the men not to drink, smoke, or carouse. After a few days they ran
out of money and tried to raise funds from Vancouver's citizens, a test of
local sympathy. "It was a happy day, like a gala occasion," reported Ronald
Liversedge, who was among the strikers. "Vancouver responded to the
rattle of nickels and dimes. Vancouver was with us to the tune of four
thousand six hundred dollars."

A few weeks later, Vancouver women held a picnic to raise more
money, making sandwiches and carrying signs that declared these men to be
their sons. Police estimated that twenty thousand people attended. "The
Tory government of R. B. Bennett had decided a role for the single unemployed," Liversedge noted. "They were to be hidden away to become
forgotten men, the forgotten generation. How naive of Mr. Bennett. Never
were forgotten men more in the public eye."

Over time, the goodwill they had built up began to flag. Their marches
interrupted traffic, and in May there was a fight between marchers and
police in front of the Hudson's Bay store on Granville Street, after which the
store was vandalized and looted. The strikers had been occupying the city
for six weeks, and Vancouver mayor Gerry McGeer wrote to Bennett: "Situation in Vancouver extremely critical. We have done everything possible

A decapitated mannequin lies on the sidewalk after the May 1935 riot in Vancouver. (*National Archives of Canada*, C-13231)

and we have no resources left and can only look to you for help." But Bennett did not want any part of this strike. "It is obviously the duty of that municipality to seek any assistance required from their provincial authorities," he replied, "because as you are well aware a municipality is a creation of the province."

The strike leaders knew that their welcome was wearing thin. They decided that their next move would be to send a thousand men to Ottawa by train to demand work from the federal government. This contingent left on June 3, with the ubiquitous Ronald Liversedge on board. "The train crews were co-operating with us in every possible way," he wrote, "and there was no attempt made to stop our march to the east. It seemed as though local and provincial authorities were leaving it to the federal government. And in the meantime we were quite a formidable force and beginning to snowball. Even the press was sympathetic."

A new spirit of militancy was taking hold. Arriving in Calgary, the hungry strikers met with the mayor and demanded that they be given relief support for three days. The mayor and other government officials were pinned in the city hall by the crowd of desperate men. "We told him we wouldn't let him out," Liversedge wrote. "That we were prepared to wait as long as he was prepared to go hungry. And we reminded him that we could outlast him since we'd been hungry a lot more often than he had." They received three days' worth of meal vouchers and were joined by hundreds of Albertan men. The group, now numbering almost two thousand, listened to the Knights of Harlem band at the Bow River Park, slept outside, and made further plans for what was now being called the "On to Ottawa Trek." They left town the next morning, watching the parched, empty prairie roll by from the tops of CPR boxcars.

The On to Ottawa Trek,
in Kamloops, June 1935.
(*National Archives of Canada,*
*C-29399*)

More men joined the trek in Saskatchewan; there were now three thousand in Regina, with more waiting in Winnipeg to join up. This intimidating show of strength caught Bennett's attention, and he agreed to meet with an appointed delegation, including Arthur "Slim" Evans and J. Cosgrove, who went ahead to Ottawa. The men demanded work. Bennett lectured them on Communism and said they were looking not for work but for revolution. Evans said that Bennett was not fit to be the prime minister of a Hottentot village. Bennett reminded Evans of his criminal record (for misappropriating union funds) and warned that lawlessness, on whatever scale, for whatever reason, would not be tolerated. "The police have moved west," he warned. "They have moved east; they will move in increasing numbers wherever it is necessary to maintain law. Take that down. Tell Mr. Cosgrove to take it down, Mr. Evans. Take that down." The meeting ended badly, and Bennett's promise of police action was fulfilled almost immediately.

Most of the strikers remained in Regina, and several hundred of them were meeting in Market Square on July 1 to discuss strategy when they were suddenly interrupted. "A shrill whistle blasted out a signal," Liversedge wrote, "the backs of vans were opened and out poured the Mounties, each armed with a baseball bat. In less than four minutes Market Square was a mass of writhing, groaning forms, like a battlefield. As we retreated I saw one woman standing over an upturned baby carriage, which had been trampled by these young Mounties. I saw four Mounties pulling at the arms and legs of one of our men, whom they had on the ground, while a fifth continued to beat viciously at the man's head."

The strikers erected barricades and threw stones, and the Mounties retaliated with their .38 revolvers. When it was over, one policeman was dead, 40 strikers and 5 citizens were wounded, and 130 men had been arrested. The city was a ruin, the sidewalks covered in broken glass. The On to Ottawa Trek was over. The men dispersed, and many slowly returned to

Mitchell Hepburn, Ontario premier, 1934–42. (*National Archives of Canada, c-19524*)

the relief camps. Bennett had won, but his reputation suffered. The leader of Canada's Nazi Party sent him a letter, congratulating him on the effective manner in which he had handled the riot.

Mackenzie King campaigned with the slogan "King or Chaos," and on October 14, 1935, the country voted against chaos, returning King's Liberals to office with 173 seats, compared to 40 for the Conservatives.

King inherited a dismal economy and a growing restlessness in the provinces, including a deeply disaffected Alberta. Premier Aberhart was taking drastic, dictatorial steps to deal with his province's economic problems. He had passed the Accurate News and Information Act, which gave him control of the press, and he moved to take over the banks, prompting accusations of both fascism and Communism from the hostile newspapers. "He could be an arrogant boor as I discovered when I tried to interview him," wrote James Gray, who was writing about Aberhart for the *Winnipeg Free Press*. Aberhart had a running feud with the press and referred to reporters as "sons of Satan" and "fornicators." "In my reading of the Social Credit literature," wrote Gray, "it seemed there was a resemblance between Aberhart's 'just price system' and Benito Mussolini's original blueprint for his corporate state. [I hoped] Aberhart would provide the kind of answers that would make a good interview." What began as an interview, Gray reported, ended in a shouting match.

Both the News Act and the banking law were declared unconstitutional, but Aberhart argued that the British North America Act did not give the provinces enough power, especially in times of emergency. "It's a weird business," King said of the premier's plans. "A fortunate thing for Canada as a whole that this fanatical flame has thus far been kept within the bounds of a single province."

There was a growing power struggle between Ottawa and the provinces, one that worsened when, in Quebec, the Liberals were replaced by Maurice Duplessis's party, the Union Nationale. To make matters worse, one of King's biggest supporters, Liberal Ontario premier Mitchell Hepburn, turned on him. Hepburn had been a steadfast champion of King while he was in exile, but once King was back in the prime minister's office, Hepburn challenged him repeatedly.

While Aberhart and Woodsworth preached salvation across the prairies, Hepburn embraced the devil in a suite at Toronto's stately King Edward Hotel. Hepburn was an affable, hard-drinking womanizer who was rarely far from his bodyguard-bartender and a handful of female escorts who called him "Chief." Hepburn had a broad populist appeal. One of the first things he had done on taking office was to hold a public auction in Toronto's Varsity Stadium at which he sold off the government limousines. He fired the strict provincial film censor and ridiculed the weekly criticism that came from the province's pulpits. "[These] pious so-called Christians with souls that would just fit in a peanut shell, every once in a while have to shout from the house tops to justify their existence," Hepburn said. Eddie Odette, a friend and inveterate drinker, was hired to oversee the Liquor Board, an appointment that gave the abstemious King a bad dream, which he saw as a portent: "terrible, a handing over to liquor interests in Ontario." Within weeks of his appointment, Odette issued 1,100 liquor licences.

Hepburn and King clashed repeatedly over national policy, and when King cut Ontario's relief grant by 15 per cent without any warning, Hepburn was enraged. In North Bay the destitution was so pronounced that the mayor legalized begging. Sudbury declared itself broke and shut down the relief office. In Toronto, there was an ugly fight between police and mothers outside a suburban welfare office.

The political feuds between the two opposed men were exacerbated by their mutual antagonism and came to a head over the issue of unions. Union membership was growing, and Communists were said to be involved in recruiting. "We know what these agitators are up to," Hepburn said. "We are advised that they are working their way into the lumber camps, the pulp mills and our mines. Well, this has got to stop – and we are going to stop it. If necessary we'll raise an army to do it."

Hepburn did raise an army. When the new United Automobile Workers union local at the General Motors plant in Oshawa went on strike in April 1937, Hepburn organized an anti-union security force that became known as "Hepburn's Hussars" and "Sons of Mitches." Mackenzie King, who had started his career as a labour negotiator, was critical of Hepburn's blunt approach: "Hepburn has become a fascist leader and has sought to have labour in its struggle against organized capital put into the position of being under Communist direction and control. Action of the kind is little short of criminal."

While the concepts of communism and fascism were being fearfully invoked and hotly debated around the country, touted as both salvation and damnation, capitalism was still working well for some of the country's businessmen. Eaton's was the largest department store in the country, and the family that founded it had established a kind of colonial aristocracy. Flora McCrea Eaton – who became Lady Eaton when her husband was knighted after the First World War – lived like royalty in a handful of opulent homes. She had met her husband, John Craig Eaton, at Rotherham House, a private hospital in Toronto, where Flora was working as a nurse and the young "Jack" was trying to curb his drinking. When Jack died in 1922, at the age of forty-six, Lady Eaton assumed the role of corporate director, scheduling board meetings for Tuesdays because she liked to stay in bed on Mondays. She became an outspoken dowager who returned from her annual Mediterranean vacation with praise for Italian dictator Benito Mussolini. "Italy is the brightest and happiest of lands," she told a journalist. "Mussolini has done much for the country and no more do the beggars in the streets around the cathedrals annoy everyone. The streets are clean as if they had been newly swept and all the cities look better. I have never seen such happy people as in Italy today."

Canadians were less happy during the Depression years, and Eaton's looked for ways to cheer up its customers. It sponsored radio concerts featuring classical music, and in 1933 it founded the "Good Deed Club," a Saturday morning radio show that featured children talking about how good they had been to others. The child who had done the "good deed of the week" received a fifteen-jewel watch. The company was not above cloaking its own corporate goals in the appearance of altruism. Full-page newspaper ads appeared, warning Canadians about the economic pitfalls of not spending money: "If people refrain from buying, a shrinkage in employment occurs. . . . Less spending means less work to do and more unemployment. Unemployment is universally regarded as the bane of today. Unemployment is simply consumption falling away below capacity for production." If people bought more from Eaton's, the ad suggested, it would help pull the country out of the Depression.

The Depression apparently did nothing to dampen the spirits of Flora's son and fellow Eaton's director John David Eaton. "Nobody ever thought about money in those days," he said, "because they never saw any. . . . You could take your girl to a supper dance at the hotel for $10, and that included the bottle and room for you and your friends to drink in. I'm glad I grew up then. It was a good time for everybody. People learned what it was like to work."

Ten dollars was the weekly salary for Eaton's employees in the 1930s, and it was not a good time for them, a fact that was soon made clear to the buying public. In 1934, Eaton's came under attack from H. H. Stevens, the federal trade minister. He talked Bennett into forming a commission to investigate the country's biggest companies, suspecting that they were running Dickensian sweatshops in the desperate climate of the Depression. "The law has holes big enough for millionaires to crawl through," he said, "and company laws that permit the fleecing of the public on one hand and the sweatshops on the other."

When Eaton's, Canada's most trusted retailer, was investigated by the commission, the country paid close attention. A seamstress named Annie Wells told members of Parliament that she was paid nine and a half cents for a dress that Eaton's then sold for a dollar and sixty-nine cents. She said she was under constant pressure to make more dresses more quickly. "You were badgered, harassed, and worried," she testified. "You were told to work and work and work so hard at these cheaper rates . . . and you were threatened [that] if you didn't, you would be fired. You felt insecure with your job. You had to sit at your machine from a quarter to eight until twenty minutes to one and go as hard as you could. You had not time to get up and have a drink of water or powder your nose or look at anybody. You just went on working."

Eaton's was publicly humiliated and quickly changed its policies, but its suppliers, who were small, anonymous, and not under pressure from the commission, continued their tyrannical labour practices.

John David and Lady Eaton, opening the new "Home Furnishing Store" at the corner of College and Yonge streets in Toronto, 1930. Other departments were added to the store over the years. (*City of Toronto Archives, SC244-1638*)

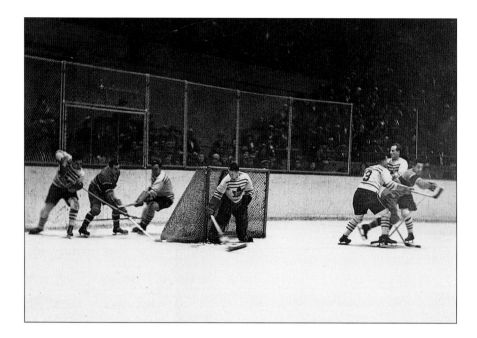

The Toronto Maple Leafs versus the Montreal Canadiens, 1934. (*City of Toronto Archives, SC266-32449*)

John David Eaton learned the family trade at the Winnipeg store, driving his Auburn roadster along Wellington Crescent, wearing a raccoon coat against the cold. While he struggled to understand the family empire, he courted Signy Stefansson, a dental receptionist who was part of the city's substantial Icelandic community. After they were engaged, the family sent Signy to London to be presented at court to King George V and Queen Mary. John David, a reluctant heir to the Eaton throne, became the fourth president of the company in 1942, and he would usher it into a long, slow decline.

A few blocks north of Eaton's flagship store in Toronto, Conn Smythe, the diminutive, combative owner of the Maple Leafs hockey team, planned to build not just a hockey arena but a shrine, "a place where people can go in evening clothes, if they want to come there for a party or dinner. We need at least twelve thousand seats, everything new and clean, a place that people can be proud to take their wives or girlfriends to." The Leafs had yet to do anything to warrant a shrine, having failed to win a Stanley Cup since the inception of the National Hockey League in November 1917. They were still playing at a crumbling mausoleum on Mutual Street. But Smythe had recently used money he had won at the track to buy the country's greatest defenceman, King Clancy, from the Ottawa Senators, and he was optimistic. "Most people think of 1930 as the first year of the Depression, the unemployed, hard times," Smythe later said. "I always think of it as the year the Leafs got King Clancy."

Eaton's had just built a new store at College and Yonge streets and Smythe convinced Eaton's executive J. J. Vaughn that it would be to their advantage to have the arena nearby, so that the store could take advantage of the pedestrian traffic. Eaton's sold Smythe a piece of land at the corner of Carlton and Church streets, a block away, and bought shares in the new

Howie Morenz in 1930.
(*Archives nationales du Québec
à Montréal*, P100.D1132.P8)

Maple Leaf Gardens as well. Smythe negotiated a deal with construction workers to take a 20 percent cut in wages in exchange for shares, a scheme that kept his costs down and eventually made some of the workers rich. Maple Leaf Gardens was built in five months and twelve days, with construction going around the clock so that it would be ready for the 1931 hockey season. Smythe had his shrine, but it was still not enough to get him the Stanley Cup. The Montreal Canadiens, led by the dauntless Howie Morenz, the Mozart of centre ice, dominated the league, winning the Cup in 1930 and again in 1931.

By 1932, the Depression had reached even the National Hockey League. Player salaries were frozen, the Ottawa Senators were on the verge of bankruptcy, and the Canadiens were at the end of an era. Leafs coach Dick Irvin introduced the concept of pre-season training, which up until that time had consisted of fishing and drinking beer. His coaching techniques paid off. That year, the Leafs, led by the "Kid Line," with King Clancy and Hap Day on defence, won their first Stanley Cup.

Smythe had a winning team, and now he wanted to market it properly. He was one of the first to recognize the importance of radio. Other owners felt that radio broadcasts of the games would cut into the gate receipts, but Smythe supported broadcaster Foster Hewitt, and every Saturday night, the Canadian Radio Broadcasting Commission network broadcast the Leafs game, beginning with Hewitt's familiar salutation, "Hello Canada!" The Gardens became a national monument, with sell-out crowds for every game.

The Montreal Canadiens would not win the Stanley Cup again for thirteen years, and in 1937 they suffered a serious blow with the tragic death of Howie Morenz. On March 8, Morenz broke his leg after crashing into the boards in a game against Chicago. He suffered an embolism the next day and died in hospital. His body lay in state in the Montreal Forum, and tens of thousands of people lined up in the sub-zero temperature to pay their respects.

The woes of the Canadiens were mirrored in Montreal's economy. A city active in international trade, Montreal felt the impact when global markets collapsed, and the effects echoed around the province. Irene Duhamel was one of fifteen children of a mill worker who lived in St-Hyacinthe, a factory town near Montreal. "I slept with two sisters and one of the babies in the same bed," she said. "We slept across the bed so there would be more room. First we had the baby at the foot of the bed, but he didn't like that so we put him at the head and we slept across. There were so many of us that the bed was warm when those who worked nights took over from those who worked days."

As the Depression deepened, the textile mills took advantage of cheap labour, and adult workers were replaced by girls as young as fifteen, who would do the job for about half of what the men earned. Irene had little choice but to join them: "I was at school and they called to tell me to come home. It was to go to work. I was so unhappy, I was devastated. I cried and

**CANADIAN RADIO BROADCASTING COMMISSION** ◆ In 1932, under R.B. Bennett, Canada inaugurated its first national radio network, the Canadian Radio Broadcasting Commission, which would later become the Canadian Broadcasting Corporation (CBC). It featured "Hockey Night in Canada," "The Happy Gang," and "*L'Heure Catholique*." In 1936, the power of the medium was made clear when the whole country (as well as 650 American radio stations) listened to the progress of the rescue efforts to save three men who were trapped underground. They had been inspecting a mine they had purchased at Moose River, Nova Scotia, when it suddenly caved in. A diamond-drill operator named Billy Bell managed to drill a small hole and a telephone was lowered down to them.

"This is the Canadian Radio Commission calling Canada from Moose River," CRBC reporter J. Frank Willis (*left*) said. "Herman Magill is dead. Others still in the depths of the mine . . . can hear the men in there working, breaking rocks to get through to them."

An estimated 50 million people in Canada, the United States, and Britain tuned in to Willis's live coverage of the disaster, which he broadcast every half hour for a total of fifty-six hours. Radios were set up in classrooms. After three days, the remaining two men were rescued, live on radio. (*National Archives of Canada*, CBC 15284)

cried. I think I cried enough to last me a lifetime. There were seventeen of us at home, I had no choice, they needed my salary. When I had my medical exam, I weighed sixty-eight pounds [thirty kilograms] but the medical examiner wrote down that I was seventy, so I was allowed to work there."

The factory supplied cloth to department stores like Eaton's, and Irene's workday was from 7:00 a.m. to 6:00 p.m. "Because I was small I had to climb into the needles and go between the threads with a little brush to lift the cotton debris. My hands were full of blood. There was no break. It was so hot in the factory. All the windows were closed to keep in the humidity so the cotton would stay soft. It could get as hot as 105 degrees [40 degrees Celsius]. You worked mindlessly without stopping. The company hired a nurse to give us salt pills if we fainted."

Irene was earning eight dollars a week, two dollars below the legal minimum wage. "We didn't have much choice," she said, "because the girls who worked at the other factories wanted to come work with us because the pay was a little better." They were closely monitored in the factory, and if an employee missed a day of work her job was in jeopardy: "It was so strict that one employee had her baby in the factory bathroom to avoid missing a day of work. Because of the heat, many employees got sick, especially with tuberculosis. One of my friends got sick and died. The guy in charge wasn't evil, it's just that he had a job to do and that was to get us working. After my little friend died, he went to pay his respects. We were inside with the mother. When the boss came to the door, she went into a mad rage, she screamed, 'You killed my daughter.' We had to hold her back.

The smashing all new revue
"SPEED"
boasts a cast that is hard to beat.

JOHNNY VIGAL — the peer of Em Cees

THE FOUR MUSKETEERS
"They run wild in singing, dancing and comedy."

EVELYN CAMPBELL
"Stunning Creole Soubrette"

BEE McCONNIE
"Teasing high-brown dancer"

— plus —

Those colored aristocrats of jazz
CANADIAN AMBASSADORS
dispensing the kind of dance music you like.

Connies
Montreal's beautiful show place
Featuring world-famous
colored attractions.

1417 St. Lawrence Blvd.
(just above St. Catherine St.)

RESERVATIONS:
Phone LAnc. 3501

Black entertainers, including Myron Sutton's Canadian Ambassadors swing band, were featured at some of Montreal's most popular night clubs during the 1930s. (*Concordia University*)

"One thing that came out of this incident, afterwards the boss listened to us if we said we were sick. He was more humane. If we were really sick, we'd get a couple of hours off to rest."

The workday was a long misery for people like Irene, but nights in Montreal were a sinful pleasure for those with money. The city had a flourishing red-light district and a taste for jazz, and during the Depression the nightclubs were a refuge. Black musicians came to town, drawn by the clubs and the women. "You have to give the French-Canadian white woman all the credit in the world," one musician said, "because she was the nicest woman to all the black musicians. If it wasn't for the French-Canadian women, all the black musicians who came from anywhere, and stayed, would have starved to death."

Myron Sutton came to Montreal from Niagara Falls to become an alto sax player, and he gravitated to the Terminal Club, with its bare floors and pot-bellied stove. "The Terminal Club was the kind of place where anything could happen," Sutton said. "I saw Johnny Hodges come in there and blow his horn. I saw that puff-jaws Dizzy Gillespie come in there. Duke Ellington came in and sat behind the bar. Anybody's liable to come in there. It was just

**MAURICE DUPLESSIS**

◆ Duplessis was premier of Quebec from 1936 to 1939, and then again from 1944 until his death fifteen years later. He was an erratic, corrupt, effective manager and a lasting political presence. A friend of Duplessis's offered this view of his early years in office: "The first Duplessis term was something of a period piece, a grotesquely parochial, wildly hilarious 'government,' largely carried on in hotel suites amidst numerous scandals, martinis, attendant ladies and bright red herrings." (*National Archives of Canada, C-178339*)

a joint, but it was a well-known joint." Rich Montrealers came in with their girlfriends and gave the band fifty dollars to keep playing after the bar had emptied and closed. Booze was delivered in the morning, seized by the vice squad in the afternoon, and bought back at a premium in time for opening in the evening.

Sutton had a band called the Canadian Ambassadors, the first organized black jazz band in the country. They played Connie's Inn on St. Catherine Street for nine months in 1933 and wore custom-tailored suits. "Our band was strictly a swing band," Sutton said. "And we just swung, that's all." They played Connie's, the Terminal Club, and the Hollywood Club but refused to play brothels, a significant and growing market.

The new premier of Quebec was Maurice Duplessis, known as "Le Chef," or "Uncle Maurice." He believed in rewarding his supporters with subsidies, loans, roads, and government jobs. During the 1935 election, Duplessis made sure that the faithful were driven to the polls, and given whisky to smooth the ride. Money or gifts were awarded to large families that voted in a bloc. Duplessis's support was concentrated in the rural areas, and he pulled money out of the cities that had elected Liberals.

St-Hyacinthe, where Irene Duhamel lived, was the site of one of the most closely fought electoral battles, a loud, angry affair. The Liberal incumbent, Télesphore-Damien Bouchard, had convinced the provincial Liberal government to give the town $4.5 million for public works, and the deal was signed in St-Hyacinthe amid great hoopla. When the election was

Children in Abitibi, Quebec, 1937. (*Archives nationales du Québec à Québec, P667.D26.P14*)

over, Bouchard still had his seat, but the Union Nationale had ousted the Liberals, and the money he had promised disappeared.

St-Hyacinthe was in decline, and rather than invest money in its renewal, the government offered incentives to citizens willing to try farming in the north. "One day a government officer came to our home because of our large family, especially the twelve boys," Duhamel wrote. "He offered my father land in Abitibi. My father would have loved some land, but not in Abitibi. Duplessis wanted people in the country, not in the cities. He said there were enough people as it was in the cities. He wanted more votes, and for that he needed strong and well-populated rural areas and that would give him more strength."

Almost fifty thousand Quebecers took the offer and moved north. But much of the land was impossible to farm, and roughly two-thirds of them moved back, defeated. Discouraged by her limited options, Irene turned to Georges-Henri Lévesque, a Dominican priest who was trying to educate the province's working poor. An organization for social reform, the Jeunesse Ouvrières Catholique (JOC), was formed by the Oblats de Marie-Immaculée, and it turned its energies to dealing with the devastating effects of the Depression.

"It was a way of focusing my energy," Duhamel said. "It got my mind off work. A lot of young girls who came to work in the factories were from the country and they didn't have a lot of education. They dreamt of pretty dresses and the Saturday night dance, or about finding a husband as soon as possible. The JOC taught me that there was life outside of St-Hyacinthe."

The JOC organized a field trip to Quebec to demand that Duplessis give the same subsidies to working youth that he gave to farmers. For Duhamel, the success of this protest held out the possibility of returning to school: "The trip to Quebec was a new challenge, it inspired me to keep on

Padlock Law protest, Montreal, 1939. (*National Archives of Canada, PA-129184*)

going. I was very impressed and moved to be there especially since we were convinced the response would be favourable." But the visit with Duplessis was another disappointment. "He called us 'my dear little children.' The encounter only lasted a few minutes. Duplessis listened nicely and then he said a very definite no. And then he added, as for the workers, pray for their eternal souls. It was over."

In Montreal, Duplessis's influence spread to the jazz clubs. "Duplessis sent two guys down to Rockheads," Myron Sutton said, "and that's when Rockheads was going great, and they told Rockhead they were his new partners, and Rockhead said no way, nobody is going to tell me what to do. Rockheads was closed for eight years after that, they took his licence. Rockheads was closed because it was making big money at the time, biggest in Montreal."

The clubs that stayed open became increasingly intolerant and politicized. "It went through a period there at the Terminal Club," Sutton said, "where English people tried to have a theme song, like 'There Will Always Be an England.' So we'd play that but the French wouldn't stand up. English would stand up at attention, French people wouldn't stand up. So when we got through playing the song, the English people wanted to fight the French people 'cause they wouldn't stand up. So then we'd have to play 'God Save the King' or 'Queen,' or whoever the hell was in power then, and they'd all stand up again! I used to carry a piece of iron under my seat. I never had to hit anybody, but I would have. Some of the guys were crazy if you get 'em half drunk."

Quebec had a $31-million debt, and Duplessis, like Bennett, seized on the spectre of Communism as a scapegoat, encouraging anti-Red rallies that

Marian Dale Scott, seen here (in the striped dress) at the Kingston Artists' Conference in 1941.

During the Depression, Marian Dale Scott wrote, "The inner necessity to paint was there, in spite of the times, in spite of the misery, the growing fear of fascism and war." (*Queen's University Archives, André Bieler Collection, 2050*)

sometimes became violent and racist. In 1937, he passed the Padlock Law, which dictated that anyone who promoted Communism could have his home and/or office padlocked. Duplessis's definition of a Communist was wonderfully flexible, a handy club to wield against political enemies. "Communism can be felt," he said. "We shall understand Communism by what everybody understands as Communism."

Communism was not the only revolutionary idea circulating at the time. Architecture, literature, and art were all in upheaval and becoming increasingly politicized. Marian Dale had been born into Montreal's English-speaking aristocracy, but she had rejected the world of a debutante to become an artist. "If man's liberation is the chief aim of action," she wrote in her diary, "the function of the creator is as essential as that of the politician or the economist. The creator liberates with the instrument of the word, the plastic organization, the rhythmic composition. His revolution aims at a complete metamorphosis of the world." She was a pretty, delicate, dark-haired woman whose early landscapes gave way to bold cubist images. She found inspiration in the shoppers in Eaton's who wandered lonely among the merchandise and incorporated them into her paintings.

When she met Frank Scott in 1925, she knew she had found a soulmate. Scott, a serious young man who looked like a rural preacher, was a legal scholar who wanted to be a poet. "We believed in forward things," Marian said. "We read Bertrand Russell's 'The Right to be Happy.' We thought we should allow each other to be free and we would be honest with each other and say if we found somebody else we wouldn't want to continue." The two were married in 1928 and left the splendour of

**FRANK SCOTT:** ◆ Scott was a noted poet as well as a legal scholar. After Mackenzie King's death in 1950, Scott wrote a poem, "W.L.M.K.," that was critical of the former prime minister's record and the legacy he had left the country.

We had no shape
Because he never took sides,
And no sides
Because he never allowed them to take shape.

He skilfully avoided what was wrong
Without saying what was right,
And he never let his on the one hand
Know what his on the other hand was doing.

The height of his ambition
Was to pile a Parliamentary Committee on a Royal Commission,
To have "conscription if necessary
But not necessarily conscription,"
To let Parliament decide –
Later.

Postpone, postpone, abstain.

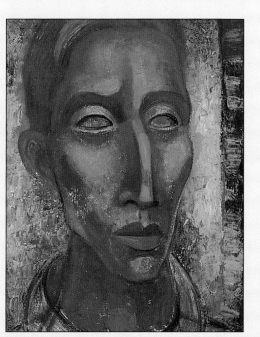

Marian Dale Scott, *Head of Frank*.
(*Firestone Art Collection, Ottawa Art Gallery*)

Westmount for a student apartment near McGill University. They had frequent parties, where they drank beer, read poetry, and argued about politics and the "New Morality."

Scott took a job with the law faculty at McGill and lobbied to overturn Duplessis's Padlock Law. (He was eventually successful, though not until 1953.) He also embraced Bertrand Russell's philosophy of guilt-free sex and began having an affair. Marian was tortured by Frank's infidelity, though determined to hold on to their shared modernism. "This pain because F is with another woman," she wrote in her diary. "Use this pain, this special pain. . . . Use this pain that wrenches me to new planes."

She found her own romantic outlet in Dr. Norman Bethune, whom she met in 1935 at a meeting of Montreal's Contemporary Art Society. Bethune was an amateur painter and the chief of thoracic surgery at the Hôpital du Sacré Coeur in Cartierville, Quebec. He was short, stocky, and balding but possessed a compelling energy and had a reputation for being a ladies' man. He had already twice married and divorced the same woman, Frances Penney, and he was a fledgling Communist. Bethune fell in love with Marian Scott, read Byron to her, and called her Pony. "Dear Pony," he wrote, "Let us go into the future together – heads up and with a smile on our lips – no real harm or injury can touch us. . . . It is only because I love you I write like this, so darkly lest I injure you with my love. In the name of love and life instead of bedecking you with jewels I load you with chains."

Opposite: Marian Dale Scott,
*Fire Escape*, 1939, (*Musée du Québec*)

Marian was drawn by Bethune's charisma and his words. "I am happy," she wrote in her diary, "impervious to those who came before, those who come after, for you, a complicated, unsatisfied creature, recognize me as a complicated unsatisfied creature, recognized each other and know that because we are what we are we need each other."

In August 1935, Bethune returned from the Soviet Union, where he had taken a first-hand look at Communism. Frank Scott left for Moscow the same month. Bethune praised the Soviet medical system and the immense scale of the Communist vision, and he joined the Communist Party a few months later. Scott went as a socialist, willing to embrace the central ideas of communism, but he rejected what he recognized as a totalitarian state. He also commented on the enigmatic national nature of the Russians. "These atheists practising Christianity," Scott wrote in his diary, "humanely brutal, and creating freedom through their ruthless dictatorship, are certainly a challenging paradox."

Marian moved Bethune the doctor to write love poetry ("Hand clasped/ Look, see us stand, with eager upturned faces / Lit by the rising sun of our new love, / Whose gentle light touches so tenderly / Eyelids and mouth"). Scott the poet turned to political commentary ("Scratch the Communist, and you find a Tartar"). But politics soon engulfed all of them.

There was a crisis looming in Spain. The republican government there was backed by the Soviet Union, while Germany and Italy were arming General Francisco Franco's fascist rebels. Bethune felt that the Spanish Civil War was the beginning of a larger world war, a political crucible that would shape the future. "The world war has started," he wrote, "it's democracy against fascism. . . . It is in Spain that the real issues of our time are going to be fought out, it is there that democracy will survive or die." In October 1936, Bethune left for Spain on the *Empress of Britain* to work for the republicans as a much-needed surgeon. He wanted Marian Scott to come with him, but she would not leave her husband. She donated some of her paintings, though, to raise money for the republican cause. Bethune felt he had lost the love of his life. "You are the *first* woman in the world I have met about whom I have felt *no doubt* that we could live together, physically & mentally & spiritually mated," he had once written to her. "This has never happened to me before . . ."

Mackenzie King worried that the Spanish war would provide a fresh opportunity to divide Canada. He had a vivid memory of the conscription crisis of the First World War, and its devastating, divisive, and lingering effects. In 1920, Canada had become one of the founding members of the League of Nations, which meant that it was committed to defend the territorial integrity and independence of all other members. King was now wondering how far he could limit this obligation, to avoid the further divisions that Canadian involvement in overseas conflicts might provoke. Franco's rebels were defenders of order and the Catholic Church, which elicited some sympathy in Quebec's conservative religious circles. King's

**NORMAN BETHUNE** ◆ Born in Gravenhurst, Ontario, the son of a Presbyterian minister, Bethune studied medicine at the University of Toronto and worked as a medical officer for the Royal Navy in the First World War. An early crusader against tuberculosis, he eventually contracted the disease himself and recovered in a sanatorium in New York State. He was in love with Marian Dale Scott, wife of the lawyer and poet Frank Scott, but he could see that there was no future for them. In a November 21, 1935, letter to her, he expressed his fears.

"I, this person you love, am nothing. Understand that firmly. I am nothing in myself. I represent and symbolize an emotion emanating from yourself – of your own being. I am merely an externalized part of your own vital self.

"We could have gone a long way together thru this maze if we had held each other's hands.

"I have been robbed of jewels."

A few days later, Bethune joined the Communist Party.

(*Bethune on the boat to Spain, National Archives of Canada, PA-160628*)

government passed the Foreign Enlistment Act, forbidding Canadians from enlisting on either side, but 1,300 French and English Canadians, many of them jobless, defied the law and went to Spain. Virtually all of them enlisted with the republican cause. Some, including Ronald Liversedge, were inspired by Bethune, whose pioneering system of providing blood transfusions on the front lines was receiving a lot of publicity. "I read a press report of how a brilliant young Canadian surgeon had resigned a remunerative position in a Montreal hospital to go to Spain to aid the embattled people of the Republic," Liversedge wrote. "This Doctor, Norman Bethune, has raised funds for, and organized, and taken to Spain the first mobile blood transfusion unit to be used in warfare. I knew then that I had to go also."

Liversedge's decision was made easier by the fact that, like thousands of other men whose lives were a wearying routine of relief camps, flophouses, railcars, and handouts, he had few options in Canada. In 1936, he travelled

Dans la lutte actuelle, je vois du côté fasciste les forces périmées, de l'autre côté le peuple dont les immenses ressources créatrices donneront à l'Espagne un élan qui étonnera le monde.

Miró.

**THE MACKENZIE-PAPINEAU BATTALION** ◆ Named for the leaders of the 1837 rebellions, William Lyon Mackenzie and Louis-Joseph Papineau, the battalion included 1,300 Canadians who joined the republican cause in the Spanish Civil War (July 1936 to March 1939). Led by Edward Cecil-Smith, a Toronto labour journalist, the "Mac-Paps" fought in five major campaigns, losing half of their number to casualties. They were part of the Battle of the Ebro during the last summer of the war (July to November, 1938), which ended with a republican defeat and seventy thousand casualties. Upon returning to Canada, members of the Mac-Paps received no official recognition for their efforts because of the Foreign Enlistment Act, which forbade Canadian volunteers from fighting in foreign wars. The decision to let them back into the country was itself controversial, and their role in the war remained obscure and unheralded for forty years. (*National Archives of Canada, C-67460*)

*Joan Miró, Aidez Espagne,*
*(Collection Eduardo Arroyo*
*Giraudon/Art Resource, N.Y.)*

to New York using false papers and then sailed to Marseilles on board the *President Roosevelt*. In Marseilles he met up with other Canadians bound for Spain. "Tommy and I did the rounds of a few bistros," he wrote, "drinking vermouth and listening to some good accordion music. It was pleasant, the cafes were bright, cheerful, but as a farewell celebration it was a flop. I am afraid that I took my responsibilities as group leader too seriously and I know that I spoiled the night for Tommy. At one of the cafes two very attractive girls for whom we had bought a drink wanted to sell us some love, and although I wanted to go with them I refused and also dissuaded Tommy from doing so. My scruples were not moral ones, but some of the volunteers had gone into Spain having contracted venereal disease on the way. . . . Had I known that Tommy would be dead within a week I would have acted otherwise."

On board the ship to Spain, Liversedge met men he had known from the On to Ottawa Trek. As they reminisced, the ship was hit by an Italian torpedo, and it quickly sank. Among the survivors, holding on to pieces of the ship, Liversedge recognized Ellis Fromberg, a friend from the Vancouver demonstrations. Together they clung to the wreckage, their bodies cramping, fearful of sharks, waiting nervously for rescue.

A week later Liversedge was in Spain, fighting with the Mackenzie-Papineau Battalion, which, along with other volunteers in the International Brigade, fought on the side of the Soviet-backed republicans. They had little food, clothing, medical supplies, or weapons, and they lived in shallow trenches under the Spanish sun, lice ridden, without water, surviving on cat meat, and taking terrible casualties. "All were changed," he wrote of his

The destruction of the Basque village of Guernica in April 1937 was one of the most brutal incidents of the Spanish Civil War. In a massacre that lasted three hours, German bombers killed or wounded 1,600 civilians. Picasso's mural depicting the atrocity was unveiled at the Paris World's Fair in June 1937. (*Museo Nacional Centro de Arte Reina Sofía, Madrid, Spain, Bridgeman Art Library NUL-10313*)

battalion. "Even facial expressions changed, besides being haggard the men seemed to be nursing unwelcome thoughts. War is an obscene atrocity, and no man comes out of it the same as before."

Liversedge contracted pleurisy and was moved to a hospital in a Spanish village. He and other casualties were taken to a room above a chemist's shop to be X-rayed. The fluoroscope was embraced as entertainment by local villagers, who crowded into the room and watched the picture of his bones move subtly on the square screen, amazed at the new toy.

By 1937, Bethune was drinking heavily, at war not just with the fascists but also with the Spanish doctors and his own Communist Party. His brilliance in the triage tents near the front lines was matched by his arrogance and his temper. He began to withdraw even from friends. "I am a solitary,"

Mackenzie King receiving
the Nazi salute in Berlin, 1937.
(*National Archives of Canada,*
*PA-119013*)

he wrote, "loving privacy, my own satisfactory aloneness . . . I didn't need any
woman, or any man."

In 1937, Bethune's clashes with local doctors and Communist authorities finally led to his being recalled from Spain. Shortly afterward all the
volunteers of the International Brigade were ordered home, and Franco
was victorious. Liversedge arrived back in Halifax, "the place where I had
started my journey into Spain from, and with the same amount of money in
my pocket that I started my journey with a little under two years ago. I
thought, 'Well Ron, home from the wars, but with no home to go to.'"

Fascists were now at the head of three European governments – Spain, Italy,
and Germany – and western democratic leaders feared a world war. In 1937,
Mackenzie King went to Europe to assess the situation himself. In Germany,
he was given a tour of the ordered splendour that was the Third Reich,
viewing its dramatic architecture, the near-identical rows of Hitler Youth
on parade, and the smooth promise of the autobahns. He and Hermann
Goering, the air minister, had coffee together and discussed big-game
hunting in the Rocky Mountains.

King's meeting with Adolf Hitler left him satisfied that war was not
imminent. "He smiled very pleasantly," King wrote in his diary, "and indeed
had a sort of appealing and affectionate look in his eyes. My sizing up of the
man as I sat and talked with him was that he is really one who truly loves his
fellow man and his country. . . . His face is much more prepossessing than
his picture would give the impression of. It is not that of a fiery over-strained
nature but of a calm, passive man, deeply and thoughtfully in earnest. His
skin was smooth; his face did not present lines of fatigue or weariness.

**CAIRINE WILSON** ◆ Born into the wealth of Montreal's Scottish commercial aristocracy as Cairine Mackay, she was an unlikely choice to become Canada's first woman senator. Nellie McClung, who had been lobbying for women to be represented in the Senate, was the obvious choice, but the cautious Mackenzie King was wary of McClung's forceful personality. In return for appointing Cairine Wilson, King suggested that she donate her entire salary to the Liberal Party. He had hoped that she would be politically pliant, but this did not turn out to be the case.

In 1938, after the Munich Agreement had awarded Hitler the Sudetenland, the German-speaking part of Czechoslovakia, there was general relief that war had been averted. Both the British prime minister, Neville Chamberlain, and Mackenzie King were elated. But Wilson felt that this attempt at appeasement was a disastrous mistake, and a prelude to war. As King presided over a ceremony to celebrate the peace, Wilson issued a statement that was picked up by newspapers. "Our leaders," she warned, "continue to subscribe to a concept of anarchy which actually permitted the World War of 1914 and which might well have permitted its repetition in the last few hours. . . . The new barbarism represented by Germany may now be free to extend to the Black Sea and other continents." (*National Archives of Canada*, PA-136906)

His eyes impressed me most of all. There was a liquid quality about them which indicated keen perception and profound sympathy (calm, composed) – and one could see how particularly humble folk would come to have a profound love for the man."

King was also convinced that Hitler, like himself, was guided by his dead mother. "I am convinced he is a spiritualist," he wrote in his diary. "That he has a vision to which he is being true . . . his devotion to his mother – that Mother's spirit is I am certain his guide. . . . I believe the world will yet come to see a very great man – mystic, in Hitler."

King was not alone in being seduced by Hitler's personal charm and rehearsed simplicity; a British diplomat compared him to Gandhi. But in March 1938, Germany annexed Austria, and in October, Hitler's army walked into the Sudetenland, the German-speaking part of Czechoslovakia, where it was welcomed with swastikas and the Nazi salute. A month later, on November 9, anti-Semitism exploded in Berlin when young Nazis went on a rampage in the Jewish quarter, killing ninety people and destroying hundreds of businesses, homes, and synagogues. *Kristallnacht* (Crystal Night), named for the broken glass, was a turning point in the fate of European Jews. But even this display of brutality was not going to open Canada's doors to Jewish refugees. Frederick Blair, Canada's deputy minister of immigration, announced: "Pressure on the part of the Jewish people to get into Canada has never been greater than it is now, and I am glad to be able to add, after thirty-five years experience here, that it was never so well controlled."

Australia had already admitted fifteen thousand Jewish refugees, and Canadian senator Cairine Wilson argued that Canada, with its vast, unfilled spaces, could accommodate even more. "We must be big enough and courageous enough to admit to Canada a fair share of the unfortunate persons involved," she said in a speech. "We hear constantly that people must not be admitted to Canada when we have several hundred thousand persons on relief. . . . Canada's ratio of population to the square mile is the second lowest of any country in the world yet she is possessed of enormous wealth in natural resources and with a vigourous and enterprising people is surely able to assume this responsibility which can be defended on economic as well as on humanitarian grounds."

Blair ignored Wilson's arguments and raised the amount of capital an immigrant needed to enter the country from $5,000 to $15,000. As well, immigrants had to prove that they were farmers, which he hoped would further winnow the Jewish applicants, as most were coming from cities. "I often think that instead of persecution it would be far better if we more often told them frankly why many of them are unpopular," he said. "If they would divest themselves of certain of their habits I am sure they could be just as popular in Canada as our Scandinavians."

Cairine Wilson mocked Blair's anti-Semitic reasoning. "The stories circulating against the Jew are so astounding and contradictory that no thinking person could believe them," she declared. "In the same breath, the Jew is accused of being a Communist as well as controlling the money bags of the world." She lobbied King to overrule Blair, but King himself practised a quieter prejudice: he bought all the land around his country house, Kingsmere, in part to prevent having a Jewish neighbour. "We must seek to keep this part of the continent free from unrest," he wrote in his diary, "and from too great an intermixture of foreign strains of blood." But King also recognized a larger moral obligation, and his solution reflected his governing style: he would shift the responsibility to the provinces, asking each premier how many refugees he could take.

Wilson tried another tack, turning the League of Nations Society – a body established to promote international peace by educating the public about the work of the League – into the Canadian National Committee on Refugees, which was linked to the Canadian Jewish Congress. She worked to get Jews admitted to Canada, starting with a request for 5,000, which proved unpalatable, then 1,000, and then for the 907 Jewish refugees on board the *St. Louis*, a ship that had already been rejected by the United States, Argentina, Paraguay, Panama, and Cuba as it sailed the west, seeking asylum. They too were rejected. Wilson finally tried to have one hundred Jewish orphans admitted to Canada, but Blair's regulations banned all but two of them. Most of the others died in Europe. Thanks to government inaction and bureaucratic anti-Semitism, Canada emerged from the war with one of the worst records of Jewish refugee resettlement in the world.

**JOSEPH STALIN** ◆ Born Iosif Vissarionovich Dzhugashvili, Stalin (meaning "man of steel") served under Lenin after the revolution in October 1917. A decade later he was the unopposed dictator of the Soviet Union. During the 1930s, Stalin initiated a purging of any rivals and a forced collectivization of farms that resulted in the deaths of as many as ten million people. In his seventies, Stalin's encroaching paranoia and psychosis renewed his taste for mass executions. He died of a stroke in 1953. (*National Archives of Canada*, PA-802610)

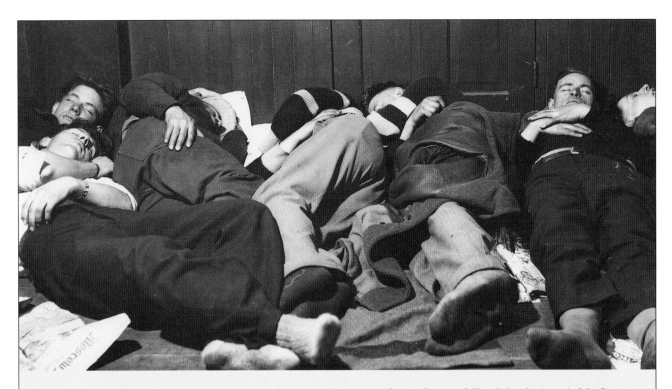

**HUGH MACLENNAN** ◆ A Montreal author whose best-known work was the novel *Two Solitudes* (1945), MacLennan wrote dispassionately about the 1930s, a decade that was given to grand passions.

"In the Thirties what looked like successful revolutions were merely putsches, and these were all reactionary. . . . In retrospect it seems to me that the young Left in the countries which remained democratic only thought they were revolutionary. Did not most of them accept, either in keeping with their natures or against their natures because this was the fashion, the nineteenth century materialist idea that a civilization must be judged solely in materialistic terms, particularly by the efficiency in production, distribution and consumption? Was their quarrel with the Establishment based on anything deeper than the tradition of nineteenth century humanitarianism, coupled with the socialist view that the economy should be planned, and not left to chance? It seems pretty evident, and the next three decades have proved it to the hilt, that radical Youth in the Thirties was in no fundamental revolt against the superego of the society they had inherited. No matter how much we pretend to the contrary, we were still puritanical enough to feel guilty about sex. No matter how violently they claimed it was the Establishment's fault that they were not successful, nearly all of us felt guilty because we were failures." From "What It Was Like to Be in Your Twenties in the Thirties." (*Glenbow Archives, NC-54-4078*)

On September 1, 1939, General Walter von Brauchitsch led 1.25 million German troops into Poland. The next day, Mackenzie King conducted a seance at Kingsmere, where his deceased father was conjured and reassured the prime minister that Hitler was already dead, "shot by a Pole." King also spoke to his mother, his grandfather William Lyon Mackenzie – who warned that Hitler was desperate – Wilfrid Laurier, and William Gladstone, the giant of nineteenth-century liberalism. The seance was interrupted by a phone call informing King that the British cabinet had issued Germany an ultimatum: if they did not withdraw from Poland, the nations would be at war. On September 3, Britain and France declared war on Germany, and King abandoned the spirit world, staying away (with a few exceptions) for

**FRÈRE ANDRÉ** ◆ Born in 1845 as Alfred Bessette in St-Gregoire, Quebec, he was accepted in the Congrégation de Sainte-Croix in 1870, and took the name Frère André. He was uneducated and relegated to manual work, but he showed a gift for healing the sick who came for help. In 1904 Frère André built a small chapel on Mount Royal in honour of Saint Joseph. It was too small to accommodate those who came to see him, and in 1908 it was expanded to seat one hundred people. Seven thousand people showed up at the opening of the new chapel, so it was again rebuilt, this time on an enormous scale as the St. Joseph Oratory. Frère André became the keeper of the oratory, where he would give the sick a St. Joseph medal and some healing oil. He died on January 6, 1937, in one of the worst winters of the Depression, and his death was grieved by the whole province. He lay in state for five days and 700,000 people paid their respects. (*La Presse*)

the duration of the fighting, worried that mischievous forces had corrupted his communications with the dead.

King called a special session of Parliament to vote on the question of Canada's participation, and on September 10, the country was once again at war. At this point, King's plan was to ensure that Canada played only a limited role. It would provide pilot training programs, war supplies, raw materials, and volunteers, this time under Canadian command, but there would be no conscription for service outside Canada. King pursued a program of "limited liability." There was no shortage of volunteers; thousands of single, unemployed young men with no prospects welcomed the offer of a coat, new boots, three meals, and $1.30 a day. In the first four months, more than 58,000 Canadians signed up.

The war intensified the friction between Ottawa and the provinces. Duplessis hastily announced a provincial election, one of the few missteps he would make in his lengthy political career. On October 4, 1939, drunk on gin and champagne, he delivered a speech in Trois-Rivières, where he told his audience that "a vote for the Liberals is a vote for participation [in the war], conscription and assimilation." Conscription was still a powerful symbol from the First World War, and the Liberals seized it, arguing that Quebec's best hope of avoiding it lay with King's Quebec cabinet ministers, who would resign if Duplessis were elected. Voters agreed, and Duplessis was ousted by the new Liberal premier, Adélard Godbout.

King still had to deal with Mitch Hepburn, who was critical of the prime minister's cautious approach to the war. "When the real fury of this

**LETTERS FROM EUROPE** ◆ In the late 1930s, Canadian Jews began to receive desperate letters from relatives in Nazi-occupied Europe:

Dear Cousins,

You know the situation in Germany – we cannot stay – and where in the world shall we go? You will understand that we look for relatives and you are the cousins nearest to us.

I am an able tailor, understand my work thoroughly, my brother is a small businessman and we have confidence that we shall make our way in Canada.

Dear cousins, you would do a high act of humanity by helping us to enter Canada . . . we do hope to hear from you very soon as our quick emigration is a dire necessity.

Yours sincerely,
Adolf Schaffer

(*A Nazi Rally in Berlin, 1937.
National Archives of Canada, C-16791*)

thing strikes us," Hepburn said, "the people of Canada will realize they have made a tremendous mistake in endorsing King and his half-hearted war effort." He passed a resolution in the Ontario legislature denouncing the federal Liberals' war effort. On the other side, Frank Scott warned against military fervour. "Canada's participation in this war must be strictly limited if we are to emerge as a nation," he wrote in a letter to King. "No enemy will be able to cross the Atlantic to attack us; but we can be destroyed by internal stresses and strains." Scott saw an emerging Canadian national sentiment that he feared would be threatened by the war.

On April 9, 1940, Hitler's army marched into Denmark and Norway, meeting no resistance. Hepburn was drinking more than usual, and his health was poor. Suffering from a high fever, he listened nightly to the radio and offered a glum prediction. The Germans, he said, would easily march through the Low Countries, the French army would collapse, and Hitler's troops would be in Paris by May 15, in London a month later, and on the shores of Canada by September 15.

In May, it looked as though his prediction would come true. The *blitzkrieg* moved easily through Luxembourg, the Netherlands, Belgium, and into France. With its army of six million, France was one of the most powerful military forces in the world and was expected to be the bulwark for western democracy. But on June 14, ten days after engaging the French army, the Nazis walked into Paris unopposed. Little more than a week later the French premier, Marshal Henri Philippe Pétain, signed an armistice with Germany, ceding half the country and agreeing to pay the expenses of the invading army. The hope that Germany could be beaten was shattered, and Benito Mussolini brought Italy into the war, adding to the despair. The

**THE DIONNE QUINTUPLETS** ◆ Born near Corbeil, Ontario, on May 28, 1934, the Dionne quintuplets (Emilie, Cécile, Marie, Yvonne, and Annette) immediately became a commercial property. Within weeks of their birth, the destitute parents had signed a contract with an American promotional company giving them the right to tour the quints as a sideshow. Ontario premier Mitch Hepburn stepped in to have the contract annulled and made the quints wards of the Crown in 1935. Labour minister David Croll acted as their guardian and negotiated thirty-six contracts on their behalf. The girls endorsed syrup, were the subject of media rights, and appeared in the 1936 film *Reunion* (which was banned by Chicago's Board of Censors, as it featured both an adulteress and a pickpocket). By 1937, they had earned $535,000, though none of it found its way to the girls themselves.

In 1938, Frank Scott went to the Sydney Conference of the Institute of International Affairs to present a paper. On board the *Mauganui* there was a costume party to break the ice among various delegates, and five Canadians dressed as the Dionne quintuplets, with Scott as Emilie. He described his outfit as "the most loathsome sight I've ever seen." (*Archives of Ontario, C9-6*)

Axis powers – Germany and Italy, soon to be joined by Japan – suddenly seemed unstoppable. The Allied forces were evacuated from Dunkirk, and King's dream of "limited liability" vanished. Canada was now Britain's most important ally against the Germans, and the country geared up for a full war effort.

"It is really appalling how completely masses of people have miscalculated Germany's strength," King lamented. "They are behind in everything. It is an appalling day for Britain when she has to seek from one of the dominions ships, ammunition, aircraft, additional land forces, etc." Canada was even further behind. When asked about the country's military stockpile, General McNaughton, the chief of staff, replied, "Except as regards rifles and rifle ammunition, partial stocks of which were inherited from the Great War – there are none."

The British prime minister, Neville Chamberlain, had been in favour of a policy of appeasement in Britain's relations with Germany. Faced with the disastrous failure of that approach, he resigned and was replaced by the fierce, articulate, hard-drinking warrior Winston Churchill. King

**WINSTON CHURCHILL AND MACKENZIE KING** ◆ In his first statement
in the British House of Commons as prime minister, Winston Churchill
announced his war policy: "Victory at all costs, victory in spite of all terror,
victory however long and hard the road may be; for without victory there
is no survival." (*Library of Congress*)

described him as "tight [drunk] all the time" and disliked his imperious-
ness, while Churchill was impatient with King's natural caution and referred
to him as "the little son of a bitch." They formed an uncomfortable
and fragile alliance. "The battle of France is over," Churchill said. "The battle of Britain is about to begin. On this battle depends the survival of
Christian civilization."

America was reluctant to join the fight to save civilization. President
Roosevelt phoned King and they conversed under aliases – "Mr. Kick" for
King and "Mr. Roberts" for Roosevelt – to confuse any eavesdropping spies.
Roosevelt thought that Churchill would have to consider surrender, and
King was disappointed by the president's position. "It seems that the United
States was seeking to save itself at the expense of Britain, that the British
might have to go down," King lamented. "I instinctively revolted against
such a thought. My reaction was that I would rather die than do aught to
save ourselves or any part of this continent at the expense of Britain."

**NEWFOUNDLAND** ◆ In the tiny, splendidly isolated Dominion of Newfoundland, the Depression was particularly devastating. By 1932, more than half the workforce was unemployed. An enraged mob of ten thousand people descended on Prime Minister Richard Squires, hoping, at the very least, to drive him from office. Squires was rescued from physical harm by a young politician named Joseph Smallwood, who dressed Squires in a monk's robe and spirited him out of town. Two years later, with the government facing bankruptcy, a referendum was held. The desperate citizens voted to suspend their own right to democratic self-government, and an unelected commissioner was selected by Britain to govern the territory indefinitely. (*The Knee Family, Badger's Quay, Newfoundland. Provincial Archives of Newfoundland and Labrador, VA 14-127*)

In London, Churchill was being pressed to consider a deal with Hitler. His position was delivered in a memorable speech: "We shall never surrender, and even if . . . this Island or a large part of it were subjugated and starving, then our Empire beyond the seas, armed and guarded by the British fleet, would carry on the struggle, until, in God's good time the New World, with all its power and might, steps forth to the rescue and liberation of the old."

Among the Canadian volunteers who responded to Britain's crisis was the Winnipeg reporter James Gray. But the army doctor recognized him from the dole lines. "Jimmy Gray," he said. "What the hell are you doing in this man's army? At your age? With your T.B. history? My God, look at you. Get on the scales." Gray now weighed sixty kilograms [134 pounds]. "Get the hell out of here," the doctor said. "And don't come back."

Gray's hometown of Winnipeg had started to recover from the Depression, and the surrounding farmland was benefiting from the heroic

**"La Bolduc," Mary Travers-Bolduc**

◆ Born on the Gaspé Peninsula, Mary Travers was the daughter of an Irish father and French-Canadian mother. In 1907, at the age of thirteen, she moved to Montreal to work as a domestic, then took a job in a factory. She married Edward Bolduc and had eleven pregnancies, though only four children survived. When her husband was injured and could not work, Mary, at the age of thirty-four, took to the stage, first playing violin and harmonica and later singing. Encouraged by the response, she made her first record in 1929, "La Cuisinière," which sold ten thousand copies in a month. In the next decade she made thirty-nine records and wrote ninety songs, which spoke of the daily life of Quebecers. She became the voice of the province, a folk hero who sang of factory workers and women with ten children, the poor and the disenfranchised. She became wealthy in the process, able to pay $1,200 cash for a new 1931 Dodge. In 1937 she was in a serious car accident, and the next year she developed cancer, but she continued to sing. In 1941, she fainted after a show and was taken to hospital. She died a month later at the age of forty-six, mourned by all of Quebec. (*Archives nationales du Québec à Montréal*, P175.P71)

efforts of the Prairie Farm Rehabilitation Administration, a federal initiative created in 1935 to combat erosion and drought. Farmers ridged their fields to prevent land erosion and planted the newly developed Fairway crested wheat grass to anchor the soil. By 1939, the farms were again producing viable crops, and those young men who had battled nature for so long enlisted in the army to fight a new enemy.

Because Ronald Liversedge had fought Spanish fascists he was ineligible to fight the German fascists; the government remained suspicious of any Communist leanings held by those veterans. Liversedge returned to Vancouver, where he worked in the shipbuilding yards as the country desperately tried to build a military force.

In St-Hyacinthe, five of Irene Duhamel's brothers joined up. One of them brought home a friend, George Graveline, who courted Irene. They were engaged, and she quit her job in the cotton factory. But Graveline enlisted in the army, and Irene once more put her life on hold.

Norman Bethune went to China to help in their fight against Japanese occupation, implementing the wartime medical innovations he had introduced in Spain. He joined the Eighth Route Army in the Shanxi-Hobei region and worked tirelessly as a surgeon, teacher, and propagandist. In 1939, he died of septicemia, having become infected after slicing his finger open while operating on a Chinese soldier. Mao Zedong wrote an essay, "In Memory of Norman Bethune," which praised his efforts and established him as a role model: all Communists should embrace his internationalism and commitment. A statue of Bethune was erected in China, where to this day he is celebrated as a national hero. In his will, Bethune left all his diaries, photographs, and the films he had made to Tim Buck, still the leader of Canada's Communist Party.

Marian Scott's paintings were exhibited at the 1939 New York World's Fair. A year earlier, Hitler had confiscated all the "degenerate art" in Germany and now only bland, noble, Nordic images that functioned as propaganda were allowed to be exhibited. In 1935, Bethune had given Marian a self-portrait as a gift, with a note suggesting that her husband, Frank, might object to it being hung in their home. She put it up after Bethune's death and later donated it to McGill University, which in turn presented it to the People's Republic of China.

Mackenzie King remained the calm – some would say inert – centre of the swirling political and cultural movements that swept across the country. His political skills were subtle, and he intuitively understood the delicate task of holding together a culturally diverse and politically tormented country. As Frank Scott had observed, Canada was experiencing a growing nationalism, and now more than half of its citizens had no ties to Great Britain. The face of the country was changing, and King had to find a way to accommodate that. King shared with Frank Scott the idea of an autonomous country free of its colonial roots. But independence from Britain did not release Canada from international obligations. What role would the country play in international affairs – in the war that was now engulfing the world – and what price would it be willing to pay?

# We're in the army now

## A NEW WORLD ORDER

CHAPTER 5

Gladys Arnold left Saskatchewan in 1935, during the bleakness of the Depression, and went to Europe to work as a reporter for the Canadian Press news service. In May 1940, she was on a train headed to Paris when she encountered a Belgian refugee train that had been attacked by German fighter planes. "It had been carrying whole school classes of children, hospital patients, old people, women," she wrote. "On top of the cars and along the sides were painted large red crosses and the words 'hôpital' and 'enfants.' I walked through the train. Blood was spattered everywhere, broken glass and tufts of hair were partially embedded in the back of a seat. The silence was awesome and the eyes of the remaining, untouched passengers and children were blank. I rushed to a washroom and retched. It was the first and only time I vomited. Such scenes were to become familiar."

German armies were moving through Luxembourg, Holland, and Belgium in Hitler's promised "*blitzkrieg*" (lightning war), and refugees streamed toward Paris. On May 14 the Netherlands surrendered, and two weeks later King Leopold of Belgium ordered his soldiers to lay down their arms. "Refugees arriving by trains had been joined by those in cars," Arnold wrote. "Soon they were arriving on foot. . . . Their stories were horrifying. One woman in her sixties, who had never been on a bicycle in her life, rode from Antwerp to Paris. Another woman who was almost mad with grief told me how she had buried two of her children by the roadside after a raid on the [refugee] column. . . . The human river stretched across the road, across the sidewalks and hugged the fence of Luxembourg Gardens. . . . They were locked together in the common, grey weariness of their faces and shocked eyes."

Paris offered only a temporary refuge. The French army had collapsed, and Nazi troops were heading for the capital. Ten million people were on the roads of France, without food or shelter, Gladys Arnold among them. She had left Paris only days before the German army entered its silent streets on June 14, parading its tanks through the Place de la Concorde. A sign was raised on the Eiffel Tower: "Germany Conquers on All Fronts." Arnold managed to get to the port of Le Verdon, along with thousands of others. "Bicycles, carts and mountains of luggage lay scattered along the beach. . . . French officials, British officers and dock hands tried to keep order and told us that when our turn came to embark we could take on board 'only what we could carry.' People frantically clawed through trunks and boxes, tossing out the contents. Women were throwing away valuable furs, gowns, coats and treasured trinkets."

Arnold crowded onto a small car ferry with three hundred others. For four hours they approached every ship in the harbour, trying to find one that would take them across the Channel to England. A Dutch freighter finally agreed. The crossing was slow and hampered by the German planes that were dropping mines into the Channel, but the freighter finally reached Falmouth safely. "It was at the moment a little Girl Guide offered me a cup of tea at the Falmouth quay that I realized that, in the eyes of everyone there, I was a refugee," Arnold wrote. "Then I realized the difference. I was not a refugee like the others. Unlike those men and women in the queue for aliens, I could go home."

By winter, Arnold was in Ottawa, still working for the Canadian Press but writing now about the home front. "People were pouring into Ottawa from all parts of Canada to fill war jobs," she wrote. "The YMCA was filled with western girls arriving with one slim suitcase, thrilled to have a job in Ottawa, and thrilled at the prospect of buying a new dress after the long years of depression."

By the end of June 1940, Hitler had control of continental Europe, and his army was massed at the Channel, intent on invading Britain. Prime Minister Mackenzie King worried that England could fall, and Canada would be the next target. "There is a real possibility of invasion of our shores," he wrote. "We have, therefore, changed now to the stage where defence of this land becomes our most important duty. It will involve far-reaching measures." King had been re-elected on the promise that he would not impose conscription for military service overseas, but he still had to prepare for war. His compromise was the National Resources Mobilization Act, which required all men over the age of sixteen to register. King

Opposite: By May 20, 1940, Hitler's Panzer divisions had reached the English Channel near Abbéville, France, effectively trapping the British Expeditionary Force. A huge flotilla of Royal Navy vessels and small civilian boats managed to evacuate 338,000 British and French soldiers, preventing an early end to the war. This concerted effort inspired one of Winston Churchill's most memorable speeches: "We shall not flag or fail. We shall go on to the end. We shall fight in France, we shall fight on the seas and oceans, we shall fight with growing confidence and growing strength in the air, we shall defend our island, whatever the cost may be, we shall fight on the beaches, we shall fight on the landing grounds, we shall fight in the fields and in the streets, we shall fight in the hills; we shall never surrender." – From Churchill's speech in the British House of Commons, June 4, 1940. (*Richard Eurich,* The Evacuation from Dunkirk. *The Grange Collection, GR-479*)

stipulated that Canadians would be called up for home defence only, but some felt that registration was the first step toward sending conscripts overseas.

Camillien Houde, the mayor of Montreal, told citizens to defy the law. "Parliament, according to my belief," he said, "has no mandate to vote for conscription. I do not believe that I am held to conform to the law, and I have no intention of doing so. And I ask the population not to conform, knowing full well what I am doing presently and to what I expose myself. If the government wants a mandate for conscription, let it come before the people without, this time, fooling them." His comments were banned from publication. Two days later, on August 5, he was arrested by the RCMP as he left city hall and imprisoned without trial. He spent the next four years in Canadian internment camps but remained a popular figure.

After the German invasion of France, King wrote, "It is now left to the British peoples and those of British stock to save the world." But the Canadian military was ill equipped to save anything; its army was small and untrained, its weapons outdated and inadequate. And now the country was called on to produce military machinery not just for its own army but for Britain's as well. The task fell to the minister of munitions and supply, Clarence Decatur Howe, a former engineer who had made a fortune building grain elevators. In accordance with the War Measures Act, Howe was allowed to produce weapons and supplies without parliamentary approval or budget constraints. "We have no idea of the cost," he said of the military buildup, "but before the war is over everything will be needed so let's go ahead anyway. If we lose the war, nothing will matter. . . . If we win the war the cost will have been of no consequence and will have been forgotten." Howe hired businessmen at a dollar a year to run the Crown corporations that were involved in the rapid transformation to a war-time economy.

One of Howe's first priorities was fighter planes, and the job of building them fell to the Canadian Car and Foundry Company in Fort William, Ontario, a railway boxcar manufacturer. The work was directed by thirty-five-year-old Elsie MacGill, an aeronautical engineer who had been the first woman to graduate from the University of Michigan with a master's degree. To produce forty Hawker Hurricane fighter planes first required retooling the factory, designing new tools and equipment, and hiring and training hundreds of inexperienced workers. There were 3,600 blueprints outlining the specifications for the plane's 60,000 parts. The factory had 3,000 workers, 500 of them women. It took a year to produce the first plane, but with that accomplished they began building three or four a week.

Hitler was preparing to invade England and Winston Churchill delivered the first of the many stirring speeches that would distinguish his tenure as wartime prime minister. "The whole fury and might of the enemy must very soon be turned on us," he told the British House of Commons. "Hitler knows that he will have to break us in this island or lose the war. . . . Let us therefore brace ourselves to our duties, and so bear ourselves that, if

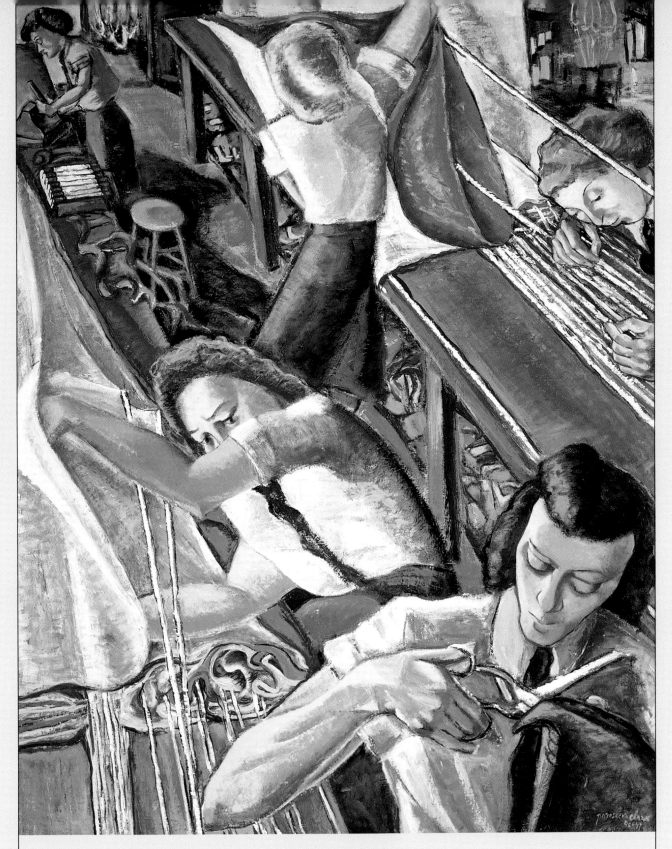

**WOMEN AT WAR** ◆ On the home front, women were recruited en masse into the new war industries, and by 1943, 261,000 Canadian women were manufacturing various war goods. For the first time, women were allowed in the armed forces in roles other than as nurses, and 45,423 enlisted. They took over support functions, allowing the men to be sent into combat. (*Paraskeva Clark*, Parachute Riggers. *Canadian War Museum*, CN14086)

the British Empire and its Commonwealth last for a thousand years, men will still say: 'This was their finest hour.'"

The Battle of Britain began in July 1940 and raged for two months. Britain's Royal Air Force was defending its coastal targets from a series of German air attacks targeting radar and shipping. Among the squadrons of British fighter pilots there were more than one hundred Canadians, including Ernest McNab. McNab was a short, stocky engineer from Rosthern, Saskatchewan, a member of Canada's first aerial acrobatic team and the country's most experienced fighter pilot. He had joined the No. 1 RCAF squadron, which flew up to seven sorties a day during the heaviest fighting.

On September 15, 1940, the German Dornier and Heinkel bombers came in waves over London at night and hit civilian targets, leaving thousands dead and the city in ruins. The Allied pilots scrambled to their Hurricanes and Spitfires. "It was a terrific spectacle," McNab recalled. "There were more than a thousand aircraft in the sky just south of London. So many that there was as much danger of colliding with another fellow as there was of being shot down."

Churchill was in the RAF Operations room, a bunker deep below the streets of London. "I asked Air Vice Marshall [Park] what other reserves have we," he wrote. "'There are none,' he replied. The odds were great; our margins small; the stakes infinite."

The German planes retreated but came back two hours later. "It was a quick shot and away for someone was sure to be on your tail," Ernest McNab remembered. "I counted nine aircraft falling at one time, and there were parachutes everywhere. After fifteen minutes there was hardly a plane in the sky – the Germans had run for home."

*The Battle of Britain* by Commodore Norman Hood of the RAF. (*The Granger Collection, AV66*)

By the end of October, the Royal Air Force had won the Battle of Britain, a critical siege that claimed the lives of twenty Canadian pilots. Though the RAF had lost 900 aircraft, the Germans had lost roughly 2,300. It was their first major failure in the war.

Howe's war machine had begun to send supplies to Britain, but the merchant ships carrying them were being torpedoed daily by German U-boats. These submarines, by preventing food and military supplies from reaching Britain, were effectively hastening a German victory. In December 1940, the British freighter *Western Prince* was torpedoed and sunk; its survivors were left bobbing in the frigid water nearly five hundred kilometres off the coast of Iceland. The ship's convoy was under strict orders not to stop under any circumstances, and so these men watched the faint hope of rescue steam eastward without them. Among them were C. D. Howe, Toronto tycoon E. P. Taylor, and Montreal financier Gordon Scott. In an open lifeboat, their chances of survival were poor. When news of the sinking reached Ottawa, King despaired at the loss of his munitions minister. "Through the day I have been turning over in my mind possible men to take his post," he wrote in his diary, "but I can think of no one available."

A U-boat surfaced next to Howe's lifeboat but moved on, seeking larger prey. Then, at dusk, a small tramp steamer returned, its captain disobeying orders, and picked them up.

By 1941, Allied ships were being lost to U-boats faster than they were being built, and the Germans launched eight new submarines for every one sunk. They attacked in packs of six or more, invisible, well-armed (each carried twenty-one torpedoes), and difficult to defend against. "The only thing that ever really frightened me was the U-boat peril," Churchill wrote.

*Torpedoed, North Atlantic* by Flight Lieutenant Paul Alexander Goranson. (*Canadian War Museum, 11469*)

"How much would the U-boat warfare reduce our imports and shipping? Would it reach the point where our life would be destroyed?" Churchill feared that the U-boats could gradually strangle England by continually sinking Canadian supply ships.

The main craft available to protect the merchant ships was the corvette, a cheap, leaky, unstable ship that would "roll in wet grass," as the seamen joked. "I cannot imagine a more miserable existence than this of being caught on a corvette in the Atlantic," wrote Frank Curry, who joined the navy at the age of twenty. "I grew up in Winnipeg, Manitoba, thousands of miles from both the Pacific and Atlantic Oceans. A prairie boy, through and through. And yet, like thousands upon thousands of others, from the farms, villages, small towns and cities of the prairies, I ended up on a corvette in the North Atlantic."

Curry was an ASDIC (sonar) operator on HMCS *Kamsack*. His job was to search for submarines as the corvette escorted merchant ships across the Atlantic. A hundred men were crowded into facilities for fifty – a damp, dismal existence: "Mess deck is a terrifying place to venture near, knee-deep in sea water, tables smashed, clothes floating around in it, breakfast stirred in, the crew in an almost stupor from the nightmarishness of it all. . . . If only they could portray all this in their recruiting posters."

Each month, hundreds of ships left Canada, bringing tonnes of food, lumber, iron, steel, and oil to England. The odds were grim: up to one hundred ships were sunk each month. "It was the merchant seamen who suffered most," a dock worker noted. "They couldn't fight back and they were the best targets. They never knew when they would be singled out for extinction. The suspense must have been awful."

The sea itself was enough to deal with. "Mountainous seas are breaking completely over the ship and it is turning into massive coatings of ice as it hits," Curry wrote in his diary. "We are sheathed in sixteen inches of ice and I do not know what keeps us from going to the bottom of the Atlantic as we pitch, toss, roll and do everything else imaginable."

Allied planes tried to bomb the U-boats, but the submarines waited in packs in mid ocean, out of range of the planes. "Sharp alteration of course on emergency signal," read Curry's diary entry for May 10, 1942. "Six to eight German U-boats in pack formation, laying across our course, 300 miles ahead. Flocks of messages pouring in from Convoy W-8 under heavy attack to our north; they lost six ships last night and still under heavy attack." Seven days later, his own convoy was under attack. "We lost ship on the far side during the night. Nothing we could do about it; terrible feeling of helplessness."

On December 7, 1941, 360 Japanese warplanes bombed the American naval base at Pearl Harbor, Hawaii, killing thousands of people, destroying 200 aircraft, and sinking more than a dozen ships. The United States immediately declared war on Japan.

Canada had already declared war on Japan, and the existing anti-Asian sentiment reached new depths. Within days, Canadian Pacific Railways had fired all its Japanese workers, and most other Canadian industries followed suit. Japanese fishermen in British Columbia were ordered to stay in port, and 1,200 fishing boats were seized by the Canadian navy. Curfews were imposed on Japanese Canadians and enforced by soldiers. "We are so used to wars and alarms," Muriel Kitagawa, a twenty-nine-year-old writer and mother of two, wrote to her brother Wes. "And we have been tempered for the anti[-Japanese] feelings these long years. It has only intensified into

In 1941, as many as 1,200 fishing boats owned by Japanese Canadians were impounded and later sold. (*Vancouver Public Library, 3190*)

overt acts of unthinking hoodlumism like throwing flaming torches into rooming houses and bricks through plate glass."

The anti-Japanese sentiment intensified after Japanese forces invaded Hong Kong a few hours after the attack on Pearl Harbor. Among the 20,000 Allied troops posted there were 2,000 poorly equipped Canadian soldiers. The Winnipeg Grenadiers and the Royal Rifles had been in Hong Kong less than a month when they were overrun by Japan's 38th Division. There were 800 casualties among the Canadians. But what followed their surrender on Christmas Day was worse. The Japanese murdered the wounded, raped and killed nurses, and brutalized those who were surrendering. "We walked with our hands up and they nicked us in the back with bayonets," one private wrote. "They took out DeLaurier and two or three others and used them for bayonet practice all night long. We could hear them." The survivors went to prison camps, where the brutality and privation continued.

When news of the Hong Kong campaign reached Canada, the premier of British Columbia, fearing that Japanese Canadians remained loyal to Japan, announced that Canada should "remove the menace of Fifth Column Activity from B.C." On January 14, 1942, all male Japanese Canadians between the ages of eighteen and forty-five were taken to camps in the interior, and the coast was designated a "protected area." Ian Alistair Mackenzie, a cabinet minister from British Columbia, called for even stricter measures. "It is the government's plan," he said, "to get these people out of B.C. as fast as possible. Every single man, woman and child will be removed from the defence areas of this province and it is my personal intention, as long as I remain in public life, to see they never come back here."

On February 26, 21,000 Japanese Canadians were told to pack a single suitcase each. They were taken to livestock barns, photographed, fingerprinted, given identification numbers, and told to wait for trains to take them inland. Vancouver's Hastings Park was one of the holding areas where families waited, sometimes for months, to be relocated. "Hundreds of women and children were squeezed into the livestock building," remembered

**Japanese Relocation** ◆ Before being sent to this camp at Slocan, B.C., or other locations in the interior, Japanese Canadians were held at Hastings Park in Vancouver. Muriel Kitagawa described the conditions there after a visit in April 1942: "Eiko sleeps in a partitioned stall. . . . This stall was the former home of a pair of stallions. . . . The whole place is impregnated with the smell of ancient manure and maggots. . . . The toilets are just a sheet metal trough, and up till now they did not have partitions or seats. . . . Eiko is really sick. The place has got her down. There are 10 showers for 1500 women. Hot and cold water. The men looked so terribly at loose ends." (*The Slocan City camp. National Archives of Canada, c-29464*)

Yukiharu Misuyabu, a teenager at the time, "each family separated from the next by a flimsy piece of cloth hung from the upper deck of double-decked steel bunks. The walls between the rows of steel bunks were only five feet high, their normal use being to tether animals."

In Ottawa, the RCMP and military believed that British Columbia's Japanese Canadians posed little threat to security, but a racist mood gathered momentum within the province. There was a fear of invasion and of "fifth columnists," a fear that increased in June 1942 when Japan invaded and occupied the Aleutian Islands off Alaska. "B.C. is falling all over itself in the scramble to be the first to kick us out from jobs and homes . . . it has just boiled down to race persecution, and signs have been posted on all highways . . . JAPS . . . KEEP OUT," Muriel Kitigawa wrote to her brother. "We are tightening our belts for the starvation to come. The diseases . . . the crippling . . . the twisting of our souls . . . death would be the easiest to bear."

Some families were divided, with the men sent to work camps while women and children were sent to defunct mining towns in the province's interior. Other families went to Manitoba or Alberta to work on beet farms.

Franklin Roosevelt, Mackenzie King, and Henry Stimson, the U.S. secretary of war, the day after signing the Ogdensburg Agreement, which committed Canada and the United States to a continental defence policy. (*Library of Congress, 569960*)

Yukiharu Misuyabu and his family went to Lemon Creek, where about 1,700 Japanese lived in shacks. The government had sold the family's boat and house and offered them $75 per month if his father would sign consent papers agreeing to the sale. "Refusal to comply meant that we would starve . . . My father finally gave in. . . .Thus, we were forced to pay for our imprisonment out of our own pockets – a requirement not even imposed upon hardened criminals." On January 19, 1943, the federal government passed a law authorizing the sale of all seized properties without the owners' consent, a measure aimed at the Japanese.

In the United States, a military zone was created along the west coast, and 100,000 Japanese Americans who lived in the area were relocated to camps in the interior. A 2,451-kilometre road was hastily built from northern Alberta to Alaska, to facilitate the movement of military forces in the event of invasion. Mackenzie King worried that the road was simply another encroachment of American influence. "The road was less intended for protection against the Japanese than as one of the fingers of the hand which America is placing more or less over the whole of the Western hemisphere," he wrote in his diary, "which would mean hemispheric immunity from future wars but increasing political control by U.S." He felt that Canadians should maintain control of the new Alaska Highway.

The highway symbolized a dramatic political shift during the war that moved Canada away from its political alignment with Britain and toward the United States. On August 17, 1940, King had met with American president Franklin Roosevelt on his private railway car near Ogdensburg, New York. The two drafted an agreement that created a permanent board responsible for the joint defence of the two countries. King told Parliament that the Ogdensburg Agreement was "part of the enduring foundation of a new world order, based on friendship and good will. In the furtherance of this new world order, Canada is fulfilling a manifest destiny." Britain could no longer guarantee Canada's security; it was necessary to tie Canada's fate to that of the Americans.

This alliance with the United States presented obvious problems. Lester Pearson, who was at the time Canada's second-highest ranking officer in Washington, articulated the delicate nature of the relationship: "When we are dealing with such a powerful neighbour, we have to avoid the twin dangers of subservience and truculent touchiness. We succumb to the former when we take everything lying down and to the latter when we rush to the state department with a note every time some congressman makes a stupid statement about Canada, or some documentary movie about the war forgets to mention Canada." The task of finding an acceptable partnership would prove to be an ongoing challenge.

As the war escalated, voluntary recruitment began to slow, and there was a resurgence of conscriptionist sentiment, both in the press and from Arthur Meighen, an old political foe of King's who was now leader of the Conservative Party. "This nation is in the throes of a crisis," Meighen said. "That Britain is doing its mightiest few will dispute. Who will dare to say that Canada is even in sight of a total war? I shall, therefore, urge with all the power I can bring to bear compulsory selective service over the whole field of War." It was Meighen who had drafted the Military Service Act, which had brought to a boiling point the 1917 conscription crisis, Wilfrid Laurier's most bitter political defeat. King detested him. "I am getting past the time when I can fight in public with a man of Meighen's type who is sarcastic, vitriolic, and the meanest type of politician," he wrote in his diary.

King had campaigned on a promise not to impose conscription for overseas service, but now even some members of his own cabinet were adding their voices to the call for conscription. The prime minister was in an impossible political position. "I, myself, could not continue at the head of any Government which as much as considered conscription," he wrote, "unless I were released from all commitments in that connection made before the war had reached the proportions it has today."

Attempting a compromise, King announced that a national non-binding plebiscite would be held on the issue. In Montreal, ten thousand members of a newly formed organization called the Ligue pour la défense du Canada gathered at the Saint James Market to protest. André Laurendeau, one of the leaders, addressed the crowd: "French-Canadian nationalists are opposed to the very principle of the plebiscite. They deny the government the right to ask the majority to cancel a promise made to the minority." The gathering turned into a riot, and police arrested twenty protesters.

On April 27, 1942, Canadians voted on the plebiscite: 80 per cent of Canadians outside Quebec voted in favour of conscription, and 73 per cent of Quebecers voted against. "Together, we have lived through . . . an hour of unanimity the like of which has never been known in our history," Laurendeau announced. "In its own way, English Canada has also demonstrated its unity: they had as a rallying cry the pursuit of total war. But French-Canadians refused to let themselves be pushed around."

King viewed the polarized results and sought, as always, a middle way, adopting a slogan from a *Toronto Star* editorial: "Not necessarily conscription, but conscription if necessary."

By August 1942, Canadian troops had been in England for almost three years, training, and waiting to see action. Everitt Hill, a twenty-one-year-old private from Valentia, Ontario, was training in southern England with the Third Anti-Tank Regiment. When a nearby school was bombed and eighteen children killed, Hill wrote to his brother Albert: "I think by all laws of human nature we should dread going into action but we are the opposite we can hardly wait to get going. It takes the army a little while to make you want to kill but a few things like the bombing of those kids can make a killer out of any man overnight."

Hill was disappointed not to be part of the raid at Dieppe on August 19. "Well I guess the radio and newspapers would be full of talk about our boys being in France yesterday," he wrote to Albert. "Gee I wish I had been with them. I was talking to some of them last night and they said they wouldn't miss it for the world. We don't know how many were lost on our side but they tell us they really knocked the Jerries over."

The optimistic news that Hill reported was at odds with the facts: Dieppe was a military disaster. The raid on the French coast had been intended as an experiment, allowing the Allies to test their amphibious equipment and develop invasion strategies. It would also indicate whether cross-Channel assaults were feasible. Beyond that, it was felt that a landing on continental Europe would demonstrate support for the beleaguered Soviets on the eastern front. It was decided by both British and Canadian generals that the eager Canadian soldiers would make up most of the assault force. The attack was originally scheduled for July but was cancelled due to rough water and rescheduled for August 19.

Code-named "Jubilee," the landing force was made up of six thousand men, five thousand of them Canadians. As the troops approached the beach at 5:10 a.m., it was clear that they had lost the element of surprise. German tracers lit up the sky, and the Canadians were faced with devastating fire from fortified, elevated German positions.

Captain Denis Whitaker and a platoon of Royal Hamilton Light Infantry were among those who landed on the beach at dawn. "The ramp dropped," Whitaker recalled. "I led the thirty odd men of my platoon in a charge about twenty-five yards up the stony beach. We fanned out and flopped down just short of a huge wire obstacle. Bullets flew everywhere. Enemy mortar bombs started to crash down. Around me, men were being hit and bodies were piling up, one on top of the other. It was terrifying."

The raid on Dieppe, 1942.
(*Canadian War Museum,*
*AN-19830136-001*)

Dieppe had been a French resort town, its stony beach and casino popular among Parisians seeking relief during the sticky summer months. Whitaker's men moved toward the casino and routed the Germans who were using it for cover. Casualties were already high, and the invading forces were crippled by confusion and the unexpected carnage that not even three years of training could have prepared them for. Their radio communications were broken, and on the command ship in the Channel Major-General J. Hamilton Roberts was not aware that his troops were being slaughtered. He ordered the reserves to land, and they waded to shore through water that was red with the blood of the first wave of Canadian soldiers, their corpses moving in the surf. "I noticed a handful of soldiers spread out on the ground," one soldier recalled, "with their heads turned toward the parapets, as if waiting for the order to move. . . . So I crawled toward one of them, I shook him and spoke to him, but he didn't answer. He was dead. I did the same with a few others, but in vain. They were all dead."

Six hundred soldiers with the Fusiliers Mont-Royal waded toward the beach under heavy fire. "I think that I must have made no more than three steps before I was hit by a bullet for the first time and knocked to the ground," remembered Lieutenant-Colonel Dollard Menard, the twenty-nine-year-old commander. "A bullet hits you head-on, like the blow of a hammer. At first you don't feel the pain. . . . I was hit a second time. It seemed to explode all around me. I was no longer sure I was still in one piece. The second bullet hit me in the right cheek and tore my face pretty badly. I had just reached the parapet when I was hit for the third time, this time in my right wrist."

He was on the beach, exposed to mortar and gun fire, and he tried to find cover. "I was trying to leave the beach when I was hit in the right leg just below the knee. . . . The last bullet hit me below the right ankle and nailed me to the ground for good. I couldn't feel the pain anymore and I began to pray harder and harder."

Captain Whitaker was trying to lead his surviving men back from the casino, toward the beach, to pull out. "The worst part was the dash for the boats amid a hail of bullets and mortar or shellfire. Apart from trying to help the wounded, it was every man for himself. I expected every step to be my last." Whitaker made it back to the boats, the only Canadian officer to survive unscathed. Menard was pulled to safety by his men and survived his five bullet wounds. But of the 5,000 Canadians who left England for Dieppe, 907 were dead, 586 wounded, and 1,874 taken prisoner, making the failed invasion the bloodiest nine hours in Canadian military history.

Able Seaman Albert Kirby was back in England by night, torn by different emotions: "So relieved to be home. So happy to be in one piece. So ashamed to have come home alone. So proud of the way the Camerons went to their deaths. So sad that they seemed to have been wasted. So angry that I was even a part of something so confusing, agonizing, demanding, and apparently unrewarding, without even knowing what I was doing or exactly where I had been."

The debacle had produced much valour, provided an expensive lesson in amphibious assaults on a fortified position, and given the Canadians their first tragic infantry experience on European soil.

On January 31, 1943, the German army that was occupying Stalingrad surrendered after 90,000 Nazi soldiers starved to death, more died of exposure, and 100,000 were killed by the Soviet army. Hitler had forbidden surrender – it was to have been a fight to the last man – but Field Marshal Freidrich von Paulus had disobeyed orders. The Nazis received another blow in March when Field Marshal Erwin Rommel, the celebrated "Desert Fox," retreated from North Africa after losing battles in Egypt and Tunisia. Hitler had again denied the possibility of surrender, saying to Rommel, "As to your troops, you can show them no other road than that to victory or death." Rommel returned to Europe, sick and exhausted, and Hitler's mania and desperation grew. The German army was now recruiting boys as young as sixteen.

In July, Canadian soldiers saw action once again when they invaded Sicily and successfully drove the Germans out. They continued on to the Italian mainland, to Ortona on the Adriatic coast, where, five days before Christmas, they engaged the German elite paratroopers and tanks in a street-by-street battle. "The Seaforths and the Edmontons were still embarked on the bloody task of flushing the enemy from fortified houses in hand-to-hand fighting which asked and gave no quarter," reported Charles Comfort, an artist commissioned to document the war. "Tired, drenched and mud-covered men blasted and tunneled their way from one house to the next like demon moles. . . . Undoubtedly Canadians were joined in the most bitter and costly fighting of the campaign on this Christmas eve." The Canadians took Ortona on December 27, but suffered 2,339 casualties in the process.

**CANADIAN WAR ARTISTS** ◆ In 1943, Canadian artists serving in the armed forces were commissioned by the Department of National Defence to depict the war. Thirty artists eventually took part in the War Art Program, including Charles Comfort and Group of Seven member Lawren Harris. (*Charles Comfort*, Via Dolorosa, Ortona. *Canadian War Museum, 12402*)

Everitt Hill had missed Dieppe, but he found a way to relieve the boredom by courting a twenty-year-old Englishwoman named Joan Kitchell who was serving as a farm worker in the Women's Land Army. The two met regularly at Kitchell's parents' home in Brighton. "Look at me when I came overseas I said oh no – no girl will ever hook me," Hill wrote to his brother, "yet here I am sunk hook line and sinker and really liking it. I must admit this

### THE ITALIAN CAMPAIGN

◆ "What were once proud
Tiger and Churchill tanks are
now blackened twisted hulks.
Whole towns and villages have
disappeared, except for ugly
piles of rubble. . . . To veer off
the trail means instant destruction. Fresh graves show where
some of the fiercest battles
have raged. On some, the only
indication of whether the grave
is friend or foe is a Canadian or
German helmet atop a rifle or
rough wooden marker. Ahead,
the sounds of battle grow louder
and fiercer. . . . The mass of San
Fortunato looms before us in the
failing light. . . . The ground
ahead is being heavily shelled
by everything the Germans have
in their arsenal." – Lieutenant
Charles Sydney Frost of Princess
Patricia's Canadian Light Infantry,
September 1944. (*Charles Comfort,
Canadian Field Guns Near Ortona.
Canadian War Museum, 12246*)

though that if Joan hadn't come into my life when she did I might have been a pretty hard boiled case by now cause I had no mean start when I met her. This life of being overseas will do that to a fellow if somebody doesn't snap you out of it."

He spent his fourth Christmas at an English camp, tired of war without ever having seen it. "I'm so darn restless," he wrote to his sister. "I guess the trouble is I'm not contented in an army camp anymore. I want a home and Joan. Can you blame me?"

In March, he had more news. "I'm to become a daddy in August bet you have a hard time getting over that shock. . . . I'll be damned if this war is going to ruin our lives completely." Hill's desire for battle had waned, but he would soon find himself in the fighting.

By June 1944, "Operation Overlord" had sent 130,000 men across the Channel to France's Normandy coast on seven thousand ships to liberate Europe. Fifteen thousand of the troops were Canadians. Frank Curry, who was now aboard the *Caraquet*, a minesweeper that left Portland Harbour for Normandy at 10:00 p.m. on June 5 described the scene: "The moon played hide and seek with the clouds and we expected any moment to be the target for shore batteries. . . . RAF blasting away all along the coast, so close that we could feel the jar of the bombs continuously. . . . [G]reat fires started all along and over fifty planes came down in flames throughout the long and terrible night." At dawn on June 6, the Allies, having learned a lesson at Dieppe, used their battleships to bombard the German fortifications. "British, American and French cruisers and battleships . . . opened up like the very gates of hell, blasting away all around us, the concussions of 16 inch guns practically tossing us out of the water."

By nightfall, the Canadian troops had advanced farther inland than any other Allied force. They initially engaged the Wehrmacht troops, but they were soon facing fanatical teenaged members of the Hitler Youth, and the 25th SS Panzer-Grenadier Regiment led by the ruthless Colonel Kurt Meyer. Meyer ordered the murder of Canadian prisoners, and the bodies of soldiers in the Queen's Own Rifles and other regiments were later found with bullet holes in their temples.

By August 8, the Canadians had advanced thirty kilometres. In a pincer movement with the Americans and British, they trapped the German 7th Army, leaving only a small opening. Several hundred thousand German troops fought toward what was called the Falaise Gap, which was to be closed by the Canadians and a Polish armoured division. "It was as if the Americans and British were huge brooms sweeping the Germans into the dustpan which at that moment was the Canadian Army," wrote one artillery officer. Strafed by Spitfires and bombed by Typhoons, the Germans were taking a heavy hit. Between August 8 and 21, they suffered 5,500 casualties. The bombardment tested Nazi loyalties, but soldiers who tried to surrender were shot in the back by SS troops.

(*From* The Canadian Home Journal, *August 1944*)

In the confusion, the Canadian troops were mistakenly bombed by Allied planes. They were also losing men to battle exhaustion as they moved toward the town of Falaise. Major David Currie had sixteen tanks and 175 men of the South Alberta Regiment to seal off the road. "In the distance we could see rising clouds of dust," he recalled. "We were witnessing the remnants of the German forces in France trying to escape the pocket. The column stretched as far as we could see. It was an awe-inspiring sight, and from the distance, it appeared to be a crushing force."

By Sunday, August 20, Currie was down to 120 men and five tanks, but they still managed to kill, wound, or capture 2,900 Germans. The role of the

Polish Armoured Division was to block the other side of the exit route, and they fought for seventy-two hours to keep the German army at bay. The Polish commanding officer was shot and died on the battlefield. "I shall never forget his words," wrote Pierre Sévigny, a liaison officer from Quebec. "'Gentlemen,' he said, 'everything is lost. I do not think the Canadians can come to our rescue. We have too few men. No more supplies, very little ammunition: five shells per gun and fifty rounds per man. . . . Still you must fight all the same. To surrender to the SS is useless, you know that. I thank you: you have fought a good fight. Good luck gentlemen, tonight we shall die.'"

The following day, the Germans advanced on the weakened Polish position with their oversized Tiger tanks. Sévigny called in an artillery barrage and prayed it would arrive before the tanks did: "The steel monsters were still moving forward with all their guns firing. . . . The first tank was only 500 metres away, now 400, 300, 250, 200 . . . 100. I jumped into the bottom of the hole, and with my face to the ground, I did not make a move; in a second death would come, of that I was certain. There was no hope. Instinctively I murmured a prayer. . . . All of a sudden, a hurricane, the noise of thunder, the earth was quaking. Was this death? Was this life? Was it possible? . . . Our guns were firing. . . . I laughed and cried! We were saved."

The Canadian tanks had arrived, and the Falaise Gap was closed, but the four-day siege had left 325 Canadian troops dead and 1,002 wounded. The landscape was a wasteland of scorched earth, corpses, and dead and dying horses. The German army in Normandy was effectively destroyed, having lost 300,000 men and most of their equipment. The fabled 12th SS Panzer Division had started with 20,000 men and 150 tanks and ended with 300 men and 10 tanks.

At Caen, near the coast, Everitt Hill finally saw the action he had been awaiting for more than three years. On his first day in battle, he was hit by a mortar. He was buried by fellow soldiers, and his grave became a shrine in Caen, a symbol of the Canadian effort. Eight days later, a government telegram arrived at the Hill farm in Ontario, announcing that their twenty-three-year-old son had been killed in action. Albert Hill was in England, with Everitt's wife, Joan. "At Joan's," he telegraphed his parents. "Not telling Joan until baby born. Be brave as you can. All my love. Albert." Within weeks, Everitt's daughter, Lynn, was born.

Two months later, Canadians were fighting in the damp misery of Holland's Scheldt Estuary, driving the Germans away from the key port of Antwerp. The Canadian forces were thinned by casualties, and replacements were under-trained. Colonel J. L. Ralston, the minister of national defence, went to Europe to investigate the state of the Canadian fighting force and was shocked at their depleted condition. "He was terribly despondent and lonely," his aide-de-camp said of Ralston. "His mind was completely made up. He had been deeply moved by seeing hundreds of badly wounded

The Canadian assault on Caen, depicted by Captain Orville Norman Fisher. (*Canadian War Museum, 1016526*)

men in field hospitals, men who had gone into action with regiments at half strength. He would either force the government to bring in overseas conscription or he would resign."

Ralston met with King but succeeded only in reviving all the prime minister's doubts and fears regarding conscription. "Considering all aspects of the situation more harm than good would be done with any attempt to force conscription at this time," King wrote in his diary. "I could not bring myself to being the head of a Government which would take that course – a course which might, after five years of war in Europe, and preparation for a year and a half of another war in the Pacific – lead to spurts of civil war in our own country. It would be a criminal thing, and would destroy the entire war record. . . . This is going to be a trying experience for me. Indeed, Ralston has been a thorn in my flesh right along. However, I have stood firm before and shall do so again."

Ralston also presented his case to cabinet, which made King uneasy. "It is perfectly plain to me that in pretty much all particulars my position is becoming identical to that of Sir Wilfrid Laurier," King wrote, "where his supposedly strongest colleagues left him, one by one, and joined their political enemies and became a party for conscription."

King's calculating political solution was to produce a resignation that Ralston had offered two years earlier and failed to withdraw, and announce that he was now accepting it. He replaced Ralston as minister of defence with retired general Andrew McNaughton, who was popular, provided a political advantage (he was being courted by the Conservatives as a political candidate), and was opposed to conscription. McNaughton felt he could raise enough troops voluntarily, but his confidence was shaken somewhat when he was booed and pelted with debris at an Ottawa rally. Shortly afterward he announced himself the most hated man in Canada, though King offered stiff competition for the title.

On November 22, the military high command told King that the campaign for voluntary enlistment would not work. King finally reversed his stand on conscription, worried that the army might actually revolt. The home defence conscripts would be sent overseas. He wrote: "It was apparent to me that it was only a matter of days before there would be no Government in Canada and this in the middle of war with our men giving their lives at the front." To get his Quebec lieutenant, Louis St. Laurent, on board, King told him that the army was about to stage a coup. But St. Laurent's reluctant endorsement did nothing to help in Quebec, where there was widespread protest, and the rest of Canada quickly joined in. There were desertions among the home defence conscripts, and King had to consider the depressing prospect of calling in the American army to deal with possible revolt. Of the 16,000 infantry reinforcements needed, 12,908 were sent overseas, and 2,463 reached the front lines.

By the spring of 1945, Canadian soldiers were forcing German troops out of Holland, and in April, Berlin was surrounded by Soviet troops. The end was in sight. On April 20, Benito Mussolini, the squat Italian dictator who had promised his nation prosperity, was executed: shot several times in the head and hanged by his feet with his dead mistress in a Milan square. Ten days later, Adolf Hitler committed suicide in his bunker, his dream of ushering in a thousand years of German glory vanished. The death camps were liberated, the awful scale of their horror glimpsed for the first time. Among the first journalists to witness the tragedy was René Lévesque, then a correspondent with the U.S. Seventh Army. "I felt as if I were in another world," he said on seeing the prison camp at Dachau. "What we discovered was anti-Semitism, but above all it showed where the descent into barbarism can lead. This was not a chance mishap, but a systematic death machine, a truly scientific industry of elimination, a hell fabricated with great care. We couldn't believe what we saw. There had been rumours of what was going on in the camps, and Hitler had never hidden the fact that he wanted to apply the final solution to the 'Jewish problem,' but unless you saw it with your own eyes, you couldn't believe it."

**DEATH CAMPS** ◆ Perhaps the most devastating and horrific images to come out of the war were those of the Nazi death camps. Six camps – Chelmno, Belzec, Sobibor, Treblinka, Majdanek, Auschwitz – were designed for the systematic killing of prisoners. Heinrich Himmler described their purpose: "The Jews are the eternal enemies of the German people and must be exterminated. All Jews within our grasp are to be destroyed without exception, now, during the war. If we do not succeed in destroying the biological substance of the Jews, the Jews will some day destroy the German people." Six million Jews were victims of Nazism. (*Library of Congress*)

In Europe and the Soviet Union the fighting was essentially over, but the last act of the war was still being played out in the Far East – and also in the isolation of the New Mexico desert. In 1942, a group of scientists led by Enrico Fermi had built a pile of uranium and graphite in an abandoned squash court at the University of Chicago and demonstrated the first controlled nuclear chain reaction. The experiment launched the "Manhattan Project," the race to build an atomic bomb.

Fundamental to the U.S. military's work on the bomb was a ready supply of uranium, and they contacted their Canadian allies to provide it. The uranium came from a mine owned by Gilbert Labine, which he had optimistically named, in the fashion of hopeful miners, Eldorado. In 1930, Labine had discovered pitchblende, the host rock for uranium, on the shores of Great Bear Lake in the Northwest Territories, but he had closed the mine at the outbreak of war. In 1942, C. D. Howe had phoned Labine. "I want you to reopen," he had told him. "Get together the most trustworthy people you can find. The Canadian Government will give you whatever money is required. . . . And for God's sake don't even tell your wife what you're doing."

By the end of 1943, Eldorado, which by now had been purchased secretly by the Canadian government, was operating at full capacity, producing the sixty tonnes of uranium oxide requested by the Americans. The ore was mined by the Dene, a semi-nomadic people who followed the migratory caribou herds. The miners were paid three dollars a day to haul forty-five-kilogram sacks of radioactive ore out to barges on the Mackenzie River. They called the grey stone the "money rock." "I was coated like flour in radium dust as it leaked from the heavy bags on my back," remembered Paul Baton, who worked at the mine for three months. "It gets into your clothes, hair, mouth and hands. During the long barge trips across the lake and down the Bear and Mackenzie we would sleep and sit on the sacks." Waste from the mine was dumped into Great Bear Lake, and Dene women used the discarded sacks to sew tents.

At Los Alamos, New Mexico, the first atomic bomb was constructed in a feverish race that brought together dozens of scientists. Howe offered Alberta as a test site, but the Americans preferred the New Mexico desert, and the bomb was successfully tested on July 16, 1945. On August 6, the American bomber *Enola Gay*, named for its pilot's mother, flew over Japan and dropped the atomic bomb code-named "Little Boy" on Hiroshima, a city with a population of 343,000. More than 60 per cent of the city was razed by the blast, and 75,000 people died immediately. Tens of thousands would die of radiation poisoning within the next several months. Nagasaki was bombed three days later. "Fat Man," as the bomb was named, missed its target by three kilometres, exploding above the largest Catholic church in the Far East. The casualties matched Hiroshima's. The suddenness and scale of the devastation overwhelmed the survivors. "It was a cruel and complete silence," wrote Japanese writer Kenzaburo Oe, "worse than any other, like a moan that cannot be voiced."

The decision to drop the bomb had not been exclusively military. Both General Dwight Eisenhower and General Douglas MacArthur felt that the bombings were unnecessary. Even Major General Curtis LeMay, who authorized the bombing, later admitted, "The atomic bomb had nothing to do with the end of the war at all." Tokyo had already been firebombed, and Japanese military targets had been severely damaged. A sea embargo was keeping supplies from reaching Japan. The nation's leaders were exploring the possibility of a conditional surrender, but neither the army nor Emperor Hirohito wanted it. "The dropping of the atomic bombs was not so much the last military act of the 2nd World War as the first major operation of the cold diplomatic war with Russia," wrote the British physicist P. M. Blackett. Stalin was already reneging on the commitments he had made at the Yalta Conference. Churchill, Roosevelt, and Stalin had met in February 1945 to discuss key issues concerning post-war Europe, and the Soviets had agreed to allow for the independence of eastern European countries liberated by their troops. Stalin was quickly evolving from ally to enemy. Jimmy Byrnes, the U.S. secretary of state, viewed the bomb as a powerful diplomatic tool, a

**THE ATOMIC BOMB** ♦ The team of scientists who worked on the Manhattan Project were thrilled about their breakthroughs in physics but ambivalent about the purpose of their creation. There was a bleak party to celebrate the success of the Hiroshima bomb, and when physicist Robert Oppenheimer left, he saw a colleague vomiting in the bushes. "The reaction has begun," he thought. While initially relieved that the Hiroshima bomb was "not a dud," Oppenheimer later had misgivings about his role in the development of the bomb, and its use in mass killings. "We had somehow thought it would not be dropped on people," he later said, disingenuously. The bombing of Nagasaki was greeted by a collective feeling of nausea among most of the scientists. Oppenheimer wondered if the living in those cities might envy the dead.

The response from Japan was oddly muted, but a survivor's poem captured the essential mood:

> I would be comforted
> if all living things
> in heaven and earth
> were to perish
> in utter desolation.

(*Hulton Archives*, HA-3664)

bargaining chip for post-war negotiations with the Soviet Union. When he met with his Soviet counterpart, V. M. Molotov, at a meeting of the Council of Foreign Ministers, he tried to use the bomb to extract concessions. Molotov embraced Byrnes and whispered in his ear, "You know we have the atomic bomb!" In fact, the Soviets did not have the bomb yet, but they were working on it, using information stolen from the Manhattan Project.

A month before the bombing of Hiroshima, the Cold War had already been glimpsed at the Potsdam Conference in June 1945, where the Allies established zones of occupation for Germany. Soviet leader Joseph Stalin was preparing to set up a Communist government in Poland (and did, on July 26, 1945), and he dismissed pleas from the west for democratic elections in Soviet-occupied Hungary, Romania, and Bulgaria. Franklin Roosevelt had died in April and the new president was Harry Truman, a "plain speaker," as his supporters would later trumpet, but unsophisticated in foreign affairs. Churchill left partway through the proceedings to attend to national

**THE COLD WAR** ◆ "From Stettin in the Baltic, to Trieste in the Adriatic, an iron curtain has descended across the continent. Beyond that line lie all the capitals of the ancient states of Central and Eastern Europe: Warsaw, Berlin, Prague, Vienna, Budapest, Belgrade, Bucharest and Sofia. All are subject not only to Soviet influence, but to a very high and in some cases increasing measure of control from Moscow." – Winston Churchill, speaking in 1946. (*National Archives of Canada, PA-136328*)

elections in England. After his triumphant leadership during the war, he reasonably expected to be returned to power, and so he was shocked to find himself voted out of office, replaced by the uncharismatic Labour leader Clement Attlee. At the end of the conference, the divide between the Soviet Union and her two allies was greater than before. The Cold War had effectively begun.

Despite the awful finality of the Japanese defeat, the Canadian government was not comfortable with the idea of Japanese Canadians returning to the west coast. At the end of the war, it offered them the choice of relocating to central Canada or being deported to Japan. "By the summer of 1946, the government was still denying us freedom of movement in this country, our native land," Yukiharu Mizuyabu wrote. "I had had enough of this shabby treatment and so I chose to be exiled to Japan along with the rest of my family." The country was in ruins; Tokyo, Hiroshima, and Nagasaki were largely destroyed. The country's infrastructure was gutted, its political

**THE NORTH ATLANTIC TREATY ORGANIZATION** ◆ At the time of its creation in 1949, NATO's unstated purpose was to keep the Germans down and the Russians out. It was criticized as being less an alliance than a guarantee that the Americans would use nuclear weapons to prevent further Soviet expansion into Europe. After he became U.S. secretary of state in 1973, Henry Kissinger said, "In the 1950s and 1960s we put several thousand nuclear weapons into Europe. To be sure, we had no precise idea of what to do with them." He thought that, both morally and politically, the United States could not actually use its nuclear weapons. NATO was a success, but the reasons were not always clear. "Was it because we conducted the right policy?" Kissinger asked rhetorically. "Was it because the Soviet Union never had any intention to attack us in the first place?" (*Hulton Archives*, HB-7277)

system in turmoil, and there was a heavy Allied presence overseeing the rebuilding. "Despite the presence of the occupation forces," Mizuyabu wrote, "I felt free for the first time since being imprisoned in Hastings Park."

The government removed the prohibition against Japanese-Canadians settling in British Columbia only in 1949, almost a year after they were given the right to vote. "We are bitter," wrote Muriel Kitigawa, "with a bitterness we can never forget, that will mark us for the rest of our lives." Yukiharu Mizuyabu finally returned to Canada in 1961. The first casualties of the atomic age were still being tallied, and not just in Japan. On the shores of Great Bear Lake, the Dene miners who had been coated in floury radium dust died of cancer at alarming rates, and the Dene settlements became known as the "Villages of Widows."

**REFUS GLOBAL** ◆ A manifesto titled "*Refus global*" (total disobedience) caused an uproar in Quebec in 1948. "The frontiers of our dreams are no longer the same," wrote painter Paul-Emile Borduas. "The shame of hopeless bondage makes way for pride in a freedom that enables us to win through brave struggle. To hell with the holy water sprinkler and tuque! Make way for magic! Make way for objective mystery! Make way for love!" Borduas was fired from his teaching post at Ecole du Meuble de Montréal and left Quebec for permanent exile, first in New York, then in Paris. (*Paul-Emile Borduas*, La Femme au Bijou. *Art Gallery of Ontario*)

**DAVID BEN-GURION**

◆ In August 1947, a United Nations Special Committee on Palestine recommended dividing the Holy Land into a Jewish and an Arab state. On May 14, 1948, Israel was created on what had been Palestinian land, and the next day Egypt invaded, bombing Tel Aviv. Syria, Lebanon, Transjordan, and Iraq also advanced on the new nation. Prime Minister David Ben-Gurion read a proclamation inviting Jews everywhere to join "the struggle for the fulfillment of the dream of generations, the redemption of Israel."

War had left Europe both physically and economically devastated. But Canada's economy was booming, and the federal government now loosened its immigration policies to make sure there would be enough workers to fill the new jobs. Between 1945 and 1960, two million immigrants would come to Canada. Among them would be 100,000 "Displaced Persons," a term pejoratively shortened to "DPs." These were refugees with no real home.

In 1947, Jan Zaremba, a Polish lawyer, his wife, Alina, and their two young children were in a Displaced Persons camp named Wildflecken in a Bavarian forest. Just a few years earlier, the camp had been an SS training centre for Hitler's troops. A reserve officer in the Polish army, Jan Zaremba had spent the war in a German prison camp while his family hid in the mountains.

Prospective Canadian employers came to Wildflecken, among them Ludger Dionne, Liberal MP for St-Georges-de-Beauce and owner of Dionne Spinning Mills. He hired two hundred Polish women and the Zaremba family. Jan was offered work as a handyman for twenty-five dollars a month, while Alina would work as housekeeper and cook for Dionne without pay.

The Zarembas arrived in Halifax in 1948 on the SS *Marine Falcon*. Jan had a tag on his coat which gave the address of Dionne Spinning Mills in Quebec. His employment there was guaranteed for at least a year; this was the condition upon which his landed immigrant status depended. After three months, Dionne's new employees went on strike for higher wages, and Zaremba and his family went to Ontario, where he found work at the Thomas Edison Company as an electrician's apprentice. "I have discovered," Zaremba noted, "that when one must get a job, any kind of job, higher education is definitely against one. I just wanted to look like a good strong man who would do well in any job I was given. After all, I knew I could not be a lawyer here."

Alina found work in the catalogue department of Simpson's department store, but the family had a difficult time becoming part of Canadian society. "What precisely do the Canadians think DPs are?" she asked. "Sometimes I feel as though we were expected to be some new strange species. Sometimes I feel that people forget that we did live quite normal, quite ordinary lives for perhaps 30 years, perhaps longer, before the war shook us out of that normality. The biggest thing will be to be normal people again. To forget we are numbers. To forget we are DPs."

Some were able to forget more quickly. Georges Lukk, an Estonian, arrived on the same ship as the Zarembas and went to the gold mines at Red Lake, a barren northern Ontario mining town. But he was happy just to be in Canada: "We had heard that our countrymen who had come here had been able to become happy without changing completely. In America, we understood, you must change into another person."

He did not mind the oppressive, underground work, but he was an untalented miner and was fired after several months. Lukk moved to Sarnia,

**THE BIRTH OF THE SUBURBS** ◆ As the demand grew for new housing in the suburbs of Canada's cities, so did demand for the labour required to build them. Frank Colantonio emigrated from Italy in 1949 and helped build the subdivisions in Toronto. While the suburbs themselves were sparkling symbols of prosperity, the construction of them involved unsafe work practices and tenuous employment. "Things were in a state of frenzied expansion," Colantonio said. "New subdivisions around the city fringes and individual houses everywhere in the city were being thrown up at a breathtaking pace. The pressure to produce was unbelievable. Houses got built. The city grew. Builders and developers made big money. And a huge pool of immigrant labourers scrambled from job to job, competing with each other while an equally desperate group of contractors, subcontractors, and even sub-sub-contractors drove down the price of labour. Time consuming and costly safety measures took a back seat to production. I saw men injured and killed. I saw paycheques bounce. Anyone who objected could be easily replaced, and the fear of deportation always festered in the background. The government had no reason to change this system. From the viewpoint of those on top, it was functioning smoothly." From *From the Ground Up: An Italian Immigrant's Story* by Frank Colantonio. (*City of Toronto Archives, 107031*)

where he found work with Imperial Oil. "I don't worry at all," he wrote. "I have a feeling I can do anything here. Anything can happen here. It is a little like being a child, with faith, again." A year after arriving, he wrote a friend: "We have left behind the DP status. We are free men in charge of our own lifes. It is good to greet each new morning as individuals, ordinary human beings."

The post-war era in Canada was one of prosperity, new alignments, immigration, and a testing of the relationship between management and labour.

**MAURICE DUPLESSIS**

◆ Maurice Duplessis, premier of Quebec (1936-39 and 1944-59), welcomed foreign investment and equated opposition to it with Communism. "When you request government intervention you eat away at liberty and rend the fabric of free enterprise, the best and only economic system for Quebecers. Hundreds of millions in capital has been invested to develop our resources. Let me repeat: American capital, English capital, French capital: Welcome!" (*Archives du Séminaire de Trois-Rivières*)

On February 14, 1949, five thousand Quebec asbestos miners went on strike. The miners' union had approached the American-owned company Johns-Manville with their demand for a wage increase of fifteen cents an hour and improved working conditions, particularly with respect to the health threat posed by asbestos dust. The company had offered only a five cent an hour increase. Johns-Manville had an ally in Premier Maurice Duplessis, who welcomed American investment and viewed any opposition to it as tantamount to Communism. The union called for a general strike.

*Le Devoir* sent twenty-nine-year-old reporter Gerard Pelletier to the town of Asbestos, Quebec. "In our official ideology at that time," he wrote, "there was just no place for the working class. Factory workers were seen as intruders. They had the bad taste to exist." He was joined by two friends, labour leader Jean Marchand and twenty-nine-year-old lawyer Pierre Elliott Trudeau. "At the time," Pelletier wrote, "he had a blonde beard, so the striking miners nicknamed him 'St. Joseph'! But when he took the floor at a meeting, they listened to him very attentively. He knew how to speak on matters of justice, democracy and freedom in a way that was highly relevant to the situation."

Union federations across the country supported the strike. And the strikers' cause was taken up by some members of the clergy, which enraged Duplessis. The archbishop of Montreal, Monsignor Joseph Charbonneau, delivered a sermon at Nôtre-Dame Basilica in which he told the congregation, "The working class is the victim of a conspiracy aimed at crushing them, and when there is a conspiracy to crush the working class, it's the Church's duty to intervene. We value people more than capital."

The strikers became more militant and blocked the roads to the town. Strikebreakers were brought in, resulting in an angry confrontation between the strikers and police. Duplessis would not tolerate any suggestion that the strikers' demands could be considered on their merits. "This is about an admitted attempt," Duplessis warned, "encouraged from outside, to challenge and break the State's authority. That is intolerable. Whoever deviates from this policy that I have established, privately or publicly, will be expelled from the Union Nationale."

On May 6, the government sent in four hundred police armed with guns, tear gas, and billy clubs. They rousted the miners, dragging some from the church where they sought sanctuary. A striker named Alphonse Vallières was questioned by police: "I told them that yesterday the cops fired at us. One of them called me a liar. He pounces and curses me, hits me in the side of the mouth with his fist. While I was trying to protect my face, the other one hit me across the ribs with his baton."

The strike lasted more than five months, with the strikers gaining a ten-cent raise and the mandatory payment of union dues. Archbishop Charbonneau resigned and spent the rest of his life as a hospital chaplain in Victoria, British Columbia. "I had felt the storm approaching for some time," he wrote to a friend. "Its violence broke my wings." It was the first glimmering of an organized opposition to Duplessis. While the strike was seen as a victory for the company, giving rise to anti-American sentiment in Quebec, it was also a victory for the labour movement, which had shown remarkable solidarity. Within a year of the strike, the Quebec miners were the highest paid in Canada.

A year after the strike, Pelletier and Trudeau launched a new publication, *Cité Libre*, which became the intellectual voice of Quebecers against Duplessis. (Soon after, the FBI began a file on Trudeau, concerned that he was at best left-leaning, and at worst a Communist.) The strike marked the first public split between both Church and State, and the intelligentsia and the government. Both of these gaps would widen.

In Canada, the Cold War was heralded by the actions of a Russian cipher clerk named Igor Gouzenko, who worked in the Soviet embassy in Ottawa, encoding communications to Moscow. In 1945 he received orders to return home, and, faced with a choice between the benign Canadian capital and the oppression of Communist Russia, he chose to stay. He plotted his escape for several weeks, stealing classified material that he could use to ingratiate himself with his Canadian hosts. "During the course of about half a month, I examined the materials so as to select the best ones that would disclose the operative work, leaving the informational telegrams on one side," he wrote, "the telegrams which I wished to take out I marked by bending over slightly one of the corners."

On September 5, 1945, Gouzenko stuffed 109 documents under his shirt, walked to the *Ottawa Journal* offices, and in a thick Russian accent said to the city editor, "It's war. It's war. It's Russia." The editor told him to go to the RCMP, but Gouzenko went to the Department of Justice instead, which was closed. He returned home, burdened with guilt and more than a hundred documents showing that the Russians had been operating an espionage ring in Canada for almost two years.

The next morning, Gouzenko went back to the *Journal* and spoke to reporter Elizabeth Fraser. By noon, Mackenzie King was faced with the unwelcome news. Canada was about to meet with the Soviets, Britain, France, China, and the United States to discuss and construct a post-war peace, and King was worried that this scandal would damage international relations. "It was like a bomb on top of everything," King wrote, "and one could not say how serious it might be or to what it might lead."

Later that day, Gouzenko applied for Canadian citizenship. Then he wandered the streets of Ottawa, unsuccessfully seeking asylum and feeling suicidal. The Soviets were now aware of the theft and were looking for him. That night, Gouzenko and his family stayed with a neighbour. In the middle of the night, four men from the Soviet embassy broke into the apartment and tried to abduct them. The Ottawa police quickly arrived, followed by the RCMP and staff from External Affairs. After threats and unanswered questions, the Soviets left without Gouzenko or the documents. His story

**IGOR GOUZENKO** ◆ After his defection, Igor Gouzenko remained in hiding with his family for the rest of his life, moving often. "My children go to Sunday school like other children. As for me, my neighbours go as often as I do – which is to say, not much. This does not seem very important. The first time I went to church it was very hard for me to grasp. I went quite often in the first years, though, and finally found some interest in it. Basically, it must be good. It is preaching love – in Russia the basic thing that is taught is class hatred. It is better to preach love, preach what is good even if we do not always do what is good when we grow up." – From a September 1, 1953, interview with *Maclean's*. (*Star Newspaper Service*)

remained secret for five months while an investigation was conducted into the activities of twenty-two suspected spies, most of them civil servants.

On the strength of the information in Gouzenko's documents, King invoked the War Measures Act, giving the police broad powers to make arrests. Israel Halperin, a mathematician, was arrested in February 1946 and detained for five weeks without charge. He was questioned by a royal commission, but he did not know whether he was there as a suspect or a witness. The procedure was uncomfortably reminiscent of the kinds of abuses that were being perpetrated under Stalin, whose paranoia regarding foreign agents had already led to millions being imprisoned, tortured, or murdered in an increasingly irrational, violent putsch. Mackenzie King was alarmed. "I thought it was wrong that those who are suspects should be detained indefinitely and that some way should be found to shorten the inquiry. The whole proceedings are far too much like those of Russia herself." Halperin did not have a lawyer, nor was he charged, and he refused to be sworn in when asked to testify. He protested and declared, "I will not open my mouth here again." Nineteen others were arrested and sent to trial, including Fred Rose, a member of Parliament for the Labour Progressive Party, and Alan Nunn May, an English physicist. Halperin was eventually acquitted, but Fred Rose was convicted of treason and sentenced to six years in prison, and Alan Nunn May was sentenced to ten years. Nine others were also convicted of treason, sending shock waves through the government and the country. The *Globe and Mail* reported that there were 1,700 Soviet spies operating in North America.

South of the border, J. Edgar Hoover, the eccentric, fanatical director of the Federal Bureau of Investigation, warned, "Something new has taken root in America in the past generation, a Communist mentality, representing a systematic, purposive, and conscious attempt to destroy Western Civilization . . ." While there was a legitimate threat from Communist espionage (as evidenced by the Manhattan Project's leaks), it was accompanied in the United States by an unreasonable national paranoia that reached a zenith in the 1950s. In February 1951, Wisconsin senator Joseph McCarthy announced, "I have here in my hand a list of 205 . . . names that were known to the Secretary of State as being members of the Communist Party and who nevertheless are still working and shaping policy in the State Department." This unfounded charge sparked a frantic search for "Reds" under every American bed. Many of the nation's actors, writers, journalists, and labour leaders were called before the House Un-American Activities Committee to answer questions about their political affiliations. Many refused, or refused to implicate others, and were then assumed to be Communists, or "fellow travellers." Those who were blacklisted saw their careers ruined. The hearings were televised in the United States, a long-running Grand Guignol that threw a spotlight on both patriotism and democracy.

The Canadian hunt for Communists was characteristically discreet: the RCMP quietly conducted security checks on seventy thousand people,

**SENATOR JOSEPH MCCARTHY** ◆ In a 1950 speech, McCarthy announced that the U.S. State Department had been infiltrated by Communists; three years later he was appointed chairman of the Senate's Permanent Subcommittee on Investigations. He used his new authority to conduct inquiries, including the Army-McCarthy hearings in 1954, which were nationally televised and witnessed daily by millions of Americans. As the hearings progressed, McCarthy's unsubstantiated accusations began to earn him more detractors than fans. His speeches became disconnected and rambling and the hearings grew increasingly unhinged. Eventually, the Senate stepped in to curb McCarthy; it voted to "condemn" but not "censure" him. (*Top: The Army-McCarthy Hearings. New York Times. Bottom: McCarthy addressing the Sons of the American Revolution. Wide World Photos.*)

and most decisions were made behind closed doors. There were victims in Canada as well as in the United States, people whose lives were interrupted or ruined by innuendo or anti-Communist zeal. Gordon Martin was a British Columbia man who had volunteered for the war in 1941. After serving in the air force for four years, he received an honourable discharge and studied at the University of British Columbia, where he graduated with a degree in law. In his 1948 application to the bar, Martin was asked about his politics. He had been a member of the Communist Party since 1938, but he responded that queries about his political affiliation violated his freedom of thought and association. The Benchers of the law society rejected Martin's application for membership, which made it impossible for him to practise law in British Columbia. They cited his membership in the Labour Progressive Party. "In the view of the Benchers," they ruled, "the Labour Progressive Party is an association of those adhering to subversive Communist doctrines."

Martin responded in the press, saying, "The Benchers' decision ignores my unblemished service record and disregards my reputation as it was established by the evidence of classmates, fellow servicemen and people who knew me in the various communities in which I have lived." He ridiculed their logic. "Marxists are not monarchists, therefore they are disloyal. Disloyal people subscribe to subversive doctrines and dictates of a foreign power. The argument is distorted and wrongly premised in both its parts. I can only answer that I see no reason why I should play Don Quixote merely because anti-Communists construct dramas around such imaginary characters." Martin found work with a logging company and later was employed in a sawmill. Eventually he set up a television repair shop in Nanaimo. He died in 1974. Twenty-four years later, the Law Society of British Columbia apologized to the Martin family.

While Canada was investigating its civil servants, wary of Reds, the Crown colony of Newfoundland was beginning its cautious dance with Confederation. During his colourful twenty-two-year reign as Newfoundland's premier, Joey Smallwood would launch many improbable and doomed schemes – the recreation of the town of Rothenburg, Germany, to attract tourists; the lining of the Trans-Canada Highway east of Port aux Basques with flowering trees; the creation of oil refineries, rubber plants, greenhouses, chocolate factories, and the Flying L Ranch, whose one thousand imported Herefords were rustled nightly or poisoned themselves on marsh grass and died in the bog. But in 1945, Smallwood was a small, bespectacled failed pig farmer and former radio broadcaster, and Newfoundland was still a British Crown colony, governed by a commission consisting of a British governor, three British commissioners, and three Newfoundlanders, all appointed by the British government.

After the war, Britain was looking for every possible economy, and Newfoundland's independence would provide much-needed savings. A National Convention was held in Newfoundland to decide the colony's future, and Smallwood was there, representing Bonavista. Most of the delegates wanted Newfoundland to be independent, but Smallwood instead suggested the possibility of joining Canada. His proposal to send a delegation to Ottawa was defeated, but five months later the Newfoundland government

**TOMMY DOUGLAS** ◆ Tommy Douglas was born in Scotland in 1904 and grew up in Winnipeg. A former boxer turned Baptist preacher, he entered politics and became leader of the Co-operative Commonwealth Federation in Saskatchewan. In the 1944 election, he delivered a parable with the message that it was time for political change: "Mouseland was a place where all the little mice lived and played. And every time on election day, they used to elect their government, a government made of big fat black cats. They were nice fellows. They passed good laws, that is laws that were good for cats. When the mice couldn't put up with it anymore, they decided something had to be done about it. They voted the black cats out. They put in white cats. You see, my friends, the trouble wasn't the colour of the cats. The trouble was that they were cats. Presently, there came along one little mouse who had an idea. And he said to the other mice: 'Look fellows, why don't we elect a government made up of mice.' Oh, they said, he's a Bolshevik, lock him up!"

Douglas was elected with a large majority, forming the first social-democratic government in North America. It ushered in a series of innovative laws, including the Trade Union Act, which allowed for collective bargaining. He also introduced paid holidays, low-cost government automobile insurance, and the Saskatchewan Bill of Rights. He revolutionized medical treatment, providing guaranteed admission to hospitals and free treatment for certain illnesses. (*National Archives of Canada*, PA-46909)

sent one to London and another to Ottawa to discuss the colony's future. The London group was told that Britain was in no position to help them. But Prime Minister Mackenzie King saw the opportunity to become a latter-day Father of Confederation. "I believed some day – the dream of a great country – a British country, extending from the waters of the Atlantic to the Pacific, all one, united . . . would come to pass," he wrote in his diary. "Whether this was the moment or later, one could not say. I was sure, however, that our present gathering would bring us one step nearer that result." King offered Smallwood $15 million in new capital and the absorption of most of Newfoundland's debt if the colony joined Confederation. There was also the inducement of existing Canadian welfare programs, such as the "baby bonus."

Smallwood was elated. "Let no man dare to crush that hope that has arisen in our people's hearts," he said. But most men did, and at the next National Convention, on January 29, 1948, the option of joining Canada was not even on the ballot: the only two options were independence as a Dominion or remaining under the rule of the British commission. Smallwood launched a petition asking that the possibility of joining Canada be added as a third option, and he got almost fifty thousand signatures. In the June 3 referendum, it was included on the ballot.

In the campaign that followed, Smallwood flew from town to town in an old seaplane, tirelessly arguing the merits of joining Canada, and he launched a newspaper, *The Confederate*, that supported the cause. But when the votes came in, none of the three options had obtained a clear

**JOSEPH SMALLWOOD**

◆ "We all love this land.
It has a charm, it warms our
hearts, go where we will, a
charm, a magic, a mystical
tug on our emotions that
never dies. With all her
faults we love her. We
might manage, precariously,
to maintain independent
national status. We can
resolutely decide to be poor
but proud. But if such a
decision is made it must be
made by the sixty thousand
poor families, and not by the
five thousand families who
are confident of getting
along pretty well in any
case." (*Smallwood signing
the agreement admitting
Newfoundland into Confederation. National Archives of
Canada, PA-128080*)

majority. The option of remaining a colony had received the fewest votes, and so it was eliminated; the next referendum would offer a simple choice between independence or Canada. "It would surely be the supreme tragedy of our history," Smallwood wrote in an editorial, "if by apathy, indifference, lack of enlightened leadership, or the influence of sinister propaganda we were to alienate irretrievably the inheritance which was won for us by our patriotic forebears."

During the campaign preceding the next referendum, Smallwood would be cheered and encouraged at one stop, threatened with violence at the next. He hired two bodyguards and carried a gun. At a rally in St. John's he escaped a mob only by hanging on to the top of the car that drove him to safety. The referendum succeeded in splitting Irish Catholics (against union with Canada) and English Protestants (in favour), but also divided families, towns, and neighbours. The business and professional class fought Smallwood, worried that Confederation would diminish its power.

The option to join Canada won by the narrow margin of 7,000 votes, or 52 per cent (the count would be protested by the losing side for a generation), and on March 31, 1949, Newfoundland became Canada's tenth province. The next day, Joey Smallwood was asked to form an interim government and so became the province's first premier, a singular and stubborn political force. "We are not archangels and we are not supermen," he said. "I think I can say we are a bunch of Newfoundlanders determined to do their best for the toiling masses of Newfoundland, to make Newfoundland fit for Newfoundlanders."

The United States and the Soviet Union, the two new superpowers, squared off against one another in a moody, dangerous staring contest that would define the next forty years. Mackenzie King did not view the Soviets with the same blunt distrust and fear that Washington did, but the Cold War nevertheless brought Canada closer into the American orbit, completing the transition that had begun with the Ogdensburg Agreement. Lester B. Pearson, who became Canada's ambassador to the United States on January 1, 1945, was an observer at the San Francisco conference where the Allied nations were meeting to draft the charter for a new international body, the United Nations, which was to replace the League of Nations. "Between Russian deviousness and U.S. ham-handedness," Pearson wrote, "this conference is going to have a bad time."

Canada hoped to define a role for itself as a middle power, a reasonable voice, and more than any other Canadian, Lester Bowles Pearson came to personify this unique position. He had been a professor of history before joining the Department of External Affairs in the 1928. "A good many of the worries and hesitations which I feel, as a Canadian, about certain aspects of United States policy can be expressed in private to my American friends (and this is done) but not always so frankly in public," Pearson wrote. "We are constantly faced with the problem of trying to influence United States

**LESTER BOWLES PEARSON** ◆ "I was reading in bed, and to drown out or at least to take my mind off the bombs, I reached out and turned on the radio. I was fumbling aimlessly with the dial when the room was flooded with the beauty and peace of Christmas carol music. Glorious waves of it wiped out the sound of war and conjured up visions of happier peace-time Christmases. Then the announcer spoke – in German. For it was a German station and they were Germans who were singing those carols. Nazi bombs screaming through the air with their message of war and death; German music drifting through the air with its message of peace and salvation. When we resolve the paradox of those two sounds from a single national source, we will, at last, be in a good position to understand and solve the problem of war." – Lester Pearson on December 11, 1957, in his speech after receiving the Nobel Peace Prize, describing his experience in London during the Second World War. (*National Archives of Canada, PA-117624*)

policy in a manner which will protect our interests and our conception of what is good for the world, but which will not involve us in public quarrels with a great and friendly neighbour." This was one of the essential issues facing post-war Canada, and Pearson's quiet diplomacy emerged as the solution, a way to define the country on the international stage. By this time, Mackenzie King had retired, to be followed by another Liberal prime minister, Louis St. Laurent. (King died of pneumonia on July 22, 1950, at the age of seventy-five.)

The Cold War grew dangerously colder after the Soviets successfully tested their first atomic bomb, "Joe I," in 1949. A year later, on June 25, 1950, with Stalin's blessing and the promise of Soviet weapons, North Korea invaded South Korea. The United Nations condemned the action, and the United States offered American naval and air support. Lester Pearson, who was now external affairs minister, was confronted by his American counterpart, Dean Acheson, who asked Pearson for Canadian military support in Korea. It was a private, rather than an official request, a sounding of the Canadian commitment. Pearson deferred the matter to a three-day cabinet meeting, at which it was decided that St. Laurent would call for a voluntary force willing to go to Korea under the auspices of the United Nations and under U.S. command. There was an immediate response: hundreds of men lined up at recruiting centres that were not scheduled to open for another twenty-four hours. The first Canadians were sent in November 1950, arriving a few days after the Communist Chinese army, which had been building at the border, attacked, driving the United Nations forces back.

Though Canada was allied with the United States in Korea, the political relationship between the two nations was strained. In the spring of 1951, Pearson addressed the Empire and Canadian clubs in Toronto. "The days of relatively easy and automatic political relations with our neighbour are, I think, over," he told them. "While we are most anxious to work with the United States and support her in the leadership she is giving to the free world, we are not willing to be merely an echo." The speech launched a controversy and elicited hate mail from Americans and expressions of concern from the U.S. government. Pearson was surprised at the response: "This, however, confirms my thesis that we never get much attention down there unless we say something critical, and then the attention becomes surprised, pained and irritated."

Throughout the Korean War, which was billed euphemistically as a "police action," there were attempts at negotiation. "Peace talks were initiated in early 1951 in the middle of the battlefield," wrote Private D. A. Strickland. "For more than two years front-line commanders tried to conduct effective military operations without prejudicing the diplomatic activities at the ever-apparent tents of Panmunjom."

By war's end, 25,000 Canadian soldiers had served in Korea, enduring fierce firefights and mortar attacks and the surprising cold, all to little end. "I left my hillside battle position to come back to Canada," wrote Private Strickland, "and when I returned almost two years later for a second tour of duty, I was astonished to be assigned to the same hill I had left. The trenches were deeper, the defences and the barbed wire seemed more permanent and the possibility of military victory was all but forgotten."

The peace talks, two years of bickering and horse-trading, finally ended with an armistice on July 27, 1953, which effectively divided the country into a Communist North and an anti-Communist South. "Months of pent-up emotions were released and loud shouting echoed across the valleys," remembered Strickland. "Their reaction was similar to ours. Flares and illuminations went up in all directions. . . . We unloaded our weapons, maintained the barest of vigilance and settled down for our first night's sleep in many weeks." More than 2 million Koreans had died in the conflict.

The Korean War was over, but the Cold War dragged on. Igor Gouzenko was now living in the countryside under another name, making occasional public appearances wearing a pillowcase over his head. He wrote a lengthy novel about life in the Soviet Union, *The Fall of a Titan*, which won the Governor General's Award for Fiction. A curious celebrity, virtually unrecognizable, with a heavily accented speech, he was nevertheless a powerful symbol of Canada's role in the Cold War. He spent his time painting portraits of those in charge of his security and listening to music on the record player he had bought with money the Canadian government had given him. He and his wife had eight children, and Gouzenko flirted with Christianity in a mild, suburban way, living happily in seclusion.

The chain reaction of anti-Communist sentiment Gouzenko had unleashed had yet to play itself out. After arresting Israel Halperin, the RCMP had seized his address book and submitted it as evidence. One of the names in the book was that of an old school friend, Herbert Norman, a scholar and diplomat. Norman had been educated at the University of Toronto, at Harvard, and at Cambridge and had joined External Affairs in the 1930s as an expert on Japan. On his return to Ottawa in 1950, he found himself under suspicion for his left-wing associations. His name was raised in the U.S. Senate in 1951 by an associate of Senator Joseph McCarthy's. Norman was running the U.S. desk at External Affairs, and the Americans were concerned that he had access to secret material. An RCMP inquiry followed, and though Norman was cleared, he felt his reputation had been compromised. "You can't wash off the poison," he complained. "How can you fight back against this sort of thing?"

Pearson, who was particularly sensitive to matters of American influence and Canadian sovereignty, came to Norman's defence. He also refused to allow Igor Gouzenko to testify before the House Un-American Activities Committee. "Let us by all means remove the traitors from positions of trust," Pearson had said in 1949 with some prescience, "but in doing so, I hope we may never succumb to the black madness of the witch hunt." This decision was viewed as impertinence by the United States. J. Edgar Hoover warned that "Pearson had better stop mouthing his half truths as pertain to the FBI," and he requested Pearson's FBI file, which was 243 pages long and labelled "Espionage R," the R standing for "Russian." Hoover threatened to make the file public, and Pearson dared him to do it; Hoover reconsidered and the file remained secret. But Colonel Robert S. McCormick, the publisher of the *Chicago Tribune* (and a friend of Hoover's) publicly denounced Pearson, citing "Communist infestation . . . in Canada where Lester Pearson is the most dangerous man in the English-speaking world." The image of the soft-spoken Pearson as the most dangerous man in the English-speaking world showed McCarthyism at its most giddy and irrational.

Stalin died of a stroke in 1953 and was succeeded a few months later by the shrewd peasant Nikita Khrushchev, who was elected first secretary of the Communist Party. In Canada, Prime Minister Louis St. Laurent was re-elected in August, after campaigning on his "Uncle Louis" charm. Dwight Eisenhower had assumed the U.S. presidency in January of that year. This new framework for the Cold War was accompanied by a disturbing military development: the successful (and secret) testing of a hydrogen bomb. On November 1, 1952, the Americans exploded a hydrogen bomb in the Pacific Ocean that was one thousand times more powerful than the Hiroshima blast. The Soviets tested their own hydrogen bomb in September 1954, renewing the fear of nuclear war and spawning a fresh, unprecedented possibility: the complete destruction of the planet.

**LOUIS ST. LAURENT** ◆ Louis St. Laurent succeeded Mackenzie King as prime minister in 1948 and continued the Liberal policy of French-English accommodation and a strong central government. The Trans-Canada Highway, initiated in 1948, made the country more accessible to its own citizens. Six years later, the St. Lawrence Seaway, another grand project, was undertaken, making the Great Lakes accessible to ocean freighters. St. Laurent's unifying ideas didn't initially extend to culture, however. In 1951, Vincent Massey produced a report that recommended the creation of a council to provide grants for arts and scholarship. St. Laurent responded that the government's job did not extend to "subsidizing ballet dancing," but by 1956 he had changed his mind, and he created the Canada Council. (*National Archives of Canada*, PA-128080)

In 1955, Canada and the United States agreed to build a network of radar stations in the Canadian north, the Distant Early Warning (DEW) line, which would detect any Soviet planes armed with H-bombs coming over the pole. It was manned by one thousand Americans. In one incident, Canadian parliamentarians were expected to secure permission from the Pentagon before visiting DEW line stations. This revived worries about northern sovereignty that had first been expressed during the wartime construction of the Alaska Highway. To balance this new foreign population in the far north, the federal government initiated a well-meaning, disastrous plan to relocate Inuit to settlements near the DEW line. "The Canadian government is anxious to have Canadians occupying as much of the north as possible," announced a federal spokesman, "and it appears in many cases the [Inuit] are the only people capable of doing this."

A group of Inuit who lived in Inukjuak on the eastern shore of Hudson Bay were moved to Ellesmere Island, 6,900 kilometres away, above the Arctic Circle. "The RCMP came to us and they told us that we had to leave," remembered Simeonie Amagoalik. "When the *Qallunaat* or white men spoke, we were afraid of them. . . . The white man was all powerful, next to God, actually, and you don't argue with him if he insists on something."

Ten families went north on a supply ship, the *C D Howe*. "I was crying all the time," said Anna Nungaq. "I was wondering how can I do this. They left us there and we saw the ship sailing away and we were just dumped in a place where there was absolutely nothing."

They had experience hunting caribou and ducks but none with polar bears. There was no school or medical care at Grise Fjord, as the settlement was named, and many families had been separated. "The first ten years . . . were the most terrible years of our lives," John Amagoalik said. "We spent years without mothers, without fathers, without brothers, without sisters, who were all sick in southern hospitals. I remember my parents always yearning for food." The experiment was an abject failure, a dismal version of early contact being recreated in the atomic age.

Igor Gouzenko might have initiated Canada's entree into the Cold War, but it was Herbert Norman who personified the tragic second act. In August 1956, Norman was sent to Cairo as Canada's ambassador to Egypt, hopeful that the spy innuendo that had plagued his career was finally behind him. But his new post presented a challenge. Egyptian leader Gamal Abdel Nasser was slouching toward Moscow, accepting Soviet arms and denouncing the west. The foreign investment he had sought to construct the ambitious Aswan High Dam on the Nile River quickly disappeared, withdrawn by France, Britain, the United States, and the World Bank (an agency of the United Nations). Nasser then seized control of the Suez Canal, a critical shipping route, which had previously been run by foreign interests, mostly British and French. Egypt would no longer be under "the domination of the Imperialists," he announced.

In October, Israel invaded Egypt, and within days British and French bombers had devastated Egyptian airfields. Nasser appealed to Khrushchev, who threatened to shower the west with nuclear weapons if the British and French did not withdraw. The world appeared to be on the brink of war.

When the United Nations met to discuss the situation, Pearson proposed a plan that called for the British and French to withdraw but would allow for a United Nations Emergency Force to remain in the area, stabilizing the situation. The British were unhappy with the proposal, but when it was tabled, all fifty-seven member nations voted for it. There were some in Canada who were critical of it as well, angry that Canada had not sided with Britain.

It was the first time the United Nations had dispatched such a large international peacekeeping force, and it was commanded by a Canadian, General E. L. M. Burns, a national triumph. Herbert Norman had helped mediate between Nasser and the west, and he hoped that the resolution of the Suez crisis would be his political redemption. It was, but only briefly. In March 1957, the U.S. House Un-American Activities Committee again attacked him for being a Communist.

Pearson vigorously defended Norman in the House of Commons, arguing that his friend had already been subjected to an exhaustive security check: "Nothing he has done since has affected – unless to increase – the confidence we have in him as a devoted, efficient and loyal official of the Government, who is doing extremely important work at a very difficult post in a way which commands my wholehearted admiration and deserves my full support." But the attack itself was too much for the beleaguered diplomat. On the morning of April 4, 1957, Norman jumped off the Wadi el Nil Building in Cairo, overlooking the Nile. He left two notes on top of his discarded jacket and more at home. One read: "Never have I violated my oath of secrecy. But how the issues will be obscured and twisted! But I am too tired of it all. The forces against me are too formidable, even for an innocent man, and it is better to go now than to live indefinitely pelted with mud – although so much of it will be quite incorrect and false. My loved ones will regret this act but I believe they will understand the reasons for it."

Norman's death prompted a wave of anti-American feeling in Canada. Editorials and angry letters blamed the United States for Norman's death, and the relationship between the two countries deteriorated. Pearson, however, emerged from the Suez crisis as a hero and was awarded the Nobel Peace Prize for his role in its resolution. This provided him with a platform from which to make a run for the Liberal Party leadership.

Canadians who had lived through the Depression and the war were now sharing an unbridled optimism and an economic surge. The most dramatic symbol of the boom came in Alberta.

By 1947, Alberta had been haunted by the spectre of oil and its transformative properties for more than forty years. There had been false booms and minor strikes, but it was an industry defined more by possibility than reality. Since 1917, Imperial Oil had spent $20 million drilling 133 dry holes. Dozens of companies had formed and disappeared without ever seeing oil. But on February 13, 1947, the promise was finally delivered in a farmer's field near Leduc, twenty-seven kilometres southwest of Edmonton, when Imperial Oil's Leduc No. 1 well came in. It was the most significant field yet discovered, and it would eventually support 1,278 wells. A year later the field's potency was seen in spectacular fashion when Atlantic No. 3 blew wild for six months, spewing millions of litres of crude oil on surrounding fields, then caught fire, sending up a blaze visible for 150 kilometres. It provided a brief tourist attraction and a fitting symbol for the prosperity and waste that

"That swooshing sound you just heard was the Imperial Oil Limited No. 1 well at Leduc, Alberta, coming into production. The oil started flowing under its own pressure at four o'clock this afternoon in what may be a momentous occasion in the oil world." – Hal Yerxa of CJCA radio, Edmonton, 1947. (*Drilling at Leduc. Hulton Archives*, HK0338)

the oil business brings. The image was a favourite in newsreels around the world.

Towns were created in the wake of the Leduc discovery – Devon, Redwater, Drayton Valley, High Level – and both Edmonton and Calgary were transformed, with each vying for the title of "oil capital." American money flooded in, and the population soared as immigrants arrived to take advantage of the bonanza. After Leduc, oil companies increased their exploration activity, and larger reserves were found. In the next thirty years, the province's economy went from one based primarily on agriculture to one dependent on oil.

One of the benefits of the oil boom was that it became cheaper to heat homes with oil, eliminating the messy ritual of hauling coal. Residential construction, which had been dormant during the Depression and then through the war, suddenly took off. Returning veterans married, and their prosperity and need for housing led to that hopeful, much maligned development: the suburb.

Don Mills was the first comprehensive suburb. Named for a mill on the Don River, it was constructed eleven kilometres northeast of downtown Toronto in 1954 under the auspices of E. P. Taylor, the owner of O'Keefe Breweries. As conceived by planner Macklin Hancock, Don Mills was a community arranged along a series of curved, discontinuous roads that effectively blocked outside traffic. Within its boundaries were a shopping mall (the modernist "Convenience Centre" designed by John Parkin), green space, churches, schools, and homes that were linked by their design and materials. It was hermetic, prosperous, and designed for the automotive age, with streets lacking sidewalks. A few years after the first stage was completed, similar developments appeared on the edges of cities across Canada.

Don Mills was created with the idea that it would attract a diverse population: the working class would live in its many apartments and work in the nearby mills and factories, while the middle class would commute to downtown Toronto. But the popularity of the new development quickly drove prices up, and the suburb became home to a largely uniform white middle class.

In 1954, Toronto was the fastest-growing city on the continent, and new suburbs began to push out in all directions. Between 1945 and 1956, one million houses were built in Canada. The millionth house was a three-bedroom brick bungalow on lot 121 in Scarborough, and it was celebrated as a symbol of post-war affluence. On September 14, 1956, a procession of limousines left the Wishing Well Shopping Centre carrying politicians, businessmen, and the Camisso family, who were moving into the house. The entourage was accompanied by motorcycles and majorettes. The Camissos were given the keys to the home, and neighbours brought roses, served coffee, and welcomed the new family to Wishing Well Acres under the glare of the press. "Everything was just about the way we wanted it," said Mr. Camisso. "Conventional layout, six rooms and a wonderful heating system. . . . No more coal shovelling. We swore that if we ever got a house it would have an automatic heating system, a good one."

Along with oil furnaces, these new homes soon had televisions. In 1932, Sir John Aird had addressed the Royal Commission on Radio Broadcasting, which he chaired. "It is coming, gentlemen," he said, "and we should be prepared, in dealing with this question of radio broadcasting, to keep the question of television well before us." The United States had introduced regular television service in 1939, though its progress was largely halted by the war. In Canada, the inaugural broadcast came from the Canadian Broadcasting Corporation's Montreal affiliate, CBFT, which began operations on September 6, 1952. Two days later, CBLT in Toronto began broadcasting. Quebec had the drama "La Famille Plouffe" and a current affairs program, "Point de Mire," hosted by René Lévesque, as well as

"Hockey Night in Canada." Toronto had hockey, but most of its dramas were imported from the United States, shows like "Father Knows Best," which followed the domestic life of an American insurance man burdened with normalcy. Canadian shows began to appear: "Country Hoedown" debuted in 1956, and two years later "The Friendly Giant" arrived and began its twenty-six-year run. "Don Messer's Jubilee," a musical variety show, came in 1959. This homely, beloved program was cancelled a decade later while it was still one of the country's most popular shows. It was desperately unhip at a time when the CBC wanted to appeal to a younger demographic, and its cancellation became a cultural focal point. John Diefenbaker, a fan, raised the issue while sitting in Opposition in the House of Commons. "Many people are asking that this show be continued," he implored, "and they are not particularly pleased with the fact that the Black Panthers and the like apparently have an inside track at the CBC." Diefenbaker's link between a militant African-American organization and the plaid-clad, smiling fiddlers of "Don Messer" provided a jarring and fanciful image, but it reflected a broader sentiment: that local cultural products were being muscled aside by American shows.

Back in 1956, Diefenbaker was railing in the House against another outrage, and it, too, had to do with unwanted American influence. The contract to construct a natural gas pipeline linking Alberta with Quebec and Ontario had been awarded to a U.S.-financed company, TransCanada Pipelines, which wanted an $80-million loan from the Canadian government to fund the project. Diefenbaker felt that the loan simply added insult to injury. C. D. Howe, now known as the "Minister of Everything" because of his power in the St. Laurent government, wanted to get the legislation authorizing the pipeline and the loan through the House in time to begin construction in the summer. He invoked the rarely used rule of closure to limit debate to two weeks. What followed was fourteen days of accusations, threats, and screaming matches, ending finally in an ugly and expensive victory for St. Laurent's Liberals.

Diefenbaker was infuriated by the decision, and by the undemocratic way it had been arrived at: "I could not believe that stubborn stupidity would be carried to the limit and that the bill would be engineered through the House regardless of consequences. The government trod on the Opposition and in doing so, they trod on the rights of the people of Canada."

When Louis St. Laurent called an election in 1957, the Conservative campaign tapped into the anti-American mood in the country. If the Liberals were elected, Diefenbaker warned, the country would become "a virtual forty-ninth economic state in the American union." The campaign was the first to be seen on television, and at seventy-five, St. Laurent looked old and static. Diefenbaker understood the new medium, and his demagogic energy played well on the black-and-white television sets in the nation's living rooms. On June 21, 1957, John George Diefenbaker became

**JOHN DIEFENBAKER** ◆ "I come before you today as a defender of the faith of the Fathers of Confederation in *One Canada*. I come to you to unite, not to disunite. I come to heal, not to wound. To raise up your eyes to the future, to build, not to tear down. . . . I have no ambition that is unsatisfied, everything that one could have has been given to me.... We have a responsibility as a party which Macdonald and Cartier tried to achieve – bringing about a new unity in this country. . . . I do not come before you to ask you, to appeal. I come before you knowing you will decide a question I want decided." – John Diefenbaker on February 3, 1964, in a speech to Conservative delegates. Diefenbaker carried the day within his own party but never regained the support of the Canadian electorate. (*National Archives of Canada*)

prime minister, ending twenty-two years of Liberal rule. Louis St. Laurent stepped down as Liberal leader in 1958 in favour of Lester B. Pearson.

Though Diefenbaker's margin of victory was narrow, six months later he dissolved Parliament, called an election, and beat Lester Pearson in a landslide (208 Conservative seats to the Liberals' 49). Despite his trumpeted distaste for American involvement in Canadian affairs, Diefenbaker

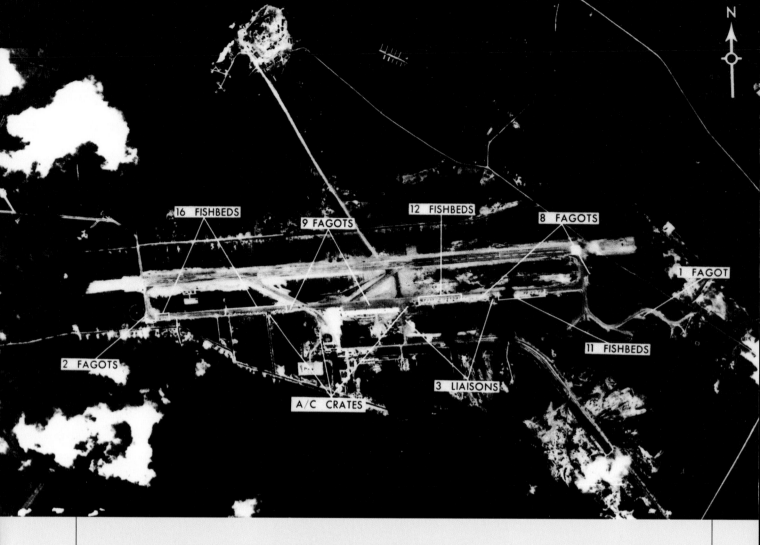

16 FISHBEDS

9 FAGOTS

12 FISHBEDS

8 FAGOTS

1 FAGOT

2 FAGOTS

11 FISHBEDS

3 LIAISONS

A/C CRATES

N

## THE CUBAN MISSILE CRISIS

◆ In August 1962, the Americans became aware that the Soviets were involved in a large missile buildup in Cuba. President John F. Kennedy demanded the removal of the missiles on October 21, initiating a tense standoff between the world's two nuclear powers. Curtis LeMay, chief of staff for the United States Air Force, favoured bombing Cuba, believing that the Soviets, who were far behind in the missile race, would not respond. LeMay was concerned with the leadership of General Thomas Power, the commander of Strategic Air Command, who had the authority to initiate a nuclear strike if the president was not available. "I used to worry about General Power," LeMay later admitted. "I used to worry that General Power was not stable. I used to worry about the fact that he had control over so many weapons and weapons systems and could, under certain conditions, launch the force." Top: Soviet missile sites being prepared in Cuba. (*Hulton Archives, HH9540*). Bottom: An American P2V Neptune patrol plane flying over a Soviet freighter during the Cuban missile crisis. (*Hulton Archives, JE5088*)

**JOHN F. KENNEDY** ◆ When President Kennedy was assassinated on November 22, 1963, he was mourned by the world. Canadian poet Al Purdy wrote a commemorative poem, "Death of John F. Kennedy":

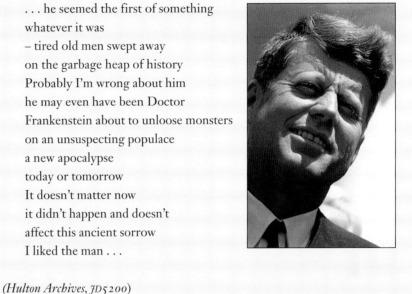

. . . he seemed the first of something
whatever it was
– tired old men swept away
on the garbage heap of history
Probably I'm wrong about him
he may even have been Doctor
Frankenstein about to unloose monsters
on an unsuspecting populace
a new apocalypse
today or tomorrow
It doesn't matter now
it didn't happen and doesn't
affect this ancient sorrow
I liked the man . . .

*(Hulton Archives, JD5200)*

quickly signed the North American Air Defence (NORAD) agreement, putting the country's air defences under joint Canadian-American control. He also invested heavily in weapons that required nuclear warheads. The majority of Canadians did not want to become a nuclear power, something Diefenbaker was slow to grasp. Along with the threat of nuclear holocaust, his tenure was plagued with a recession at the end of the decade that produced unemployment levels of more than 11 percent. By the early 1960s, Diefenbaker's prairie populism, which had looked like a vibrant alternative to the musty central Canadian power of the Liberals, was starting to look merely rustic. "Dief the Chief" appeared indecisive, particularly on the issue of nuclear arms.

In August 1962, the U.S. government learned that the Soviets had been putting nuclear missiles in Cuba that were capable of targeting America. On October 22, President John F. Kennedy demanded that the missiles be removed. The next thirteen days of nuclear brinksmanship kept the world in chilling suspense as Khrushchev and Kennedy exchanged threats, armed their warheads, and weighed their options (Kennedy's military advisers wanted to bomb Cuba). Diefenbaker was the last of America's allies to offer support, a fact that dismayed both Washington and, for the most part, Canadians. It did not help that Kennedy and Diefenbaker did not like one another personally.

It was the only direct confrontation of the Cold War, and after a week that saw Canadian schoolchildren scurrying under their desks in bomb drills as sirens wailed, Khrushchev backed down. Diefenbaker was politically wounded by the affair, and stung by a message from the U.S. State Department: "The Canadian government has not as yet proposed any arrangement sufficiently practical to contribute to North America's defense."

Later that year, Diefenbaker reluctantly performed the ceremonial kickoff at the Grey Cup football game at Toronto's Exhibition Stadium, and he watched from the stands as the game became increasingly obscured by fog. It was the first time the rights to a Canadian football game had been sold to American television, and by the second quarter, the black-and-white screens in Rochester, Buffalo, and Detroit showed only dull, dark shapes moving in a whitish cloud. The Canadian Football League commissioner, G. Sydney Halter, stopped the game in the fourth quarter, and Diefenbaker, along with thirty thousand other dejected fans, filed out of the stadium.

Three months later, Diefenbaker was again campaigning, crossing the country like an addled prophet. In the election of April 1963, he was defeated by the Liberals and Lester Pearson.

# All Canadians are equal

## THE AWAKENING

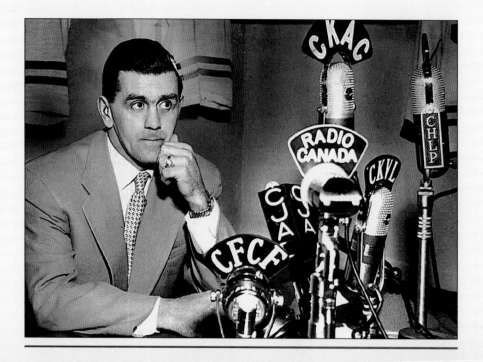

In 1958, television was still a hopeful, unmaligned medium, and its grainy, black-and-white images were a fixture in thousands of Canadian homes. The first stars of Canadian television had already emerged, and on Dominion Day, July 1, 1958, two of the most popular, Joyce Davidson, a host with the English-language network of the CBC, and René Lévesque, a journalist with the French-language Radio-Canada, teamed up for a live, bilingual celebration of the country's birthday. It was called "Memo to Champlain/Si Champlain Vivait" and was intended to showcase the rising stars of each network to the other's audience.

When the show began, both hosts began speaking at once, stepping over each other's words until both broke out laughing.

"We have a problem," Davidson finally acknowledged in English.

"If we keep going like this, we'll have more than a problem on our hands," Lévesque replied in French, with a characteristic shrug. "It'll be a catastrophe."

They quickly recovered and Lévesque gallantly allowed his co-host to go first. "After all, this is what we are: two nations united. So, after you, madam. Not because you speak English, but because you are you." The broadcast went on as planned, another brave, stumbling exercise in linguistic politics.

Maurice Richard asks for calm during the Richard Riot in Montreal, on March 17, 1955. During a game between the Montreal Canadiens and the Boston Bruins, Richard was involved in an altercation with a linesman and was subsequently suspended by NHL president Clarence Campbell. The decision caused outrage in Montreal, where thousands rioted in protest. (*La Presse Canadienne*)

Television had a far greater impact in Quebec than in the rest of Canada. Even before the advent of CBC Television, English Canadians had been exposed to American programs. By the time the CBC went on the air in 1952, there were already 146,000 television sets in Canada, most tuned to American border stations. But until Radio-Canada started broadcasting there were no French-language television programs. From the start, Radio-Canada relied on local programming. It allowed all opinions in Quebec to be expressed, and it delivered news and images from around the world and across the country. Talk shows and interview programs won massive ratings, and TV journalists like Lévesque, host of "Point de Mire," a current-affairs program, became stars, as popular as the actors from the *télé-romans* such as "La Famille Plouffe" and "La Pension Velder." By 1958, television had become a showcase for Quebec's creative artists and a lively forum for political debate. Montreal was the third-largest television production centre in North America, after Hollywood and New York, providing work to more than four thousand people. After decades of relative isolation, millions of Quebecers were suddenly being exposed to all kinds of new information and new currents of thought; television became a mirror of the times, in which Quebec society could see itself begin to change and evolve.

The mirror suddenly ceased reflecting on the evening of December 29, 1958, when Quebecers turned on their television sets and found nothing but blank screens; the Radio-Canada producers had gone on strike. Seventy-four producers were involved, seeking the fairly mundane goal of union recognition and the right to bargain collectively with their employer. They had no job security, no benefits, and no protection from what they considered arbitrary decisions by their bosses. But the management of Radio-Canada rejected their demands, insisting that the producers exercised managerial functions and so could not unionize.

When the strike began, the producers were convinced it would last no more than a few hours. Surely, they reasoned, given the immense popularity of the programs they produced, it would not be allowed to drag on. But the producers at CBC's English network, whom the strikers had counted on for support, did not see it as their fight and continued to work. "We did not feel they were our colleagues; back then, the world was divided between French-speakers and English-speakers," one CBC producer recalled.

The strikers also believed that the Conservative government of John Diefenbaker would respond to public pressure and force Radio-Canada's managers to settle quickly. Again, they were mistaken; Ottawa refused to get involved. The strike began to assume a political dimension: the apathy of the federal government and the indifference of English-speaking Canada stirred up the feeling that what happened in Quebec was of little importance to the rest of the country. "We come face to face once more with the tragedy of the French-Canadian situation," André Laurendeau wrote in *Le Devoir*, on January 19, 1959. "French Canada is not master of its own institutions, and,

**THE PRODUCERS' STRIKE** ◆ René Lévesque was escorted out of a downtown Montreal police station after being arrested during a demonstration in support of striking producers at Radio-Canada. On January 17, 1959, 1,500 demonstrators boarded a train to Ottawa, among them Lévesque, Pierre Trudeau, the actor and broadcaster Pierre Bourgault, and journalist Jeanne Sauvé. Their encounter with labour minister Michael Starr did nothing to bring an end to the strike, but it helped politicize Lévesque. "Starr did not even know what we were talking about," he wrote. "They were not really bothered in Ottawa, it was just the French network that was blacked out. We came back empty handed, but thinking that had the strike occurred in Toronto, twenty-four hours is all that would have been needed to mobilize Parliament, the whole government, and even send in the troops if need be to solve the issue." (*The Montreal Gazette*)

in times of crisis, the outside support on which the very idea of Canadian unity should depend is not forthcoming."

The strike quickly attracted broader support, especially among the Quebec intelligentsia. Until now, René Lévesque had been interested mainly in international affairs, but his focus shifted to national politics – especially to the question of Quebec's place in Canada. His charisma and power as an orator made him a natural leader of the strike supporters. Lévesque later said that the strike was a political turning point in his life: "I had never really identified with federalism, but I had never been anti-federalist either, until then."

After sixty-eight days, the producers finally won the right to organize and bargain collectively. But that was the least of the strike's significance; for those involved, it had thrown the gulf between French- and English-speaking Canadians into sharp relief. For Lévesque, the harsh political comments he had made during the strike effectively ended his broadcasting career. "Point de Mire" was not renewed that autumn.

Joyce Davidson's CBC career did not last much longer. A few months after the strike ended, Davidson was host of a special program to commem-

**MAURICE DUPLESSIS** ◆ Duplessis ran the province of Quebec with an iron hand for eighteen years. He is seen here in Montreal in one of the last pictures taken before his death on September 7, 1959. (*Archives nationales du Québec, Centre de Montréal*)

orate the opening of the St. Lawrence Seaway. Constructed between 1954 and 1959, the Seaway was a huge undertaking, one of the engineering megaprojects that transformed the face of the country in the 1950s and symbolized the post-war economic boom. Through a network of locks and deep-water canals, huge ocean-going ships could now sail directly into the heart of the continent. A joint Canada-U.S. undertaking, the Seaway underscored the growing integration of the two North American economies. The opening ceremony was attended by Prime Minister John Diefenbaker, U.S. President Dwight Eisenhower, and Queen Elizabeth II, who was in Canada for her longest visit since her coronation. Speaking in careful French, the young and surprisingly glamorous queen described the Seaway as a force for national unity: "This important achievement opens a new chapter in the history of Confederation, by creating new links between the two main ethnic groups whose presence confers to the Canadian nation its singular identity."

But a few days earlier, Joyce Davidson had made a casual comment that brought some underlying tensions to the surface. In an appearance on NBC's "Today" program, she was asked about the significance of the queen's visit to Canada. "Most Canadians are indifferent, as I am," she replied. "I think the majority of Canadians do not care much about her visit." There were eight hundred calls from Canadian viewers, all but a hundred of them demanding Davidson's resignation. The controversy damaged her career at the CBC. She left Canada and went to work in American television.

In the spring of 1960, René Lévesque decided to leave journalism and go into politics. His timing was fortuitous; after fifteen years, Maurice Duplessis's hold on Quebec was starting to weaken. Even so, because the province's electoral map favoured rural areas at the expense of urban ridings, tipping the scale in his favour, and because he was adept at stuffing ballot boxes and buying votes where necessary, Duplessis had little fear of the Liberals and their new leader, Jean Lesage. "He does not know the people," Duplessis growled when reminded that elections would have to be held soon. "I am in dangerously [good] shape."

He was, in fact, in dangerously poor shape, and on September 3, 1959, Duplessis collapsed. For four days, his entourage imposed a total blackout on his condition; a vivid illustration of the rigid control that characterized his regime. Duplessis died during the night of September 7, the victim of four cerebral hemorrhages. The era of *duplessisme* – a period his opponents called "*La Grande Noirceur*" (the Great Darkness) – was suddenly over.

Paul Sauvé, the designated successor, quickly distanced himself from his former boss, promising a new approach to education and social affairs. But only 118 days after becoming premier, Sauvé also died. When a provincial election was called, on April 27, 1960, Jean Lesage had his campaign slogan ready: "*Il faut que ça change*" (Things have to change).

Lesage wanted to field a strong team of Liberal candidates, and he was reputedly going after some of the most prominent figures in the province:

**THE QUIET REVOLUTION** ◆ Jean Lesage (left) had promised the Catholic bishops that he would never create a secular ministry of education in Quebec. But he bowed to the prevailing nation that the existing system was holding the province back and reneged on his promise. In 1964, one of his most trusted ministers, Paul Gérin-Lajoie (right), was given the daunting task of carrying out the sweeping recommendations of a royal commission on education, which entailed a radical overhaul of the province's education system, from elementary school through university. (*La Presse Canadienne*)

the union leader Jean Marchand, Gérard Pelletier, the editor of *Le Travail*, Pierre Trudeau, one of the founders of the influential magazine *Cité Libre*, and René Lévesque. In his memoirs, Lévesque wrote, "Marchand was more interested [in running] than Pelletier who, in turn, was more interested than Trudeau. In fact, Trudeau was not interested at all. I think he caught a whiff in the Liberals' rhetoric of the Quebec nationalism that he so opposed." Both Marchand and Pelletier declined to leave their jobs. But other high-profile figures joined Lévesque, creating what Lesage called his "*Equipe de tonnerre*" (his thunderers). He promised to reform the government of Quebec and to reorganize the outmoded and patronage-ridden civil service. It was a hard-fought campaign, but Lesage's Liberals managed a slim majority, capturing fifty-one of the province's ninety-five ridings, and 51 per cent of the popular vote. René Lévesque, their star candidate, won his Montreal riding of Laurier by a mere 129 votes.

The Liberal government enjoyed a wave of goodwill after taking power, as intellectuals, labour leaders, politicians, and even the business community endorsed its plans to modernize Quebec's institutions. Lesage

During the 1962 provincial election campaign in Quebec, the now legendary slogan "*Maîtres chez nous*" was used for the first time. (*The Montreal Gazette*)

made the most of this honeymoon, immediately initiating sweeping reforms. He set up a medicare program and created new ministries for cultural affairs and federal–provincial relations. After years of decrying the electoral corruption of the Duplessis regime, the Liberals quickly imposed tough limits on election spending.

Lesage's most radical reform, however, was in education. The Liberals were determined to modernize the system, which, until then, had been tightly controlled by the Catholic church. The system – and the curriculum – were archaic, obsolete, and wide-open to criticism, and also produced the highest drop-out rate in the country; half of all students were leaving school by the age of fifteen. But criticizing the school system was tantamount to attacking the Church directly, still a risky undertaking. Eventually, the charges against Church-run education came from within. In a vitriolic book, *Les Insolences du Frère Untel* (The Impertinences of Brother Anonymous), a Marist brother named Jean-Paul Desbiens brought the debate over Church-run schools into the public eye in 1960. "We must close down the department," he wrote. "Let's give all the officials all the medals there are. . . . Let's create some special ones, such as one for Solemn Mediocrity. Let's give them all a comfortable and well-paid retirement and send them home to their mamas." He denounced the school system as inadequate, marked by "far-reaching incompetence," and demanded the abolition of the Duplessis-era Department of Public Instruction. His book was an unprecedented success, selling over 100,000 copies. It gave Lesage the encouragement he needed to set up the province's first ministry of education – greatly weakening the Church's control of education – and to reorganize the hundreds of school boards.

Lévesque also convinced Lesage to nationalize Québec's electrical power companies and merge them with the Crown corporation Hydro-Québec, despite strong disagreement within the party and from the Union Nationale Opposition. Lesage called an election on the issue, two years into his mandate. The nationalization of hydro was seized as a symbol of

Quebec's determination to control its own destiny. In Shawinigan, a banner appeared: "The era of economic colonialism is over in Quebec. Now or never: masters in our own house."

Quebec was not the only province caught up in the throes of change in the early 1960s. A few months before Lesage took power in Quebec, Louis Robichaud was elected premier of New Brunswick. Robichaud, the first Acadian to become premier, launched his own set of reforms, designed to raise the standard of living in the province's poor, predominantly French-speaking rural areas. He also overhauled the province's schools and health-care system. With Robichaud's push for what he called "equal opportunity," Acadians started to enjoy better access to public services and began playing a more active role in the province's political life. The wave of reform culminated ten years later, when New Brunswick became Canada's only officially bilingual province.

In June 1960, the Co-operative Commonwealth Federation premier of Saskatchewan, Tommy Douglas, called an election and made medicare the centrepiece of his campaign. It was an issue that sparked militant opposition from the province's doctors.

The attempt to bring medicare to Saskatchewan was the latest in a series of measures adopted across Canada and throughout the western world in the post-war years, based on the premise that governments owed their citizens a reasonable standard of living and access to basic services. The federal government had already introduced such pillars of the welfare state as old age pensions in 1927, unemployment insurance in 1940, and mothers' allowances – the so-called baby bonus – in 1945. The right to collective bargaining had been recognized in 1943, and the principle of equalization was adopted in 1957, a measure intended to help poorer provinces provide the same services as wealthier provinces did, through a redistribution of tax revenues by the federal government.

In Saskatchewan, the CCF had been in power since 1944 and had been the first government in the country to provide hospital insurance for its citizens. Now, in 1960, Douglas was ready to take the next step and introduce universal, publicly funded medical care, not just in hospitals, but also in clinics and doctors' offices. Douglas was bitterly opposed by the province's physicians and private health-care insurers. The doctors complained that they would be turned into civil servants, unable to follow their own judgment about what was best for their patients. They argued that medicare was another step down a slippery socialistic slope.

Despite the $115,000 spent during the election on an anti-medicare campaign, Douglas and the CCF won a commanding majority and a clear mandate to proceed. After a long debate, the law was adopted in November 1961, to take effect the following July 1. The day medicare was born, about 90 per cent of the province's doctors went on strike. The government – headed by Woodrow Lloyd after Douglas left for Ottawa in 1961 to lead

**THE DOCTORS' STRIKE** ◆
Ted Tulchinsky, from
Brantford, Ontario, had just
finished his medical-school
internship when he heard
of the doctors' strike in
Saskatchewan. "I phoned
this [medical-care]
commission guy. . . . I said
I'm Doctor Blah-blah-blah
and I hear you need some
help. He said, yes . . .
bring your credentials,
take the next plane."
(*Courtesy of Joel Tulchinsky*)

the newly formed New Democratic Party – had planned for this contingency, recruiting doctors from Britain and other provinces as temporary replacements.

One of them was Ted Tulchinsky, from Brantford, Ontario. He was immediately sent to the small town of Preeceville, north of Yorkton, where a child had died of meningitis on the first day of the strike. Soon after he arrived, Tulchinsky walked into a restaurant, and no one would speak to him. "It was during the first week of the strike," he said. "There was violence in the air, one could feel it. I slept with a lead pipe under my mattress."

The next week, a huge rally to support the striking doctors and denounce the strikebreakers was held in Regina. That night, three people showed up at the hospital in Preeceville, asking that a doctor come to issue a death certificate for their mother. Tulchinsky drove off into the darkness with them, despite his fears of being on his own and far from help among evidently hostile people. "After I had delivered the death certificate," he recalled, "they treated me with an icy politeness that was almost unbearable. They hated my very presence there, but I was happy I could be of assistance when they needed a doctor."

The Saskatchewan doctors' strike lasted twenty-three days. The strikers won some minor concessions but conceded the main point: they would accept medicare. As part of the settlement, the out-of-province recruits were supposed to leave Saskatchewan, but Tulchinsky decided to stay. With a group of friends and colleagues, he opened a health clinic in Saskatoon. They also opened a café called the Louis Riel – where a young singer named Joni Mitchell first performed. Tulchinsky eventually married Tommy Douglas's daughter Joan. As Douglas had predicted, in less than a decade medicare was adopted across the country.

In August 1957, Prime Minister Diefenbaker had signed the North American Air Defence (NORAD) agreement with the United States, committing Canada to continental air defence. As part of the agreement, Canada was to build two Bomarc missile bases. Persuaded that the Bomarcs were a cheap alternative to the costly but Canadian-designed Avro Arrow fighter plane then being built at Downsview, Ontario, Diefenbaker cancelled the Arrow in 1959 and, to the dismay of aeronautical engineers, ordered the planes destroyed. A year later it became public knowledge that the fifty-six class B Bomarcs in Canada were supposed to be armed with nuclear warheads. After heated debate, the Diefenbaker government decided against allowing nuclear weapons on Canadian soil, a position supported at the time by the Liberals.

On May 16, 1960, at the start of the Big Four summit in Paris among the United States, the Soviet Union, France, and Britain, Soviet premier Nikita Khrushchev torpedoed the proceedings. Two weeks earlier, an American spy plane manned by Francis Gary Powers had been shot down over Russia. The Americans initially denied that Powers was on an espionage mission (then later admitted he was spying, but claimed it was justified), and the Canadians denied the plane had been refuelled on Canadian soil. After delivering a blistering statement, Khrushchev left Paris and went home, leaving behind apocalyptic headlines, bomb drills in schools throughout North America, and renewed fears of the imminence of nuclear war.

A *Toronto Star* journalist named Lotta Dempsey angrily responded to the failure of the talks in a column. Nuclear war suddenly seemed a real possibility, and Dempsey argued that women had to do everything they could to prevent it. "I have never met a woman who did not hate war and its procession of dead, the loss of a husband, or the unbearable tragedy of children killed, maimed, abandoned and starved," Dempsey wrote. "That is what makes us strong." Dempsey received six hundred letters of support within a few days. The idea of a women's organization to fight for nuclear disarmament was born, and it quickly attracted supporters from all across the country.

One of them was Peggy Hope-Simpson, who lived in Halifax, quietly worrying about nuclear annihilation, afraid for her children. "I was having nightmares," she said, "regular nightmares [which] took the form of being in the water with my children, and I knew I could not hold on to all of them, and always I would wake up just at the point when I was going to have to abandon one of them, and I would wake up in a sweat, just in terror." The nuclear menace occupied the national consciousness, invading the dreams of millions. When Hope-Simpson was invited to join the new group, called the Voice of Women (VOW), she quickly accepted. Within months, two thousand women had signed up, including Maryon Pearson, wife of Liberal leader Lester Pearson. "Men are so used to war," she said. "This is why it's so important for women to bind together and take a stand."

For both sides in the debate, the stakes became dramatically higher during the Cuban missile crisis of October 1962, when, for two harrowing weeks, the world was on the brink of nuclear war. The confrontation eventually ended peacefully, but for the anti-nuclear activists of the Voice of Women, here was stark proof of the nuclear insanity that threatened the world. "We have been a hair's breadth from war," wrote Thérèse Casgrain, president of VOW. "I was sure the question was in everyone's mind – tomorrow will my children, my family, my home, my neighbours, my city be here? Or will we be in the death throes of radiation agony, or more mercifully dead? Facing the ultimate crisis forces us to reevaluate what is important in life, what do I stand for? These questions are easy for any mother to answer."

A few weeks later, VOW organized a major rally, intended to stiffen Diefenbaker's resolve to keep nuclear weapons out of Canada. Three hundred women from across the country descended on Ottawa to make their views known. They believed they could count on support from both the prime minister and Lester Pearson, the leader of the Opposition.

But in the wake of the Cuban crisis, public opinion was shifting – and Pearson's with it. He now demanded that Diefenbaker allow the Bomarc to

**THE VOICE OF WOMEN** ◆ In the fall of 1962, the Voice of Women organized an anti-war rally in Ottawa, demanding that the Diefenbaker government not arm Bomarc missiles stationed in Canada with nuclear warheads. VOW counted on Opposition leader Lester Pearson to support them, but Pearson later reversed his stand, prompting a letter from Kathleen Macpherson of VOW.

Dear Mr. Pearson,

Voice of Women/La Voix des Femmes is shocked and disheartened by your announcement this week . . . permitting the United States to store missiles in [Canada]. . . . When international tensions have  become somewhat relaxed as a result of the test ban agreement, why is it that Canada has to move in the opposite direction, diminishing the spirit of international cooperation we hoped so much would grow?" – from an October 11, 1963, letter. (*National Archives of Canada*, PA-209888)

be armed with nuclear warheads, reversing his earlier position. Peggy Hope-Simpson, among others, was cruelly disappointed. "We had put our faith in Pearson," she recalled. "I was shocked and angry that he could do such a thing. I felt betrayed." Pierre Trudeau, then a law professor in Montreal, was also critical, denouncing Pearson as "the defrocked priest of the peace movement," a quip he borrowed from a Quebec nationalist intellectual, Pierre Vadeboncoeur.

The controversy over arming the Bomarc missiles continued to plague Diefenbaker's government, and in February 1963, his minister of defence resigned over the issue, followed by two others. Diefenbaker set himself up as the victim of a conspiracy. "There are great interests against me – national and international," he said. "Everyone is against me, but the people." But the people were against him as well, and in the April general election, the Liberals under Pearson were voted in. On October 9, the new prime minister reached an agreement with the United States to bring nuclear warheads onto Canadian soil. Diefenbaker accused Pearson of making Canada a "burnt sacrifice" to American nuclear interests. Maryon Pearson quietly gave up her membership in the Voice of Women.

In Canada, almost 10 million children were born between 1947 and 1966, forming that immense demographic bulge: the baby boomers. Many were coddled right from birth, as their parents embraced the theories of a growing army of child specialists. The most famous was Dr. Benjamin Spock, an American pediatrician whose book, *The Common Sense Book of Baby and Child Care*, preached a new gospel to millions of young mothers: corporal punishment should be replaced by affection and understanding.

Lester Pearson and John F. Kennedy at the president's family retreat at Hyannisport, Massachusetts, May 1963. (*John F. Kennedy Library*)

Doris Anderson, then the managing editor of *Chatelaine* magazine, recalled, "Some women just made a fetish out of having a baby. There was no end of reading about it, and reading to the baby, and singing to the baby, and playing certain music to the baby, and, you know, being the best mother in the world. That was the aim of an awful lot of women back then because that was the only game in town."

Television and advertising idealized the image of the smiling, suburban wife, well-coiffed, flanked by obedient children, greeting her hard-working husband. In the early 1960s, women made up only one-third of the workforce, mostly as secretaries, receptionists, waitresses, grade-school teachers, and nurses. Twenty per cent of the women in the workforce were either maids or babysitters. In 1961, women were earning 59 per cent of a man's pay for comparable work. One labour union suggested that "behind each woman in the workforce we find an unemployed man." Women risked losing their jobs if they married. A year later, *Chatelaine* ran an article by Christina McCall entitled "All Canadians are Equal Except Women," which detailed the vast gap in professional salaries paid to men and women. When Anderson became pregnant, her boss broke the rules at Maclean-Hunter (*Chatelaine*'s owners) in allowing her to continue to work. Anderson came and went during off-hours through the back door so that the male executives at Maclean-Hunter would not have to deal with the disturbing sight of a pregnant woman in the office.

At *Chatelaine*, Anderson published articles on such previously forbidden

Christina McCall's 1962 article in *Chatelaine* first revealed the big gap between men's and women's wages. (*Chatelaine*)

subjects as contraception. Until the early 1960s, the only contraception methods widely tolerated by the Catholic Church were natural means: abstinence, combined with the use of a thermometer to determine when a woman was most likely to be fertile. It was illegal to sell condoms and diaphragms, and the chairman of a Canadian pharmaceutical company was fined $100 for having mailed, to married customers, catalogues depicting them. The subject of contraception was taboo, despite opinion polls showing that 55 per cent of Canadians approved of birth control. But women were becoming better educated, and there was great interest in news of new, artificial means of contraception. Enovid, a pill that was being sold as a contraceptive in the United States, appeared in Canada in 1961. In its first year on the market, ten thousand Canadian women started to use it. Five years after its introduction, 750,000 women were "on the pill."

In the fall of 1966, Laura Sabia, the founder of the Committee for the Equality of Women in Canada, headed a delegation of seventy-five women who went to Ottawa, demanding that Prime Minister Pearson launch an inquiry into the status of Canadian women. A few months later, upset by the inaction of the Prime Minister's Office, Sabia threatened to mobilize 3 million

**THE PILL** ◆ 1966 marked the tenth anniversary of the first clinical trials of the birth-control pill (conducted in Puerto Rico). It was now used by an estimated 750,000 Canadian women, and 7 million American women. Since 1958, the birth rate had fallen from 28 babies per 1,000 to 21.4 per thousand. Side effects of the pill were reported: 15 per cent of women cited nausea, swelling of limbs, or changes in their skin and hair. In Winnipeg, 225 indigent mothers, some with as many as fourteen children, were given free prescriptions for birth-control pills by a private welfare agency, the first program of its kind in western Canada. (*MD of Canada*)

lowest dosage form proven 100% effective for the control of conception

YORKVILLE ◆ "We, the villagers, were sick of gawking tourists traipsing through our special place, destroying the love vibe. In the Spirit of the Love Generation, hundreds of us . . . sat in the middle of Yorkville Avenue chanting, "Close our street." . . . The cops were not amused. They came at us on horseback." Carole Pope, from *Diva Diaries.* (*The Globe and Mail*)

women in a march on Ottawa. On February 16, 1967, Pearson announced the creation of the Royal Commission on the Status of Women, headed by Ottawa journalist Florence Bird. The commission held public hearings in fourteen cities, visited all ten provinces and both territories, and received 468 briefs, 1,000 letters, and heard 870 witnesses. The commission's 500-page report was tabled in the House of Commons in 1970, and its 167 recommendations included equal pay for work of equal value, a national day-care network, and paid maternity leave. Two years later, the National Action Committee on the Status of Women was founded to monitor and press for government action on the commission's recommendations.

The ethos of sexual liberation that the birth-control pill engendered corresponded to a wider sense of liberation throughout Canadian society. As the first of the baby boomers reached their mid-teenage years, a distinct and vast youth culture emerged, and it contributed to a burgeoning arts scene. In Toronto, poets gathered in Yorkville village, in cafés like the Bohemian Embassy, where a young Margaret Atwood first read her poems in public. "It was a bit frightening, although the room was cramped and dark," she said. "You could always find someone worse than yourself. . . . We all wanted to be poets, so we would end up applauding one another."

Yorkville had a folk music scene that attracted Ian and Sylvia Tyson, Gordon Lightfoot, Joni Mitchell, and Neil Young, who sang at the Riverboat, the Mousehole, or the Home of the Blues. At the Mynah Bird, go-go girls danced in the windows, trying to attract crowds. Marijuana smoke drifted through the dense summer crowds, the police stepped up their patrols, and tensions mounted. In August 1967, hippies demanding that the street be closed to traffic staged a sit-down demonstration in the middle of Yorkville Avenue. The police tried to break up the protest with force, and a riot ensued,

The government of Newfoundland closed 250 outports and relocated 30,000 of the province's inhabitants to larger communities in the late 1950s and early 1960s. Recorded on film by the National Film Board, large families huddled on the decks of tiny boats, towing their houses – quite often their only possession – toward a new life in town. (*National Archives of Canada, P-154122*)

leaving two policemen stranded on top of a car, surrounded by hundreds of people. Twenty constables waded in with clubs and rescued them.

In 1964, the Beatles had arrived in North American with an appearance on "The Ed Sullivan Show." Later that year, they played two Canadian concerts – in Vancouver and Toronto – before thousands of screaming fans. It was dubbed "the British Invasion" and it signalled the sea change in the attitudes of youth. Change echoed throughout the country; church attendance in the 1960s was half what it had been in the previous decade. Divorce rates had doubled. Society was redefining itself. The population was wealthier, better educated, and fast distancing itself from the moral constraints of the previous generation.

The fresh promise and prosperity of the 1960s was not shared everywhere in Canada, and it largely bypassed the Atlantic provinces. In 1957, a Royal Commission on Canada's Economic Prospects alerted the federal government to the region's distress. The average annual income was 37 percent lower than in the six other provinces. The literacy rate was the lowest, unemployment was twice the national average, and the school systems were inadequate. When a coal mine in Springhill, Nova Scotia, collapsed in 1958, killing seventy-four miners, Ottawa did not send relief to the families of those who died, a wound that never quite healed. They felt abandoned by the federal government.

Newfoundland's dependence on the fishery made it the poorest province. Over the course of five hundred years, fishermen had established hundreds of small, isolated communities along the rocky shoreline. But in the 1950s, the provincial government decided that it could not afford to bring modern amenities and services to these outports, many of which could be reached only by sea. Premier Joey Smallwood seized on a Draconian solution:

between the mid 1950s and the early 1970s, the Newfoundland government closed 250 villages. Thirty thousand people were uprooted and relocated to larger villages and towns. Smallwood argued that this would make it more economical to provide education, health care, and social services to them. He also wanted to wean them from the cyclical and risky business of fishing, to retrain them for other work.

Many Newfoundlanders welcomed the government's initiative. "We have re-settled at last," said Charlie Parish, one of the uprooted villagers. "We have a new house, and I will soon be able to buy a car. I am grateful." The massive program introduced many Newfoundlanders to the amenities of modern, urban life: electricity, telephone, schools, roads. But it also meant the end of an era, and the death of a distinct culture. "Most people in my village were fishermen," said Bruce Wareham. "Maybe 90 per cent of them. They just moved these people away from their fishing grounds. I do not know what will happen next. I think it is very sad."

Fishing was not the only industry that was troubled. Hawker Siddeley Canada closed its iron-ore mine on Bell Island in 1966, dramatically altering the economic and social landscape. A short boat trip from St. John's, the island was home to 18,000 people, many of whom had depended on mining. Hubert Butler was a nineteen-year-old living there, looking for his first job. Butler's fiancée, Margaret, was still in school, training to be a secretary, but she was not optimistic about the future. "The mine closed in 1966 just when I finished high school, and the fishing was not doing well either. Everyone knew that unless you were a professional teacher, nurse or doctor, there was no future for you in Newfoundland. It's beautiful, a beautiful island, but it is just not a healthy way for people to live."

Between 1956 and 1973, close to one million people left the Atlantic provinces, seeking work elsewhere. Hubert Butler went to Ontario, looking for work at an automobile factory. In 1970, the Auto Pact between Canada and the United States was already in its fifth year, and Ford, Chrysler, and General Motors had all built factories in southern Ontario, offering lucrative jobs. "I was nineteen!" Butler said. "Arriving at Toronto, looking at those buildings, you know, until you could not turn your neck any further down, right? . . . Me and my buddy Sweeney . . . both of us were very naive, did not really have a clue what we were up against, and really thinking that the world was one big family."

Butler went on to Windsor, where he had an uncle. "He decided to go to Windsor because his uncle had got work there at the Ford Motor company," Margaret recalled. "Imagine, being nineteen, a young nineteen from a small town, going all the way to Windsor to seek your fortune! And he went up to Windsor, and stayed with that uncle and, the next week, he applied for a job at Ford, and he got it!" A full-time job was a rarity back home, and Butler was elated. Margaret made her first trip out of the province to join Butler in Windsor and marry him. Eighty per cent of Bell Island's inhabitants eventually left, following the trail of easterners seeking work.

Located in the north end of Halifax, Africville was created as a separate black community through a land purchase in 1848. Initially a thriving community, it became the location for every unwanted aspect of urban life (railway tracks, sewage disposal pits, and a dump site were all located nearby). "They say the people in Africville encroached on the government," one resident said, "but I say the government encroached on the people." (*Nova Scotia Archives and Records Management*)

In Halifax, a derelict neighbourhood called Africville was the ramshackle home to the descendants of the American slaves who had fled to Canada more than 150 years earlier. They had found freedom in Canada, but little else. By 1960, decades of racism and neglect by civic administrations had turned Africville into the most miserable urban ghetto in the country. As early as the 1850s, nearby land had been expropriated for railway tracks and sewage disposal pits, a policy that continued for a century. In the 1950s, city council moved an open dump to the edge of the community. Not long afterward, a report by the city of Halifax described Africville as "a jumble of shacks, where 70 negro families live in deplorable conditions. There is only one thing to do: these families must be moved out, and the land must be made available to future city needs."

The mayor of Halifax, John Lloyd, explained that the decision to bulldoze Africville had been made for sanitary reasons, and he stressed the move would mean an end to race segregation in Halifax: "It is clear to me that Africville must be redeveloped, but sometimes we have to explain to people that we are acting in their interest. We have taken our decision in the interest of the public, and in the best interest of the people [of Africville] and of their children."

But the city of Halifax offered the inhabitants of Africville nothing more than a symbolic lump-sum compensation for their houses. Daisy Carvery, a mother of five, was outraged: "The meanest part that they did to Africville is, they got the old people together, because they simply knew that the older people did not have an education. What is $500 to a 75-year-old Negro? He thinks he is rich. They took our homes, they moved us out of Africville. The city moved us out of Africville in the city's garbage trucks. We had it a lot better out there than in some of the places they put us in the city."

In Quebec, Jean Lesage's Liberals rode to an easy victory on November 14, 1962, winning sixty-three ridings, twelve more than in 1960, which gave them a clear mandate to forge ahead with their reforms. Brian Upton, a *Montreal Star* journalist, coined the phrase "Quiet Revolution" to describe the changes being wrought in Quebec. But the rapid change and nationalist slogans raised the spectre of an independent Quebec. Separatist groups took to describing federalism as a form of colonialism that hampered the growth of the French-Canadian nation. The early groups, such as the right-wing l'Alliance laurentienne, launched by Raymond Barbeau in 1957, were moderate to start, but the rhetoric quickly hardened and the factions multiplied.

English was still the language of business in Montreal, and anglophones a dominant minority. Sixty per cent of francophones did not speak English and were largely excluded from economic power. The term "Westmount Rhodesians" was a popular but unflattering comparison of Montreal's anglophone aristocracy to the white ruling class in southern Africa. The Lesage government had undertaken a series of initiatives to promote a more dynamic francophone business class, but foreign companies invited in by Duplessis still dominated the economy, and the executive class was almost exclusively anglophone.

A stormy debate in a Commons commitee on November 19, 1962, between a Quebec MP and an English-speaking business leader propelled the language issue onto the national agenda. Donald Gordon, the chairman of the board of Canadian National Railways, tabled his company's annual report in a committee of the House of Commons. Gilles Grégoire, an MP for the Ralliement des Créditistes, said, after reading the report, "I see here that CN has one chairman, seventeen vice-presidents, and ten directors, and that none of them is French Canadian."

"How do you know?" Gordon replied.

"Then which ones are?" asked Grégoire.

"I want to know how you define French Canadian," said Gordon.

"Could you name for me the ones who are?" Grégoire asked.

"I do not know how to define a French Canadian. But I will say this: these are all Canadians, every one of them."

To a roomful of surprised MPs, Gordon said he had tried repeatedly, but had been unable to find one French-speaking Canadian competent enough to fill a high-level management position at CN. But he tried to reassure them by saying, "Any man who . . . is considered by management to be the best person for a job will receive the promotion – and we do not care whether he is black, white, red or French."

Gordon was hanged and burned in effigy by demonstrators in Ottawa, Quebec City, Montreal, and Trois-Rivières and decried in the Quebec media. "No other event," said the *Montreal Star*, "short of the conscription crisis, has triggered so much animosity between the two ethnic groups." Opposition leader Lester Pearson demanded a royal commission into the state of bilingualism in Canada.

**DONALD GORDON** ◆
Gordon, the chairman of the board of Canadian National Railways, appearing before the Railway Committee of the House of Commons on November 19, 1962. (*National Archives of Canada*, PA-209754)

The Front de Libération du Québec, formed in March 1963, set off some 200 bombs of increasing power during its seven-year terrorist campaign. (*National Archives of Canada.* PA-157323)

"Recent events have clearly indicated that we are going through yet another crisis of national unity," Pearson said in the House of Commons. "Technically, Confederation may not have been a treaty signed between [founding] states, but it constituted nonetheless an agreement, a pact between the two founding nations of Canada, based on the principle of a fair and equal association. . . . If we refuse, or if we forget, or neglect the obligations that come with our true association, we will keep on drifting from one crisis to another, until a majority of the population, on both sides, becomes jaded with this unique, Canadian experience. The end result will be separatism."

On the night of March 7, 1963, the most radical separatist group to emerge so far – the Front de Libération du Québec (FLQ)– proclaimed its existence by placing bombs in mailboxes at three federal armories in Montreal and Westmount. The next morning, the FLQ introduced itself as a revolutionary movement, whose members were prepared to die in their fight to bring about the total independence of Quebec.

A month later, Pearson was elected prime minister, and, as one of his early initiatives, he created the Royal Commission on Bilingualism and Biculturalism. The B&B commission, as it came to be known, was co-chaired by André Laurendeau, editor-in-chief of *Le Devoir*, and Davidson Dunton, former chairman of the CBC. Together they oversaw the often turbulent public hearings held throughout the country.

While the commission was at work, Pearson launched a debate on the nation's flag, or its lack of one. He was hoping for a symbol that would unite Canadians. Canada had existed for ninety-six years and still did not have a

**THE NEW FLAG** ◆ "I believe that today a flag designed around the maple leaf will symbolize – will be a true reflection of – the new Canada. Today there are 5 million or more Canadians whose tradition is not inherited from the British Isles, but who are descendants of the original French founders of our country. There are another 5 million, or more, who have come to Canada from other faraway lands, with a heritage neither British or French.

"I believe that a Canadian flag – as distinctive as the maple leaf in the Legion badge – will bring them all close to those of us of British stock and make us all better, more united, Canadians." – Lester Pearson, in a May 17, 1964, speech to the national convention of the Royal Canadian Legion in Winnipeg. It was his first speech introducing the new flag to the public, and he was repeatedly booed by the Legionnaires. (*National Archives of Canada, PA-117488*)

flag to call its own. The flag floating over Parliament and all official places in Canada was the Union Jack, a British emblem, or the Red Ensign, a modified version of the flag of the British merchant fleet. But instead of uniting the country, the flag became yet another divisive issue. John Diefenbaker insisted that the Union Jack be part of the new flag, to reflect Canada's British heritage. And those who supported the idea of a new flag that had no associations with the country's colonial past were bitterly divided over what it should look like.

Pearson's insistence on the need for a new flag provoked editorial controversy across the country. "If this is his idea of unity," read an article in the *Vancouver Province*, "it is doubtful whether the country can swallow much more of it." Support, laments, and threats poured in as the country revealed an untapped and unsuspected passion for its national symbol. There was also a healthy pocket of apathy. "Quebec does not give a tinker's dam about the new flag," Pierre Trudeau said. "It's a matter of complete indifference." As many as 5,900 alternative designs were sent to Ottawa. The parliamentary debate was lengthy and ugly. It consumed thirty-seven sitting days: the Conservatives made 210 speeches, the Liberals 50, the NDP 24, Social Credit 15, and the Créditistes 9. Pearson's preferred design of three maple leaves was finally rejected in favour of a design proposed by the historian George Stanley that featured a single leaf flanked by red bars. Diefenbaker dismissively said that it looked like the Peruvian flag. On December 15, well after midnight, Pearson used the rules of closure to settle the matter. "You have done more to divide the country than any other prime minister," Diefenbaker charged. When Diefenbaker died, in 1979, his coffin was draped with both the Red Ensign and the new flag.

As opportunities for post-secondary education expanded in the early 1960s, a restless generation of university students emerged, increasingly aware of international issues, and newly militant. "That was the whole revolution," said James Laxer, a member of the Student Union for Peace Action, "beginning with cars and Elvis and music and then movements like SUPA. This huge generation that went to university meant that we felt like we were beginning the world again. We felt like a powerful generation. I had the feeling [of being] part of a huge movement that existed all over North America, and I had a vague sense that it also existed in Europe, and that in some ways, we really were going to change the world."

Laxer was a student at the University of Toronto in 1962, when three thousand students protested Donald Gordon's comments about not being able to find a qualified French Canadian for his board. Their March for Canada ended at Queen's Park, where Ontario premier John Robarts came out and spoke to them.

Students also organized a demonstration at the American Consulate in Toronto in 1965 to denounce the brutal repression of Dr. Martin Luther King, Jr., and civil rights activists in Selma, Alabama. "The civil rights movement in the United States was an inspiration for the New Left," said Laxer. Student radicals opposed the Vietnam War and organized the first teach-in ever to take place in Canada, at the University of Toronto. For three days, students, professors, and intellectuals analysed the implications of the Vietnam War. The teach-in mirrored a rising tide of protest on American campuses; millions of students demonstrated against the war throughout the United States.

For James Laxer, the Vietnam protest was a defining moment: "On one hand, you had America, with its advanced technology, its economic power, its military might, bent on promoting liberalism, and standardizing the planet, and whose sideshow of the moment was the war in Vietnam. But on this side, Canadians lived a more conservative life, in a more organized society, and with a different set of values. Suddenly, preserving these Canadian values became our most pressing objective."

Student militancy spread across the country. In February 1968, students at the Université de Montréal and the Université de Moncton walked out of their classes, protesting a hike in tuition fees. In Moncton, the strike quickly escalated into a battle by Acadians to gain the right to live and work in French. They demanded the immediate and full implementation of the sweeping recommendations of the Bilingualism and Biculturalism commission.

Led by Bernard Gauvin, twelve hundred Acadian students demonstrated in front of city hall in Moncton. "Bystanders were shouting at us: 'Go back to France! Go back to Quebec!'" said Gauvin. "But we had

**MARSHALL MCLUHAN** ◆ McLuhan was born in Edmonton, raised in Winnipeg and went to the University of Toronto where he became a professor of English literature. During the 1960s and 1970s, his theories on media and technology earned him the title of guru (and a cameo in Woody Allen's 1977 film *Annie Hall* as himself). Of television, McLuhan wrote in 1971, "When the news team seeks to become the news source by means of direct dialogue rather than by remote report of the event, they are being true to the immediacy of the TV medium in which comments outrank the event itself." In 1970, he foreshadowed the emergence of the Internet, predicting that personal computers would change the economic and social landscape. "In terms of, say, a computer technology, we are headed for cottage economics, where the most important activities can be carried on in any individual little shack anywhere on the globe." (*CP Picture Archive*)

been here since 1604." Moncton mayor Leonard Jones treated the demonstrators, and their demands, with contempt and condescension. A few days later the students delivered a five-kilogram pig's head to his door.

In May 1968, students in Paris, demanding the overthrow of the "capitalist establishment," occupied the Sorbonne and set up barricades in the streets. Hundreds were injured in clashes with riot police. The students' rallying cry was "*L'imagination au pouvoir*" (Let imagination run the world). It was a more abstract concept than rising tuition costs, but nevertheless the students' militancy galvanized support throughout France. On May 11, labour unions called a general strike, shutting down trains, airports and the post office. By May 20, millions of workers were occupying their factories, in some cases holding the managers hostage. The government responded with a 35 percent increase in the minimum wage.

Unrest was at the boiling point and not only in the West. In Czechoslovakia, the hope that the new leader of the Communist Party, Alexander Dubcek, would allow reforms and a return to a free press – "socialism with a human face" – was crushed that summer by Soviet tanks. In August, they rumbled through the streets of Prague, along with thousands of Soviet soldiers. Thirty people were killed and three hundred injured when Soviet troops stormed the national radio station.

Seven days later, on August 29, there was a riot in Chicago outside the convention centre where Hubert Humphrey was being nominated as the Democratic presidential candidate. Thousands were demonstrating against the war in Vietnam, and more than one hundred were injured when police charged their ranks. Eight people were indicted on charges of incite-ment to riot.

Throughout 1968, television screens were filled with images of riots (or at least their aftermaths), of war and revolution. The footage of bombs dropping on rice paddies, of wounded soldiers and dead Vietnamese civilians, of bloodied protesters and weeping students, was punctuated by advertisements for the new Ford Mustang and "new and improved" detergents. Marshall McLuhan, a professor of English at the University of Toronto, became the inscrutable sage of the electronic age, interpreting its imagery and assessing its power. He coined his famous phrase, "The medium is the message," on July 30, 1959, at a Vancouver symposium on mass media and music. Five years later, *Understanding Media* was published to some confusion and great acclaim. McLuhan argued that the sequential, linear experience of reading print was being challenged by powerful, more arbitrary, and constantly changing images that were television. Television demanded a greater degree of involvement on the part of the viewer and allowed the broadcaster a greater opportunity for manipulation. Often quoted, much celebrated, and poorly understood, McLuhan was occasionally ridiculed for being too abstruse. ("I don't pretend to understand it," he once said of his own work.)

His theories embraced almost everything, including nationalism. "Look a bit closer at both nationalism and industrialism," he said in a *Playboy* interview, "and you'll see that both derived directly from the explosion of print technology in the 16th century. . . . The printing press, by spreading mass-produced books and printed matter across Europe, turned the vernacular regional languages of the day into uniform closed systems of national languages – just another variant of what we call mass media – and gave birth to the entire concept of nationalism." But television was an auditory and tactile experience, he argued, and we were united by its ubiquity and its immediacy. "The human family now exists under the conditions of a global village," he wrote. "We live in a single constructed space resonant with tribal drums."

The most compelling model of the global village was Expo 67 in Montreal. The World's Fair was a celebration of Canada's centennial and a showcase for the world. Sixty countries erected pavilions, from the sober to the fanciful, on two islands in the St. Lawrence River, Ile Ste-Hélène and Ile Nôtre-Dame, a man-made island created out of landfill from the building of the city's new subway system.

Originally a Diefenbaker initiative, Expo had been inherited by a doubtful Pearson, who worried that the four and a half years Canada had would not be enough time to mount an exposition of such magnitude. The fear of an unprecedented disaster hung in the air right until opening day; what if the country stumbled on the world stage? But the Expo village was a gleaming paean to the future, with Buckminster Fuller's oversized geodesic

**EXPO 67** ◆ Perceptions of Expo 67 varied greatly from one end of the country to the other. It boosted patriotic sentiments for English-speaking Canadians during the year the country was celebrating its centennial. For many Quebec francophones, Expo was a spectacular showcase for their newly developed capabilities. Expo commissioner Pierre Dupuy wrote, "The people of today, confused by the turmoil of progress, were reminded that there are ties of interdependence between them, a common destiny. What united them was much more fundamental than what divided them." (*National Archives of Canada, C-18536*)

dome, Moshe Safdie's innovative Habitat housing, pulsing electronic images, and a monorail snaking through all of it. The *Montreal Star* described it as "the most staggering Canadian achievement since this vast land was finally linked by a transcontinental railway." It was sleek, sexy, and visited by more than 50 million people, a stunning international success. "Ca-na-da," Bobby Gimby's catchy, song, reverberated among the pavilions, and Canadians everywhere seized upon Expo as a symbol of unity and national pride.

French president Charles de Gaulle was invited to Expo by Ottawa and given a hero's welcome in Quebec. On July 24, from the balcony of Montreal's city hall, flanked by Premier Daniel Johnson and Montreal mayor Jean Drapeau, he addressed a crowd of thousands, delivering his famous four-word contribution to national unity: "*Vive le Québec libre!*" Below him, the crowd erupted with cheers.

René Lévesque watched the performance on a television monitor and pondered its consequences: "For some of us, including me, it [was] a red alert. And rather premature. We were not ready to imitate those young people marching down the street chanting: '*Québec libre, oui, oui, oui! Québec libre, de Gaulle l'a dit!*' In fact, their exuberance filled me with a vague uneasiness, for it did not seem to me to be at all advisable to have recourse to some external authority, no matter how prestigious." Lévesque left the provincial Liberal party a few months later, after his proposal for a modified form of independence, which he called "sovereignty-association," was defeated at the party's policy convention. Within a year, he launched the separatist Parti Québécois, with a platform that outlined an economic union with Canada in the event that voters supported sovereignty. Canada was very much like a couple, Lévesque said: "If both are able to sleep in the same bed, then, fine, it can bring good results. But if they are unable, then they should sleep in different rooms."

Pierre Elliott Trudeau was Lévesque's natural opponent. "Nationalism is a backward force," he said, "that is to blame for the worst of all wars." Trudeau had come to Ottawa in 1965 when federal Liberals were looking to invigorate their party. He explained his move by quoting Plato: "The price to pay for those who shy away from public life is to be governed by people worse than themselves."

As justice minister under Pearson, Trudeau had a high profile and was keen to tackle the delicate issues of abortion, homosexuality (both of which were still offences under the Criminal Code), and divorce. "With laws dating back to 1870, in a society which has moved so quickly and so far in the intervening years," he said, "it is not astonishing that the present divorce laws and the way in which they govern our society are highly unsatisfactory, and indeed produce some very evil results." Until this time, a couple seeking divorce had few legal grounds to do so, and were sometimes reduced to the

On April 4, 1967, Pierre Trudeau, John Turner, and Jean Chrétien joined Lester Pearson's cabinet. They all went on to become prime ministers. (*CP Picture Archive*)

Pierre Elliott Trudeau's campaign quickly developed a glamour previously unknown in Canadian politics. Quebec welcomed a French-speaking candidate, and the rest of the country embraced his style as much as his politics. He won the majority that had eluded Lester Pearson, winning 155 seats to Robert Stanfield's 72. (*CP Picture Archives*)

charade of bringing a witness to find one or the other spouse in bed with someone else. New legislation was introduced on December 9, 1967, which substantially broadened the grounds for divorce. Two weeks later, Trudeau announced an omnibus bill that would legalize homosexuality and permit abortion if a committee of doctors determined that the pregnancy threatened the life or health of the mother. "The state has no business in the nation's bedrooms," he said the next day when asked about the bill. The legislation was finally enacted in May 1969.

After Pearson stepped down as Liberal leader in April 1968, Trudeau won the job. In the wake of the giddy spirit of Expo 67, Trudeau's leadership campaign had a contagious glamour. He was charismatic, the antithesis of his staid predecessors, Lester Pearson and John Diefenbaker, and his earnest Conservative opponent, Robert Stanfield. Television's insistence on the primacy of images focused attention on the leader, rather than on the party or its policies. "The medium [can't] take a real face," McLuhan observed of Trudeau's television presence. "It has to have a mask." Television emphasized conflict and delivery, it showcased charm and punished dullness. Did the country want Robert Stanfield's academic gawkiness or the cool grace of Trudeau?

On June 24, the last day of the federal election campaign, Trudeau attended Montreal's celebration of St-Jean Baptiste Day, sparking controversy. "We take a tough stance against Mr. Trudeau because he has the arrogance to show up at a celebration of the French-Canadian nation," said Pierre Bourgault of the Rassemblement pour l'indépendance nationale. "But Mr. Trudeau himself refuses to acknowledge the existence of a French-Canadian nation! He said there is only one nation in Canada. That is why he has no business showing up at these celebrations, to play the dandy." Hard-core separatists pelted the grandstand where he sat with rocks and bottles. Mayor Jean Drapeau implored Trudeau to leave, but he refused to be intimidated, and the clashes escalated into a riot beamed into the living rooms of Canadians watching on television. Three hundred demonstrators were arrested and a hundred injured. The Liberals were returned to office with a comfortable majority on June 25, 1968.

In 1969, Trudeau pulled half of the country's NATO contingent out of Europe and reduced the armed forces by a third, cost-cutting moves that were criticized both within and outside the country. Among those who applauded the move were John Lennon and Yoko Ono, who met with Trudeau in Ottawa in December 1969, after meeting with Marshall McLuhan in Toronto. Trudeau and the former Beatle spent forty minutes chatting about fame and peace. Afterward, Lennon said, "If there were more leaders like Mr. Trudeau, the world would have more peace."

As prime minister, Trudeau introduced his concept of a "Just Society" for Canada, one supported by a Charter of Rights and Freedoms. He was in favour of a centralized political system, with a strong, activist federal government. His main interests lay in Quebec, in language and constitutional issues, which he pursued to the exclusion of issues of concern to the west, giving rise to increased western alienation and his personal vilification there. But it was not just the west that felt ignored; native people were also becoming increasingly militant.

For a century, the federal government had assumed the responsibility for the education of aboriginal people, a job it had delegated to the churches. They had set up a series of residential schools, which in the 1960s were coming under attack by natives for their educational limitations and reported abuses. "My first memory of education is being trucked into the school," said Leona Makokis, from Alberta's Saddle Lake Reserve. "We were all lifted into a big truck box, where we lay looking up at the sky. There were kids screaming and hollering around us, and we were driven away from our families." In 1957, there were reports of critical shortages of food, clothing, heat, and furniture in the residential schools. In 1962, two years after native people finally won the right to vote, the federal government increased funding to the schools, but the curriculum dismissed native history and forbade teaching in their languages. By 1966, the high-school drop-out rate among natives was 94 per cent.

In 1969, Indian Affairs minister Jean Chrétien delivered a White Paper that proposed to end the long-standing practice of treating Indians differently from other Canadian citizens. Among other things, it would provide a fund of $50 million to compensate for the termination of the treaties, eliminate the Department of Indian Affairs within five years, and reshape the Indian Act. It would also integrate many native children into white schools.

One of the native leaders who protested the paper was Harold Cardinal, the twenty-four-year-old president of the Indian Association of Alberta. He had grown up in Sucker Creek, Alberta, attended residential schools and then St. Patrick's Oblate College in Ottawa. "The federal government engaged in an extensive process to change the Indian Act," he said. "We, leaders all over the country, made extensive proposals. Everyone assumed they were going to deal with the recommendations that were brought in. The White Paper resulted in a lot of anger, anger in the sense of betrayal."

Cardinal felt that Chrétien's proposed legislation would mean the assimilation of native people into the white mainstream. One of the casualties would be the Blue Quills school near St. Paul, Alberta, if its students were streamed into a regional school in town. Blue Quills was twenty-six kilometres from the Saddle Lake reserve, one of the few places where students could go to school and remain relatively close to their own families.

"We went through Alberta, community by community," Cardinal said, "talking to people, beginning to draft a response. The White Paper was read in June 1969, and we did not bring our response to the government until June 1970." *Citizens Plus*, also called the Red Paper, was presented in person to Trudeau and his cabinet. "It was, for us, in political terms, extraordinary," Cardinal said. "Because, you see, up until then you saw Native leaders in full regalia only when they danced for the Queen. There had never been a face-to-face meeting between the country's ministers and First Nations leaders. It was a breakthrough."

They met with Trudeau and his cabinet, telling them they rejected the White Paper. They demanded instead a "truly impartial claims commission appointed after consultation with the Indians," as well as recognition of treaty rights. They also wanted control over the native education system: "Our theory was that if we had greater control over the educational system, if we were able to set up our own institutions, we would have better success."

Trudeau responded to the assembled chiefs, "We were not, as Mr. Cardinal suggests, perhaps pragmatic enough or understanding enough . . . and let me just say, we're in no hurry if you're not. . . . We'll take two,

On June 4, 1970, Harold Cardinal (standing) and two hundred other native leaders met with Pierre Trudeau and his cabinet to present their Red Paper, which called for serious land-claims negotiations and community control of native schools. (*CP Picture Archive*)

three, five, ten or twenty years – the time you people decide to come to grips with this problem."

But the Blue Quills school was still slated to close, and on July 14, the parents in Saddle Lake occupied the school. The two-week sit-in inside the school's new gymnasium involved as many as two hundred people, among them Charles Wood. "We have been told that native culture was not good, and that our customs were no-good pagan rites for so long that it was hard for us to believe we were good enough [to run our own schools]," he said. "But, one evening, one of the elders stood up and asked: 'How many of you have studied up to grade 12?' No hand showed. Then, 'How many of you have studied up to ninth grade?' A few hands. 'See?' the old man said, 'almost none of us can claim to have received an education. But the white man, the clergy, have been in charge of our education for over a century. We can't do worse than them.'"

Margaret Quinney was involved in the occupation. "This was our school," she said. "We did not want them to close it. Some of the older kids had tried integrated schools. They were saying it was even tougher than residential school. We thought we could manage the school, and educate our own children."

Harold Cardinal was at Saddle Lake with the protesters when Chrétien sent him a telegram saying that he thought the parents were moving too quickly with their protest. Cardinal wrote back, "The situation at Blue Quills is serious and not a matter for political manoeuvring on the part of anybody. In view of your lack of response, and, indeed, misrepresentation of these people's legitimate aspirations, we cannot in good faith

In July, 1971, the Blue Quills school near the Saddle Lake reserve in Alberta became the first in Canada to be managed by native people. Margaret Quinney (fourth from left) was one of the members of the first board. (*Provincial Archives of Alberta, Grey Nuns collection*)

counsel moderation on their part." The protest was getting international media attention, and the following week César Chávez, leader of the California farm workers' union, sent a crate of grapes in a gesture of solidarity. At the end of July, Cardinal and fifteen other protesters were flown to Ottawa for three days of meetings with Chrétien and his officials.

In the end, the federal authorities relented, and on September 1, 1971, native people celebrated the creation of the first native-run school in Canada. "We wanted to re-introduce our children to their native culture, and, above all, to make them proud of their heritage," Margaret Quinney said. In 1972, the National Indian Brotherhood formally proposed local community control of schools and teaching in local languages, a policy subsequently adopted by the Department of Indian Affairs. The following year, the Supreme Court of Canada ruled that treaties signed as much as two hundred years earlier gave native people a strong legal basis for their current territorial claims. Faced with this ruling, the federal government had little choice but to enter land-claims negotiations.

Despite the softening of the abortion law in 1969, it remained a difficult issue, legally, morally, and politically. Desperate women were still subjecting themselves to illegal, sometimes dangerous abortions or resorting to risky and usually ineffective homemade methods. A thirty-two year old woman with six children, and another on the way, described the experience: "Our youngest daughter was just at the two-year-old stage. . . . And I thought, I can't do this. I can't do it mentally and I can't do it physically." One of her neighbours, an intern in a hospital, recommended she douche with laundry soap, although it was dangerous. "I went up into the bathroom and about once an hour I did this. . . . I was crazy. I should never have done it. . . . But when I saw that menstrual blood, I could have clicked my heels and jumped up to the ceiling, I was so happy and relieved."

Women protesting against the arrest of Dr. Henry Morgentaler, in front of the Montreal court-house on June 10, 1970. (*National Archives of Canada*, PA-164027)

In October 1968, a booklet written by a group of students at McGill University, *The Birth Control Handbook*, contained detailed descriptions of all the known abortion techniques, while warning women against those that could harm their health. The booklet, which was quickly translated into French, came out three months after the papal encyclical *Humanae Vitae*, in which Pope Paul VI stressed the Church's steadfast opposition to contraception. Ignoring the pope's injunction, Catholic women snapped up copies of the booklet. By 1971, *The Birth Control Handbook* was in its tenth printing.

In 1969, in defiance of the law, Dr. Henry Morgentaler started offering only abortions at his family practice clinic on Beaugrand St., in a French-speaking neighbourhood in east-end Montreal. After lagging behind the times for so long, Quebecers had moved to the vanguard in the fight for

**ABORTION CARAVAN** ◆ "We really took [the abortion debate] out of the closet. We did this, remember, a year after Trudeau had liberalized the law. But what had happened was that women still had to go to a psychiatrist and say, 'I'm psychologically unstable and so you have to give me an abortion.' And so what going across the country did, and quickly, within six months, was that those [abortion] committees changed. . . . The idea changed to women consciously choosing to have an abortion, the idea of 'every child a wanted child.' . . . What our caravan succeeded in was challenging this notion of paternalism, moving past the legal to the moral areas." – Marcy Cohen, one of the leaders of the Abortion Caravan that travelled from Vancouver to Ottawa. (*Provincial Archives of Alberta, J-446/8*)

birth control. Family-planning clinics had opened, despite the fact that they were still illegal under the Criminal Code. "Illegal abortions involve enormous hazards to women's lives and health: this fact is indisputable and even the archfoes of abortion themselves acknowledge it," Morgentaler wrote. "Unfortunately, the extent of the illegal abortion phenomenon and its consequences have never been properly assessed: we have to be content with rough estimates. . . . [But] apparently one out of every three illegal operations had serious enough consequences to require a stay in hospital."

The protest against restrictive abortion laws was also gathering momentum on the west coast, and on April 27, 1970, a caravan of vehicles left downtown Vancouver. It included a Pontiac convertible, a station wagon, and minivan with a coffin on its roof, symbolizing the hundreds of women who had died after botched illegal abortions. Aboard the Abortion Caravan were seventeen women, headed for Ottawa. In each city the caravan passed through – Calgary, Edmonton, Regina, Saskatoon, Winnipeg, Sudbury – the small group staged a play that satirized the law against abortion and the hypocrisy of the medical profession. "We'd do guerrilla theatre about back-street abortion," said Marcy Cohen, one of the leaders of the group. "It was incredible. Across the country, waitresses in restaurants, for instance, would open up to us and tell us stories about what they had gone through."

The Abortion Caravan picked up supporters as it moved across the country. When the group finally reached Ottawa, on May 9, hundreds of women demonstrated in the streets of the capital. The coffin, covered with the symbols of illegal abortions – garbage bags, knitting needles, vacuum-cleaner accessories, cans of Drano – was laid in front of 24 Sussex Drive, the prime minister's official residence. Shortly before Question Period, thirty-five women entered the visitors' gallery in the House of Commons. At 3:30 p.m., they demanded, in one voice, the legalization of abortion and locked themselves to their seats. "We had our own chains in our purses," Cohen said. "We went in twos. By the time they got around to all of us, it took them an hour. They suspended Question Period. We thought the media had covered us so much they did not want to arrest us." Abortion remained a political landmine, resulting in bitter, emotional battles both in Parliament and in the streets.

At the time there was only one woman – Grace MacInnis – in the House of Commons. Two years later, in April 1972, Monique Bégin, a sociologist who had been executive secretary of Florence Bird's Royal Commission on the Status of Women, was called to Trudeau's office. The prime minister wanted her to run for Parliament. She said she would, but only if there were at least three other female candidates, running in ridings safe enough for them to be elected. Jeanne Sauvé and Albanie Morin joined her in Quebec, and other women stepped forward: Aideen Nicholson in Toronto, Mary Casey and Margaret Dunn in Nova Scotia, Peggy Thatcher and Stephanie Poposki in Saskatchewan. "As one of the few women in politics, I had, from the start, the impression of being barely tolerated in a restricted area," Bégin said. Five women were elected in 1972, Bégin among them – a small but significant political start.

In 1965, the Laurendeau-Dunton Royal Commission on Bilingualism and Biculturalism issued a dire warning to federal authorities: "Canada is, without being fully conscious of the fact, passing through the worst crisis of its history. . . . The time has come to make hard decisions, and to contemplate real change." We must reorganize the way this country works, the commissioners said, or contemplate the possible break-up of Canada. The commission's final report outlined a wide range of reforms aimed at ensuring the survival of French culture in Canada and easing French-English political tensions. It recommended that all federal government offices nationwide offer services in both English and French, and that French-language education in English-speaking parts of the country be expanded (and vice versa). The tabling of the commission's report went almost unnoticed in Quebec, where public opinion was gripped by the rise of nationalism, the radicalization of labour, and the bombs of FLQ terrorists. Elsewhere, it was cheered by French-speaking communities that were struggling against assimilation. But the recommendation to introduce bilingualism outside Quebec was viewed with suspicion by many anglophones, who felt they were being forced to learn French to pacify excited separatists in Quebec.

**THE B&B COMMISSION** ◆ After Donald Gordon, chairman of the board
of Canadian National Railways, announced that it was impossible to find
qualified francophones to sit on the board, André Laurendeau (left) responded
in *Le Devoir*, "Mr. Gordon has one quality: he is blunt. He says out loud what
others besides him do, but without saying so. . . . 23 of 78 public bodies of
the federal government also practice the same form of total exclusion [of
francophones]. Mr. Gordon is the noisy exponent of a policy that is usually
kept quiet." Laurendeau, along with Davidson Dunton (right), co-chaired
the Royal Commission on Bilingualism and Biculturalism created by
Lester Pearson. (*National Archives of Canada*, PA-209871)

In 1969, the federal government passed its Official Languages Act,
giving French and English equal status in Canada. It also proclaimed that all
federal agencies, departments, institutions, and organizations must operate
in both languages. Financial incentives were offered to provincial governments and private businesses to review their own language policies.

It quickly became apparent that Ottawa's official languages policy was
not satisfying its main target: Quebec's middle-class, nationalist francophones. The rising separatist unrest in Quebec was seen as essentially a
language-based problem, one that could be addressed with language-rights
legislation. Ottawa had hoped to appease and reassure Quebec francophones
by making federal institutions bilingual everywhere, and by promising that
the small, isolated francophone communities scattered across Canada would
receive adequate protection. But for a majority of Quebec francophones, the
issue was not the survival of French in North America. They were not concerned with the fate of francophones in Moncton, Sudbury, or St. Boniface;
they were concerned with Montreal, the only large city French-speakers

could hope to call their own. At the time of the B&B commission, a visitor to Montreal might not have realized that francophones were the in the majority. Most immigrants to the city aligned themselves with the English-speaking minority – 90 per cent of them sent their children to English schools – and the birth rate among francophones, which had been very high just two generations earlier, was now one of the lowest in the world. Alarmist projections had Montreal becoming a majority English-speaking city by the turn of the millennium.

In the spring of 1970, the Parti Québécois was second in the polls behind the Liberals, and its leader, René Lévesque, with his fiery, nationalist rhetoric, was fast becoming a cult figure among the province's younger voters. But on voting day, the PQ won just 24 per cent of the popular vote, and elected only seven members to the National Assembly. Lévesque's campaign had stressed democracy and patience and denounced the use of violence in politics. After the disappointing showing, some of his most militant supporters decided it was time to split from the party, and pursue their political goals another way.

On the morning of October 5, 1970, one of four men posing as deliverymen pointed a gun at the head of the Portuguese maid who opened the door of a plush residence on Redpath Crescent in Montreal. Minutes later, British trade commissioner James Richard Cross was in the hands of a cell of FLQ terrorists, who detained him for fifty-nine days in a secret hideaway in the city.

News of the kidnapping did not break until later that afternoon. In exchange for Cross's release, the FLQ demanded the release of twenty-three people charged with crimes committed in the name of the Front – people they called political prisoners – and an airplane to take them to Cuba or Algeria. They also wanted their manifesto to be read on national television.

At first, both the federal and provincial governments downplayed the kidnapping. Premier Robert Bourassa stuck to his announced schedule and boarded a plane for New York City, where he was trying to sell Wall Street brokers on his plan to build mammoth power-generating stations on rivers flowing into James Bay. Bourassa put justice minister Jérôme Choquette in charge of dealing with the crisis.

Two days later, on October 7, the federal and Quebec governments relaxed their hardline stance and allowed the FLQ manifesto to be read on Radio-Canada television. Gaétan Montreuil, the network's stone-faced news anchor, read the text, which was written in *joual*, the Quebec vernacular, heavily laced with Marxist rhetoric. The manifesto was staunchly separatist and filled with hatred for the English-speaking elite: "We have had enough of promises of work and prosperity, when in fact we will always be the diligent servants and bootlickers of the big shots, as long as there is a Westmount, a Town of Mount Royal, a Hampstead and an Outremont, all these veritable fortresses of the high finance of St. James Street and Wall Street; we will be slaves until Quebecers, all of us, have used every means, including

**THE OCTOBER CRISIS** ◆ For two months, from October to December 1970, the army was deployed in Montreal. Montrealers became used to seeing armed troops guarding official buildings and the houses of political leaders. Since 1963, the FLQ terror campaign had killed six people and injured twenty-one, including Wilfrid O'Neil, a night watchman killed by a bomb in April 1963, and Walter Leja of the RCMP, who lost an arm while trying to defuse an FLQ bomb hidden inside a mailbox in May. Most of the deaths and injuries were caused by a bomb that went off in the Montreal Stock Exchange building on February 13, 1969. In 1970 alone, 3,600 pounds of explosives were stolen, in twenty-nine different robberies.

FLQ member Paul Rose was sentenced to life imprisonment in 1971 for the kidnapping and murder of Quebec cabinet minister Pierre Laporte. His brother Jacques received eight years for being an accessory after the fact. Both were released on parole between 1978 and 1982. (*CP Archives*)

dynamite and guns, to drive out these big bosses of the economy and of politics, who will stoop to any action, however base, the better to screw us. . . .

"Workers of Quebec, begin from this day forward to take back what is yours; take what belongs to you. Only you know your factories, your machines, your hotels, your universities, your unions; do not wait for some organization to produce a miracle."

Jérôme Choquette ordered a cot and a special telephone for his office and let the kidnappers know he was ready to discuss with them, at any hour, the release of James Cross. The telephone never rang, and on October 10, Choquette promised that the kidnappers would be allowed to leave the country in exchange for Cross's freedom.

Twenty minutes after Choquette made this announcement, the FLQ struck again, kidnapping Pierre Laporte, Quebec's labour minister. The news sent ripples of panic through the public and gave the impression that the FLQ was a large, powerful organization. Bourassa, who had just arrived back from New York, took over from Choquette. He asked Trudeau to put the Armed Forces on alert. "As of Sunday," Trudeau recalled, "the Quebec government was saying it would ask us to apply the War Measures Act. We could hold back for a few days, in agreement with them, in the hope that police would find the kidnappers."

There were no direct negotiations between the authorities and the FLQ. The kidnappers used radio stations to communicate and sent reporters on tortuous chases all over town to find press releases taped inside phone booths. The government responded through press conferences. These communications led nowhere, and some Québécois, taken by the working-class brashness of the FLQ's manifesto, were growing sympathetic to their cause. "There was nothing new or noteworthy in their famous manifesto," Gérard Pelletier, a federal cabinet minister, said later. "All this propaganda was just a rehash of well-known facts. But the dramatic circumstances [of the kidnapping] gave the public the impression they were hearing these things for the first time."

On October 14, a group of high-profile opinion leaders in Quebec, including René Lévesque, Claude Ryan, the influential publisher of *Le Devoir*, and several labour leaders, urged the government to open direct talks with the kidnappers. They condemned the use of violence, but sanctioned the idea of exchanging the two hostages for jailed FLQ members.

The next day, students and some teachers walked out at the Université de Montréal and at some Cégeps (junior colleges) to show support for the terrorists' demands. At noon, the Canadian army started to deploy forces around public buildings and some private houses, to protect public figures from any possible kidnapping attempts.

That evening, three thousand people gathered at Paul Sauvé Arena to show support for the FLQ. All signs indicated that the Front was a powerful force in Quebec. Premier Bourassa glumly considered asking Ottawa to invoke the War Measures Act. "What else can I do?" he reportedly told MNA Guy Joron. "I personally know a great number of the people who will be arrested. . . . I know that my political career is over. The economic recovery, the foreign investment, the 100,000 new jobs, all that has just gone up in smoke."

Both Bourassa and the mayor of Montreal, Jean Drapeau (whose residence had been bombed the year before), urged the federal cabinet to invoke the War Measures Act. On October 16, it was proclaimed, granting police the right to arrest anyone without a warrant. Early that morning, the police arrested 405 people. Some were kept behind bars for twenty-one days, the full period allowed under the act, but most were released after a few hours without being charged.

The following day, Pierre Laporte's body was found in the trunk of a car. He had been murdered, and his death abruptly shifted sympathy away from the FLQ. James Cross was held for almost two more months; when he was eventually released his kidnappers received safe passage to Cuba. On December 28, four members of the FLQ cell that killed Laporte were charged with kidnapping and murder.

Several years later, after extensive investigation, it became apparent that the FLQ was not the major paramilitary organization it had led many to believe it was. It was an informal group, organized in small, autonomous cells, whose members dreamed of a separate and socialist Quebec. At the time of the October Crisis, the FLQ had no more than thirty-five members.

Despite the political fallout from the events of October 1970, most of the country continued on the path of prosperity it had known for almost a generation. The personal income of Canadians doubled between 1955 and 1970, and the nervous thrift of the previous generation was abandoned as Canadians began to spend freely on luxuries such as televisions, cars, and travel. The welfare state provided for its citizens' basic needs; government spending on social programs had tripled in the 1960s. In 1971, $9 billion was spent on health care alone.

British Columbia was among the most prosperous provinces, its economy flowering under its Social Credit premier, W. A. C. "Wacky" Bennett. A high-school dropout who had come to politics via the hardware business, Bennett first came to power in 1952. He was a sober, churchgoing man who tried the Conservative Party before turning to Social Credit. He was both premier and minister of finance, an enthusiastic, glad-handing salesman who exercised a firm control over the province and harboured grandiose plans. Bennett recognized the economic potential of the province's resources, opening the interior for mining and logging and building a grid of modern highways. During his twenty-year reign, the value of B.C.'s exports jumped from $675 million to $3.3 billion. Using the revenues from the sale of resources, he was able to retire the public debt in 1959. In a flamboyant gesture, he put $70 million worth of cancelled bonds on a barge in a lake in Kelowna, doused it with gasoline, and fired a flaming arrow at it. The arrow bounced off the chicken wire holding the paper in place, but an RCMP officer discreetly lit the pyre.

Bennett developed both the Columbia and Peace rivers simultaneously for hydroelectric power, constructing massive dams. The W. A. C. Bennett Dam on the Peace River was one of the largest in the world, and it created a lake (named for Ray Williston, Bennett's minister of lands and forests) that was the largest in the province. B.C. Hydro president Gordon Shrum compared the engineering feat to the building of the pyramid of Giza. "But the pharaoh went bankrupt building the pyramid," he said. " We intend to make it pay." In the Columbia project, Bennett cunningly exploited the political weakness of a succession of minority federal governments, as well as the United States' vast appetite for electricity. He signed a thirty-year

Paul Rose leaves court in Montreal on January 7, 1971, after being charged with kidnapping and murder. (*CP Picture Archive*)

supply contract with Washington State, for which the province received $275 million in advance.

He also oversaw the creation of a personality for the province: a mini-state with the swagger of wealth. B.C. was the embodiment of progress in the post-war era. It was rich, pleased with itself, and the weather was mild: perfect conditions for a counterculture to thrive. Dan McLeod was a graduate student in mathematics at the University of British Columbia in the 1960s when he became caught up in the counterculture. There was an influx of draft dodgers from the United States, who brought the mores of San Francisco's lively anti-authoritarian scene with them. Bennett's aggressive exploitation of the province's natural resources was producing an inevitable backlash, and there were small protests against his policies. "If Wacky ever got into trouble," McLeod said, "he'd just build another dam or another bridge or another highway or ferry line and he'd survive." Most voters ranked jobs over environmental concerns, and Bennett suggested that the protesters themselves constituted a form of pollution. "You see a whole bunch of people who do not pay too much attention to hygiene, you know, dirty feet and stuff. They are polluting the countryside even while carrying banners against pollution." B.C. highways minister Phil Gaglardi summed up the government's philosophy: "God put the coal there for our use. So, let's dig it up."

In 1967, McLeod and a few friends met and decided to start an anti-establishment newspaper; in May that year, the first issue of the *Georgia Straight* was published. Modelled on New York's *Village Voice*, it railed at politicians, featured poetry and fiction, and kept a running watch on idealists who left Vancouver to get back to the land. Vancouver mayor Tom Campbell tried to rid the city of its remaining hippies, whom he saw as a blight. By the summer of 1967 – the "summer of love" – the *Georgia Straight* had a circulation of 65,000, with 700 vendors selling it on the street.

In 1971, the newspaper organized a "smoke-in," an event that advocated the legalization of marijuana. Hundreds of hippies congregated in Maple Tree Square in Gastown, which they called "Grasstown." Vancouver police rode in on horseback, beating the protesters with clubs. The Gastown Riot was a watershed event, marking Vancouver as the centre of the counterculture.

Vancouver was also a launching ground for the environmental movement. In the fall of 1971, a small Vancouver group called Don't Make a Wave was recruiting volunteers to sail to Alaska to protest against American nuclear tests scheduled to be conducted underground at Amchitka, one of the Aleutian islands. Among the volunteers was Patrick Moore, who had returned home to Vancouver after going to college in St. Louis, Missouri. "I knew right away I wanted to join it," he said. "I wanted to do something, I wanted to do something about ecology and peace." He became a member of the crew on the boat, the *Greenpeace*.

Amchitka was four thousand kilometres north of Vancouver, but all along the Pacific coast people were concerned that the nuclear blast could

**GREENPEACE** ◆ Patrick Moore (inset) was one of the twelve crew members who sailed from Vancouver on September 15, 1971, aboard a twenty-five-metre halibut trawler originally called the *Phyllis Cormack*, then rechristened the *Greenpeace*. They hoped to prevent the detonation of an American nuclear test on Amchitka Island, but the test was delayed; the bomb was finally triggered on November 6, only a few days after the *Greenpeace* had sailed away. (*City of Vancouver Archives*)

trigger a giant tidal wave. "As of midnight," read a *Vancouver Sun* article, "a blockade will be thrown around Amchitka Island, near the tail end of the Aleutians. Sometime between tomorrow and October 15, a 1.2 megaton atomic bomb will be triggered at the bottom of a hole. . . . No one knows what the consequences will be, but scientists in Canada, the U.S., Japan and Hawaii have warned that there is a distinct danger that the blast might set in motion earthquakes and tidal waves which could sweep from one end of the Pacific to the other."

The *Greenpeace* neared Amchitka on September 24, but the blast, scheduled for October 2, was postponed. Moore was convinced the Americans were delaying the test to throw them off their plan. "The U.S. Atomic Energy Administration, in order to thwart us, postponed the test for

**INFLATION** ◆ By 1966, inflation was becoming a concern to consumers, and workers started demanding and receiving commensurate wage increases (workers on the St. Lawrence Seaway got 30 per cent over two years; railway workers won a 24 per cent increase over three years). This trend increased into the 1970s: in 1973, the cost of living went up 9 per cent, and the following year it was in double digits. Housing prices rose 20 per cent in some cities. During the 1974 election campaign, Opposition leader Robert Stanfield argued for a wage and price freeze to combat inflation, an idea that was ridiculed by Pierre Trudeau ("Zap! You're frozen!"). The following year Trudeau and the Liberals adopted wage and price controls themselves. (*The Montreal Gazette*)

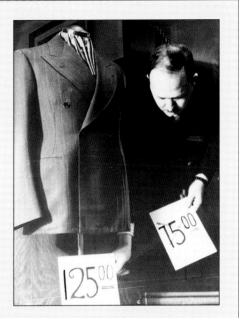

a month for no other reason than to put it in November, when it was virtually impossible to be in the vicinity of Amchitka island on a boat without sinking." They turned around and sailed back to Vancouver. "The big problem for us was to have to wait for a month," crew member Robert Hunter wrote. "We had food and fuel supplies to last only six weeks. We would have been stuck up there, a few hundred miles from the Russian coast, without food and drink."

The bomb was finally exploded on November 6. There was no tidal wave, but shortly afterward, the House of Commons in Ottawa voted to condemn nuclear tests. The vote was one shy of being unanimous. The Greenpeace movement was launched.

On the prairies, perhaps spurred by Bennett's success in B.C., provincial governments were also pursuing megaprojects, their solution to growing unemployment and economic ills. In Manitoba, the Red River Floodway Project was started in 1962. Two bulldozers, driven by Premier Duff Roblin and the federal minister of national resources, Walter Dinsdale, broke the ground just south of Winnipeg on October 6. Called "Roblin's Folly" and "Duff's Ditch" by locals, the channel to divert the flood-prone Red River from Winnipeg was more than 46 kilometres long, 9 metres deep and, in places, more than 150 metres wide. Its construction employed 1,000 people, cost $63 million, and displaced 100 million cubic metres of earth, more than the St. Lawrence Seaway. It was a belated and not entirely popular response to the 1950 flood, when the Red River had risen more than nine metres, inundating Winnipeg. The disaster had been a favourite subject of international newsreels, which showed the floodwaters creeping higher and Winnipeggers being evacuated.

There were other projects: the western world's first integrated nickel-mining, smelting, concentrating, and refining complex was opened at Thompson in 1957. Elsewhere in the west, hydroelectric projects were initiated and forestry development increased. Some megaprojects were less successful than others: a $100-million, four-thousand-job project to develop a pulp and paper complex at The Pas in the late 1960s collapsed, at a cost of $40 million in public funds, when its Swiss investors pulled out.

The need for the megaprojects was being fuelled by the shrinking of the region's agricultural base. The number of farms in Canada had dropped dramatically – of the 732,832 farms that existed in 1941, only 289,089 remained in 1986. In the 1960s, mechanization had radically altered the way people farmed. But the costs were steep, as farming became a capital-intensive rather than a labour-intensive business.

In 1965, Jack Pawich of Cartwright, Manitoba, bought his first combine. To pay for it, he drove it down to the Texas border each May with a four-man crew, then followed the harvest season north through Oklahoma, Kansas, Nebraska, and South Dakota, charging American farmers to harvest their crops. By the time he had finished in North Dakota it was time to take his own crop off. The low interest rates were seductive, and Pawich, like many prairie farmers, borrowed to buy more land and more machinery. The trend stopped in the late 1960s with rising interest rates, falling wheat prices, grain surpluses, and subsidy wars between the United States and Europe. Former grain-buying nations such as France and India began to produce so much wheat that they did not need to import it. Wheat prices had risen marginally since the 1930s, but the cost of machinery had skyrocketed. Fertilizers, pesticides, herbicides, and new techniques improved yields, but not enough to pay for the extra fuel and chemicals it took to achieve them. Farm operating expenses in 1976 were five times higher than they had been in 1956, but income had risen only threefold. In 1969 and 1970, there were near-depression conditions for wheat.

"Why should I sell the Canadian farmers' wheat?" Trudeau rhetorically asked when the farmers urged Ottawa to help. He told them to reduce their acreages instead, an attitude that fuelled western alienation. The prairie population had made up 23 per cent of the Canadian population in 1931; by 1971 it had fallen to 16 per cent. The message Trudeau seemed to be relaying, that a national party need only carry Quebec and Ontario, grated, and it prompted many westerners to take a long look at how well federalism was serving their needs.

In the 1960s and 1970s, Ontario remained the economic powerhouse of Canada, fuelled by the Automotive Products Agreement with the United

States. The Auto Pact, as it was known, was devised as an alternative to a potentially destructive trade war between the two countries. The 1957 Royal Commission on Canada's Economic Prospects, chaired by Walter Gordon, a partner in the Toronto accounting firm Clarkson Gordon, had catalogued a disturbing amount of foreign ownership in Canada (nine out of every ten factories employing more than five thousand people were owned by Americans). By 1965, there was $17.3 billion in foreign investment in Canada, most of it American. The automobile industry became a focus for a rising fear of economic colonialism.

In the early 1960s, most Canadian branch plants were tooled for short production runs appropriate for Canada's small market, which put them in a perennially disadvantaged position. The Auto Pact was a way of rectifying this imbalance in one industry. The Americans were not anxious to give up their advantages; they owned the industry. When the two sides met, Walter Gordon, by then the Liberal finance minister, said that if Canadians did not get what they wanted, they would walk away from the table and build their own all-Canadian cars or impose Canadian content requirements on the American factory owners. The solution was a limited free trade agreement. The automobile companies pledged to maintain a substantial and steady proportion of the continent's automobile and parts production in Canadian factories. New cars and parts could cross the border duty free (though consumers could not go across the border and return with a new Ford without paying duty). Canadian companies would invest $260 million in new plants and infrastructure and were guaranteed the same share of North American production they enjoyed when the agreement was signed, which meant that if the auto market weakened, the auto-makers could not simply close Canadian plants as a cost-cutting measure.

The Auto Pact was signed by Lester Pearson and American president Lyndon Baines Johnson down at LBJ's Texas ranch on January 16, 1965. Johnson and Pearson were not close, continuing a tradition of mismatched leaders (Diefenbaker and Kennedy; Trudeau and Nixon; Trudeau and Reagan). Johnson told the assembled press that he was thrilled to have his good friend "Drew Pearson" down at his ranch. They ate steak and catfish for dinner, and the next morning signed the pact.

On April 2, Pearson went to Temple University in Philadelphia to accept an award. Johnson had just authorized the bombing of North Vietnam, and in his speech, Pearson suggested that a temporary cessation of the bombing might bring the North Vietnamese back to the bargaining table. Johnson was furious, and the next day, when the two met at Camp David, he harangued Pearson for hours

The Auto Pact was a boon for Canadian employment. By 1975, there were 106,000 people working in the auto industry, most of them in Ontario. Total trade between the countries had grown to $13 billion. The pact was a significant step in strengthening the economic links between the two economies, confirming each as the other's largest trading partner.

In 1971, Ottawa and the provinces thought they had reached an agreement on a formula to amend the Constitution, which would have cleared the way for its patriation from Great Britain. The amending formula hammered out in Victoria said the Constitution could be changed if at least six provinces – representing at least half of the population of Canada – agreed. Furthermore, provinces would have the right to opt out of certain federally sponsored social programs with compensation if they chose. Before arriving in Victoria, Premier Bourassa said he supported the agreement, but once there he refused to sign the document. On his return to Quebec, Bourassa was greeted by a political storm. Public opinion had been whipped up against the Victoria agreement by Parti Québécois leaders, and by Claude Ryan at *Le Devoir*. For them, it was essential that Quebec have the right to opt out of *any* federally funded social programs with full compensation. In the face of strong opposition, Bourassa chose to backtrack, and he scuttled the Victoria agreement.

Federal Liberals never forgave Bourassa for his last-minute about-face. And his foes in Quebec used his reversal as an opportunity to depict him as a dithering, unreliable leader. So when Bourassa called an election for October 1973, PQ strategists thought they were in a position to make significant gains. The FLQ's terrorism during the October Crisis was still a handicap for the separatist cause, but René Lévesque had repeatedly condemned the use of violence to reach political goals, and he had convinced several high-profile candidates to run. On October 29, the PQ won 30 per cent of the vote, but ended up with only six MNAs, one less than in the previous election, compared to the Liberals' 102.

The language issue continued to plague Bourassa, and he attempted to defuse it by introducing Bill 22, which would make French the only official language in Quebec, while still recognizing the legal status of English. It also stipulated that the children of immigrants who wanted to attend an English school would have to be tested, and demonstrate fluency in the language. This meant that most immigrants would be channelled into the French system, a policy that outraged anglophones and immigrants. Francophones complained that the law was too soft. The bill passed into law on July 30, 1974, but no one was pleased with Bourassa's compromise.

Language tensions entered a new, national forum in 1976, when the Canadian Airline Pilots Association and the Canadian Air Traffic Control Association opposed a federal plan to introduce French into air traffic control in Quebec. In 1974, Ottawa had authorized the use of French in five small Quebec airports. When the pilots' association opposed the changes, francophone pilots left the association in protest and formed their own, Les gens de l'air. In June 1976, just as the world was preparing to fly to Montreal for the Olympics, the air traffic controllers went on strike, claiming that bilingualism was a threat to the safety of air travellers. Anglophone pilots joined the controllers on the picket line, wreaking havoc in

**ROBERT BOURASSA** ◆ Bourassa was thirty-six when he became premier of Quebec in April 1970. "The leader people were looking for was a young businessman, with a very detailed knowledge of the economy," a senior provincial Liberal told journalist Graham Fraser. " The man who best corresponded to the picture was Bourassa. I barely knew him at the time, but without knowing him, I agreed he should become leader." *(CP Picture Archive)*

**THE PARTI QUÉBÉCOIS VICTORY** ♦ "The most urgent task was, so to speak, to decolonize ourselves day by day, proving to ourselves and to others that we were as capable as anyone of running our own affairs, at least that part of them we were permitted to look after ourselves." – René Lévesque, from *Memoirs*. (*CP Picture Archives*)

major Canadian airports. To resolve the crisis, Ottawa signed an agreement with the air traffic controllers, who gained the right to review and manage the implementation of bilingualism in the air. Transportation minister Jean Marchand resigned to protest the federal government's waffling on its bilingualism policy. The controversy polarized public opinion in Canada, and deepened suspicion between French- and English-speakers.

Millions of people arrived in Montreal that July for a somewhat listless Olympics. There was a boycott by African nations over the issue of apartheid in South Africa, and intrusive security everywhere. The Olympic Stadium, unfinished at the time of the games, nevertheless rose from its concrete pedestal in east end Montreal as an elegant, revolutionary structure. Designed by French architect Roger Taillibert, it had already cost $700 million, roughly $650 million more than any other covered stadium in North America. Jean Drapeau's famous utterance that an Olympics could no more lose money than a man could get pregnant turned sour as the cost of the stadium continued to rise after the games to well over $1 billion. Over the years, the stadium and its perennially dysfunctional retractable roof steadily crumbled – a lingering monument to debt and mismanagement.

Quebec nationalists used the air traffic controllers' strike as evidence that bilingualism in Canada was a hollow notion, at best, and that English Canada had no real interest in promoting it. The controversy helped pave the way for the first Parti Québécois government. In 1976, the PQ's campaign slogan, "*C'est le début d'un temps nouveau*" (This is the beginning of a new era), reflected the current political zeitgeist. "It spelled hope," said Laurent Leclerc, a volunteer party worker in Montreal. "The feeling was that everything was possible now. We felt we were helping things happen. On election night, I was a poll worker in Claude Charron's riding, and the place was demented. We were going crazy as the results started to come in."

On November 15, 1976, the PQ swept to victory, winning seventy-one ridings to the Liberals' twenty-six. Lévesque celebrated the historic win with a utopian message: "If everyone puts forth his best effort we can make Quebec a country that is a happy place to live in, a country that cultivates harmonious relations with its neighbours, a country that treats its minorities with justice and equity, a country that develops its resources while respecting the environment."

It was no accident that Lévesque spoke of a country; many of his supporters hoped that the victory would be quickly followed by a declaration of independence. But Lévesque would not be stampeded. The stage was set for a chess game between Quebec and Ottawa that would last for the next four years.

# A Nation in Question

In the fifteenth century, the New World represented resources. Gold, furs, fish, and the race to control them led, eventually, to colonization, and domination of the natives. Five hundred years later, the issue of who would control Canada's vast resources – oil, lumber, minerals – would remain unresolved.

In 1971, the oil companies operating in Canada were 65 per cent owned by foreign interests. Their profits became not only an issue between Canada and the foreign investors, but the source of an extended grudge match between Ottawa and Alberta. As oil wealth was being allocated, the call for environmental awareness increased, and in the Arctic, the Dene Nation questioned the impact that oil exploration and the construction of a pipeline would have on native lands and their traditional way of life. On the east coast, the cod fishery that had attracted Portuguese and Spanish fishermen in the fifteenth century was in crisis. By the end of the 1980s, the resources were waning, and Canada's 200-mile (321-kilometre) boundary off the coast was being questioned by European powers.

As resources were being debated over and claimed, Canada's political geography was being disputed by Quebec's premier, René Lévesque, who was seeking a new arrangement with Canada, one that he described as "sovereignty-association." And the country's traditional relationship with

Britain was under review by Prime Minister Pierre Trudeau, who believed that it was imperative to "patriate" and renew the constitution: "I had a real sense that the country wouldn't last," Trudeau warned. "It would become a confederation of shopping centres." Canada was becoming much more racially diverse, a trend that was accompanied by economic dislocation as the spectre of globalization appeared and the free-trade issue, so hotly disputed seventy-five years earlier, was dividing Canadians again. Native land treaties were being scrutinized, and in 1990 in Quebec, Mohawk natives staged a militant challenge at Oka. As the twentieth century moved to a close, centuries-old issues, conflicts, and prejudices flared.

The transformation of Alberta through the 1970s was personified by its leaders. After thirty-six years of unglamorous, rural-based Social Credit rule, the Conservatives came to power in 1971, led by native son Peter Lougheed, a square-jawed former football player, grandson of Senator James Lougheed. Premier Lougheed took an immediate interest in the province's oil, increasing the tax on oil revenues and provoking a hostile response from Alberta oilmen. But the province's fortunes were soon given a boost from an unlikely source.

On October 6, 1973, on Yom Kippur, Egyptian tanks crossed into the Israeli-occupied Sinai Peninsula and Syrian troops entered the Golan Heights, moving toward Jerusalem. Israel, backed by the United States, rebuffed the attack. On October 16, there was a meeting in Kuwait at which Arab oil producers discussed the prospect of using their oil resources as leverage, hoping to get western nations to back away from their commitment to Israel. They cut production initially by 25 per cent, with plans for further cuts of 5 per cent a month until a Middle Eastern settlement could be reached. The price of oil quickly soared; it had been selling for three dollars a barrel, and it climbed to fifteen. Non-Arab producers raised their prices to take advantage of the shortage. The Alberta oil industry boomed, transforming the cities of Calgary and Edmonton and creating brash millionaires, new confidence, and renewed tensions with governments, both provincial and federal.

Lougheed began an economic program that captured more of the oil benefits for the province, imposing tougher measures on foreign investors, increasing the price of Alberta's natural gas, and establishing a two-price system that protected Alberta's consumers but excluded the rest of the country from preferential rates. He gave the province the power to set oil prices and demanded a greater share for the government, but he also helped Albertan oil entrepreneurs.

At the same time, Lougheed played up provincial-federal divisions, clashing with Pierre Trudeau and setting up a Manichaean model: Albertans were conservative and independent, while Trudeau and his eastern Liberals were grasping, coddled pirates. It was an effective political image, one that Albertans cherished during the oil boom. Between 1971 and 1981, the

Opposite: "Anglo-Canadian nationalism produced, inevitably, French-Canadian nationalism. As I have said before, speaking of the roots of our nationalism and the futility of its tendencies: Defeated, occupied, leaderless, banished from commercial enterprise, poked away outside the cities, little by little reduced to a minority and left with very little influence in a country which, after all, he discovered, explored and colonized, the French Canadian had little alternative for the frame of mind he would have to assume in order to preserve what remained of his own. So he set up a system of defence-mechanisms which soon assumed such overgrown proportions that he came to regard as priceless anything which distinguished him from other people; and any change whatever (be it for the better or not) he would regard with hostility if it originated from the outside . . . The nationalists' idealism itself has been their downfall. 'They loved not wisely but too well.'" – Pierre Trudeau, *Federalism and the French Canadians*, 1968. (*Blaise Edwards, CP Picture Archives*)

province's population increased by a third, its wealth mushroomed, and it became wary of sending Liberal MPs to Ottawa. In eight years, the price of oil rose from less than three dollars a barrel to almost forty, and Alberta's Bible belt image was replaced by the notion of oil wealth, with all its attendant perks and vices.

At the height of the boom, Calgary issued more than $1 billion worth of construction permits annually, more than Chicago or New York. Apartment vacancy rates approached zero as Ontarians and Maritimers arrived daily in search of high-paying jobs. The housing market boomed, oil stocks rose, and an entrepreneurial spirit, once exclusive to businessmen, was awakened in professors, lawyers, and dentists, who began speculating in real estate and experimenting with oil ventures.

Among the most visible of the new oil entrepreneurs was Jack Gallagher, who, with his Hollywood smile and silver hair, looked like a B actor from the 1950s. He was a shrewd, abstemious geologist who had travelled the globe in pursuit of oil before establishing his own company, Dome Petroleum Ltd., in 1950. Bill Richards, a Manitoba lawyer, joined the company and quickly rose to become its president. Richards engineered an aggressive expansion through clever recruitment and careful acquisitions so that, by the end of the 1970s, Dome was the largest oil company in the country.

Gallagher's passion was the development of the Arctic. "My greatest love is exploration," he said. "My real interest in Dome is the Beaufort [Sea] and Arctic islands." Dome had drilled the first hole in the Arctic in 1962. Fourteen years later, they still had not found oil, though Gallagher said he anticipated a twenty-five-year wait to profitability.

While many western oilmen were openly antagonistic to Ottawa, Gallagher was a gifted lobbyist who learned how to get what he needed from the government. "He probably understood better than almost any other businessman how the government worked and what the government's objectives were," said Alastair Gillespie, minister of energy, mines, and resources in 1976. "He always had a very positive suggestion: 'Here's a way of gaining your objectives.'" Dome was seeking rights to drill in the Beaufort Sea. The Liberal government wanted to achieve energy self-sufficiency and had an interest in discovering the extent of Arctic reserves. Arctic oil would also challenge Alberta's monopoly on oil and gas; it would strengthen the federal government's position. After heated debate in the House of Commons, in 1976 Dome got permission to drill, provided it undertook an adequate set of environmental studies.

While Gallagher was working the government with such success (he obtained a 125 per cent tax write-off for Arctic exploration, among other concessions), another oilman, Jim Gray, made a remarkable find. Gray was a geologist and devout Mormon from Kirkland Lake, Ontario. He and his partner, John Masters, discovered Elmworth Deep Basin, a gas field west of Grande Prairie, Alberta, which turned out to be the second largest in North

**PETER LOUGHEED**
♦ "Perhaps some people see my position as too harsh. Look, I want to see progress towards a more united Canada but I want to know what the actual terms of such an arrangement are. There is complete justification – if not for suspicion of the federal proposals – at least for caution. It's simple. If Ontario owned the oil you can be assured that we in Alberta would be buying it at the world price." – Peter Lougheed, speaking after a federal-provincial conference in Ottawa, October 1978. (*Pat Humphries, CP Picture Archive*)

In 1981, just as the oil boom was about to be overtaken by a severe recession, vacancy rates in Calgary were 0.2 per cent and unemployment rates were the lowest in the country. Calgary was the youngest city in Canada, with 37 per cent of its population (compared to the national average of 27 per cent) between the ages of twenty and thirty-four. It had the highest per capita disposable income and was home to 638 oil companies. (*Mike Ridewood, CP Picture Archive*)

America. Gray quickly joined the wild pace of Calgary's oil world. "There are over seven hundred oil and gas companies here," Gray said. "It's heavy competition. Some people can't keep up with it. We've got a high incidence of social stress. Divorce, drinking, suicide. But there's a lot of us who thrive on it." He felt that federal interference in the oil industry (including the tax incentives for Arctic drilling that were going to Dome) was counterproductive. "But the prices were going up so rapidly that they masked what was happening." Everyone was getting rich.

Peter Lougheed was not happy with the existing federal energy policy: Trudeau had frozen oil prices, established a federal oil export tax, and announced that provincial royalties were non-deductible. The political rhetoric of Alberta's premier emphasized Alberta's historic alienation from Ottawa. "Our destiny," he said, "was formed by outside forces – the railways, the pipelines, the banks, and above all, the federal government – acting on matters of direct importance to us but without consultation. Not all of these forces were negative all of the time. But our overall feeling was that the west had not had a fair deal in the Canadian federation." Lougheed and Trudeau picked away at each other with retaliatory policies through the 1970s, girding for the inevitable showdown.

Amid the oil riches, there were concerns about the effect that all the new oil exploration was having on the environment. In 1974, Judge Thomas Berger was appointed to head an inquiry into the environmental impact of a proposed Mackenzie Valley pipeline. The line would carry American oil and gas from the Prudhoe Bay field in Alaska south through the Mackenzie River Valley to the United States. Berger was a judge of the British Columbia Supreme Court and conversant with both native and civil rights issues, so he was a logical choice to head the inquiry. The expectation was that it would follow the formula of many royal commissions and result in a dull, plodding, extended investigation that would demonstrate political concern but yield negligible results.

Instead, Berger held meetings in thirty-five northern communities, as well as several southern cities, throughout 1976. One thousand people participated in the meetings, which received widespread media coverage. "Berger served to politicize a lot of people," said John T'Seleie, a member of the Indian Brotherhood of the Northwest Territories (later the Dene Nation). "It focused the attention of Canadians for the first time on First Nations people and some of their issues, related to the land, culture. . . . People from here spoke about their land, were allowed to appear on television and talk about their own history." The importance of the debate became dramatically apparent with the death of Nelson Small Legs, Jr., who committed suicide two days after testifying on May 14, 1976, leaving a public suicide note that decried the treatment of natives in Canada.

The Berger Commission was proving to be about more than a pipeline; it had provided a rare opportunity to air long-held grievances on a national and sometimes international stage. Georges Erasmus, who would eventually become head of the Assembly of First Nations, spoke at the hearing, addressing the issue of assimilation. "Before the coming of the Europeans we the Dene defined history in our own terms. We decided the kind of communities we wanted to be. We decided the way we wanted to live. With the coming of the Europeans we felt the experience of a way of life in which we were supposed to be inferior. . . . History was being defined for us. . . . The whole experience up to now has been that we Dene should forget who we are and assimilate into a superior way of life. We should become Canadians."

Erasmus noted that the north was the only part of the country that did not operate as a democracy. "The Yukon and the Northwest Territories were

**THE BERGER INQUIRY** ◆ "The important thing is that the Liberal government at the time supported the pipeline. They were probably hoping that Berger wouldn't be too honest, that he'd hold a few meetings and say that people were in favour of it. But he ended up not doing that. You could have had a very different inquiry." – John T'Seleie, a member of the Indian Brotherhood of the Northwest Territories, at the time of the Mackenzie Valley Pipeline inquiry, presided over by British Columbia Supreme Court Judge Thomas Berger. (Berger, left, and John Amagoalik of the Inuit Tapirisat of Canada during the Berger inquiry hearings in Ottawa in June 1976. *Fred Chartrand, CP Picture Archive*)

regions with powerful commissioners [who were] appointed," he later said. "I don't think it's a coincidence that these were also regions rich in resources that we couldn't control. We were hearing about pipelines, more pipelines, mines would surely follow, roads. Everyone wants to work for the good life for their people, but the pace really made us stop to take a look."

Bob Blair was a prominent Calgary oilman whose company had applied for pipeline rights as a part of a consortium called Canadian Arctic Gas Study Ltd. He attended the hearings, and was singled out by Frank T'Seleie, who accused him of plotting genocide, bringing a dramatic shift to the tone of the meetings. "You are like the Pentagon, Mr. Blair, planning the slaughter of the innocent Vietnamese," he accused. "Don't tell me you are not responsible. You are the twentieth-century General Custer. You are coming with your troops to slaughter us and steal land that is rightfully ours. You are coming to destroy a people that have a history of thirty thousand years. Why? For twenty years of gas? Are you really that insane?"

Blair waited until the next day to respond. He invited T'Seleie to inspect the pipeline system in Alberta. "A natural gas pipeline really does not destroy the country or make it unclean or kill all animals or kill all vegetation," he said.

**RENÉ LÉVESQUE** ◆ Regarding Bill 101, Lévesque wrote that it corrected previous legislation and ensured the promotion of French: "Everywhere outdoor advertising continued to throw down on us the unilingual sneer of a dominant minority. Nothing seemed able to stop the assimilation of immigrants. Our economic inferiority continued to be carefully maintained from the highest echelons to the level of simple foreman. We weren't told to 'Speak white!' any more but we were still obliged to do so in many cases, right here in our own home. One day, if we wanted it badly enough, French would be at home everywhere in Quebec and, as in any normal country, we could finally toss aside the crutches of legislation that have always seemed to me to be deeply humiliating. But for the time being, the prosthesis remained necessary." – From *Memoirs*, 1986. (*Jacques Boissinot, CP Picture Archive*)

In 1977, Berger's final report appeared. Its strong position was that the north was a native homeland and not simply a frontier resource for the federal government. It recommended a ten-year wait before construction of the pipeline to allow time for further study and settlement of native land claims. The project was put on hold, and ultimately an alternative route was chosen. The Berger Commission report was published in 1977 as *Northern Frontier, Northern Homeland* and became an unlikely bestseller. Public sympathy and interest in both native and environmental concerns were heightened as a result, but few concrete gains were realized. Native politicians began making dire predictions about what might happen if their voices went unheard in future.

Trudeau had other problems. The Parti Québécois, which was committed to Quebec's independence, won the 1976 provincial election, defeating the Liberals under Robert Bourassa. René Lévesque was now premier, and he promised a referendum on Quebec sovereignty before the end of his first term.

One of the new government's first actions was to introduce a language law, Bill 101, which declared French to be the only official language of Quebec, entrenching the right of workers to work in French and the rights of consumers to be served in French. It also placed limits on the use of English, especially in education; immigrants were prevented from enrolling their children in English schools. Trudeau denounced Bill 101 as a "bad

**JOE CLARK** ◆ In the 1976 leadership convention, Joe Clark emerged as the leader of the Progressive Conservative Party. It was a fractious convention that left Brian Mulroney bitter for several years. "I'm not the greatest," Clark declared. "I'm the best available." This modest claim was disputed in 1980 when his government lost power after less than a year in office. "Anyone who can bring the Conservative Party together can bring the country together," Clark said. His prediction was borne out when the party united under Brian Mulroney and the country followed suit, giving Mulroney two majority governments. (*CP Picture Archive*)

law," but its author, Camille Laurin, the minister of cultural development, argued that it was necessary to protect the French language. Angry, emotional debates over how threatened the language actually was raged in the editorial pages of the province's newspapers, a leitmotif that would define the next two decades. Recriminations, volumes of statistics, and an anglophone exodus all followed. Between 1976 and 1981, the English-speaking population of Quebec declined by 90,600.

By the late 1970s, both Lévesque and Trudeau were approaching the end of their terms. "I had decided we should avoid mixing the referendum debate with the excitement of an election," Lévesque wrote. "Knowing this, and also seeing himself doomed to almost certain defeat, Trudeau spun out his term of office from month to month. At last he had to resign himself to take the plunge, and in May was beaten hands down, except in Quebec."

In May 1979, Trudeau and the Liberals were replaced by Joe Clark's Conservatives. The existing energy deal between Ottawa and Alberta was due to expire the following summer, and Clark was confronted with the task of restructuring it. He was also facing possible oil shortages, resulting from a revolution in Iran, and he had inherited the enormous issue of the referendum.

On December 19, 1979, Lévesque and his cabinet worked out the referendum question. The Parti Québécois would be asking for the mandate to negotiate an agreement with the rest of Canada that would give Quebec "the exclusive power to make its laws, levy its taxes and establish relations abroad – in other words, sovereignty – and at the same time to maintain with Canada an economic association including a common currency." The question would be posed in three short paragraphs, but it was criticized by federalists as being convoluted. Opponents pointed out that Lévesque's request for a mandate to negotiate left the issue open-ended and ill defined. In a speech in Quebec City, Trudeau complained that Lévesque did not "have the courage to ask a simple question, Do you want to separate from Canada, YES or NO?"

The referendum was scheduled for May 20, 1980, but in February, Clark's first budget was rejected in the House by a non-confidence motion, triggering an election. Clark's government was rejected by voters, who had been unimpressed with his brief, bland tenure, marked by frightening interest rates (20 per cent) and threatened oil shortages. Trudeau was re-elected with a majority government, ready to face Lévesque.

In April, six weeks before the referendum, the "Oui" side was ahead in the polls by three points. Lévesque and his team worked to keep the momentum going, overseeing every detail and providing media coaching for those who were not adept at television interviews. But the case for separatism had been weakened slightly by the government's own Bill 101, which had eased francophone language concerns, and voters, who were growing tired of the debate, felt that they were being hectored by both sides. The crucial undecided vote was becoming increasingly nervous of the

**REFERENDUM QUESTION**

◆ The full question in the 1980 referendum was: "The government of Quebec has made public its proposal to negotiate a new agreement with the rest of Canada, based on the equality of nations; this agreement would enable Quebec to acquire the exclusive power to make its laws, levy its taxes and establish relations abroad – in other words, sovereignty – and at the same time to maintain with Canada an economic association including a common currency; no change in political status resulting from these negotiations will be effected without approval by the people through another referendum; on these terms do you give the Government of Quebec the mandate to negotiate the proposed agreement between Quebec and Canada?" (*Journal de Québec, CP Picture Archive*)

sovereignty-association proposal, which held too much uncertainty. And while Lévesque's team worked to deliver the message that an independent Quebec would prosper, the federal government assessed the various debts the province would depart with and warned of higher taxes, insignificance on the international stage, and economic calamity. Days before the final vote, Trudeau delivered a speech at Paul Sauvé Arena in Montreal, speaking to the need for change in Quebec's position in Confederation and hinting that the province's constitutional issues would be addressed, that independence was drastic and unnecessary. "But what change?" Lévesque asked. Trudeau would not be pinned down. "The sphinx kept his secret," Lévesque complained.

The referendum produced a provincial split along predictable fault lines, but also divided friends and families. In 1980, Laurent Leclerc was a thirty-year-old Montrealer. "In my family I was the only nationalist. The night of the referendum, I went [to the arena] with my wife and son. It was the night of the century, the night of my life. I was going to be thirty years old, and since the age of fifteen I had always been *indépendantiste*, nationalist, sovereigntist. The terms changed, but there was always the same objective, the same vision." On May 20, the night of the vote, he took his son to Paul Sauvé Arena, where the "Oui" camp was gathered.

His mother was in the "Non" camp, swayed by Trudeau, trusting that constitutional change could be achieved without the wrenching process of separation. On the night of the referendum, she was with her husband at the "Non" headquarters in Saint Bruno.

The province voted 60 per cent for "Non," 40 per cent for "Oui." "I felt I was falling apart," Laurent Leclerc said. "I had a son who was five years old, another who was three months. The country I wanted to give them had slipped through my fingers and it was very painful." Addressing the emotional crowd at Paul Sauvé Arena, Lévesque promised another attempt at independence. "I must admit that tonight I would be hard pressed to tell you when or how. In the meantime, we must live together." Lévesque began to sing "Gens du pays," the Gilles Vigneault song that had become a nationalist anthem. At its conclusion, he said, "*A la prochaine*" ("Until next time") and left the arena.

A year later, Lévesque's Parti Québécois was re-elected, winning a comfortable majority with eighty seats, nine more than in 1976. "We felt the euphoria of the resurrected whom most people had written off as dead and buried a short time before," he wrote. "Yet I had to remind the thousands of supporters come to celebrate this rising from the tomb that it would fade with the dawn." There was another battle looming: Trudeau's determination to give Canada full control over its own constitution.

The British North America Act, which had brought Canada into being in 1867, was a statute of the British Parliament. While Canada had achieved independence during the twentieth century, any constitutional change still had to be approved by Britain. This was a vestige of colonial status that Trudeau felt had to end. He had raised the issue in 1974, saying, "I think we'll have to consider bringing back the constitution from Great Britain and make it a Canadian constitution, we will do it ourselves. . . . I don't see how Quebec can object." But when he announced that he would bring it home, Quebec did object, strenuously, at least to the way Trudeau planned to do it. "Trudeau represents the centralizing of Canada," Lévesque observed, "literally crushing provinces into a federal mode. That cannot go for Quebec."

The battle was defined as much by the two opposing personalities as by the issues. "I like to think that [Lévesque] appealed to the emotions of the Quebec people, while I was trying to appeal to their reason," Trudeau later wrote. "In any case, I knew it would be a good fight." Trudeau's vision of the Constitution included a Charter of Rights and Freedoms, which would protect citizens against arbitrary actions by their governments. He was looking for support from the premiers, but only William Davis of Ontario and New Brunswick's Richard Hatfield endorsed it. The rest of the premiers saw nothing but a diminution of their own influence. "Under the pretext of giving citizens a new Charter of Rights," Lévesque wrote, "the Ottawa project is, in fact, an unprecedented attack on the powers of the National Assembly of Quebec, designed to limit and restrict it, especially with regard to the language of education."

Without the support of most premiers, Trudeau threatened to take his case to London alone. "I'm telling you gentlemen," Trudeau said to the

**CONSTITUTIONAL TALKS** ◆ In 1955, Pierre Trudeau paddled the Mackenzie River to the Beaufort Sea with poet and political thinker F. R. Scott. Scott observed Trudeau standing in shallow rapids and wrote a poem that could be applied to Trudeau's approach to the constitutional crisis twenty-five years later.

> Leaning south up the current
> To stem the downward rush,
> A man testing his strength
> Against the strength of the country.

(Trudeau alone at the 1979 Federal-Provincial Conference in Ottawa. *Robert Cooper, CP Picture Archive*)

premiers at an official dinner at the governor general's residence on September 7, 1980, "I've been warning you since 1976 . . . we're going to go it alone . . . we'll go to London and we won't even bother asking a premier to come along with us."

"If you do that," warned Manitoba's Sterling Lyon, "you're going to tear the country apart."

Trudeau's plan to patriate the Constitution without the provinces' consent was challenged in court. The premiers were disappointed, however, when the Supreme Court, while declaring that Trudeau's initiative would be in contravention of constitutional conventions, did not rule it illegal. It was a judgment that left almost everyone dissatisfied. "Having said that our plan didn't conform with conventions," Trudeau complained in his *Memoirs*, "the majority of the court had to state what the convention was. But their answer was only that there had to be a 'substantial number' of the provinces agreeing with the federal government. They never defined 'substantial.' . . . This was in my view a faulty judgment. . . . I just said, 'Well . . . we have to live with it.' But, privately, I didn't have to like it, or agree with it."

Lévesque was equally doubtful. "What did this hocus-pocus amount to . . .? Now that he knew his constitutional monster was legal after all, Trudeau had to find a way to get the other provinces to adopt it. He couldn't turn up at Westminster flanked by Bill Davis and Dick Hatfield."

**TERRY FOX** ◆ Terry Fox had his right leg amputated above the knee after a malignant tumour was discovered there in 1977. Two years later he began training for a cross-country run called the Marathon of Hope to raise money for cancer research. On April 12, 1980, Fox dipped his artificial leg into the Atlantic Ocean at St. John's, Newfoundland, and began his run, averaging forty-three kilometres a day. After 143 days and 5,373 kilometres, he was forced to abandon the run in Thunder Bay, Ontario, after discovering that the cancer had spread to his lungs. His Marathon of Hope raised $24.17 million dollars and inspired the annual Terry Fox Run. He died on June 28, 1981, in New Westminster, British Columbia, at the age of twenty-two. (*CP Picture Archive*)

Lévesque condemned Trudeau's intransigence but was worried that public opinion was moving toward the prime minister's position. "This damned 'repatriation' created the image of some kind of treasure on the verge of being brought home after a long exile. Even in Quebec quite a few people were beginning to fall for the magic of this symbol." Lévesque met with the seven other premiers who were opposed to Trudeau's plans in April 1981. The "Gang of Eight," as they became known, agreed to remain a bloc, and they drafted some resolutions. "Faced with a common front of eight premiers out of ten, Trudeau didn't stand a chance," Lévesque said, "as long as everyone stuck to his guns and respected his signature."

In November 1981, Trudeau met with all the premiers in Ottawa, in the old railway station across the street from the Château Laurier Hotel. "Lévesque's goal was to keep the Gang of Eight intact to thwart me, and mine was to make a certain number of concessions that would split their ranks and bring some of the others on-side," Trudeau wrote. "That was the spirit in which we began the negotiations." He thought the premiers were feeling cocky as a result of the Supreme Court's decision. "I could either prove to the Canadian public that the eight were being completely unreasonable and then go ahead alone . . . or I could break the solidarity among the eight and go . . . with the support of a substantial number of premiers, which I supposed would be anywhere between five and nine of them."

Lévesque felt that the premiers' alliance was already showing signs of strain on the first day of meetings. Allan Blakeney of Saskatchewan and Bill Bennett of British Columbia now appeared to be slouching toward Trudeau's

**THE CONSTITUTION** ◆ Left to right: Bill Davis (Ontario premier), Jean Chrétien (federal justice minister), Pierre Trudeau, Allan MacEachen (deputy prime minister), and René Lévesque at the 1981 Constitution conference. (*Ron Poling, CP Picture Archive*)

brand of federalism. "They seemed to be saying to Trudeau: 'Find something or other, if you possibly can, to let us reach a compromise.' The common front was decidedly beginning to crack."

On the second day, Trudeau goaded Lévesque, daring him to put the idea of a Charter to a referendum, something the Gang of Eight had agreed to avoid at all costs. "You, the great democrat," Trudeau said, "don't tell me you're afraid to fight."

"All right," Lévesque responded, surprising both Trudeau and the seven other premiers.

Peter Lougheed, who had been Lévesque's closest ally, took him aside to talk. "We went outside and met in the side room," Lougheed said, "and I made it very clear to Mr. Lévesque that I thought that he had either misunderstood that question, because we had agreed to hang together as a group with regard to the whole question . . . to move to a referendum as distinguished from a negotiation was different than we agreed to."

But the damage had been done – the cohesion of the Gang of Eight was unravelling. Trudeau addressed the press, announcing that "Canada and Quebec have a new deal . . . the cat is among the pigeons."

On the night of November 4, the premiers retired to their rooms in Ottawa's Château Laurier, except Lévesque, who was staying across the river at the Hôtel de la Chaudière in Hull. In his memoirs, Lévesque recalls telling the others before he left for the hotel, "If anything new comes up, don't forget to call us."

After midnight, the minister of justice, Jean Chrétien, who was the point man for the federal government, worked with the attorneys general from Saskatchewan and Ontario, Roy Romanow and Roy McMurtry, to find an acceptable deal. Their solution was to allow their governments

**BOAT PEOPLE** ◆ In 1975, seventy thousand South Vietnamese fled when the Communist North overran their country, putting to sea in small, ill-equipped vessels. Some were accepted in Canada as political refugees. Among them were members of the Trang family, who had lived a privileged life in Saigon and now settled into an overcrowded two-bedroom apartment in Quebec City. "My mother worked at night as a waitress, cashier, house-cleaner," said her son Phan. His father was still in Vietnam, a political prisoner. "At that time we had a lot of Québécois friends, we spoke more French than Vietnamese. That made my mother crazy . . . I listened to the radio, the television, I knew all the shows." When his father was finally released, after eleven years, he came to Canada to meet with his now unfamiliar family. "He got off the plane, I didn't have a strong reaction. I didn't hug him. . . . My mother was very moved. She cried, she was very content. . . . But the children, my brothers, my sister, are less taken with that. . . . It was a very difficult period. I follow traditions but I don't think like a Vietnamese. One evolves with the society. My mother changed. I see my future here. I love the culture, the society." (*CP Picture Archive*)

to override the Charter of Rights, preserving provincial rights, a provision that would be known as the "notwithstanding clause." Trudeau was not convinced that it was necessary. "I had little sympathy for provincial demands for an override," he wrote. "The notwithstanding clause violated my sense of justice: it seemed wrong that any province could suspend any part of the Charter." But his only two allies, premiers Hatfield and Davis, agreed to the compromise position. Davis called Trudeau. "I think that our people have worked out something pretty good," he said. "What do you think, Pierre?"

"I don't like it," Trudeau responded. "We're giving away too much."

"Look, Pierre, I've been talking this thing over with Hatfield and I think we have to tell you that we won't go to London to support you if you don't accept some sort of compromise of this nature." In danger of losing his only two allies, Trudeau would be forced to give ground.

When Lévesque arrived late for a premiers' breakfast the next morning, caught in rush-hour traffic, he found that a new deal had been drafted during the night. However, it omitted Quebec's central demand, which would have allowed the province to opt out of shared federal-provincial programs but receive equivalent funds to set up its own programs. This provision would have greatly increased the provincial government's power, at Ottawa's expense. Brian Peckford handed Lévesque the document.

"The others literally were starting to leave because we didn't know he was going to even show," Peter Lougheed said. "I stayed and chatted with him about it, told him what had happened. He was very angry about it."

"We had been betrayed, in secret, by men who hadn't hesitated to tear up their own signatures, and without their even taking the trouble to warn us," Lévesque said, though he, too, had broken their pact by agreeing to a referendum. The new deal was signed by Trudeau and nine of the premiers that morning. Only Lévesque refused to endorse it.

"Behind his Oriental impassivity," Lévesque observed, "one could feel Trudeau literally rejoicing. He had put one over on us."

There were conflicting interpretations of what had happened. Trudeau's supporters argued that Lévesque was committed to separation and would not have accepted any agreement to patriate the Constitution. "Lévesque was a gambler," Trudeau responded. "He had taken a huge gamble, and he had lost." But Lévesque and his supporters saw the agreement as a betrayal, one in which English politicians had conspired against Quebec. Lévesque left the conference, denouncing the premiers and their role in what would be characterized as "the night of the long knives." "I have been stabbed in the back during the night by a bunch of carpetbaggers," he wrote.

Mary Eberts in 1978.
(*CP Picture Archive*)

The drafting of a Charter of Rights and Freedoms had a great many hurdles to overcome. Doris Anderson, former editor of *Chatelaine* magazine, was at that time head of the Canadian Advisory Council on the Status of Women. She realized that the Charter presented a crucial opportunity to advance women's rights. "It was clear a Charter would profoundly affect women," she said. "Its wording had to be strong, or we would be saddled with a bad and useless document for generations to come." To prepare the legal case for a strong acknowledgment of women's rights in the Charter, Anderson hired Mary Eberts, who had grown up in St. Thomas, Ontario, and studied constitutional law at Harvard. Once a Trudeau supporter, she had broken with the prime minister over his 1970 invoking of the War Measures Act. "A famous revolution was once fought because of taxation without representation," Eberts argued. "If governments do not see our place and our voice in their assemblies, it is up to women to bring the point home. . . . We have a special historical relationship to the constitution, as we had to fight so hard for so long to be included in even its minimal provisions. Let us not stop now."

When the government cancelled a conference on the issue of women's rights in the new constitution with the assurance that "they would look after things," Doris Anderson resigned her position on the Canadian Advisory Council. An ad hoc conference was planned, and women across the country responded, meeting on Parliament Hill. "The ad hoc committee was possibly one of the most important things to happen for the equality of Canadian women in the last fifteen or twenty years," Mary Eberts said. "It confirmed that the Constitution was a people's instrument."

Eberts presented briefs to a Special House-Senate Joint Committee, arguing that the Charter had to include an endorsement of sexual equality,

**THE WOMEN'S MOVEMENT** ◆ In 1967, the government of Lester B. Pearson established a Royal Commission on the Status of Women, chaired by Florence Bird, who went across the country collecting information. Progress in women's rights was slow over the next decade. Legislative gains were made, but they were not always reflected in women's experience. The case of Irene Murdoch, an Alberta housewife, became one of the precedents for Canadian family law.

Murdoch lived on a ranch near Turner Valley with her husband of twenty-five years, Alex. In 1968, he broke her jaw in three places during an argument over whether to sell the ranch and start over. He drove her to the Holy Cross Hospital, where her jaw was repaired, leaving her mouth partially paralyzed. When she returned home, the locks on the house had been changed and her credit cut off. She hired a lawyer to arrange a legal separation and settlement, but in the judgment she was awarded only $200 per month. Her work on the ranch was discounted and her husband retained the land, farm machinery, house, furniture, car, and all revenues. Murdoch appealed the decision to the Supreme Court, which offered its decision on October 2, 1973, ruling that she had made "only the normal contribution to the farm that most farm or ranch wives make" and had no claim to the property. In a dissenting view, Supreme Court Justice Bora Laskin argued, "In making a substantial contribution of physical labour, as well as financial contribution, to the acquisition of successive properties . . . the wife has, in my view, established a right to an interest which it would be inequitable to deny."

Murdoch was crushed by the decision and burdened with debt, but her case drew media attention and helped move the courts toward a more equitable position. "One of the most defining examples of this court/media domino effect is the Murdoch case," Justice Rosalie Abella later wrote, "galvanizing this generation's women's movement. . . . The media grabbed the story, and jolted the public out of its complacency about family law. Most Canadians at the time thought universes and laws unfolded as they should, and were generally unaware of the economic consequences of marriage breakdown. Irene Murdoch, through the media, introduced those consequences to the wives of this country and the reaction was swift. By the end of three years, even before any statutes were changed, the Supreme Court reversed the principles in Murdoch with a 1978 case called Rathwell, and most provincial legislatures subsequently changed their family property law regimes to recognize marriage as a social and economic partnership with a more equitable distribution of entitlements on separation."

The Murdoch case was one development in a multi-faceted international movement. In 1969, Canadian courts ruled that the advocacy of birth control was no longer a criminal offence. Germaine Greer published the *The Female Eunuch* in 1970, in which she argued that marriage is a legalized form of slavery for women. The following year the Women's Press was founded in Toronto by a collective of several women who began publishing material "by, for and about Canadian women." In 1974, the Royal Canadian Mounted Police hired its first female officer. Three years later, the Canadian Women's Movement Archives were founded by an independent feminist collective to preserve records (it is now held at the University of Ottawa). In 1978, the first "Take Back the Night" march was held in Toronto, with marchers protesting violence against women. Alexa McDonough became the first woman to lead a provincial political party in Canada when she was elected leader of the New Democratic Party in Nova Scotia. By 1983, the majority of undergraduate students in Canadian universities – 56 per cent – were women, up from 37 per cent in 1970. (International Women's Day March in Toronto, 1979. *Dennis Robinson, The Globe and Mail, CP Picture Archive*)

*Queen Elizabeth II signing Canada's Constitutional Proclamation. (Ron Poling, CP Picture Archive)*

women's right to control reproduction, and other guarantees of women's rights. As a result, an "equality clause" was added. Section 28 read, "Notwithstanding anything in this Charter, the rights and freedoms referred to in it are guaranteed equally to male and female persons." The explicit acknowledgment of equality between men and women was something American feminists had struggled unsuccessfully for years to achieve. But the section would be subject to an override, making it legally toothless. This sparked a national campaign on behalf of women to have the override removed. Support from across the country flowed in – a show of solidarity that received a lot of media attention. Ultimately, the override was abandoned.

On April 17, 1982, Queen Elizabeth II came to Ottawa to sign the patriated Constitution with its Charter of Rights and Freedoms. "The day began sunny and warm," Trudeau wrote, "but ended in a downpour – an omen, I suppose, of things to come."

Oil remained a divisive political issue. Bill Twaits, the president of Imperial Oil, described the struggle between the federal and provincial governments to work out a coherent oil policy as "two pigs battling under a blanket for the same acorn." The struggle became a war in October 1980, when Pierre Trudeau announced the National Energy Program (NEP). Designed by energy minister Marc Lalonde, it had the express intention of moving the

In 1981, 515 oil wells were drilled in Alberta; by 1987, the figure had dropped to 260. The number of people receiving welfare payments in Edmonton in April 1978 was 12,447; by 1987 it had almost doubled to 23,894. (*CP Picture Archive*)

country toward energy self-sufficiency, increasing Canadian ownership, and promoting national unity. It introduced a series of new federal taxes on petroleum, kept prices in Canada below world levels, and included conservation clauses, among other things. The program offered benefits for Canadian companies drilling within Canada, but most Alberta oilmen saw it as a unilateral, heavy-handed money grab. When the NEP was announced, Jim Gray was in Ottawa on business, and he was outraged by its audacity: "It capped the price of oil and gas, gave all kinds of Canadian incentives in the north that were devastating, took away opportunity, imposed all kinds of taxes, and tried to manage the industry from Ottawa." Gray publicly tackled Trudeau on the issue of natural gas, and though it was a subject the prime minister knew little about, he won the debate. "He was a marvellous intellectual debater," Gray acknowledged grudgingly.

Peter Lougheed was equally outraged. The Alberta premier appeared on television, a medium that emphasized his western sheriff image, decrying the NEP. "Our forefathers fought hard to obtain these resources," he told the viewing audience. "We now have a responsibility to manage them well and preserve our ownership rights. . . . The Ottawa government – without negotiation and without agreement – simply walked into our homes and occupied the living room." Lougheed's image of prairie homesteaders fending off the predatory (and distant) federal government played well. Bumper stickers appeared: "Let the Eastern Bastards Freeze in the Dark" and "This car doesn't brake for Liberals." Lougheed cut the flow of oil to the east by 15 per cent in 1981. He and Trudeau finally agreed to a modified NEP agreement, in which Ottawa would not tax oil and gas exports to the United States. The listless compromise was made just in time for the industry to begin its jarring decline.

By 1982, Dome Petroleum had grown to enormous proportions and its debt load was reaching a critical mass. Interest rates were high, and Dome's aggressive expansion under president Bill Richards had become insupportable. Rumours of the company's instability began to move around the

Petroleum Club, sending a collective shudder throughout the industry. Richards and CEO Jack Gallagher were barely speaking. "If Bill has a weakness," Gallagher said in 1982, "it's his impatience to grow."

By the spring, Dome was in crisis. "We felt we needed $600 million just to survive the summer," Richards said, "and we really couldn't see any way out of it. . . . It was just fancy footwork that carried us through the whole of summer. . . . At times we were just hours from going under. Sometimes we had one or two instances a *day* where we could have gone under. . . ." On June 30, Dome's debt stood at $7.03 billion, owed mostly to the four major Canadian banks (as well as thirty-six foreign banks).

The fallout from a Dome collapse would be unprecedented in Canadian corporate history. In addition to the losses suffered by investors, the Calgary real estate market would certainly falter, and even the Bank of Commerce, a big lender, was thought to be in jeopardy. All eyes turned to the government for help. On a radio show, Pierre Trudeau said, "The government did not force the banks to lend money to Dome. The banks thought they were going to make a buck and Dome was investing this money because it thought it was going to make a buck. Are we going to bail it out? The answer is no, we're not going to bail it out." Dome's stock dropped 10 per cent that morning.

Despite Trudeau's hard line, Jean Chrétien, who had taken over the energy portfolio from Marc Lalonde, helped work out a bailout package that involved the banks and the federal government. The giddy expansion was over. "What is required is a 180-degree change in approach," said Bill Richards in November 1982. "The virtues of yesterday are the vices of today. Management must develop and apply the pedestrian qualities of caution and restraint." Alberta had been defined by growth and risk for more than a decade; now, the downturn was more than simply economic, it affected the provincial personality. Within two years, mirroring trends elsewhere in the country, unemployment in the province rose from 3.8 per cent to 10.2 per cent. For the first time in more than a decade, Alberta had a net out-migration. The province led the nation in housing foreclosures, bankruptcies, and suicides. The *Calgary Herald*'s classified section bulged with homes for sale, sometimes including the contents and cars. By 1984, the city of Calgary had 2.3 million square metres of vacant office space, and its real estate speculators and oil investors had reverted to teachers, dentists, and taxi drivers.

"This industry is like a complex tapestry," Jim Gray said, "intricately woven over the past three or four years. . . . It is unravelling before our eyes. It is being torn apart by vandals. It is happening far faster than I thought possible. It is a sad spectacle. It cannot and will not be rebuilt quickly." Gray's company, Canadian Hunter Exploration, was hit hard as well, as a result, he said, of the NEP. "We had gained enough momentum that it didn't kill us," he said. But the oil patch was littered with other casualties. On October 17, 1986, Gray held a meeting in his office that included Ted Byfield, the pugnacious publisher of *Alberta Report* magazine, and Preston Manning, the son of former premier Ernest C. Manning, and they talked about the

**RONALD REAGAN** ◆ Ronald Reagan came to power in the United States with a unique blend of Hollywood charm, calculated nostalgia, and free-market theory. While campaigning for the presidency, Reagan, who at sixty-eight would be the oldest president elect, recounted this story: "Not so long back a little boy came up to me – he must have been, why, no more than eleven or twelve years of age. He looked at me and he said, 'Mister, you're pretty old. What was it like when you were a boy?' And I said . . . 'Well, son, when I was a little boy, America was the strongest country in the world. When I was a little boy, every working American could expect to buy his own home. When I was a little boy, gasoline was twenty cents a gallon.' The little boy looked up at me and he said, 'Hey mister. You ain't so old. Things were like that when I was a little boy too.'"

Reagan's ability to simplify issues and present them as parables (he often quoted lines from films, including an uncredited speech from *The Bridges of Toko-Ri*, delivered in Normandy on the anniversary of D-Day) earned him the title of "the great communicator." Where Carter had magnified the complexity of the job, Reagan was visibly relaxed. He tried, like Margaret Thatcher, to get government out of the way (though he increased spending in his first term), to lower taxes, and to let free enterprise work. He had the performer's gift for knowing what his audience wanted. (Ronald Reagan taking the oath of office, January 20, 1981. *CP Picture Archive*)

possibility of creating a new political party, one that would address western concerns. Gray did not commit at that time, but the seeds of the Reform Party were sown.

It was not just Albertans who were unhappy with the NEP. In the United States, President Jimmy Carter's humanitarian spirit had lost to Ronald Reagan's isolationist view in the election of 1980 (Reagan won 489 electoral votes to Carter's 49). Trudeau's attitude toward the United States had been characterized for the most part by a lack of interest. He was unaware of American popular culture, and of the several presidents he dealt with, only Carter could have been called an ally. Nixon, with his combination of Quaker righteousness and blithe corruption, had detested Trudeau. Reagan was incurious, anti-intellectual, effortlessly warm, and defiantly provincial – the antithesis of Trudeau – and the two were never comfortable with one another. Reagan felt that the NEP and the Foreign Investment Review Agency (FIRA), which sharply restricted the ability of foreign investors to take over Canadian businesses, were both threats to American interests, and he wanted changes.

The aspect of the energy policy that was most objectionable to the Americans was a "back-in" clause, which stated that a 25 per cent equity interest in new oil development on federally owned land would go to the Crown – in effect, to the government – without compensation to the company paying for the exploration. Reagan had come to power as a champion of free enterprise, and this provision rankled. Concessions were made in May 1981, but the Americans remained unhappy with the deal. While the

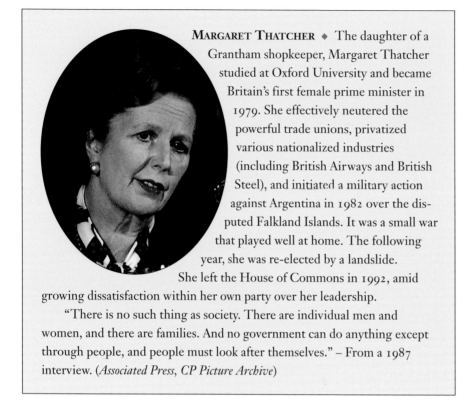

**MARGARET THATCHER** ♦ The daughter of a Grantham shopkeeper, Margaret Thatcher studied at Oxford University and became Britain's first female prime minister in 1979. She effectively neutered the powerful trade unions, privatized various nationalized industries (including British Airways and British Steel), and initiated a military action against Argentina in 1982 over the disputed Falkland Islands. It was a small war that played well at home. The following year, she was re-elected by a landslide. She left the House of Commons in 1992, amid growing dissatisfaction within her own party over her leadership.

"There is no such thing as society. There are individual men and women, and there are families. And no government can do anything except through people, and people must look after themselves." – From a 1987 interview. (*Associated Press, CP Picture Archive*)

relationship between the two countries was not particularly good, Canada had demonstrated that it was willing to pursue its own economic course, even if it angered the powerful United States.

Ronald Reagan and Britain's Margaret Thatcher (who had come to power in 1979) ushered in an era of neo-conservatism. Their belief that the free market should operate with as few restrictions as possible constituted an attack on the "welfare state" that had grown up during the post-war boom. The period of sustained growth that had characterized the 1950s and 1960s had now been replaced by a much more difficult economic climate, one that would persist for a decade. "So let us have no truck with those who say the free enterprise system has failed," Thatcher told her Conservative Party in her first speech as its leader. "What we face today is not a crisis of capitalism but of socialism. . . . It will take time to reduce public spending, to rebuild profits and incentives, and to benefit from the investments that must be made. But the sooner that time starts, the better it will be for Britain's unemployed and for Britain as a whole."

By 1983, Thatcher's stringent policies had begun to transform Britain. She was cheered by the nation's business class, who had felt persecuted and vilified under the Labour government, and criticized by the Labour Party as leading "the most reactionary, right-wing, extremist government in all of British history." Her personal popularity soared in 1982 when Britain won a brief, occasionally televised war with Argentina over the ownership of the Falkland Islands, and in 1983 she was re-elected in a landslide victory.

**RENÉ LÉVESQUE** ◆
Lévesque began
to keep a diary in 1984.
His entry for Sunday,
January 22, was: "So here
we are at the end of
January. Not doing so
hot. With election
defeats in Mégantic-
Compton, and especially
in Jonquière, that makes
seven by-elections lost since our 1981 win. And it seems quite clear that even
an old tugboat like me isn't pulling the weight he used to. According to the
confidential memo I was given for Christmas, even what I'm leaving in my
wake is not all that palatable: 'even your most faithful supporters are wondering what's going on,' I read. 'We feel you are easily irritable, less open to
suggestions . . . more and more isolated.' The worst of it is that it's true,
I can feel it." The Parti Québécois lost the subsequent election to Robert
Bourassa's Liberals. (*Jacques Boissinot, CP Picture Archive*)

In the United States, Ronald Reagan cut personal taxes by 25 per cent
and lowered corporate taxes in his first months in office. He concentrated on
domestic policy, increasing defence spending and the deficit, and had a
talent for reducing complex issues to heartwarming parables. His combination of folksiness, tax cutting, and optimism won him wide approval. In
1984, Reagan was decisively re-elected, winning forty-nine of fifty states.

In Canada, the rebirth of conservatism arrived in the form of Brian
Mulroney, the son of a millworker in Baie Comeau, Quebec, a company
town that owed its existence to an American pulp and paper company. At
Laval University, Mulroney had worked ceaselessly on developing contacts.
He had a natural charm, made friends easily, and was a quick study. "As you
got to know him better," said classmate Lucien Bouchard, "his ambition
became more apparent, as well as his determination to follow the path of
politics. . . . His ambition had a romantic aura: he saw the world as something to conquer rather than to change, as a place where cruelty spared a few
individuals who happened to be more resourceful or fortunate than others."

In 1976, Mulroney took a run at the leadership of the Conservative
Party, but his defeat at the hands of Joe Clark left him demoralized and
bitter. He turned to the private sector, where he became president of the Iron
Ore Company, one of the largest mining companies in Canada, with headquarters in Cleveland. There he bided his time, making money and new
contacts and revising his political persona, preparing for another run at the
leadership. At the Conservatives' leadership convention in 1983, he finally beat
Clark and took his place as leader of the Opposition in the House of Commons.

**BRIAN MULRONEY** ◆ After John Turner approved nineteen Liberal patronage appointments (most actually made by outgoing prime minister Pierre Trudeau), Mulroney announced at a press conference, "It's something out of an Edward G. Robinson movie. You know, the boys cuttin' up the cash. There's not a Grit left in this town. They've all gone to Grit heaven." At the televised election debate between Turner and Mulroney two weeks later, Turner surprisingly raised the issue of patronage, prompting a tirade from Mulroney.

"Mr. Turner, the only person who has ever appointed around here, for the last twenty-odd years, has been your party, and 99 per cent of them have been Liberals. And you ought not to be proud of that. . . . The least you should do is apologize for having made these horrible appointments. . . ."

"I told you and told the Canadian people, Mr. Mulroney, that I had no option."

"You had an option, sir. You could have said, 'I'm not going to do it. . . .'"

"I had no option. I was able –"

"That is an avowal of failure. That is a confession of non-leadership and this country needs leadership. You had an option, sir. You could have done better."

That moment in the television debate was the turning point in the campaign, a brief exchange in front of 7.5 million Canadians that underlined the power of the medium. Turner's stuttering and panicked look were his undoing. (Mulroney being sworn in as prime minister, September 17, 1984. *CP Picture Archive*)

A few months later, Trudeau was contemplating his future in politics. On the evening of February 28, 1984, in the middle of a Montreal blizzard, Trudeau took a thoughtful walk around his neighbourhood on the southern slope of Mount Royal. He then returned to his art deco mansion, enjoyed a sauna, and slept soundly, having made the decision to retire.

While Trudeau was taking his walk in the snow, Mulroney was in West Palm Beach, Florida, taking a much-needed vacation, trying to quit smoking, and considering his own political career. With Trudeau gone, Mulroney's new Liberal opponent would be John Turner, a handsome corporate lawyer who had been out of active politics for ten years, a man who was awkward and tentative in the limelight. An election was called, and Turner stumbled in the televised candidates' debate, which helped Mulroney's cause. Campaigning against years of interventionist economic policies imposed by successive Liberal governments, Mulroney was able to capitalize on the neo-conservative successes of both Thatcher and Reagan.

In 1984, the Conservatives won the general election, carrying 211 seats. It was the first Tory majority since Diefenbaker's, and the third-largest in Canadian history. President Reagan called Mulroney the next day to congratulate him, and the two joked that now there were two Irish leaders in North America. Although Mulroney was never as hardline a conservative as Reagan, their relationship was one of political alignment and personal familiarity, and it marked the beginning of a new relationship with the United States. One of Mulroney's first major speeches was to the Economic

**REFORM PARTY** ◆ The first meetings to define a western political party took place in 1986 and included oilman Jim Gray, Ted Byfield, the publisher of *Alberta Report* magazine, and Preston Manning. "We met for the whole evening," Byfield said, "and came to two conclusions: one was that there had to be another party, and the other was that such a party would have little chance of success." Byfield felt that Confederation was unfair. "We gave the provinces control over resources. But for one hundred years, control of resources was not sufficient . . . to outweigh the weight of central Canada. Then in the 1970s, this OPEC thing came along, oil and gas were worth an enormous amount of money. So finally the rules began to work for the other side – the smaller provinces. And what the hell do they do? They come along and change the rules just when they began to work for the smaller provinces! These guys aren't running a country, they're running an empire." (Preston Manning during the 1988 federal election campaign in which he ran for the Reform Party against former prime minister Joe Clark in the Alberta riding of Yellowhead. *Larry Johns, CP Picture Archive*)

Club in New York, where he told the assembled business leaders that FIRA was dead, and the NEP was next. "Our message is clear," he told an appreciative crowd. "Here and around the world, Canada is open for business again." But while Canada was open for business, the United States was closing: under Reagan, more protectionist measures were passed than at any time since the 1930s.

The new relationship was cemented publicly at the "Shamrock Summit," a meeting between Mulroney and Reagan that was held in Quebec City. Mulroney once again emphasized a spirit of hospitality toward the Americans: "People who criticize from the bleachers are the same people who for twenty years were in charge of Canadian-American relations, our largest trading partner, friend and ally, treated them like enemies, barraged them with insults, never gave them the benefit of the doubt, and then wondered why we never got along." Mulroney, by contrast, went so far as to support the U.S. invasion of Grenada, which even Margaret Thatcher had advised against, and which was broadly criticized as a cynical military exercise designed to increase popularity. The summit ended with the maudlin image of Mulroney and Reagan together singing "When Irish Eyes are Smiling," an ill-rehearsed hymn for a new era.

**JOHN TURNER** ◆ After being drubbed in the televised election debates in 1984, Turner returned in 1988, having learned the lessons of the medium, and he effectively attacked Mulroney on the issue of free trade: "A hundred and twenty years ago we built this country east, west, north, we built it on an infrastructure that deliberately resisted the continental pressure of the U.S. For a hundred and twenty years we've done it. With one signature of a pen, you've reversed that, thrown us into the north-south influence of the United States, and will reduce us to a colony . . . because when the economic levers go, the political independence is sure to follow." In a Gallup poll taken after the debate, Turner's Liberals rose from third place to first with 43 per cent of respondents, compared to 31 per cent for the Conservatives. Mulroney, however, was returned to power in the election. (*Fred Chartrand, CP Picture Archive*)

Mulroney tempered the conservative message for a cautious Canadian electorate, and initially his leadership met with approval. His pledge to cut the deficit was lauded, his overtures to the business community were welcomed, and some social cuts (the reduction of family allowances, among others) were grudgingly accepted, although he retreated from a proposal to deprive old age pensioners of protection against inflation. With FIRA dismantled, foreign investors faced far less government scrutiny. The possibility of free trade with the United States, Canada's largest trading partner, was gaining political momentum.

It was an issue that was older than Confederation, and it had contributed at different times to the downfall of two prime ministers who favoured it – Alexander Mackenzie and Wilfrid Laurier. In 1983, Mulroney himself had been against it. "We'd be swamped," he said. "We have in many ways a branch-plant economy in certain important sectors. All that would happen with free trade would be the boys cranking up their plants throughout the United States in bad times and shutting their entire branch plants in Canada. It's bad enough as it is." But within a few years, the prime minister had changed his mind, prompted by mounting U.S. protectionism, the recommendations of the Macdonald Commission on the economy, and pressure from the business community.

In 1986 and 1987, Canadian and American negotiators hammered out a wide-ranging free-trade deal that phased out customs duties on all goods crossing the Canada-U.S. border. Canada also promised not to restrict U.S. investment, or unfairly subsidize its exports, and agreed not to charge Americans a premium on Canadian oil and gas. Canada did not, in return, get the exemption from U.S. protectionist laws that it had demanded. Instead, there was a mechanism to ensure that American laws would be applied fairly.

By the time Canadians went to the polls again in 1988, free trade had become the sole election issue, engendering strong emotions on both sides. Supporters saw it as the country's best chance of succeeding in the increasingly competitive global market. It would create jobs, attract foreign investment, and provide access to American consumers. Opponents argued that Canadian manufacturers who relied on tariff protection would be decimated by free trade, leading to unemployment, and that small cuts in tariffs would not benefit consumers by much. Canadian culture, social policies, and the environment would be threatened as well. American branch plants would move back to the United States and take advantage of cheaper, non-union labour. Opposition leader John Turner decried the free-trade agreement: "I'm not going to let Brian Mulroney destroy the Canadian dream, and that's why this election is more than an election, it's your future."

The election pitted two mythologies against one another: the anti–free trade side held up the historical idea of Canada as a place of social justice and inclusiveness, a country where the state had the authority to direct and constrain the free market – ideas, they argued, that were not held dear in the United States. The pro side stood by the idea that Canadians could compete effectively, and promoted free trade as the ticket to a brighter economic future. Popular opinion waffled: in 1986, the majority of Canadians opposed free trade. By 1988, a poll showed that 70 per cent were in favour. Mulroney won the election and once again formed a majority government, though the Conservatives had won less than half the popular vote. The country remained divided on the issue.

On the front lines of the free trade issue were the workers, among them Mike Hersh. Hersh was president of the United Steelworkers of America union local at Inglis, an appliance manufacturer which, by the mid 1980s, had its head office in Ohio and a plant in Toronto. After attending the University of Massachusetts, where he was active in the anti-war movement, Hersh came to Canada in 1967. In Montreal, he enrolled at McGill University and safely avoided the draft. Then in 1969 he moved to Toronto and started working on the assembly line at Inglis. By the time free trade was being proposed, he had worked at Inglis for almost twenty years, watching the wave of immigration that filled the plants and factories, observing the decline in the standard of living for workers, and preparing for the worst.

"Whatever leverage [the union] had before, in the '60s and '70s when the economy was always booming," Hersh said, "the '80s changed all that. The unions were on the run and management went for the jugular and it had

**LABOUR STRIKES BACK** ◆

"Management wants to maximize profit and workers want to get a bigger share. I mean that's always going to be. In the '80s there was talk of teams and quality circles and all these good things. But in the '70s there was none of that stuff, you know. That was the boss, you're the worker. I'm the foreman, you do what I say. And it was very simple. Everyone understood. If you don't like what I say, you grieve it, but you do it first. All the stewards, we were all taught that, this is the way life is. Totally adversarial and the workplace was very volatile because of that." – Mike Hersh, president of the United Steelworkers of America local at the Inglis manufacturing plant. (Striking workers from the Gainers meat-packing plant in Edmonton join forces with workers on strike against Inglis, an appliance manufacturer in Toronto, during September 1986. *Thomas Szlukoveni, The Globe and Mail, CP Picture Archive*)

an impact at every negotiation throughout the '80s. . . . Management became far more aggressive and the unions far more intimidated and defensive than they had been before. It was something that all of us noticed."

He watched as his own plant withered and died. "We made a washing machine for $320, and they would sell it to Leon's [furniture and appliance chain] for $450, and you poor suckers would pay $650 for it," he said. But as trade barriers were dismantled, and the value of the Canadian dollar rose, it became cheaper to import the washing machines from the United States, where they could be manufactured at a lower cost because of longer production runs. The branch plants, which had not received any new investment to make them more efficient, were in danger of being closed, as Mulroney had warned in 1983. "You can't make a machine for what they do in the States," Hersh said. "Before free trade, Inglis was still a cash cow without any investment of capital, but take away the tarriffs and protection . . . forget it. What free trade did was expose Canadian manufacturing. The [plants] that succeeded were the ones where the industry was not foreign-owned and controlled." The branch plants were vulnerable, and on February 15, 1989, Inglis announced that it was closing its Toronto plant. "Globalization was inevitable," Hersh said, although he felt it had not been adequately prepared for. "The plant is gone. It's now a parking lot. But it was a training ground for other people to fight for the rights of their friends and fellow workers. It's not for naught."

During the years that Hersh worked in the plant, he also noticed the effects of immigration. "There were changes in the workplace," he said, "particularly in the '70s and then into the '80s, when you had an influx of East Indians and West Indians. Up to that point it was primarily Scottish, Irish, Canadian East Coasters, that's what Toronto plants looked like. Then in the '70s you started getting West and East Indians and you started getting Portuguese and you started getting Greeks and it wasn't just Italians from Europe. And so that brought some volatility to the workplace too. Prejudices and flare-ups, we almost had race wars at Inglis sometimes." For most of the century, Canadian immigration policy had explicitly discriminated against non-white immigrants, but in 1967 and 1978, revisions to the Immigration Act had removed most of the racist barriers. For those who did get into the country, though, racism remained a problem.

Baltej Dhillon was a Sikh who came to Canada in 1983 at the age of sixteen. Thousands of Sikhs had emigrated to Canada, and their visibility – beards, turbans, saris – often made them the objects of racist attacks. In 1984, the fight for a Sikh homeland in Kashmir led to violent clashes between Sikhs and the Indian army, and this distant battle had repercussions in Canada. In June 1985, 329 people aboard an Air India flight were killed by a terrorist bomb, and the suspects were a group of Sikhs in British Columbia dedicated to a winning independence from India for Sikhs. "I felt the effect here," Dhillon said. "I felt the effect of how we were viewed in Canada. When we went out into the community, people looked at you in fear, what you might do to them."

Dhillon applied to the Royal Canadian Mounted Police and was accepted, though tradition held that he could not wear his turban as part of his uniform. He asked that an exception be made, arguing that the wearing of a turban is a religious duty that no devout Sikh can shirk, and that preventing him from wearing one was a violation of his religious rights. The issue was picked up by the media, which solicited opinion from across the country. Some who responded were in favour of allowing the turban; many were opposed. An Alberta man named Herman Bittner created a crude, unflattering calendar that mocked Sikhs. "Am I really a racist," Bittner said in an interview, "or am I standing up and trying to save something that you know can be lost forever?" In the face of tens of thousands of new immigrants, Canadians would have to decide how far they were willing to go to accommodate the customs and beliefs of the newcomers.

Barbara Frum interviewed Dhillon on "The Journal." "Their argument to you, of course, is there's a great long tradition here. This goes back over a hundred years. . . . You want to be a Mountie. Why don't you join their tradition?"

"I have been practising my religion for the last twenty-three years," he replied. "Now, is somebody really asking me to protect a tradition, or are they asking me to sacrifice my religion, my principles, my disciplines, my respect in the community, the respect I have from my family, and all the other things that tie into this religion?"

**AIDS** ◆ AIDS entered the language in the early 1980s, progressing quickly from rumour, to grim reality, and finally to plague. "Plagues are invariably regarded as judgments on society," noted essayist and critic Susan Sontag, and judgments were quickly forthcoming. U.S. President Ronald Reagan's speech-writer wrote in 1983, "The poor homosexuals – they have declared war upon Nature, and now Nature is exacting an awful retribution." This position was largely abandoned in the following decade as heterosexual men, women, and children increasingly also fell victim to the disease. The health costs mounted: in 1987, the

direct cost of treating HIV-infected people in Canada was $129 million, while the indirect cost (lost production) was estimated at $500 million.

Eric Smith was a teacher in Clark's Harbour, Nova Scotia, who drove three hours to Halifax and a gay disco called Rumours on the weekends. In 1981, he heard the first whispers of a new disease: "Once the statistics began to pile up . . . I think it dawned on a lot of us slowly . . . that chances are we were probably already infected." Smith's

doctor tested his blood (without Smith's consent) and found him to be HIV-positive. He was pressured to accept a retirement package and leave his teaching post. "I became my own spokesperson . . . I came out of my shell enough to give appearances on television . . . do speaking engagements before six hundred people. I found it the easiest way to fight back. So while I may not be educating people by teaching them to read or do mathematics . . . you go out and do presentations about AIDS and HIV. You're doing another kind of education." (Members of the "Aids Committee of Toronto" meet in January 1986. *The Toronto Star, CP Picture Archive*)

**THE AIDS QUILT** ◆ A man crouches to take a closer look at one of the twelve sections of the Canadian AIDS Memorial Quilt on display at the Canadian Museum of Civilization. (*Jim Young, CP Picture Archive*)

The solicitor general, responsible for the RCMP, ruled that Dhillon could keep his turban, establishing a precedent of great symbolic power. "What is it to be Canadian, I think, ultimately becomes what is it to be a citizen of this earth," Dhillon said. "And Canada is, I believe, a petri dish for this world, where we have put all the organisms of this world. . . . And we are a test sample. And how we do as a country is going to be judged globally."

In the spring of 1987, Prime Minister Mulroney and the ten premiers met at Willson House on the shores of Meech Lake in the Gatineau Hills to re-examine the Constitution, specifically to find a way to include Quebec, which had never accepted the 1982 agreement. Robert Bourassa had replaced René Lévesque as Quebec's premier, and he had five demands, the most contentious of which were the recognition of Quebec as a "distinct society" with the right to protect and promote that distinctiveness, a Quebec veto over any subsequent constitutional change, and greater powers over immigration. The meeting began inauspiciously, as each premier laid out a list of demands: Alberta wanted Senate reform, Newfoundland wanted provincial control of the fisheries, British Columbia wanted to discuss property rights. Mulroney ran the meeting like a ringmaster, ushering demands on and off the stage, appeasing the premiers, finding ways to compromise. At the end of ten hours, an agreement in principle had been reached, one that would meet all five of Quebec's demands and grant concessions to the other provinces. The participants hugged and congratulated one another. British Columbia premier Bill Vander Zalm had the lunch menus autographed by the others to be auctioned off at a party fundraiser. Mulroney declared that "Canada is whole again. Quebec has joined the Canadian family." The deal, popularly known as the Meech Lake accord, would have to be ratified by all ten provincial legislatures within the next three years, but that seemed to be little more than a formality.

Critics soon emerged, though, among them Mary Eberts, who had reservations concerning the "distinct society" clause, fearing that it would allow Quebec to override women's rights. Judy Rebick, a member (later president) of the National Action Committee on the Status of Women, worried that if the provinces were given more authority over social programs they would impose cutbacks. Pierre Trudeau broke a three-year public silence and wrote an open letter that appeared in several newspapers, labelling Mulroney a "weakling" and warning that Canada would be governed by "snivellers" and "eunuchs" if the Meech Lake accord was adopted. He had spent his entire career in federal politics fighting against special status for Quebec, and he was not about to see this enshrined in the form of the "distinct society" clause, which, he argued, would simply move Quebec closer to sovereignty.

During the three years provided for ratification, three of the original signatories of the Meech Lake accord were defeated or resigned from politics. Gary Filmon became the new Manitoba premier, replacing the

**LUCIEN BOUCHARD** ◆ When the Meech Lake accord was amended to make it more palatable to various critics, Bouchard resigned in protest, delivering a blow to Mulroney's cause. "For two years now," Bouchard wrote, "I had been campaigning for Meech *as is*, according to government policy and the party line. . . . The prime minister would have to take the turn he had planned by himself and he would have to be happy with his new fellow traveller, Chrétien. . . . There was neither honour nor enthusiasm at the end of the torturous road the government was letting itself be pushed into taking: wheeling and dealing behind closed doors and last-minute swaps conjured up by exhausted negotiators in front of urinals."

His resignation ended both his association with the Conservative Party and his friendship with Mulroney. "I broke with so many friends," Bouchard later said. "I kept a few, but I lost many. That's politics. That's a reflection of what Canada is, a strange country where you can't keep your friends." (*Ron Poling, CP Picture Archive*)

New Democrat Howard Pawley, and in New Brunswick, Frank McKenna's Liberals took all fifty-eight seats in the legislature in a backlash against Richard Hatfield, the colourful, bon vivant Conservative leader. In Newfoundland, Conservative Brian Peckford had been replaced by Trudeau supporter Clyde Wells. All three had reservations about the accord and claimed they were not bound by their predecessors' decisions. Adding to the growing malaise was the defection from the Conservative Party of Lucien Bouchard, who had been Mulroney's Quebec lieutenant. Dissatisfied with the compromises suggested to overcome objections to Meech, he had abruptly resigned. Bouchard, who had been a member, variously, of the Liberals, the Parti Québécois, and the Conservatives, formed a new party, the Bloc Québécois. He was a political Hamlet: moody, sensitive, and plagued by ghosts. His defection left Mulroney vulnerable in Quebec.

Two weeks away from the ratification deadline, Mulroney invited the premiers to a dinner in Ottawa, where Clyde Wells restated his opposition to the accord. "I am rejecting a Canada with a Class A province, a Class B province, and Class C province," he announced. Bourassa felt he was trapped: the province's five demands had been accepted in April 1987; he could not return to Quebec with a compromise. Wells agreed to put the issue to a vote in the Newfoundland legislature, as did Gary Filmon in Manitoba.

On June 12, Filmon sought the Manitoba legislature's unanimous consent to open debate on the accord, but Elijah Harper, an Ojibwa-Cree

**ELIJAH HARPER** ◆ Harper was an NDP member of the Manitoba legislature, a largely invisible politician until he played a crucial role in blocking the Meech Lake accord by refusing his consent to open debate on the issue. An Ojibwa-Cree, Harper was advised by Ovide Mercredi and Phil Fontaine, who drafted comments for him, and by Winnipeg lawyer Jack London, who had been hired by the Assembly of Manitoba Chiefs to help block the accord. "The death of Meech was perhaps the single most important event in the history of aboriginal people in Canada," London said. (*Wayne Glowacki, The Winnipeg Free Press, CP Picture Archive*)

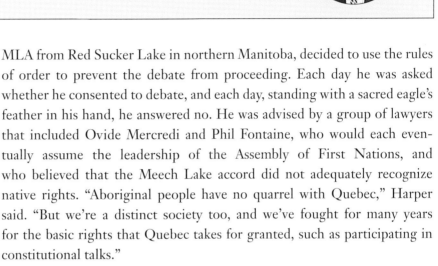

MLA from Red Sucker Lake in northern Manitoba, decided to use the rules of order to prevent the debate from proceeding. Each day he was asked whether he consented to debate, and each day, standing with a sacred eagle's feather in his hand, he answered no. He was advised by a group of lawyers that included Ovide Mercredi and Phil Fontaine, who would each eventually assume the leadership of the Assembly of First Nations, and who believed that the Meech Lake accord did not adequately recognize native rights. "Aboriginal people have no quarrel with Quebec," Harper said. "But we're a distinct society too, and we've fought for many years for the basic rights that Quebec takes for granted, such as participating in constitutional talks."

With time running out, it was suggested that the Supreme Court extend the deadline for ratification, but that move was contingent on Newfoundland putting the question to a vote. Clyde Wells declined to do that, and so, on June 23, 1990, time ran out, and the accord was declared dead. Mulroney was bitter, but he blamed Trudeau rather than Elijah Harper. "There is no doubt in my mind that the derailment of the Meech Lake accord began with a frontal assault by the former prime minister . . . the road to constitution reform is now closed."

The defeat of the Meech Lake Accord in part at the hands of an Ojibwa-Cree from an obscure northern Manitoba riding was satisfying for many natives. But the larger issues – in particular those concerning native self-government and land claims – remained unresolved. A series of incidents near the close of the decade helped fuel native discontent: the shooting of native chief J. J. Harper by a Winnipeg police officer, and the tragic case of Helen Betty Osborne, a Cree woman who had been murdered in The Pas, Manitoba, in 1971, the killers' identity kept secret for years by a number of townspeople. There was also the case of Donald Marshall, a Mi'kmaq who was wrongfully convicted of a murder in 1972 and served eighteen years in prison.

The mood on the reserves at Akwesasne and Kahnawake was becoming increasingly militant. Akwesasne straddles the borders separating Ontario, Quebec, and New York State, and the residents considered themselves to be

**MEECH LAKE** ◆ "If [Canadians] say yes to Meech Lake they know they will be getting further demands from Quebec. . . . One way or another we are not sure of what we are buying and what happens if we reject it. . . . Those who insist we sign Meech Lake despite its obfuscations are buying a pig in a poke. . . . Anyone who has to act under a threat of blackmail once will have to act under the threat of blackmail endlessly . . . I don't think we should give in to this type of reasoning." – Trudeau, responding to the Meech Lake accord in March 1990. *(Ron Poling, CP Picture Archive)*

neither Canadian nor American but Mohawk. As such, they believed that they were under no obligation to acknowledge the international boundary on their reserve. Among the other rights they claimed were tax-free tobacco products and the operation of casinos on the reserve. The issue of gambling was deeply divisive, and in the spring of 1990, two Mohawk men were killed at Akwesasne in a gambling-related incident.

The issues were given a violent focus in March when Mohawks at Kanesatake, west of Montreal, set up a blockade to prevent bulldozers from breaking ground for a golf course that would be built on a native burial ground. On July 10, the mayor of nearby Oka asked the provincial police, the Sûreté du Québec (SQ), to enforce an injunction from the Quebec superior court to have the blockade torn down. The next day, one hundred police officers with concussion grenades and tear gas, some armed with assault rifles, took up positions around the blockade. Debbie Etienne, a social worker who lived in Kanesatake, was at the barricade: "We went to the SQ line and put ashes on them. . . . We put a line on the ground and asked that no enemy would cross it."

It appeared that the 1988 prediction made by native leader Georges Erasmus was coming true. "We may be the last generation of leaders," he had warned, "who is prepared to sit down and peacefully negotiate our concerns with you."

Buried in the cemetery that was in danger of being converted to a golf course was the body of Kanawatiron, known as Joseph Gabriel, who had died in the 1930s. Kanawatiron had worked briefly in Buffalo Bill's Wild West

Show and had returned to Kanesatake at the turn of the century as a political activist, writing to politicians, warning them to honour the treaties or there would be trouble. In 1902, he left for England, hoping to be granted an audience with King Edward VII. For days he stood at the gates of Buckingham Palace dressed in a suit, fruitlessly waiting. "There is a dusky Redskin in London endeavouring to obtain an audience of the King," reported *The Times*, "and to lay before the 'Great White Father' a grievance of the Iroquois Indians of Canada, which has for generations owned a great tract of land that is being taken from them by the San Joseph Seminary of Montreal." Kanawatiron did not receive an audience, and when he returned to Canada, the Quebec provincial police treated him like a criminal, searching the woods for him, without luck. He remained a fugitive for years, hiding with friends and relatives.

In 1911, Kanawatiron was part of a native group that objected to the building of a railway through the reserve. Under the headline "Indians Threaten War Against Railroad Men," the *Montreal Star* reported: "Witnesses say there were at least forty braves armed with shotguns, revolvers and bludgeons, who with regular war cry accompaniment, informed the railroad labourers that they could proceed at their peril, as the property they were about to cross belonged to the Iroquois. The navvies [labourers] are said to have retired gracefully."

The second incident with armed natives, seventy-nine years later, would not end so gracefully.

The Mohawk Warriors at Kanesatake in 1990 were a mix of political activists and thugs, an uncomfortable alliance that did not have unanimous support on the reserve. On July 11, the tensions between police and Mohawks resulted in an exchange of gunfire. "People were screaming," Debbie Etienne said, "asking if anyone got hit. I heard somebody was shot."

Someone had been shot. Corporal Marcel Lemay had been killed, and police quickly surrounded Kanesatake. John Ciaccia was Quebec's minister of Indian affairs, and he was caught by surprise. "I never thought it would go so far," he said. "Nothing had prepared me for what would happen."

Natives at the nearby reserve of Kahnawake showed their support for the Warriors by erecting a blockade on the Mercier Bridge, effectively closing the road that carried commuters from the south shore of the St. Lawrence to Montreal. There were other incidents of violence, and pressure grew to resolve the crisis, which had now become a rallying cry for natives frustrated with political marginalization.

"The Mohawks began to make demands that had nothing to do with Oka," Ciaccia complained. "They wanted the police to leave Akwesasne, which was the scene of illegal activities that had nothing to do with Oka. Something was wrong. The stakes were now at a higher level."

Many Kanesatake residents were concerned that the conflict was escalating. "I wasn't happy with some of the things that went out of control," Debbie Etienne said. "The government used it against us." Those who were

**OKA** ◆ A Mohawk Warrior raises his weapon in triumph after a police assault to remove the barricade at the Kanesatake Reserve at Oka, Quebec, fails on July 11, 1990. One policeman was killed in the assault. (*Tom Hanson, CP Picture Archive*). Top right: A masked Warrior peers at a broken arrow hung by a soldier on the razor wire surrounding the Mohawk stronghold at Kanesatake. (*Frank Gunn, CP Picture Archive*). Bottom right: A Canadian soldier stares point blank at a Mohawk Warrior after the army surrounded the Kanesatake Reserve on September 1, 1990. (*Tom Hanson, CP Picture Archive*)

not behind the Warriors wondered how they had come to be in the middle of a war. On the other side, some of the police felt the same way. Shirley Ricard was a rookie police officer in the village of St. Donat. "At night they [the Warriors] were shooting over our heads," she said. "That's what I feared the most. We were on a barricade, in the middle of the night, in the woods: I know they see me but I don't see them. They shoot with their machine guns all around. They're not far, you know they're not far. . . . I was saying to myself, I'm twenty-two, I'm in the police, not in the army; I studied to be a policewoman. I love my job, what am I doing here?"

Many of the residents of Châteauguay (on the south shore of the river) worked in Montreal, and the road that took them to the city passed through the Kahnawake reserve. After a month of the blockade, tempers were flaring. On August 14, after a series of almost daily violent incidents in Châteauguay, Premier Robert Bourassa called upon the army for support. "The Warriors wanted the army," said Ciaccia, "because then they could say they were fighting nation against nation, the Mohawk army against the Canadian army. . . . They played it for all it was worth around the world." On August 29, the Kahnawake Mohawks dismantled the barricades at the Mercier Bridge, diffusing tension among commuters and leaving the Kanesatake Mohawks isolated. After a long and tense standoff, on September 26 the Warriors surrendered, and most of the leaders were arrested. "It was certainly one of the most difficult crises in my fifteen years of power," Bourassa confessed. "But we succeeded in reaching an end that didn't threaten the future of Quebec."

"It was really something," Ciaccia said, "a human experience . . . lessons of history . . . it was all that in seventy-eight days."

"We didn't get our land," Debbie Etienne said. "But I think on the inside we gained a lot, because our kids saw the truth. . . . It proved what my grandparents [told me] and their grandparents told them. . . . We are not a violent people; they created the violence." The only casualty was Marcel Lemay, whose wife was pregnant with their second child. No one was charged with the murder. The standoff at Oka was condemned by some native leaders, but it was cheered by others, who suggested that it was a logical and inevitable outcome of five hundred years of inequality.

In Newfoundland, there came another ancient lament: the beleaguered *Gadus morhua*, the Atlantic cod, was being overfished.

The Vikings were the first to fish the Grand Banks, followed by the Basques. Cod became a staple in Europe, in part because its low fat content made it ideal for salting, and so it preserved well. In the sixteenth century, other European nations discovered the Basques' lucrative fishing grounds, and French, Portuguese, and Spanish boats all came to fish the Grand Banks. By 1550, 60 per cent of all fish eaten in Europe was cod.

In 1883, there was an International Fisheries Exhibition in London, and the world's fishing nations met to compare information and speculation. The British scientist Thomas Henry Huxley explained why overfishing was unlikely ever to occur. "Any tendency to over-fishing will meet with its natural check in the diminution of supply," he told the fishermen. "This check will always come into operation long before anything like permanent exhaustion has occurred." Two years later, the Reverend Moses Harvey was already talking about Newfoundland's "exhausted seas," lamenting the diminishing cod catches. They rebounded, but were threatened once more in 1954 when the first factory ship, the British-owned *Fairtry*, arrived. The *Fairtry* was capable of catching and processing 600 tonnes of fish per day.

**COD CRISIS** ◆ "There isn't one decision you can take without a major battle going on as to what you should have done. For every winner, there are three losers. That's the fishery." – John Crosbie, minister of fisheries and oceans, 1991. (Fishermen at a 1991 meeting on the cod crisis at Port aux Basques, Newfoundland. *Andrew Vaughan, CP Picture Archive*)

The cod were filleted, skinned, and packed into blocks, then frozen in a factory on board – a technological innovation that increased the value of the catch dramatically. Over the next two decades the business was revolutionized by sonar devices for finding fish, bigger nets, better winches. There was no wasted effort; the offshore fishermen operated at maximum efficiency. By the 1970s there were nine hundred vessels fishing in international waters.

Politicians, scientists, and inshore fishermen united to fight the threat of European and Russian overfishing. In 1977, Canada extended the area over which it claimed exclusive fishing rights to 200 miles (321 kilometres) off shore, amid grumbling from the Spanish and Portuguese. But concessions were made to Russian trawlers, who were given a quota of 266,320 tonnes of capelin, the primary food source for cod. By 1986, there were murmurs of a crisis in the cod stocks, and blame was laid everywhere. Premier Clyde Wells, himself the grandson of a fisherman, said, "We can't say this is a God-caused disaster. This is a federal government–caused disaster. They are the ones who have the exclusive jurisdiction to manage the fisheries; they are the ones who made the management decisions that resulted in this." Other culprits were named: the inshore fishermen believed that the crisis had been precipitated by the mammoth offshore trawlers; the

**ENVIRONMENTAL ISSUES** ◆ The 1970s saw a rise in environmental concerns, sparked by increased air and water pollution, acid rain, clear-cutting of forests, massive hydro-electric projects, and fears of mercury poisoning. In the early part of the decade, the first phase of the James Bay hydroelectric project was initiated, which involved the diverting of four rivers into the La Grande River. It was completed in 1985 at a cost of about $16 billion and included the construction of 9 dams and 206 dikes, covering an area of 11,355 square kilometres. The rotting of flooded vegetation contaminated the water of the rivers and reservoirs with unsafe levels of methyl mercury. At the mouth of the La Grande River, 64 per cent of the Cree have unsafe levels of mercury in their bodies.

Perhaps the most enduring public face of the environmental movement was the baby seal, as the annual seal hunt was challenged by groups like Greenpeace. French actress Brigitte Bardot took up the cause and appeared on the cover of a 1977 *Paris Match* magazine nuzzling a baby seal. (Greenpeace activist Patrick Wall spraying a baby seal with dye, to spoil its pelt, during the 1982 seal hunt in the Gulf of St. Lawrence. *CP Picture Archive*)

offshore fishermen thought it was due to the predations of seals; and plant workers blamed foreign trawlers for overfishing. The scientists who had come up with the estimates for the cod population were also singled out, and their research, with its large margin of error (up to 50 per cent), was criticized. Between 1988 and 1990, the federal government slashed the annual quota for cod by more than one-quarter.

The pending collapse of the cod fishery posed an insoluble problem: if the total allowable catch (TAC) was reduced too drastically, processing plants would close and thousands of jobs would be lost. If the TAC was not reduced, the stocks could collapse entirely, resulting in both an ecological disaster and, inevitably, an economic one. John Crosbie, the witty, embattled Newfoundland MP who would become minister of fisheries and oceans in 1991, was in the middle of the impossible situation. "I was now faced with what became the greatest challenge of my years in political life," he said. "I was now faced with a biological and economic disaster of unprecedented proportions, and as the Newfoundland minister in the government of Canada, which had full responsibility under the constitution to manage the fisheries, I and the government of Canada would be looked to for the solutions and assistance and had to accept the responsibility for the situation and any blame that attached to it."

Compounding the problem was an ongoing territorial battle with the French, who had claimed a 200-mile limit themselves, citing their ownership of St. Pierre and Miquelon, the two tiny islands that had been retained by the French in the 1763 Treaty of Paris. They were aggressively overfishing the area with impunity, and negotiations between France and Canada had broken down. In 1987, France sent a warship to patrol its waters, and a military response was urged by the Opposition in the House of Commons. In 1989, there was a mediated resolution that called for a four-year grace period before the new quotas took effect, and the French resumed their overfishing.

By December 1989, National Sea Products, the largest employer in the fishery, had closed its plants in Canso, Nova Scotia, and the district of St. John's West, Newfoundland. The pressure for a political rather than an environmental solution escalated as hundreds lost their jobs in the perennially battered Newfoundland economy. "I did not believe that we had to slavishly follow the opinions of marine biologists and I was not going to," Crosbie said. "But the Cabinet had to live with the social and economic consequences of this resource situation."

In the end, the cod stocks dropped, factories closed, jobs disappeared, and villages were threatened. The underlying problem was characterized by biologist Garrett Hardin as "the tragedy of the commons." When a common resource is shared among competing parties, each pursues his interest without limit. Faced with reduced fish stocks, no one fisherman will reduce his catch, knowing that it will simply be taken by the next fisherman. Unless common good overcomes individual need, the resource is plundered by all.

These tensions, fundamental to many environmental issues, are reflected in Canada itself. The country arose from conflict and co-operation among peoples, and it was settled by those who battled the elements and the land to survive. It is defined by ongoing regional tensions and linguistic debate, by political compromise and unsettled land claims. It is a country of refugees that continually negotiates a new equilibrium. All of this takes place against the backdrop of the vast geography, described ecstatically in immigration pamphlets and cursed by new arrivals. "I knew that this was what the land had been waiting for all these long years," wrote Nellie McClung in *Clearing in the West*. "It was for this that the rain had fallen on it in summer and the snows had covered it in winter. It was for this the grass had grown on it, withered, and grown again, that someday someone would come and claim it, not for himself alone but for all people, claim it in the name of humanity and press it into humanity's service."

## AFTERWORD BY MARK STAROWICZ

On October 22, 2000, the myth that Canadians are not interested in their history died a well-deserved death. That was the day when more than two million people watched the first episode of *Canada: A People's History* on the French and English networks of the CBC. For the rest of the series' first year, as many Canadians watched their history unfurl as have ever watched major Olympic events or Stanley Cup playoffs. Clearly, a chord had been struck, but what was the chord?

I got my first sense of what that chord was when I was watching the rushes of the Loyalist flight to Nova Scotia – images of transport ships dropping thousands of families onto a rocky Atlantic beach. I could have been watching refugees fleeing Kosovo on the news, which they were doing at the time. Then came these voices, over the achingly lonely scene of huge ships departing on the horizon:

*Sarah Frost: "It is, I think, the roughest land I ever saw. But this is to be our city, they say."*

*Sarah Tilley: "I climbed to the top of Chipman's Hill and watched the sails disappear. Although I had not shed a tear throughout all the war, I sat down on the damp moss, with my baby in my lap, and cried."*

My eyes grew moist, and when the lights came on, I saw that I wasn't the only one trying to hide my tears. The History Project staff in the theatre that afternoon were of French, Chinese, Jewish, and English descent. And I understood why the scene had moved us all: This was our story too. The experience of refuge, of arriving in a strange place of terrifying beauty, the fear of an uncertain destiny – this is the common thread of the Canadian experience. We are not linked by blood, but we are inextricably linked by the experience of refuge.

If we cast our eyes over the hundreds of years of Canada's recorded history, we can see this thread running through it, although the aboriginal story is different. New France was peopled by the landless of Brittany, Normandy, and the displaced and abandoned daughters of Paris. The American Revolution transformed this continent and created the foundations of two countries – the United States and modern Canada – by provoking one of the greatest human migrations of the continent's history: the Loyalists who sailed to Nova Scotia, crossed rivers and swamps into Quebec, sailed on to the Thousand Islands and to the Niagara Peninsula. English Canada was born in a blink of an eye, historically speaking – just thirty years – creating the French–English duality which has governed Canada's destiny ever since.

Modern Canada was founded by two unwanted peoples. The first: the French of two separate colonies – Acadia and Quebec – both occupied by the British and abandoned by the French, who didn't even want Quebec back after the Seven Years' War and traded it in 1763 for the tiny sugar island of Guadeloupe. The second: their ancestral English enemies from the American colonies, driven out of their homes in the years after 1776.

Thus, the experience of refuge is at the core of the Canadian identity. We are refugees, or the descendants of refugees, who have come to our shores like the recurring tides: the Scots left landless by the Highland Clearances, the marginalized English gentry of Susannah Moodie's generation, the hundreds of thousands of starving Irish families ousted by landlords and famine. Countless Black people came here too, refugees from the American Revolution and the Civil War. In turn, they were followed by the landless from eastern and northern Europe: the Galicians, the Mennonites, the Poles and the Jews, the Russians, the Scandinavians, the Dutch – all fleeing war, persecution, economic devastation, or famine. Thousands of young Chinese men crossed the Pacific Ocean to escape poverty and sent their paltry earnings home to families they would never see again. Thousands of British orphans were sent here in a systematic relocation of the abandoned.

After the end of the Second World War came the people the war had displaced (among them, my parents), and survivors of the Holocaust. Then came the Sikhs, the Italians, and the Portuguese, in search of a better life; the boat people of Vietnam; people from the Caribbean. Today, the refugees from war still arrive – from the Sudan, from Somalia, the Balkans.

They were all the debris of history. The expelled, the persecuted, the landless, the marginalized, the victims of imperial wars, of economic and ideological upheavals. In a sense we are all boat people. We just got here at different times. Every one of us has the same story in our past, whether we are descended from the *filles du roi* – the street children of Paris – or from Galician villagers.

This makes us different from the peoples of the Old World. We are disdainful of class and privilege – there is no greater social sin here than trying to pull rank or jump the queue. It is unacceptable to be rude to waiters or waitresses, because our sons or daughters could likely be in that position at some point in their lives. We are suspicious of government and ideology because we are refugees from governments, armies, and ideology. We are vigilant that no one claim more rights than we have. Canada – cranky, forever courting and rejecting a breakup – is a perpetual negotiation of its constituent parts. To the frustrated question: "When are we finally going to settle all this?" the answer is, of course, "Never." The negotiation is not the problem, it's the point. The genius of Canada is the constant search for equilibrium, where no one ever fully gains the upper hand.

Some people suggest we have a tepid history because we don't have a civil war or a revolution in our past. But we are not chauvinists. Instead, the Canadian experience has bred a grumpy civility that has given rise to one of the great mysteries of history. We have all the ingredients, all the toxins, to create a Kosovo or a Northern Ireland: two major religions, two languages, contested land, racial and ethnic divisions. How we didn't become the Balkans, or the West Bank, or Vichy France, is far more intriguing than any civil war, and far more pertinent to the modern world.

The collective experience of refuge and redemption that underlies our identity has its different currents, however. The idea that "we are all boat people, we just got here at different times" applies to, but doesn't fully take account of, the French experience on this continent. Hubert Gendron, the senior producer of the series for Radio-Canada, and I have talked much about this over the four years we have worked together on the series.

Hubert has told me about the severance from the French mother country that is at the base of Quebec's cultural survival. Unlike the English, the Irish, the Scots, the Ukrainians, and the Chinese – to name just some immigrant groups – the Canadiens, and the Acadians before them, were an orphaned people. There were no waves of French immigrants to nourish the colonies, so the Canadien and Acadian experiences became exclusively indigenous, non-European survival stories. Many Québécois and Acadians consider themselves an indigenous American people. Today, the homeland of the French in North America lies within Canada.

The major diverging current is the story of the aboriginal people, the only ones who became refugees on Canadian soil. Even the most cursory reading of our history leads one to conclude that the peoples of the First Nations were systematically robbed and degraded in their own homelands. An equally cursory reading of Canadian history will show that there would be no Canada today without Donnacona, who saved Jacques Cartier's expedition, without the Huron allies of the French, without Kondiaronk of the Great Peace, without Tecumseh's warriors, who defended Canada's territorial integrity, without Brant, without the Six Nations Confederacy, without the Mi'kmaq, without the Plains Indians who saved the Selkirk Settlers, and the nations of the Northwest who formed great trading empires. The Canadian idea of redemption and equality will never be realized, and the nation made whole, until this great wrong is righted.

Those of us at the Canadian History Project have learned a great deal from some extraordinary people, two of whom I must mention here. Serge Turbide, an Acadian from the Îles de la Madeleine, died too young, of cancer, the month after his episode, "Battle for a Continent," aired. Gail Boyd, despite her English name, was a francophone from the Acadian shore of New Brunswick. She was the brilliant assistant director on Serge's and other episodes, and she died equally young from leukemia four months later. Their contributions will never be forgotten.

Finally, I hope my daughters' generation learns from this series how Canadian history is still molten and shaping itself. In the words of one writer: "The future is not some place we are going, but one we are creating. The paths to it are not found but made, and the activity of making them changes both the maker and the destination."

# AFTERWORD BY GENE ALLEN

Now that the second and final volume of *Canada: A People's History* is in the printer's hands, all of us involved in its production can finally catch our breath and look back on the past two years' work. Preparing the two volumes has been an enormous task, one that could never been carried out without the help and hard work of dozens of people.

Our academic and other outside advisers have saved us from many errors of fact and interpretation. In particular, I would like to thank Ramsay Cook and Jean-Claude Robert; they have patiently gone through innumerable draft scripts and draft chapters, always balancing their scholarly rigour with an appreciation of the challenges of popularization. We have also benefited greatly from comments by Serge Bernier, Craig Brown, Olive Dickason, Gerald Friesen, J. L. Granatstein, Desmond Morton, and Geoffrey Stevens. Any errors that may remain are our responsibility, not theirs.

Despite tough deadlines of their own, the directors, producers, and researchers who worked on the television episodes of *Canada: A People's History* have generously given their time to provide the essential raw material for this book. An especially heavy load has fallen on the shoulders of our visual researchers: Ron Krant, Hélène Bourgeault, Marque Landells, Darren Yearsley, and Mia Webster. Elizabeth Kalbfleisch did an excellent job of writing the picture captions for Chapter Three on very short notice. Rachel Brown has helped in many ways, not least by keeping her sense of humour as deadline pressures mounted. Several last-minute complications could not have been overcome without the support of Anne Emin, our esteemed project manager.

A special word of thanks must go to Mario Cardinal, my counterpart at Radio-Canada and editor of the French-language version of this book. Mario has been an ideal colleague whose gentlemanly and decent nature shone through at every moment – including the occasional difficult and frustrating ones. I can only hope I have the good fortune to work with him again. Likewise, Dinah Forbes of McClelland & Stewart has been a model of professionalism, good humour, and hard work.

As in my foreword to Volume One, my final thanks go to our principal author, Don Gillmor. Don's talent as a writer, his resourcefulness, and his unfailing curiosity and enthusiasm for Canadian history are reasons enough for praise. But the stamina and professionalism he displayed during the final months of producing this book are nothing short of amazing. He deserves the lion's share of the credit.

# BIBLIOGRAPHY

**GENERAL:**

Barman, Jean. *The West Beyond the West: A History of British Columbia.* Toronto: University of Toronto Press, 1991.

Bliss, Michael. *Northern Enterprise: Five Centuries of Canadian Business.* Toronto: McClelland & Stewart, 1987.

Bothwell, Robert, Ian Drummond, and John English. *Canada, 1900-1945.* Toronto: University of Toronto Press, 1987.

—— *Canada Since 1945: Power, Politics and Provincialism.* Toronto: University of Toronto Press, rev. ed., 1989.

Brown, R. Craig (ed.). *Illustrated History of Canada.* Toronto: Key Porter Books, 2000; rev. ed..

*The Canadian Encyclopedia.* Toronto: McClelland & Stewart, 1999.

*Canadian History: A Reader's Guide.* Toronto: University of Toronto Press, 1994.

   – Vol. 1, *Beginnings to Confederation.* M. Brook Taylor (ed.)

   – Vol. 2, *Confederation to the Present.* Doug Owram (ed.)

Cook, Ramsay (general ed.) and Jean Hamelin (directeur général adjoint). *Dictionary of Canadian Biography,* 14 vols. Toronto, Buffalo, and London:

University of Toronto Press, 1966-1998.

Dickason, Olive Patricia. *Canada's First Nations: A History of Founding Peoples from Earliest Times.* Toronto: Oxford University Press, 1997; 2nd ed.

Forbes, E. R., and D. A. Muise (eds.). *The Atlantic Provinces in Confederation.* Toronto, Buffalo, London, and Fredericton: University of Toronto Press / Acadiensis Press, 1993.

Friesen, Gerald. *The Canadian Prairies: A History.* Toronto: University of Toronto Press, 1984.

*Guide d'histoire du Québec, du régime français à nos jours: Bibliographie commentée,* sous la direction de Jacques Rouillard. Laval, Québec: Éditions du Méridien, 1993; 2nd ed.

*Historical Atlas of Canada.* Toronto: University of Toronto Press, 1987-1993.

   – Vol. 2, *The Land Transformed, 1800-1891.* Geoffrey Matthews (cartographer), R. L. Gentilcore (ed.)

   – Vol. 3, *Addressing the Twentieth Century.* Geoffrey Matthews (cartographer), Donald Kerr and Deryck W. Holdsworth (eds.)

Linteau, Paul-André, René Durocher,

Jean-Claude Robert. *Quebec: A History, 1867-1929.* Toronto: James Lorimer & Co., 1983.

Linteau, Paul-André, René Durocher, Jean-Claude Robert, François Ricard. *Quebec Since 1930.* Toronto: James Lorimer & Co., 1991.

Magocsi, Paul R. (ed.). *Encyclopedia of Canada's Peoples.* Toronto: Published for the Multicultural History Society of Ontario by the University of Toronto Press, 1999.

Morton, Desmond. *A Military History of Canada.* Toronto: McClelland & Stewart, 1990; new, rev., and updated ed.

Palmer, Bryan D. *Working-Class Experience: Rethinking the History of Canadian Labour, 1800-1991.* Toronto: McClelland & Stewart, 1992.

Strong-Boag, Veronica, and Anita Clair Feldman. *Rethinking Canada: The Promise of Women's History.* Toronto: Oxford University Press, 1997; 3rd ed.

**CHAPTER 1**

Artibise, Alan F. J. *Winnipeg: A Social History of Urban Growth, 1874-1914.* Montreal and Kingston: McGill-Queen's University Press, 1975.

Beal, Bob, and Rod Macleod. *Prairie Fire: The 1885 North-West Rebellion.* Edmonton: Hurtig, 1984.

Berton, Pierre. *The Great Railway: The National Dream, 1871-1881.* Toronto: McClelland & Stewart, 1970.

—— *The Great Railway: The Last Spike, 1881-1885.* Toronto: McClelland & Stewart, 1971.

Bradbury, Bettina. *Working Families: Age, Gender, and Daily Survival in Industrializing Montreal.* Toronto: McClelland & Stewart, 1993.

Creighton, Donald. *John A. Macdonald: The Old Chieftain.* Toronto: Macmillan, 1955.

Fingard, Judith. *The Dark Side of Life in Victorian Halifax.* Potter's Lake, N.S.: Pottersfield Press, 1989.

MacGregor, James. *Edmonton Trader: The Story of John A. McDougall.* Toronto: McClelland & Stewart, 1963.

Macleod, R. C. *The N.W.M.P. and Law Enforcement, 1873-1905.* Toronto: University of Toronto Press, 1976.

Miller, J. R. *Skyscrapers Hide the Heavens: A History of Indian-White Relations in Canada.* Toronto: University of Toronto Press, 1991; 2nd ed.

Owram, Doug. *Promise of Eden: The Canadian Expansionist Movement and the Idea of the West, 1856-1900.* Toronto: University of Toronto Press, 1992; 2nd ed.

Siggins, Maggie. *Riel: A Life of Revolution.* Toronto: HarperCollins, 1994.

Sprague, D. N. *Canada and the Métis, 1869-1885.* Waterloo, Ont.: Wilfrid Laurier University Press, 1988.

Stanley, G. F. G. *The Birth of Western Canada: A History of the Riel Rebellions.* Toronto: University of Toronto Press, 1960.

Stonechild, Blair, and Bill Waiser. *Loyal Till Death: Indians and the North-West Rebellion.* Calgary: Fifth House, 1997.

Waite, P. B. *Canada, 1874-1896: Arduous Destiny.* Toronto: McClelland & Stewart, 1971.

**CHAPTER 2**

Abella, Irving. *A Coat of Many Colours: Two Centuries of Jewish Life in Canada.* Toronto : Key Porter Books, 1999.

Bélanger, Réal. *Wilfrid Laurier. Quand la politique devient passion.* Québec / Montréal: Presses de l'Université Laval / Entreprises Radio-Canada, 1986.

Berger, Carl. *The Sense of Power: Studies in the Ideas of Canadian Imperialism, 1867-1914.* Toronto: University of Toronto Press, 1976.

Brown, Robert Craig. *Robert Laird Borden: A Biography: Vol. 1, 1854-1914.* Toronto: Macmillan, 1975.

—— and Ramsay Cook. *Canada 1896-1921: A Nation Transformed.* Toronto: McClelland & Stewart, 1974.

Chan, Anthony B. *Gold Mountain: The Chinese in the New World.* Vancouver: New Star Press, 1983.

Graves, Diane. *A Crown of Life: The World of John McCrae.* St. Catharines, Ont.: Vanwell Publishing Ltd., 1997.

McClung, Nellie L. *In Times Like These.* Toronto: University of Toronto Press, 1972.

Mills, Allen George. *Fool for Christ: The Intellectual Politics of J. S. Woodsworth.* Toronto: University of Toronto Press, 1991.

Roy, Patricia. *A White Man's Province: British Columbia Politicians and the Chinese and Japanese, 1858-1914.* Vancouver: University of British Columbia Press, 1989.

Rumilly, Robert. *Henri Bourassa: La Vie publique d'un grand canadien.* Montréal: Éditions de l'Homme, 1953.

Skelton, Oscar Douglas. *Life and Letters of Sir Wilfrid Laurier: Volume II, 1896-1919.* Edited and with an introduction by David M. L. Farr. Toronto: McClelland & Stewart, 1965.

Svarich, Peter. *Memoirs: 1877-1904.* Translated by William Kostach. Edmonton: Ukranian Pioneer's Association, 1999.

Tulchinsky, Gerald. *Taking Root: The Origins of the Canadian Jewish Community.* Toronto : Stoddart, 1997.

**CHAPTER 3**

Brown, Robert Craig, and Ramsay Cook. *Canada 1896-1921: A Nation Transformed.* Toronto: McClelland & Stewart, 1974.

Bumsted, J. M. *The Winnipeg General Strike of 1919: An Illustrated History.* Winnipeg: Watson and Dwyer, 1994.

Crowley, Terry. *Agnes Macphail and the Politics of Equality.* Toronto: James Lorimer & Co., 1990.

Gutkin, Henry, and Mildred Gutkin. *Profiles in Dissent: The Shaping of Radical Thought in the Canadian West.* Edmonton: NeWest Press, 1997.

Kitz, Janet. *Shattered City: The Halifax Explosion and the Road to Recovery.* Halifax: Nimbus Press, 1989.

Lacoursière, Jacques. *Histoire populaire du Québec, 1896-1960, Tome IV.* Sillery: Septentrion, 1996, 1997.

Lapointe, Arthur-Joseph. *Souvenirs et impressions de ma vie de soldat (1916-1919).* Montréal: Éditions Edouard Garand, 1919; 2e édition.

Macfie, John. *Letters Home.* Parry Sound, Ont.: J. Macfie, 1990.

McClung, Nellie. *The Stream Runs Fast — My Own Story.* Toronto: Thomas Allen Limited, 1945.

Morton, Desmond. *When Your Number's Up.* Toronto: Random House, 1993.

—— and J. L. Granatstein. *Marching to Armageddon: Canadians and the Great War, 1914-1919.* Toronto : Lester & Orpen Dennys, 1989.

Pettigrew, Eileen. *The Silent Enemy: Canada and the Deadly Flu of 1918.* Saskatoon: Western Producer Prairie Books, 1983.

Roby, Yves. *Les Québécois et les investissements américains, 1918-1929.* Québec: Les Presses de l'Université Laval, 1976.

Thompson, John Herd, and Allen Seager. *Canada 1922-1939: Decades of Discord.* Toronto: McClelland & Stewart, 1985.

Wilson, Barbara (ed.). *Ontario and the First World War 1914-1918: A Collection of Documents.* Toronto: University of Toronto Press, 1977.

**CHAPTER 4**

Abella, Irving, and Harold Troper. *None Is Too Many: Canada and the Jews of Europe, 1933-1948.* Toronto: Lester & Orpen Dennys, 1982.

Betcherman, Lita-Rose. *The Swastika and the Maple Leaf.* Toronto: Fitzhenry and Whiteside, 1975.

Black, Conrad. *Duplessis.* Toronto: McClelland & Stewart, 1977.

Glassford, Larry. *Reaction and Reform: The Politics of the Conservative Party under R. B. Bennett, 1927-1938.* Toronto: University of Toronto Press, 1992.

Gray, James. *Troublemaker!* Toronto: Macmillan, 1978.

—— *The Winter Years: The Depression on the Prairies.* Toronto: Macmillan, 1966.

Liversedge, Ronald. *Recollections of the On To Ottawa Trek.* Toronto: McClelland & Stewart, 1973.

Neatby, Blair H. *The Politics of Chaos: Canada in the Thirties.* Toronto: Macmillan, 1972.

—— *William Lyon Mackenzie King: The Lonely Heights, 1924-1932.* Toronto: University of Toronto Press, 1963.

—— *William Lyon Mackenzie King: The Prism of Unity, 1932-1939.* Toronto: University of Toronto Press, 1976.

Pickersgill, J. W. *The Mackenzie King Record, Vol. 1, 1939-1944.* Toronto: University of Toronto Press, 1960.

Safarian, A. E. *The Canadian Economy in the Great Depression.* Toronto: University of Toronto Press, 1959.

Saywell, John T. *Just Call Me Mitch: The Life of Mitchell F. Hepburn.* Toronto: University of Toronto Press, 1991.

Thompson, John H., and Allen Seager. *Canada, 1922-1939: Decades of Discord.* Toronto: McClelland & Stewart, 1985.

**CHAPTER 5**

Arnold, Gladys. *One Woman's War.* Toronto: James Lorimer & Co., 1987.

Bercuson, David J. *Maple Leaf against the Axis: Canada's Second World War.* Toronto: Stoddart Publishing, 1995.

Bishop, Arthur. *The Splendid Hundred: The True Story of Canadians Who Flew in the Greatest Air Battle of World War II.* Toronto: McGraw-Hill Ryerson, 1994.

Bothwell, Robert, and J. L. Granatstein. *The Gouzenko Transcripts.* Ottawa: Deneau, 1982.

Curry, Frank. *War at Sea.* Toronto: Lugus, 1990.

Granatstein, J. L. *Canada's War: The Politics of the Mackenzie King Government, 1939-1945.* Toronto: Oxford University Press, 1975.

Gwyn, Richard. *Smallwood, the Unlikely Revolutionary.* Toronto: McClelland & Stewart, 1968.

Hiller, J. K., and M. F. Harrington (eds). *The Newfoundland National Convention, 1946-1948, Volume One: Debates.* Montreal and Kingston: McGill-Queen's University Press, 1995.

Kitigawa, Muriel. *This Is My Own: Letters to Wes and Other Writings on Japanese Canadians, 1941-1949.* Edited by Roy Miki. Vancouver: Talonbooks, 1985.

Pickersgill, J. W., and D. F. Forster. *The Mackenzie King Record, Vols. 1-2.* Toronto: University of Toronto Press, 1968.

Sawatsky, John. *Gouzenko: The Untold Story.* Toronto: Macmillan, 1984.

Whitaker, Reg, and Gary Marcuse. *Cold War Canada: The Making of a National Insecurity State, 1945-1957.* Toronto: University of Toronto Press, 1994.

Whitaker, W. Denis, and Shelagh Whitaker. *Dieppe: Tragedy to Triumph.* Toronto: McGraw-Hill Ryerson, 1992.

**CHAPTER 6**

Childbirth by Choice Trust. *No Choice: Canadian Women Tell their Stories of Illegal Abortion.* Toronto: Childbirth by Choice Trust, 1998.

Clairmont, Donald H., and Dennis William Magill. *Africville, the Life and Death of a Canadian Black Community.* Toronto: McClelland & Stewart, 1974.

Collectif Clio. *Quebec Women: A History.* Toronto: Women's Press, 1987.

Desbiens, Jean-Paul. *Les Insolences du frère Untel / préface d'André Laurendeau.* Montréal : Éditions de l'Homme, 1960.

Fournier, Louis. *FLQ: The Anatomy of an Underground Movement.* Toronto: N.C. Press, 1984.

Godin, Pierre. *René Lévesque.* Montreal: Boréal, 1994 and 1997.

Granatstein, J. L. *Canada 1957-1967: The Years of Uncertainty and Innovation.* Toronto: McClelland & Stewart, 1986.

Horton, Donald J. *André Laurendeau: French Canadian Nationalist, 1912-1968.* Toronto: Oxford University Press, 1992.

Hunter, Robert. *Warriors of the Rainbow: A Chronicle of the Greenpeace Movement.* New York: Holt, Rinehart and Winston, 1979.

Lévesque, René. *René Lévesque: Memoirs.* Toronto: McClelland & Stewart, 1986.

Owram, Doug. *Born at the Right Time: A History of the Baby Boom Generation.* Toronto: University of Toronto Press, 1996.

Rowe, Frederick W. *A History of Newfoundland and Labrador.* Toronto: McGraw-Hill Ryerson, 1980.

Thomson, Dale C. *Jean Lesage and the Quiet Revolution.* Toronto: Macmillan, 1984.

Trudeau, Pierre Elliott. *Memoirs.* Toronto: McClelland & Stewart, 1993.

**CHAPTER 7**

Anderson, Doris. *Rebel Daughter: An Autobiography.* Toronto: Key Porter Books, 1996.

Bashevkin, Sylvia. *True Patriot Love: The Politics of Canadian Nationalism.* Toronto: Oxford University Press, 1991.

Clarkson, Stephen, and Christina McCall. *Trudeau and Our Times.* Toronto: McClelland & Stewart, 2 vols., 1990 and 1994.

—— *Canada and the Reagan Challenge.* Toronto: James Lorimer & Co., 1985.

Cohen, Andrew. *A Deal Undone: The Making and Breaking of the Meech Lake Accord.* Vancouver: Douglas & McIntyre, 1990.

Granatstein, J. L. *Yankee Go Home? Canadians and Anti-Americanism.* Toronto: HarperCollins, 1996.

Harris, Michael. *Lament for an Ocean: The Collapse of the Atlantic Cod Fishery: A True Crime Story.* Toronto: McClelland & Stewart, 1998.

Hart, Michael, Bill Dymond, and Colin Robertson. *Decision at Midnight: Inside the Canada–U.S. Free-Trade Negotiations.* Vancouver: University of British Columbia Press, 1994.

Hustak, Alan. *Peter Lougheed: A Biography.* Toronto: McClelland & Stewart, 1979.

Kome, Penney, *The Taking of Twenty-eight: Women Challenge the Constitution.* Toronto: Women's Press, 1983.

Masters, John A. *The Hunters: Searching for Oil and Gas in Western Canada.* Vancouver: Canadian Hunter Exploration Ltd., 1980.

Miller, J. R. *Skyscrapers Hide the Heavens: A History of Indian–White Relations in Canada.* Toronto: University of Toronto Press, 1989; rev. ed.

O'Malley, Martin. *The Past and Future Land: An Account of the Berger Inquiry into the Mackenzie Valley Pipeline.* Toronto: Peter Martin & Associates, 1976.

Pierson, Ruth Roach, et al. *Canadian Women's Issues.* Toronto: James Lorimer & Co., 1993.

Sobel, David, and Susan Meurer. *Working at Inglis: The Life and Death of a Canadian Factory.* Toronto: James Lorimer and Co., 1994.

Wood, David G. *The Lougheed Legacy.* Toronto: Key Porter, 1985.

# INDEX